MODERN CULTURE AND THE ARTS

Cover and frontispiece: Ungaro's studio.
Photographs by André Kertész

MODERN CULTURE AND THE ARTS

James B. Hall

Provost, College V
University of California, Santa Cruz

Barry Ulanov

Professor of English
Barnard College

Second Edition

McGraw-Hill Book Company

New York   St. Louis   San Francisco   Düsseldorf
Kuala Lumpur   London
Mexico   Montreal   New Delhi   Panama
Rio de Janeiro   Singapore   Sydney   Toronto

MODERN CULTURE AND THE ARTS

Library of Congress Catalog Card Number 79-177373

1 2 3 4 5 6 7 8 9 0   HDBP   7 9 8 7 6 5 4 3 2

This book was set in Janson by Monotype Composition Company, Inc., printed by Halliday Lithograph Corporation, and bound by The Book Press, Inc. The designer was Barbara Ellwood. David Edwards was sponsor. Editors were Judith Mallinson and Susan Gamer. Peter D. Guilmette supervised production.

ACKNOWLEDGMENTS

Berenice Abbot, "Eugene Atget," reprinted with the kind permission of the author.

W. H. Auden, extract of pp. 5–13, *Making, Knowing and Judging* (Inaugural Lecture 1956), Clarendon Press, 1956. Reprinted by permission of the Clarendon Press, Oxford.

Roland Barthes, "Science Versus Literature," reprinted from *The Times* of London, September 28, 1967, by permission of the publishers.

Andre Bazin, "The Ontology of the Photographic Image," from *What is Cinema?* by Andre Bazin, selected and translated by Hugh Gray, University of California Press, Berkeley, 1967. Reprinted by permission.

Charles Belz, "Rock as Folk Art," from *The Story of Rock*, by Charles Belz, reprinted by permission of Oxford University Press.

Ingmar Bergman, "Film Has Nothing to Do with Literature," from *Four Screen Plays of Ingmar Bergman*, copyright © 1960 by Ingmar Bergman and reprinted by permission of Simon and Schuster, Inc.

Bertolt Brecht, "Theatre for Pleasure or Theatre for Learning?", trans. by Edith Anderson, *Mainstream*, XI (June, 1958), pp. 1–9.

Luis Buñuel, "A Statement," from *Film Culture*, No. 21, Summer 1960, reprinted with the permission of the publisher.

Anthony Burgess, excerpts from "Our Bedfellow, the Marquis de Sade," by Anthony Burgess. Copyright © 1969 by American Heritage Publishing Co., Inc. Reprinted by permission from *Horizon Magazine*, Winter 1969.

Michel Butor, "The Crisis in the Growth of Science Fiction," from *Inventory*, by Michel Butor, copyright © 1961, 1962, 1965 by Michel Butor. First published in French in Repertoire (1960) by Les Editions de Minuit and reprinted by permission of Simon and Schuster.

John Cage, "Experimental Music," copyright © 1958 by John Cage. "Experimental Music: Doctrine," copyright © 1955 by John Cage. Both reprinted from *Silence* by John Cage by permission of Wesleyan University Press.

Ernest Callenbach, "Acting, Being, and the Death of the Movie Aesthetic," from *New American Review*, No. 8, reprinted with the kind permission of the author.

Henri Cartier-Bresson, from *The World of Henri Cartier-Bresson*, copyright 1952, © 1968 by Henri Cartier-Bresson. All rights reserved. Reprinted by permission of the Viking Press, Inc.

Joyce Cary, "The Artist and the World" from *Art and Reality* by Joyce Cary. Copyright © 1958 by Arthur Lucius Michael Cary and David Alexander Ogilvie, Executors, Estate of Joyce Cary. Reprinted by permission of Harper & Row, Publishers, and Curtis Brown Ltd.

Henry Steele Commager, "Television: The Medium in Search of Its Character," *TV Guide*, June 25, 1966.

Aaron Copland, "How We Listen," Chapter 2 from *What to Listen for in Music* by Aaron Copland, rev. ed., 1957. Copyright © 1939 and 1957 by McGraw-Hill Book Co. Used by permission of McGraw-Hill Book Company.

Kenneth Coutts-Smith, "Theatre Takes Place All the Time, Wherever One Is," from *The Dream of Icarus* by Kenneth Coutts-Smith, copyright © 1970 by Kenneth Coutts-Smith. Reprinted with the permission of George Braziller, New York, 1970.

E. E. Cummings, "Three Statements," from *Poets on Poetry*, ed. Charles Norman, copyright, 1926, by Horace Liveright; renewed, 1934 by E. E. Cummings. Reprinted from POEMS 1923–1954 by permission of Harcourt Brace Jovanovich, Inc.

Merce Cunningham, "Space, Time and the Dance," *Transformation*, 1:3, Wittenborn & Co., 1952, pp. 150–151. Also by permission of the author.

Martin Esslin, "The Theatre of the Absurd" from *Theatre in the Twentieth Century*, ed. by Robert Corrigan, Grove Press, 1963.

Walker Evans, selected essay from *Quality: Its Image in the Arts*, ed. Louis Kronenberger. Copyright © 1969 by Balance House. Reprinted by permission of Marshall Lee and Atheneum Publishers.

Leslie Fiedler, "The End of the Novel," from *Waiting for the End* by Leslie Fiedler. Copyright © 1964 by Leslie A. Fiedler. Reprinted with permission of Stein and Day/Publishers.

E. M. Forster, "Art for Art's Sake" from *Two Cheers for Democracy*, copyright 1949 by E. M. Forster. Reprinted by permission of Harcourt, Brace & World, Inc., and Edward Arnold (Publishers) Ltd.

Northrop Frye, "Design as a Creative Principle in the Arts," from *The Hidden Harmony*, by Northrop Frye The Odyssey Press. Reprinted with the kind permission of the author.

Jean Giraudoux, "Eternal Law of the Dramatist" from *Visitations*, published by Bernard Grasset, Paris, 1952, pp. 115–122. Trans. by Haskell M. Block and reprinted in *The Creative Vision*, copyright Grove Press, Inc., 1960.

E. H. Gombrich, "Meditations on a Hobby Horse or the Roots of Artistic Form," pp. 1–11 from *Meditations on a Hobby Horse and Other Essays on the Theory of Art* by E. H. Gombrich, published by Phaidon Press London and distributed in the U.S.A. by New York Graphic Society, Greenwich, Conn.

Clement Greenberg, "Avant-Garde and Kitsch" from *Art and Culture* by Clement Greenberg. Reprinted by permission of the Beacon Press, copyright © 1961 by Clement Greenberg.

Walter Gropius, "Scope of Total Architecture," from *The Scope of Total Architecture* by Walter Gropius. Copyright © 1955 by Walter G. Gropius. Reprinted by permission of Harper & Row, Publishers, Inc.

Rene d'Harnoncourt, excerpt from foreword to *Steichen, The Photographer*, reprinted with the permission of Miss Grace M. Mayer, The Museum of Modern Art.

Andrew Hook, "Commitment and Reality" from *The Novel Today*, Programme and Notes of the International Writers Conference, Edinburgh International Festival, 1962.

Irma B. Jaffe, "Conversation with Hans Hofman," reprinted from *Artforum* with the kind permission of the publishers and the author.

Wassily Kandinsky, extract of pp. 23–26, *Concerning the Spiritual in Art*, Documents of Modern Art, A Series, George Wittenborn, Inc. Copyright 1947 by Nina Kandinsky.

Abraham Kaplan, "The Aesthetics of the Popular Arts," *Journal of Aesthetics* (Spring 1966). Based on a paper read for the American Philosophical Association, Milwaukee, May, 1964. Edited and shortened with permission.

Felix Klee, extract of pp. 151–155, *Paul Klee*, George Braziller, Inc. 1962. Reprinted with permission of the publisher.

John A. Kouwenhoven, "What Is 'American' in Architecture and Design?" from *The Beer Can by the Highway* by John A. Kouwenhoven. Copyright © 1961 by John A. Kouwenhoven. Reprinted by permission of Doubleday & Company, Inc.

Susanne K. Langer, "Deceptive Analogies: Specious and Real Relationships Among the Arts" from *Problems of Art* by Susan K. Langer. Copyright © 1957 by Susanne K. Langer. Reprinted by permission of Charles Scribner's Sons.

Richard Lippold, "Illusion as Structure" from *Structure in Art and Science*, ed. by Gyorgy Kepes, George Braziller, Inc., 1965. © 1965 George Braziller, Inc. Reprinted with permission of the publisher.

Henry Moore, "Notes on Sculpture" from *Sculpture and Drawing*, Vol. I, 4th ed., ed. by David Sylvester, Percy Lund, Humphries & Co., Ltd., Publisher.

George Nelson, "The Designer in the Modern World" *Problems of Design* by George Nelson. Copyright 1957. Published by the Whitney Library of Design, New York.

José Ortega y Gasset, extracts from "First Installment on the Dehumanization of Art," pp. 19–23; and "Art a Thing of No Consequence," pp. 49–52; *Dehumanization of Art and Notes on the Novel* by José Ortega y Gasset, Princeton University Press, 1948. Reprinted by permission of Princeton University Press.

Erwin Panofsky, "Style and Medium in the Moving Pictures," reprinted from the *Bulletin of the Department of Art and Archaeology, Princeton University*, 1934, with the permission of Princeton University Press and Mrs. Gerda Panofsky.

I. M. Pei, "The Nature of Urban Spaces," reprinted from *The People's Architects*, ed. by Harry S. Ransom, published by The University of Chicago Press for Rice University, 1964, by permission of The University of Chicago Press.

Pablo Picasso, "Statement by Picasso, 1935," from *Picasso: Fifty Years of His Art* by Alfred H. Barr, Jr., copyright 1939, 1946, by The Museum of Modern Art, New York, and reprinted with its permission. Christian

Zervos put down these remarks by Picasso immediately after a conversation with him at Boisgeloup in 1935. Picasso went over the notes and approved them informally. They were first published under the title "Conversation avec Picasso" in *Cahiers d'Art*, 1935, volume 10, number 10, pp. 173–178. The above translation is based on one by Myfanwy Evans.

Gió Ponti, "The Architect, the Artist," from *In Praise of Architecture* by Gió Ponti, translated by Giuseppina and Mario Salvadori, and reprinted by permission of Vitali e Ghianda, Genoa, Italy.

Theodore Roethke, "On 'Identity'" from *On the Poet and His Craft*, ed. Mills, reprinted with the permission of University of Washington Press.

Carl Sandburg, excerpt from *Steichen, The Photographer* by Carl Sandburg, reprinted by permission of Harcourt Brace Jovanovich, Inc.

Andrew Sarris, "The Fall and Rise of the Film Director," from *Interviews with Film Directors*, copyright © 1967, by Andrew Sarris, reprinted by permission of the publisher, The Bobbs-Merrill Company, Inc.

Roger Sessions, "The Listener" from *The Musical Experience of Composer, Performer, Listener* by Roger Sessions, Princeton University, 1950, pp. 87–106. Copyright 1950 by the Princeton University Press. Abridged and reprinted by permission of Princeton University Press and the author.

Paolo Soleri, "Arcology: The City in the Image of Man," from *Arcology: The City in the Image of Man*, reprinted by permission of The M. I. T. Press, Cambridge, Massachusetts.

Edward Steichen, three quotations from *A Life in Photography* by Edward Steichen. Reprinted by permission of Doubleday and Company, Inc.

Wallace Stevens, "The Relations Between Poetry and Painting," copyright 1951 by Wallace Stevens. Reprinted from *The Necessary Angel* by Wallace Stevens by permission of Alfred A. Knopf, Inc.

Igor Stravinsky, "The Performance of Music." Reprinted by permission of the publishers from Igor Stravinsky, *Poetics of Music*. Cambridge, Mass.: Harvard University Press, copyright 1947 by the President and Fellows of Harvard College.

John Szarkowski, Introduction from *The Photographer's Eye* by John Szarkowski, copyright 1966 by The Museum of Modern Art, New York, and reprinted with its permission.

Dylan Thomas, "Notes on the Art of Poetry," *The Texas Quarterly*, 1961. Reprinted by permission of Harold Ober Associates Incorporated. Copyright © 1961 by Trustees of the Copyrights of Dylan Thomas.

Jerry Uelsmann, quotations reprinted with the permission of the photographer.

Barry Ulanov, "What Is Jazz?", Chapter 1 from *A History of Jazz in America* by Barry Ulanov. Copyright 1952 by Barry Ulanov. Reprinted by permission of The Viking Press, Inc.

Paul Valéry, "Pure Poetry: Notes for a Lecture," trans. by Haskell M. Block and originally published in *The Creative Vision*, copyright The Grove Press, Inc., 1960. The authorized English translations of the works of Paul Valéry rest exclusively in Bollingen Foundation, New York. Their permission to publish Mr. Block's translations is gratefully acknowledged.

Edward Weston, six excerpts from *The Daybooks of Edward Weston: California*, ed. Nancy Newhall, reprinted by permission of the publisher Horizon Press.

Mary Wigman, "Composition in Pure Movement," *Modern Music* (Jan.–Feb. 1931). Copyright by The League of Composers, Inc., and reprinted by permission of the International Society of Composers and Musicians—The League of Composers, Inc.

PHOTOGRAPH ACKNOWLEDGMENTS

Photos by Eugène Atget (pp. 431–436) courtesy The Museum of Modern Art.

Photos by László Moholy-Nagy (pp. 445–449) courtesy The Museum of Modern Art. Photo of light modulator (p. 450) courtesy The Busch-Reisinger Museum: Harvard University.

Photos by Edward Steichen (pp. 452–457) courtesy the photographer and The Museum of Modern Art.

Photos by Berenice Abbot (pp. 459–464) courtesy the photographer.

Photos by Walker Evans (pp. 467–472) courtesy the photographer.

Photos by Henri Cartier-Bresson (pp. 474–479) courtesy the photographer and Magnum Photos.

Photos by Bill Brandt (pp. 481–486) courtesy the photographer and Rapho Guillumette.

Photos by Jerry Uelsmann (pp. 488–493) courtesy the photographer.

Photos by Edward Weston (pp. 497–498) courtesy Cole Weston.

CONTENTS

PREFACE

In the Preface to the first edition of *Modern Culture and The Arts*, the editors suggested, "Coming to terms with modern culture can be an uneasy confrontation, both for the novice and for the initiate. Through a series of noble encounters between the artist and the work of art on the one hand, and the viewer, reader, or listener on the other, enlightenment comes slowly. In matters of art and understanding, yesterday's excitement may become tomorrow's tedium. Traditionally, even the brightest student proceeds by indirection.... In the end, however, the student becomes a different—and a better—person for his encounter with the arts, whatever its nature."

After five years, with the publication of the second edition of *Modern Culture and The Arts*, it is clear that certain issues raised by this text have changed, while others remain stubbornly the same. As before, materials continue to accumulate from the press, the scholar's study, the artist's studio, the theatre, and the street—and especially from the rampant visual coverage of the arts by television. The old difficulty remains: can anyone ever understand what the world is about, what art is about, and what man's place is in relationship to both? One answer is suggested by the fact that for this text itself a second edition was appropriate: the effort to understand, as always, must be attempted.

This optimistic conclusion, that the effort must be made, in no way changes the facts of the matter; nor does it alter certain basic assumptions. For example, it remains true that books of essays and photographs are not substitutes for the experience of art; at best this new collection will make the reader's confrontation with his heritage and his environment more stimulating and more enlightening. On the other hand, this new attempt at a balanced and relevant presentation will suggest useful directions for further explorations and thus help to avoid misunderstandings.

As before, out intention is to raise issues central to the arts in our time. We attempt to raise the major questions and are confident that a great many minor questions will also come to attention as a result. For example, there is only casual reference to the issue of censorship and government interference with the artist; yet this ancillary issue is implied or suggested in a great many ways throughout the text. Given the fact that this second edition —like the first—presents only a few concrete examples of art and many essays *about* art, the student and teacher alike should conclude, once more, that it is always more valuable to examine many ways of thinking and feeling and performing in the arts and the humanities than to suggest merely one "correct" way of accomodating experience.

Of course, in the past five years there have been a great many changes in the world of art. Probably the most significant change is the emergence of the image—the picture—in place of the word as a means of communication, of expression, of criticism, of entertainment. With this change of emphasis to things visual comes an increasing obligation on students and teachers in the realm of the arts and humanities. As never before they must face the demanding task of making firm distinctions about quality, significance, and long-term values. If photography, film making, and their sibling television, share in common an element of the mechanical, the technology of the machine, then an increasingly vast number of people will be almost casually enfranchised as "artists." In itself, "numbers" in relationship to artistic accomplishment may be little significance. On the other hand, in an age of image, verbal distinctions and close argument may become increasingly rare, and may seem less "important" as the means of obtaining increasingly extreme visual effects becomes more important in the arts.

Above all, the pictorial suggests the explicit. Hence there is presently a new candor about the arts. The exploitation of sex for questionable artistic effect is not uncommon; local, state, and federal laws on pornography, for example, are everywhere under new scrutiny. Neither candor nor mere disclosure, however, is necessarily the equivalent of either truth or satisfactory artistic effect.

Unquestionably, the strongest trend in the arts in the past five years has been the concern of artists and audience alike with the environment. If this concern is in part transitory, there is at the same time an apparent deep artistic commitment to these vital, and as yet emerging, problems. For the first time since the invention of printing, concerned students, teachers, and artists, and even the mass audiences, are asking themselves questions such as how many trees must be used to manufacture a book. Questions of this kind, it can be said, are only symptomatic; the larger issue concerns the nature and quality of human life, not only for the present generation, but for the generations to come.

Because the old issues and recent developments in the arts are such firm facts, the editors in this second edition attempt to focus attention on the problems. In order that the implications of the image may be brought more closely under examination, there is a new and separate section on the photographer's art; the section on film as an art form is completely reconstructed, with an emphasis on recent developments; the introductory section directs attention not so much to the relationship of art and audience as to the more stimulating area where the arts appear to meet. Finally, the concluding section of the text faces more responsibly the implications for the quality of human life; the issues of design; the planning of our cities; and the responsibilities of the designer, the architect, and the environmental "engineer." If the more difficult truths implied by a changing attitude toward candor in the arts can engage a newer generation, then the obligation of a work of this kind is to further the discussion. To that end, in this edition, there are essays dealing with pornography chosen with the intention of ensuring a more thorough grasp of that recurring problem of the arts.

Within each section the materials follow a general plan. In nearly every instance the initial essay represents a somewhat traditional point of view, often from the late nineteenth century or written by one whose education or taste was formed by that time. Doubtless, some of the essays are controversial, but so is the present state of the arts which this book seeks to explore.

Above all, this second edition of *Modern Culture and the Arts* retains and makes more dramatic the single most important proposition in the arts today, especially in America—the split between the high, or private, arts and the popular arts—the divorce of high-quality art designed for the few from the art designed for mass production and mass consumption. As we said in the first edition, "A recognition of this duality . . . is of vital importance to all students, to all teachers, to all people, and this collection addresses itself squarely to this timely issue. It may be that our nation's legacy to future generations will be, for better or worse, its contribution to the popular arts."

In any event, from the instructor's point of view, this text assumes a wide use of records, slides, films, reproductions of sculpture and painting, documents on the dance and the theater, and actual visits to the nearest available theater and concert hall, gallery or museum. The chief limitation in the matter of supplemental aids is that of local resources. Of course, there is also always the television set.

In order not to preempt the teacher's place in the classroom, we have omitted pedagogical apparatus except for headnotes of an introductory nature. To make possible the inclusion of more essays, some pieces have been edited; if the piece has been shortened appreciably, this fact is stated in the headnote, and in any event all cuts are indicated by ellipses. All the essays, of whatever length, style, or language, are intended to quicken the reader's interest in the arts and to illuminate the vital issues they both pose and reflect.

James B. Hall
Barry Ulanov

THE
MEETING
OF
THE
ARTS

THE DECAY OF LYING

Because he was a wit of renown in an age and in a city where that quality of mind was highly regarded, Oscar Wilde (1854–1900) sometimes caused attention to be diverted from his own best talents and his accomplishments in poetry, the short story, the novel (The Picture of Dorian Gray), and the drama (Salome, Lady Windermere's Fan, The Importance of Being Earnest). If his essays seem racy in tone, his ideas are nearly always worth serious consideration; indeed, Wilde's mind is far more disciplined than one at first suspects. After all, he came to imaginative writing from intensive work in classical studies, both as a scholar and as a translator. Wilde lectured in America in 1882, but to audiences that were probably not up to his sophistication. Back in London, the young Irishman became a celebrated literary lion, but his career collapsed in scandal and a public trial in 1895 for alleged homosexuality and, after two years in prison, lived out his life in self-imposed exile in Paris. The following dialogue, edited especially for this text, expounds a position concerning art and man and nature which may appear startling, but it is not entirely easy to refute.

Oscar
Wilde

A dialogue. Persons: Cyril and Vivian. Scene: The library of a country house in Nottinghamshire.

Cyril (coming in through the open window from the terrace). My dear Vivian, don't coop yourself up all day in the library. It is a perfectly lovely afternoon. . . . Let us go and lie on the grass, and smoke cigarettes, and enjoy Nature.

Vivian. Enjoy Nature! I am glad to say that I have entirely lost that faculty. . . . My own experience is that the more we study Art, the less we care for Nature. What Art really reveals to us is Nature's lack of design, her curious crudities, her extraordinary monotony, her absolutely unfinished condition. Nature has good intentions, of course, but, as Aristotle once said, she cannot carry them out. Fortunate for us, however, that Nature is so imperfect, as otherwise we should have had no art at all. As for the infinite variety of Nature, that is a pure myth. It is not to be found in Nature herself. It resides in the imagination, or fancy, or cultivated blindness of the man who looks at her.

Cyril.   Well, you need not look at the landscape. You can lie on the grass and smoke and talk.

Vivian.   But Nature is so uncomfortable. . . . If Nature had been comfortable, mankind would never have invented architecture, and I prefer houses to the open air. . . . Egotism itself, which is so necessary to a proper sense of human dignity, is entirely the result of indoor life. Out of doors one becomes abstract and impersonal. . . . Nothing is more evident than that Nature hates Mind. Thinking is the most unhealthy thing in the world, and people die of it just as they die of any other disease. Fortunately, in England at any rate, thought is not catching. . . . Shall I read you what I have written? It might do you a great deal of good.

Cyril.   Certainly, if you give me a cigarette. . . .

Vivian (reading in a very clear, musical voice).   "THE DECAY OF LYING: A PROTEST.—One of the chief causes that can be assigned for the curiously commonplace character of most of the literature of our age is undoubtedly the decay of Lying as an art, a science, and a social pleasure. The ancient historians gave us delightful fiction in the form of fact; the modern novelist presents us with dull facts under the guise of fiction. . . . He has not even the courage of other people's ideas, but insists on going directly to life for everything, and ultimately, between encyclopædias and personal experience, he comes to the ground, having drawn his types from the family circle or from the weekly washerwoman, and having acquired an amount of useful information from which never, even in his most meditative moments, can he thoroughly free himself.

"The loss that results to literature in general from this false ideal of our time can hardly be overestimated. People have a careless way of talking about a 'born liar,' just as they talk about a 'born poet.' But in both cases they are wrong. Lying and poetry are arts—arts, as Plato saw, not unconnected with each other—and they require the most careful study, the most disinterested devotion. Indeed, they have their technique, just as the more material arts of painting and sculpture have, their subtle secrets of form and colour, their craft-mysteries, their deliberate artistic methods. As one knows the poet by his fine music, so one can recognize the liar by his rich rhythmic utterance, and in neither case will the casual inspiration of the moment suffice. Here, as elsewhere, practice must precede perfection. But in modern days while the fashion of writing poetry has become far too common, and should, if possible, be discouraged, the fashion of lying has almost fallen into disrepute. Many a young man starts in life with a natural gift for exaggeration which, if nurtured in congenial and sympathetic surroundings, or by the imitation of the best models, might grow into something really great and wonderful. But, as a rule, he comes to nothing. He either falls into careless habits of accuracy——"

Cyril. My dear fellow!

Vivian. Please don't interrupt in the middle of a sentence. "He either falls into careless habits of accuracy, or takes to frequenting the society of the aged and the well-informed. Both things are equally fatal to his imagination, as indeed they would be fatal to the imagination of anybody, and in a short time he develops a morbid and unhealthy faculty of truth-telling, begins to verify all statements made in his presence, has no hesitation in contradicting people who are much younger than himself, and often ends by writing novels which are so like life that no one can possibly believe in their probability. This is no isolated instance that we are giving. It is simply one example out of many; and if something cannot be done to check, or at least to modify, our monstrous worship of facts, Art will become sterile and Beauty will pass away from the land. . . . Mr. Henry James writes fiction as if it were a painful duty, and wastes upon mean motives and imperceptible 'points of view' his neat literary style, his felicitous phrases, his swift and caustic satire. . . . Mrs. Oliphant prattles pleasantly about curates, lawn-tennis parties, domesticity, and other wearisome things. Mr. Marion Crawford has immolated himself upon the altar of local colour. . . .

Nothing in the whole history of literature is sadder than the artistic career of Charles Reade. He wrote one beautiful book, *The Cloister and the Hearth,* and wasted the rest of his life in a foolish attempt to be modern, to draw public attention to the state of our convict prisons, and the management of our private lunatic asylums. Charles Dickens was depressing enough in all conscience when he tried to arouse our sympathy for the victims of the poor-law administration; but Charles Reade, an artist, a scholar, a man with a true sense of beauty, raging and roaring over the abuses of contemporary life like a common pamphleteer or a sensational journalist, is really a sight for the angels to weep over. Believe me, my dear Cyril, modernity of form and modernity of subject-matter are entirely and absolutely wrong. We have mistaken the common livery of the age for the vesture of the Muses, and spend our days in the sordid streets and hideous suburbs of our vile cities when we should be out on the hillside with Apollo. Certainly we are a degraded race, and have sold our birthright for a mess of facts.

Cyril. There is something in what you say, and there is no doubt that whatever amusement we may find in reading a purely modern novel, we have rarely any artistic pleasure in re-reading it. . . . If one cannot enjoy reading a book over and over again, there is no use reading it at all. But what do you say about the return to Life and Nature? This is the panacea that is always being recommended to us.

Vivian. I will read you what I say on that subject. The passage comes later on in the article, but I may as well give it to you now:—

"The popular cry of our time is 'Let us return to Life and Nature; they will recreate Art for us, and send the red blood coursing through her veins; they will shoe her feet with swiftness and make her hand strong.' But, alas! Nature is always behind the age. And as for Life, she is the solvent that breaks up Art, the enemy that lays waste her house."

Cyril. What do you mean by saying that Nature is always behind the age?

Vivian. Well, perhaps that is rather cryptic. What I mean is this. If we take Nature to mean natural simple instinct as opposed to self-conscious culture, the work produced under this influence is always old-fashioned, antiquated, and out of date. . . . If we regard Nature as the collection of phenomena external to man, people only discover in her what they bring to her. She has no suggestions of her own. Wordsworth went to the lakes, but he was never a lake poet. He found in stones the sermons he had already hidden there. He went moralizing about the district, but his good work was produced when he returned, not to

Nature but to poetry. Poetry gave him *Laodamia,* and the fine
sonnets, and the great Ode, such as it is. Nature gave him *Peter
Bell,* and the address to Mr. Wilkinson's spade.

Cyril. I think that view might be questioned. I am rather inclined to believe in the "impulse from a vernal wood," though of
course the artistic value of such an impulse depends entirely on
the kind of temperament that receives it, so that the return to
Nature would come to mean simply the advance to a great personality. You would agree with that, I fancy. However, proceed
with your article.

Vivian (reading). "Art begins with abstract decoration with
purely imaginative and pleasurable work dealing with what is
unreal and non-existent. This is the first stage. Then Life becomes
fascinated with this new wonder, and asks to be admitted into
the charmed circle. Art takes life as part of her rough material,
recreates it, and refashions it in fresh forms, is absolutely indifferent to fact, invents, imagines, dreams, and keeps between herself and reality the impenetrable barrier of beautiful style, of
decorative or ideal treatment. The third stage is when Life gets
the upper hand, and drives Art out into the wilderness. This is
the true decadence, and it is from this that we are now suffering. . . .

Facts are not merely finding a footing-place in history, but
they are usurping the domain of Fancy, and have invaded the
kingdom of Romance. Their chilling touch is over everything.
They are vulgarising mankind. The crude commercialism of
America, its materialising spirit, its indifference to the poetical
side of things, and its lack of imagination and of high unattainable
ideals, are entirely due to that country having adopted for its
national hero a man, who according to his own confession, was
incapable of telling a lie. . . .

Cyril. My dear boy!

Vivian. I assure you: . . .

"Art finds her own perfection within, and not outside of, herself. She is not to be judged by any external standard of resemblance. She is a veil, rather than a mirror. She has flowers that no
forests know of, birds that no woodland possesses. She makes
and unmakes many worlds, and can draw the moon from heaven
with a scarlet thread. Hers are the 'forms more real than living
man,' and hers the great archetypes of which things that have

Oscar Wilde, 1882.
Photograph by Napoleon Sarony. The George Eastman House Collection.

David Mlinaric, 1966.
Photograph by Colin Jones. Life Magazine © Time Inc.

existence are but unfinished copies. Nature has, in her eyes, no laws, no uniformity. . . . She can bid the almond tree blossom in winter, and send the snow upon the ripe cornfield. . . .

Cyril.   I should like to ask you a question. What do you mean by saying that life, "poor, probable, uninteresting human life," will try to reproduce the marvels of art? . . . You don't mean to say that you seriously believe that Life imitates Art, that Life in fact is the mirror, and Art the reality?

Vivian.   Certainly I do. Paradox though it may seem—and paradoxes are always dangerous things—it is none the less true that Life imitates art far more than Art imitates life. . . . And it has always been so. A great artist invents a type, and Life tries to copy it, to reproduce it in a popular form, like an enterprising publisher. Neither Holbein nor Vandyck found in England what they have given us. They brought their types with them, and Life, with her keen imitative faculty, set herself to supply the master with models. The Greeks, with their quick artistic instinct, understood this, and set in the bride's chamber the statue of Hermes or of Apollo, that she might bear children as lovely as the works of art that she looked at in her rapture or her pain. They knew that Life gains from Art not merely spirituality, depth of thought and feeling, soul-turmoil or soul-peace, but that she can form herself on the very lines and colours of art and can reproduce the dignity of Pheidias as well as the grace of Praxiteles. Hence came their objection to realism. They disliked it on purely social grounds. They felt that it inevitably makes people ugly, and they were perfectly right. We try to improve the conditions of the race by means of good air, free sunlight, wholesome water, and hideous bare buildings for the better housing of the lower orders. But these things merely produce health; they do not produce beauty. For this, Art is required, and the true disciples of the great artist are not his studio-imitators, but those who become like his works of art, be they plastic as in Greek days, or pictorial as in modern times; in a word, Life is Art's best, Art's only pupil.

As it is with the visible arts, so it is with literature. The most obvious and the vulgarest form in which this is shown is in the case of the silly boys who, after reading the adventures of Jack Sheppard or Dick Turpin, pillage the stalls of unfortunate apple-women, break into sweet-shops at night, and alarm old gentlemen who are returning home from the city by leaping out on them in

suburban lanes, with black masks and unloaded revolvers. . . .
The boy-burglar is simply the inevitable result of life's imitative
instinct. He is Fact, occupied as Fact usually is with trying to
reproduce Fiction, and what we see in him is repeated on an
extended scale throughout the whole of life. Schopenhauer has
analysed the pessimism that characterises modern thought, but
Hamlet invented it. . . . Think of what we owe to the imitation
of Christ, of what we owe to the imitation of Caesar.

Cyril. The theory is certainly a very curious one, but to
make it complete you must show that Nature, no less than Life,
is an imitation of Art. Are you prepared to prove that?

Vivian. My dear fellow, I am prepared to prove anything.

Cyril. Nature follows the landscape painter then, and takes
her effects from him?

Vivian. Certainly. Where, if not from the Impressionists, do
we get those wonderful brown fogs that come creeping down
our streets, blurring the gas-lamps and changing the houses into
monstrous shadows? To whom, if not to them and their master,
do we owe the lovely silver mists that brood over our river, and
turn to faint forms of fading grace curved bridge and swaying
barge? The extraordinary change that has taken place in the
climate of London during the last ten years is entirely due to this
particular school of Art. . . . Things are because we see them, and
what we see, and how we see it, depends on the Arts that have
influenced us. To look at a thing is very different from seeing a
thing. One does not see anything until one sees its beauty. Then,
and then only, does it come into existence. At present, people see
fogs, not because there are fogs, but because poets and painters
have taught them the mysterious loveliness of such effects. There
may have been fogs for centuries in London. I dare say there
were. But no one saw them, and so we do not know anything
about them. They did not exist till Art had invented them. . . .
However, I don't want to be too hard on Nature. I wish the
Channel, especially at Hastings, did not look quite so often like
a Henry Moore [an English painter of seascapes, 1831–1896], grey
pearl with yellow lights, but then, when Art is more varied,
Nature will, no doubt, be more varied also. That she imitates Art,
I don't think even her worst enemy would deny now. It is the
one thing that keeps her in touch with civilized man. But have I
proved my theory to your satisfaction?

Cyril. You have proved it to my dissatisfaction, which is

better. But even admitting this strange imitative instinct in Life
and Nature, surely you would acknowledge that Art expresses
the temper of its age, the spirit of its time, the moral and social
conditions that surround it, and under whose influence it is produced.

Vivian. Certainly not! Art never expresses anything but itself.
This is the principle of my new aesthetics; and it is this, more
than that vital connection between form and substance, on
which Mr. Pater dwells, that makes music the type of all the
arts. . . . Remote from reality, and with her eyes turned away
from the shadows of the cave, Art reveals her own perfection,
and the wondering crowd that watches the opening of the mar-
vellous, many-petalled rose fancies that it is its own history that
is being told to it, its own spirit that is finding expression in a new
form. But it is not so. The highest art rejects the burden of the
human spirit, and gains more from a new medium or a fresh
material than she does from any enthusiasm for art, or from any
lofty passion, or from any great awakening of the human consciousness. She develops purely on her own lines. She is not
symbolic of any age. It is the ages that are her symbols.

Cyril. But modern portraits by English painters, what of
them? Surely they are like the people they pretend to represent?

Vivian. Quite so. They are so like them that a hundred years
from now no one will believe in them. The only portraits in
which one believes are portraits where there is very little of the
sitter and a very great deal of the artist. Holbein's drawings of
the men and women of his time impress us with a sense of their
absolute reality. But this is simply because Holbein compelled
life to accept his conditions, to restrain itself within his limitations, to reproduce his type, and to appear as he wished it to
appear. It is style that makes us believe in a thing—nothing but
style. Most of our modern portrait painters are doomed to absolute oblivion. They never paint what they see. They paint what
the public sees, and the public never sees anything.

Cyril. Well, after that I think I should like to hear the end of
your article.

Vivian. With pleasure. . . .

"What we have to do, what at any rate it is our duty to do, is
to revive this old art of Lying. Much of course may be done, in
the way of educating the public, by amateurs in the domestic
circle, at literary lunches, and at afternoon teas. But this is merely

the light and graceful side of lying, such as was probably heard at Cretan dinner parties. There are many other forms. Lying for the sake of gaining some immediate personal advantage, for instance—lying with a moral purpose, as it is usually called—though of late it has been rather looked down upon, was extremely popular with the antique world. . . .

Lying for the sake of the improvement of the young, which is the basis of home education, still lingers amongst us, and its advantages are so admirably set forth in the early books of Plato's *Republic* that it is unnecessary to dwell upon them here. It is a mode of lying for which all good mothers have peculiar capabilities, but it is capable of still further development, and has been sadly overlooked by the School Board. Lying for the sake of a monthly salary is of course well known in Fleet Street, and the profession of a political leader-writer is not without its advantages. But it is said to be a somewhat dull occupation, and it certainly does not lead to much beyond a kind of ostentatious obscurity. The only form of lying that is absolutely beyond reproach is Lying for its own sake, and the highest development of this is, as we have already pointed out, Lying in Art. . . . We must cultivate the lost art of Lying."

Cyril. We must certainly cultivate it at once. But in order to avoid making any error I want you to tell me briefly the doctrines of the new aesthetics.

Vivian. Briefly, then, they are these. Art never expresses anything but itself. It has an independent life, just as Thought has, and develops purely on its own lines. It is not necessarily realistic in an age of realism, nor spiritual in an age of faith. So far from being the creation of its time, it is usually in direct opposition to it, and the only history that it preserves for us is the history of its own progress. Sometimes it returns upon its footsteps, and revives some antique form, as happened in the archaistic movement of late Greek Art, and in the pre-Raphaelite movement of our own day. At other times it entirely anticipates its age, and produces in one century work that it takes another century to understand, to appreciate, and to enjoy. In no case does it reproduce its age. To pass from the art of a time to the time itself is the great mistake that all historians commit.

The second doctrine is this. All bad art comes from returning to Life and Nature, and elevating them into ideals. Life and Nature may sometimes be used as part of Art's rough material, but before they are of any real service to art they must be translated into artistic conventions. The moment Art surrenders its imaginative medium it surrenders everything. As a method Realism is a complete failure, and the two things that every artist should avoid are modernity of form and modernity of subject-matter. To us, who live in the nineteenth century, any century is a suitable subject for art except our own. The only beautiful things are the things that do not concern us. It is, to have the pleasure of quoting myself, exactly because Hecuba is nothing to us that her sorrows are so suitable a motive for a tragedy. . . . Life goes faster than Realism, but Romanticism is always in front of Life.

The third doctrine is that Life imitates Art far more than Art imitates Life. This results not merely from Life's imitative instinct, but from the fact that the self-conscious aim of Life is to find expression, and that Art offers it certain beautiful forms through which it may realize that energy. It is a theory that has never been put forward before, but it is extremely fruitful, and throws an entirely new light upon the history of Art.

It follows, as a corollary from this, that external Nature also imitates Art. The only effects that she can show us are effects that we have already seen through poetry, or in paintings. This is the secret of Nature's charm, as well as the explanation of Nature's weakness.

The final revelation is that Lying, the telling of beautiful untrue things, is the proper aim of Art. But of this I think I have spoken at sufficient length. And now let us go out on the terrace, where "droops the milk-white peacock like a ghost," while the evening star "washes the dusk with silver." At twilight nature becomes a wonderfully suggestive effect, and is not without loveliness, though perhaps its chief use is to illustrate quotations from the poets. Come! We have talked long enough.

*The title of this essay borrows a celebrated phrase
from Walter Pater and the fin de siècle inheritors
of the Aesthetic Movement; the phrase, indeed, had
become something of a benchmark for the
aestheticians—and the aesthetes—of the day. Here,
however, in finely honed and elegant prose, Forster
re-evaluates the implications of "art for art's sake"
in the light of the social and political realities of
1927. The result is an excellent example of the
informed but sceptical mind coming to a generally
pessimistic conclusion about art and the artist in the
twentieth century. E. M. Forster (1879-1970) is
held in great esteem as a novelist—his best known
works are* Howard's End *and* A Passage to India—
*although he inexplicably stopped writing
novels in his early middle age. His* Aspects of
the Novel *is a classic of fiction criticism and
his later collections of essays,* Abinger Harvest
and Two Cheers for Democracy, *offer models of
clean, clear, logical prose.*

ART FOR ART'S SAKE

**E. M.
Forster**

I believe in art for art's sake. It is an unfashion-
able belief, and some of my statements must be
of the nature of an apology. Sixty years ago I
should have faced you with more confidence. A
writer or a speaker who chose "Art for Art's
Sake" for his theme sixty years ago could be
sure of being in the swim, and could feel so confident of success that he sometimes dressed himself in aesthetic costumes suitable to the occasion
—in an embroidered dressing-gown, perhaps, or
a blue velvet suit with a Lord Fauntleroy collar;
or a toga, or a kimono, and carried a poppy or a
lily or a long peacock's feather in his mediaeval
hand. Times have changed. Not thus can I present either myself or my theme to-day. My aim
rather is to ask you quietly to reconsider for a
few minutes a phrase which has been much misused and much abused, but which has, I believe,
great importance for us—has, indeed, eternal importance.

Now we can easily dismiss those peacock's feathers and other affectations—they are but trifles—but I want also to dismiss a more dangerous heresy, namely the silly idea that only art matters, an idea which has somehow got mixed up with the idea of art for art's sake, and has helped to discredit it. Many things, besides art, matter. It is merely one of the things that matter, and high though the claims are that I make for it, I want to keep them in proportion. No one can spend his or her life entirely in the creation or the appreciation of masterpieces. Man lives, and ought to live, in a complex world, full of conflicting claims, and if we simplified them down into the aesthetic he would be sterilised. Art for art's sake does not mean that only art matters and I would also like to rule out such phrases as, "The Life of Art," "Living for Art," and "Art's High Mission." They confuse and mislead.

What does the phrase mean? Instead of generalising, let us take a specific instance—Shakespeare's *Macbeth*, for example, and pronounce the words, *"Macbeth for Macbeth's sake."* What does that mean? Well, the play has several aspects—it is educational, it teaches us something about legendary Scotland, something about Jacobean England, and a good deal about human nature and its perils. We can study its origins, and study and enjoy its dramatic technique and the music of its diction. All that is true. But *Macbeth* is furthermore a world of its own, created by Shakespeare and existing in virtue of its own poetry. It is in this aspect *Macbeth* for *Macbeth's* sake, and that is what I intend by the phrase "art for art's sake." A work of art—whatever else it may be—is a self-contained entity, with a life of its own imposed on it by its creator. It has internal order. It may have external form. That is how we recognise it.

Take for another example that picture of Seurat's which I saw two years ago in Chicago—"*La Grande Jatte*." Here again there is much to study and to enjoy: the pointillism, the charming face of the seated girl, the nineteenth-century Parisian Sunday sunlight, the sense of motion in immobility. But here again there is something more; "*La Grande Jatte*" forms a world of its own, created by Seurat and existing by virtue of its own poetry: *"La Grande Jatte" pour "Le Grande Jatte": l'art pour l'art.* Like *Macbeth* it has internal order and internal life.

It is to the conception of order that I would now turn. This is important to my argument, and I want to make a digression, and glance at order in daily life, before I come to order in art.

In the world of daily life, the world which we perforce inhabit, there is much talk about order, particularly from statesmen and politicians. They tend, however, to confuse order with orders, just as they confuse creation with regulations. Order, I suggest, is something evolved from within, not something imposed from without; it is an internal stability, a vital harmony, and in the social and political category it has never existed except for the convenience of historians. Viewed realistically, the past is really a series of *dis*orders, succeeding one another by discoverable laws, no doubt, and certainly marked by an increasing growth of human interference, but disorders all the same. So that, speaking as a writer, what I hope for to-day is a disorder which will be more favourable to artists than is the present one, and which will provide them with fuller inspirations and better material conditions. It will not last—nothing lasts—but there have been some advantageous disorders in the past—for instance, in ancient Athens, in Renaissance Italy, eighteenth-century France, periods in China and Persia—and we may do something to accelerate the next one. But let us not again fix our hearts where true joys are not to be found. We were promised a new order after the first world war through the League of Nations. It did not come, nor have I faith in present promises, by whomsoever endorsed. The implacable offensive of Science forbids. We cannot reach social and political stability for the reason that we continue to make scientific discoveries and to apply them, and thus to destroy the arrangements which were based on more elementary discoveries. If Science would discover rather than apply—if, in other words, men were more interested in knowledge than in power—mankind would be in a far safer position, the stability statesmen talk about would be a possibility, there could be a new order based on vital harmony, and the earthly millennium might approach. But Science shows no signs of doing this: she gave us the internal combustion engine, and before we had digested and assimilated it with terrible pains into our social system, she harnessed the atom, and destroyed any new order that seemed to be evolving. How can man get into harmony with his surroundings when he is constantly altering them? The future of our race is, in this direction, more unpleasant than we care to admit, and it has sometimes seemed to me that its best chance lies through apathy, uninventiveness, and inertia. Universal exhaustion might promote that Change of Heart which is at present so briskly recommended from a thousand pulpits. Universal exhaustion would certainly be a new experience. The human race has never undergone it, and is still too perky to admit that it may be coming and might result in a sprouting of new growth through the decay.

I must not pursue these speculations any further—they lead me too far from my terms of reference and maybe from yours. But I do want to emphasize that order in daily life and in history, order in the social and political category, is unattainable under our present psychology.

Where is it attainable? Not in the astronomical category, where it was for many years enthroned. The heavens and the earth have become terribly alike since Einstein. No longer can we find a reassuring contrast to chaos in the night sky and look up with George Meredith to the stars, the army of unalterable law, or listen for the music of the spheres. Order is not there. In the entire universe there seem to be only two possibilities for it. The first of them—which again lies outside my terms of reference—is the divine order, the mystic harmony, which according to all religions is available for those who can contemplate it. We must admit its possibility, on the evidence of the adepts, and we must believe them when they say that it is attained, if attainable, by prayer. "O thou who changest not, abide with me," said one of its poets. "*Ordina questo amor, o tu che m'ami,*" said another: "Set love in order thou who lovest me." The existence of a divine order, though it cannot be tested, has never been disproved.

The second possibility for order lies in the aesthetic category, which is my subject here: the order which an artist can create in his own work, and to that we must now return. A work of art, we are all agreed, is a unique product. But why? It is unique not because it is clever or noble or beautiful or enlightened or original or sincere or idealistic or useful or educational—it may embody any of those qualities—but because it is the only material object in the universe which may possess internal harmony. All the others have been pressed into shape from outside, and when their mould is removed they collapse. The work of art stands up by itself, and nothing else does. It achieves something which has often been promised by society, but always delusively. Ancient Athens made a mess—but the *Antigone* stands up. Renaissance

Rome made a mess—but the ceiling of the Sistine got painted.
James I made a mess—but there was *Macbeth*. Louis XIV—but
there was *Phèdre*. Art for art's sake? I should just think so, and
more so than ever at the present time. It is the one orderly
product which our muddling race has produced. It is the cry of
a thousand sentinels, the echo from a thousand labyrinths; it is
the lighthouse which cannot be hidden: *c'est le meilleur témoign-
age que nous puissions donner de notre dignité* [it is the best witness that we could give of our worth]. *Antigone* for *Antigone's*
sake, *Macbeth* for *Macbeth's*, "*La Grande Jatte*" *pour* "*La
Grande Jatte*."

If this line of argument is correct, it follows that the artist will
tend to be an outsider in the society to which he has been born,
and that the nineteenth century conception of him as a Bohemian
was not inaccurate. The conception erred in three particulars: it
postulated an economic system where art could be a full-time job,
it introduced the fallacy that only art matters, and it overstressed
idiosyncracy and waywardness—the peacock-feather aspect—
rather than order. But it is a truer conception than the one which
prevails in official circles on my side of the Atlantic—I don't
know about yours: the conception which treats the artist as if he
were a particularly bright government advertiser and encourages
him to be friendly and matey with his fellow citizens, and not to
give himself airs.

Estimable is mateyness, and the man who achieves it gives
many a pleasant little drink to himself and to others. But it has no
traceable connection with the creative impulse, and probably acts
as an inhibition on it. The artist who is seduced by mateyness
may stop himself from doing the one thing which he, and he
alone, can do—the making of something out of words or sounds
or paint or clay or marble or steel or film which has internal harmony and presents order to a permanently disarranged planet.
This seems worth doing, even at the risk of being called uppish
by journalists. I have in mind an article which was published some
years ago in the London *Times*, an article called "The Eclipse of
the Highbrow," in which the "Average Man" was exalted, and
all contemporary literature was censured if it did not toe the line,
the precise position of the line being naturally known to the
writer of the article. Sir Kenneth Clark, who was at that time
director of our National Gallery, commented on this pernicious
doctrine in a letter which cannot be too often quoted. "The poet

and the artist," wrote Clark, "are important precisely because they are not average men; because in sensibility, intelligence, and power of invention they far exceed the average." These memorable words, and particularly the words "power of invention," are the Bohemian's passport. Furnished with it, he slinks about society, saluted now by a brickbat and now by a penny, and accepting either of them with equanimity. He does not consider too anxiously what his relations with society may be, for he is aware of something more important than that—namely the invitation to invent, to create order, and he believes he will be better placed for doing this if he attempts detachment. So round and round he slouches, with his hat pulled over his eyes, and maybe with a louse in his beard, and—if he really wants one—with a peacock's feather in his hand.

If our present society should disintegrate—and who dare prophesy that it won't?—this old-fashioned and démodé figure will become clearer: the Bohemian, the outsider, the parasite, the rat—one of those figures which have at present no function either in a warring or a peaceful world. It may not be dignified to be a rat, but many of the ships are sinking, which is not dignified either—the officials did not build them properly. Myself, I would sooner be a swimming rat than a sinking ship—at all events I can look around me for a little longer—and I remember how one of us, a rat with particularly bright eyes called Shelley, squeaked out, "Poets are the unacknowledged legislators of the world," before he vanished into the waters of the Mediterranean.

What laws did Shelley propose to pass? None. The legislation of the artist is never formulated at the time, though it is sometimes discerned by future generations. He legislates through creating. And he creates through his sensitiveness and his power to impose form. Without form the sensitiveness vanishes. And form is as important to-day, when the human race is trying to ride the whirlwind, as it ever was in those less agitating days of the past, when the earth seemed solid and the stars fixed, and the discoveries of science were made slowly, slowly. Form is not tradition. It alters from generation to generation. Artists always seek a new technique, and will continue to do so as long as their work excites them. But form of some kind is imperative. It is the surface crust of the internal harmony, it is the outward evidence of order.

My remarks about society may have seemed too pessimistic, but

I believe that society can only represent a fragment of the human spirit, and that another fragment can only get expressed through art. And I wanted to take this opportunity, this vantage ground, to assert not only the existence of art, but its pertinacity. Looking back into the past, it seems to me that that is all there has ever been: vantage grounds for discussion and creation, little vantage grounds in the changing chaos, where bubbles have been blown and webs spun, and the desire to create order has found temporary gratification, and the sentinels have managed to utter their challenges, and the huntsmen, though lost individually, have heard each other's calls, through the impenetrable wood, and the lighthouses have never ceased sweeping the thankless seas. In this pertinacity, there seems to me, as I grow older, something more and more profound, something which does in fact concern people who do not care about art at all.

In conclusion, let me summarise the various categories that have laid claim to the possession of Order.

1. The social and political category. Claim disallowed on the evidence of history and of our own experience. If man altered psychologically, order here might be attainable: not otherwise.

2. The astronomical category. Claim allowed up to the present century, but now disallowed on the evidence of the physicists.

3. The religious category. Claim allowed on the evidence of the mystics.

4. The aesthetic category. Claim allowed on the evidence of various works of art, and on the evidence of our own creative impulses, however weak these may be, or however imperfectly they may function. Works of art, in my opinion, are the only objects in the material universe to possess internal order, and that is why, though I don't believe that only art matters, I do believe in Art for Art's Sake.

DECEPTIVE ANALOGIES: SPECIOUS AND REAL RELATIONSHIPS AMONG THE ARTS

A student of Alfred North Whitehead, Susanne Langer (1895–   ) came to national prominence with the publication of one of the most important books of the past fifty years, Philosophy in a New Key (1941). In this work Langer considers symbolic transformation, the logic of signs and symbols, and—among many other things— the genesis of artistic insight. Partly because of her training in philosophy and anthropology, partly because of her wide sympathy with all the arts, she is especially stimulating in the difficult area of interrelationships among the arts.

Susanne Langer

The interrelations among all the arts—painting, sculpture, and architecture, music, poetry, drama, fiction, dance, film, and any others you may admit—have become a venerable old topic in aesthetics. The prevailing doctrines about those relations, too, are rapidly getting gray hair or something that looks a lot like a mould. It has lately become acceptable again to assert that all the arts are really just one "Art" with a capital *A;* that the apparent differences between painting and poetry, for instance, are superficial, due only to the difference of their materials. One artist paints with pigments, the other with words—or one speaks in rhyme, and one in images—and so forth. Dance is the language of gesture, drama is "really" a dithyramb, i.e., a choric dance, architecture is (of course) frozen music. Some aestheticians merely mark the fundamental unity of all the arts, and then proceed to classify the various manifestations of art as lower and higher forms, major and minor arts. Thomas Munro lists a hundred kinds—alphabetically. Their peculiar differences, usually conceived as different limitations, are supposed to spring from the materials with which they work. Other philosophers and critics connect them in parallel rather than in an ascending order. These writers see a commonwealth of art, instead of a hierarchy of the arts. But all are agreed that the several arts are just so many aspects of one and the same human adventure, and almost every recent book in aesthetics begins with the statement that the customary distinctions among the arts are an unfortunate result of our modern tendency to departmentalize the contents of our lives.

It is true that questions of the exact compass of this or that art—poetry, music, drama, dance—are taken more seriously in the modern age than they were in times past. Scholars like Paul Cristeller have established that fact, I think, beyond doubt. Yet we have utterances by Leonardo da Vinci and Michangelo on the relative merits of painting, poetry, and sculpture, and comparisons of painting with music; and such comparisons go back to Horace, Simonides, and Aristotle.

Whether the distinction of the arts be old or new in aesthetic theory, in practice it is ancient. Praxiteles was a sculptor and Sophocles a poet; the statues of Praxiteles are no more likely to be confused with Sophoclean tragedies than Brancusi's statues with plays by Pirandello, nor did Homer slip from epic composition into composing vases or figurines of clay. Poetry and the plastic arts have always been separate, even when poetry furnished the themes of painting and statuary, or poets mentioned the pictorial decorations on a hero's shield.

Yet the fact that all artistic activities are related to each other has always been just as apparent as their distinct characters. It is these relations which, for all that has been written about them, have so far been treated only in a superficial fashion. Sometimes we hear of *the* interrelation of all the arts. Before long this one universal interrelation is described either as an original identity or as an ideal ultimate union; and there the study of it ends, perhaps with a few examples of conjoined arts—poetry and music united in song, plastic art and music in dance, poetry and painting in a play with scenery, or all the arts in the operatic *Gesamtkunstwerk*. It ends much as it began, with quotations from many authorities denouncing the customary separation, but heightened by the positive advice that art schools should teach a course in music and music schools should take cognizance of the sister arts, painting, poetry, and drama.

There seems to be an inveterate tendency of our minds, perhaps abetted by idioms of our language, to treat any two things that bear some intimate relation to each other as identical. The identity of two terms, once established, is an important but not at all interesting relation. It means that one and the same thing goes by two names, and that is all. If poetry, music, painting, etc., are all just different names for the same thing, their relation to each other is exhausted by the dictionary. But why should Art have so many names?

The answer to that question is usually that artists work with a great many materials, and as their techniques have to differ accordingly, they seem to be doing quite different things. All the arts are in essence one, but they differ in various accidents. From there on, we find ourselves on the trail of the accidents, and all interesting facts that emerge only lead further and further away from the basic unity of Art to its diversities.

The trouble with this approach to the interrelations of the arts is that it takes for granted the facts that are to be understood; but what a study takes for granted lies behind it, and hence cannot be the object of investigation that lies before it. What we begin with is not what we arrive at—discover, clarify, or demonstrate. If we start by postulating the essential sameness of the arts we shall learn no more about that sameness. We shall only skip or evade every problem that seems, offhand, to pertain to one art but not to some other, because it cannot be really a problem of Art, and so we shall forcibly limit ourselves to simple generalities that may be safely asserted (as is customary) of: "a poem, a sonata, a Raphael Madonna, a beautiful dance . . ." and so on.

My approach to the problem of interrelations among the arts has been the precise opposite: taking each art as autonomous, and asking about each in turn what it creates, what are the principles of creation in this art, what its scope and possible materials. Such a treatment shows up the differences among the several great genera of art—plastic, musical, balletic, poetic. Pursuing these differences, rather than vehemently denying their importance, one finds that they go deeper than one would expect. Each genus, for instance, creates a different kind of experience altogether; each may be said to make its own peculiar primary creation. The plastic arts create a purely visual space, music a purely audible time, dance a realm of interacting powers, etc. Each art has its own principles of constructing its final creations, or works. Each has its normal materials, such as tones for music, pigments for painting; but no art is limited to its normal materials by anything but their sufficiency for its normal creative purposes. Even when music uses spoken words or architecture enlists the paintbrush, music or architecture does not therefore wander from its own realm, the realm of its primary creation, whether the artist employs usual or unusual materials, in ordinary or extraordinary ways.

But if you trace the differences among the arts as far and as minutely as possible, there comes a point beyond which no more distinctions can be made. It is the point where the deeper structural devices—ambivalent images, intersecting forces, great rhythms and their analogues in detail, variations, congruences, in short: all the organizing devices—reveal the principles of dynamic form that we learn from nature as spontaneously as we learn language from our elders. These principles appear, in one art after another, as the guiding ones in every work that achieves organic unity, vitality of form or expressiveness, which is what we mean by the significance of art.

Where no more distinctions can be found among the several arts, there lies their unity. We need not accept this unity by faith and reject as vicious all inquiries that call it in question; its demonstration is the result of such inquiries. Here we have certainly the deepest relationship among the arts: they all exemplify the general principles of Art. I am using the word "Art" in the restricted sense sometimes delimited as "the fine arts" or "liberal arts"—plastic, musical, literary, theatrical, etc.—and not in the widest sense, in which we speak of "the arts of war and peace." Both uses are current; but I am talking about the kind of Art whose products are judged as *artistic* or *inartistic*. We do not say that a bungled surgical operation is inartistic (though we may find it unaesthetic). Using "Art" in its restricted sense, then, I venture the definition: *All art is the creation of perceptible forms expressive of human feeling.*

This definition contains several weasel words: "creation," "forms," "expressive," and even "feeling." But weasels do have holes where they may be cornered. I don't think my weasels are sliding around quite freely any more; but if I were to catch them for your inspection just now we would need more than this one hour to get on with our subject, the relations that hold among all the arts or among some of them.

Essentially, then, all the arts create forms to express the life of feeling (the *life of feeling*, not the feelings an artist happens to have); and they all do it by the same basic principles. But there the simple sameness ends. When we look at what the various arts create, we come to the source of their differentiation, from which each art derives its autonomy and its problems.

Each art begets a special dimension of experience that is a special kind of image of reality. In *Feeling and Form* I called this special dimension the "primary illusion," but "illusion" is a prejudicial word, and as we have no time to explain and justify its use here, we had better shelve it altogether. Let us call it the *primary apparition* of an art. . . .

Each one of the arts has its primary apparition, which is something created, not something found in the world and used. The materials of art—pigments, sounds, words, tones, etc.—are found and used to create forms in some virtual dimension. I call this primary apparition "primary" not because it is made first, before the work (it is not), but because it is made *always*, from the first stroke of work in any art. Everything a painter does creates and organizes—or in sad event, disorganizes—pictorial space. Where no pictorial space is created we see spots of color on a flat object, as we see them on a palette, or as we see spilled paint on the floor. But even a very bad picture is a spatial apparition.

Music, on the other hand, though it may create experiences of space, is in a completely given dimension of *virtual time*. Virtual time is its primary apparition, its dimension, in which its created forms move. I cannot go into further explanations here, but only indicate the findings of an enquiry that began by treating each art in its own terms, and became general by stepwise generalization.

Let it suffice, then, that each of the great orders of art has its own primary apparition which is the essential feature of all its works. This thesis has two consequences for our present discussions: it means that the distinctions commonly made between the great orders—the distinction between painting and music, or poetry and music, or sculpture and dance—are not false, artificial divisions due to a modern passion for pigeonholes, but are founded on empirical and important facts; secondly, it means that there can be no hybrid works, belonging as much to one art as to another. And we might add that the evolutionist's idea of one undifferentiated Art preceding, in primitive times, the several kinds of art, loses much of its offhand plausibility.

At this point most people will be ready to ask: "But is there, then, no relation whatever among the arts, except their unity of purpose? Are they historically entirely unrelated? And do you mean to say poetry and music are never used together in song, nor sculpture and architecture in a monument? How silly!"

My answer is that to say two things are distinct is not to say they are unrelated. The fact that they are distinct is what enables them to have all sorts of highly specialized, interesting relations to each other—much more interesting than the relation of pseudo-identity that we allege when we hold them to be, really, several views of the same thing, so they might melt into each other on better inspection. It is precisely by reason of their distinct primary apparitions that such complex works as song, opera, drama, or choric dance are not just the normal functions of several arts conjoined in varying proportion. In such works there are interesting, often involved relationships that one would not suspect without the guiding question: "What, in this case, is created? Only apparitions are created; what sort of apparition is this?"

The arts are defined by their primary apparitions, not by materials and techniques. Painted sculpture is not a joint product of sculpture and painting at all, for what is created is a sculpture, not a picture. Paint is used, but used for creating sculptural form—not for painting. The fact that poetry involves sound, the normal material of music, is not what makes it comparable to music—where it is comparable.

In fact, direct comparision is an over-rated method for discovering relations among the arts. Long before you can generalize by comparison of the actual processes involved in plastic, musical, poetic, and all other kinds of creation, and thus relate all the arts as species of one genus, (i.e. Art), the study of just two primary apparitions is enough to bring some interesting relations to light; for instance, what is the primary apparition in plastic art—virtual space—may appear as a secondary apparition in music, whose essential stuff is virtual time. There are spatial effects in music; and careful study—not fancy—shows that these are always effects of virtual, not actual, space, with the characteristics which painters and sculptors call "plastic." Similarly, where time-effects are achieved in the plastic arts, they always have the qualities of virtual time, the "stuff" of music. Progressively we find then that the primary apparition of any art may appear as secondary in another, and that in the arts generally all space is plastic space, all time is musical time, all impersonal forces are balletic (the word "balletic" here refers to Dance, not specifically ballet. There is no English adjective equivalent to the German *tänzerisch*), all events poetic. Everything in the arts is created, never imported from actuality; and in this way their fundamental creations meet. This is one of their exchanges.

Another, more striking (though perhaps not more important) relation between two arts obtains where a work of one art serves in the making of another work belonging to another art: the case in which two arts are usually said to be conjoined. Consider, for instance, a good poem successfully set to music. The result is a good song. One would naturally expect the excellence of the song to depend as much on the quality of the poem as on the musical handling. But this is not the case. Schubert has made beautiful songs out of great lyrics by Heine, Shakespeare, and Goethe, and equally beautiful songs out of the commonplace, sometimes maudlin lyrics of Müller. The poetic creation counts only indirectly in a song, in exciting the composer to compose it. After that, the poem as a work of art is broken up. Its words, sound and sense alike, its phrases, its images, all become musical material. In a well-wrought song the text is swallowed, hide and hair. That does not mean that the words do not count, that other words would have done as well; but the words have been musically exploited, they have entered into a new composition, and the poem as a poem has disappeared in the song.

The same thing holds for music and dance. A dance is not necessarily the better for using very good music. Dance normally swallows music, as music normally swallows words. The music that, perhaps, first inspires a dance, is none the less cancelled out as art in its own right, and assimilated to the dance; and for this many a third-rate musical piece has served as well as a significant work.

Every work has its being in only one order of art; compositions of different orders are not simply conjoined, but all except one will cease to appear as what they are. A song sung on the stage in a good play is a piece of dramatic action. If we receive it in the theatre as we would receive it in concert, the play is a pastiche, like the average revue that is not a creation at all, but a series of little creations, variously good or bad themselves.

This far-reaching principle of cross-relationships among the arts is the principle of assimilation. It sounds very radical, but I have always found it to hold. Opera is music; to be good opera it must be dramatic, but that is not to be drama. Drama, on the other hand, swallows all plastic creations that enter into its theatrical precinct, and their own pictorial, architectural, or sculptural beauties do not add themselves to its own beauty. A great work of sculpture, say the original Venus of Milo that stands in the Louvre, transported to the comic or tragic stage (perhaps in a play about a sculptor) would count only as stage setting, an element in the action, and might not meet this purpose as well as a pasteboard counterfeit of it would do.

The principle of assimilation holds usually in certain familiar ways. Music ordinarily swallows words and actions creating opera, oratorio or song; dance commonly assimilates music. But this is not a fast rule. Sometimes a poem may swallow music, or even dance; dramatic poetry quite normally does both. I have never known music to incorporate dancing, but it might. The only safe assertion is that every work has its primary apparition, to which all other virtual dimensions are secondary. There are no happy marriages in art—only successful rape.

Half-baked theories, such as I consider the traditional theories of the unity of Art to be, are apt to have sorry consequences when practice is based on them. Among such sorry consequences are the works that result from serious efforts to paint the counterparts of symphonies or parallel poems or pictures by musical compositions. Color symphonies are painted in the belief that the deployment of colors on a canvas corresponds to the deployment of tones in music, so that an analogy of structure should produce analogous works. This is, of course, a corollary of the proposition that the various arts are distinguished by the differences in their respective materials, to which their techniques have to be adapted, but were it not for these material differences their procedures would be the same. Oddly enough, the results of such translation, when it is really technically guided, have no vestige of the artistic values of their originals. Even where the parallels of structure are recognizable, as in a painted design following the verbal design of a sonnet, the visual forms may be interesting, even pleasant, but they are not creative, beyond their mere creation of virtual space (which they do create); as expressive forms they do not resemble the sonnet at all.

There is another class of translations that purports to express in one medium the emotional values of some work in a different medium; and this sort of suggestion (it is really nothing more) tends to produce works that are very weak in form. Simonides said that architecture is frozen music; but music is not melted architecture. When this musical ice cream is returned to its liquid state, it runs away in an amorphous flow of sound. The same weakness appears in painting that purports to render musical composition. I am thinking of the musical colors in *Fantasia*, and the music-paintings of students in the Boston Museum School of Art. A painting expressive of a very lyrical composition, such as Chopin's G major *Nocturne*, has no lyrical character at all, but only indistinct washes of color. The reason for such failure is that the painter is not guided by discernment of musical values, but is concentrating his attention on his feelings under the influence of sounds, and producing *symptoms* of these feelings. What he registers is a sequence of essentially uncomposed, actual experiences; symptoms are not works.

There is, however, a notable exception to these failures of artistic translation. Sometimes a poet calls certain of his poems "quartets," or a composer entitles a composition "Arabesque," and the designation seems fitting, even enlightening, although it suggests no particular model nor invites any method of comparison. That is because the artist—say T. S. Eliot, in the *Four Quartets*—creates an effect, an expressive virtual entity purely poetic, that functions in some particular way characteristic of string quartets: combining great richness of feeling with extreme economy of material. The result is a semblance of concentration together with complete articulation. In the poems it is all done by means of the proportion of material to technique, and of scope of feeling to scope its image. The poems are very brief. In quartet music it results from the complete exploitation of just four voices. A normal quartet is not very brief, but generally has four movements.

Similarly, Schumann's "Arabesque" does not copy any design of Arabic sculpture, but it achieves a feeling of elaborated thought where no thought really has beginning or end, or of motion in a maze yet without dizziness. This effect, which is characteristic of

Arabesque sculpture and architecture, is rare and striking in music.

The important point in these parallels is, that they do not coordinate materials, for instance tones with words, or phrases with sculptured forms. Interweaving of phrases is only an obvious bit of imitation in Schumann's piece; the to and fro of ambiguous or mixed harmonies and the relations of melodic to rhythmic accents are just as important, and correspond to nothing in a stone tracery. The sculptor works with light, texture, height, and many other material data of which Schumann was certainly not thinking. He probably was not even thinking of any particular arabesque, though of course we cannot know his thought.

As such successful analogues do not rest on correspondence of material factors, so also they are not comparably constructed. The similarity that justifies the borrowed title word holds between their respective *formulations* of feeling, and these are achieved in entirely different ways in different arts. There is no rule that can govern two arts, and probably no technical device that can be taken over from one to another, let alone materials that correspond. But there are comparable created forms.

Such occasional parallels would be trivial, were they not further related to one of the most exciting phenomena in the realm of the arts, which may be termed "ultimate abstraction," or "transcendence."

But this is a difficult topic, inviting philosophical speculations that had better not come into a brief single lecture, especially at its weary end: I mentioned it only because it is the most interesting and perhaps the closest relation among the arts—the point where their imaginal distinctions seem really to yield, for a moment, to their community of import, and achieve the utmost abstraction of that import for the beholder's direct intuition. It is here that all art "aspires towards the condition of music," and music becomes a timeless vision of feeling.

There are few more accessible approaches to the thought of the Spanish philosopher José Ortega y Gasset (1883–1955) than his little book on The Dehumanization of Art, *from which the following pages come. There are also few more lucid meditations on the meaning of the abstract textures of the modern arts. Reality, Ortega shows, has become something quite special for the painter—and all others who follow his example, in words or movements or sounds. There has been a great flight from vicariousness in the modern arts. The mere reproduction of the world around him no longer absorbs the serious artist. He is also, Ortega suggests, less than awed by the work of art itself. He has renounced pretentiousness. He snaps his fingers at his own procedures with the carefree manner of the young. These few pages assert all this and more, and remarkably enough, when one considers that they were first published in 1925, they do so with a confidence that the subsequent history of the arts more than justifies.*

THE DEHUMANIZATION OF ART

José Ortega y Gasset

With amazing swiftness modern art has split up into a multitude of divergent directions. Nothing is easier than to stress the differences. But such an emphasis on the distinguishing and specific features would be pointless without a previous account of the common fund that in a varying and sometimes contradictory manner asserts itself throughout modern art. Did not Aristotle already observe that things differ in what they have in common? Because all bodies are colored we notice that they are differently colored. Species are nothing if not modifications of a genus, and we cannot understand them unless we realize that they draw, in their several ways, upon a common patrimony.

I am little interested in special directions of modern art and, but for a few exceptions, even less in special works. Nor do I, for that matter, expect anybody to be particularly interested in my valuation of the new artistic produce. Writers who have nothing to convey but their praise or dispraise of works of art had better abstain from writing. They are unfit for this arduous task.

The important thing is that there unquestionably exists in the world a new artistic sensibility.[1] Over against the multiplicity of special directions and individual works, the new sensibility represents the generic fact and the source, as it were, from which the former spring. This sensibility it is worth while to define. And when we seek to ascertain the most general and most characteristic feature of modern artistic production we come upon the tendency to dehumanize art. After what we have said above, this formula now acquires a tolerably precise meaning.

Let us compare a painting in the new [abstract] style with one of, say, 1860. The simplest procedure will be to begin by setting against one another the objects they represent: a man perhaps, a house, or a mountain. It then appears that the artist of 1860 wanted nothing so much as to give to the objects in his picture the same looks and airs they possess outside it when they occur as parts of the "lived" or "human" reality. Apart from this he may have been animated by other more intricate aesthetic ambitions, but what interests us is that his first concern was with securing this likeness. Man, house, mountain are at once recognized, they are our good old friends; whereas on a modern painting we are at a loss to recognize them. It might be supposed that the modern painter has failed to achieve resemblance. But then some pictures of the 1860's are "poorly" painted, too, and the objects in them differ considerably from the corresponding objects outside them. And yet, whatever the differences, the very blunders of the traditional artist point toward the "human" object; they are downfalls on the way toward it and somehow equivalent to the orienting words "This is a cock" with which Cervantes lets the painter Orbanejo enlighten his public [in fact, not enlightening his public at all; the incident in *Don Quixote* is of a bungling painter who needs a title to identify his shoddy work]. In modern paintings the opposite happens. It is not that

---

[1] This new sensibility is a gift not only of the artist proper but also of his audience. When I said above that the new art is an art for artists I understood by "artists" not only those who produce this art but also those who are capable of perceiving purely artistic values.

the painter is bungling and fails to render the natural (natural = human) thing because he deviates from it, but that these deviations point in a direction opposite to that which would lead to reality.

Far from going more or less clumsily toward reality, the artist is seen going against it. He is brazenly set on deforming reality, shattering its human aspect, dehumanizing it. With the things represented on traditional paintings we could have imaginary intercourse. Many a young Englishman has fallen in love with Gioconda. With the objects of modern pictures no intercourse is possible. By divesting them of their aspect of "lived" reality the artist has blown up the bridges and burned the ships that could have taken us back to our daily world. He leaves us locked up in an abstruse universe, surrounded by objects with which human dealings are inconceivable, and thus compels us to improvise other forms of intercourse completely distinct from our ordinary ways with things. We must invent unheard-of-gestures to fit those singular figures. This new way of life which presupposes the annulment of spontaneous life is precisely what we call understanding and enjoyment of art. Not that this life lacks sentiments and passions, but those sentiments and passions evidently belong to a flora other than that which covers the hills and dales of primary and human life. What those ultra-objects[2] evoke in our inner artist are secondary passions, specifically aesthetic sentiments.

It may be said that, to achieve this result, it would be simpler to dismiss human forms—man, house, mountain—altogether and to construct entirely original figures. But, in the first place, this is not feasible.[3] Even in the most abstract ornamental line a stubborn reminiscence lurks of certain "natural" forms. Secondly—and this is the crucial point—the art of which we speak is inhuman not only because it contains no things human, but also because it is an explicit act of dehumanization. In his escape from the human world the young artist cares less for the "*terminus ad quem* [the purpose or goal of an argument]," the startling fauna at which he arrives, than for the "*terminus a quo* [the starting-point of an argument]," the human aspect which he destroys. The question

2 "Ultraism" is one of the most appropriate names that have been coined to denote the new sensibility.
3 An attempt has been made in this extreme sense—in certain works by Picasso—but it has failed signally.

is not to paint something altogether different from a man, a
house, a mountain, but to paint a man who resembles a man as
little as possible; a house that preserves of a house exactly what is
needed to reveal the metamorphosis; a cone miraculously emerging—as the snake from his slough—from what used to be a
mountain. For the modern artist, aesthetic pleasure derives from
such a triumph over human matter. That is why he has to drive
home the victory by presenting in each case the strangled victim.

It may be thought a simple affair to fight shy of reality, but
it is by no means easy. There is no difficulty in painting or saying
things which make no sense whatever, which are unintelligible
and therefore nothing. One only needs to assemble unconnected
words or to draw random lines.[4] But to construct something that
is not a copy of "nature" and yet possesses substance of its own is
a feat which presupposes nothing less than genius.

"Reality" constantly waylays the artist to prevent his flight.
Much cunning is needed to effect the sublime escape. A reversed
Odysseus, he must free himself from his daily Penelope and sail
through reefs and rocks to Circe's Faery. When, for a moment,
he succeeds in escaping the perpetual ambush, let us not grudge
him a gesture of arrogant triumph, a St. George gesture with the
dragon prostrate at his feet.

ART A THING
OF NO CONSEQUENCE

To the young generation art is a thing of no consequence.—The
sentence is no sooner written than it frightens me since I am well
aware of all the different connotations it implies. It is not that to
any random person of our day art seems less important than it
seemed to previous generations, but that the artist himself regards
his art as a thing of no consequence. But then again this does not
accurately describe the situation. I do not mean to say that the
artist makes light of his work and his profession; but they interest
him precisely because they are of no transcendent importance.
For a real understanding of what is happening let us compare

---

[4] This was done by the Dadaistic hoax. It is interesting to note again (see the above
footnote) that the very vagaries and abortive experiments of the new art derive with
a certain cogency from its organic principle, thereby giving ample proof that
modern art is a unified and meaningful movement.

the role art is playing today with the role it used to play thirty years ago and in general throughout the last century. Poetry and music then were activities of an enormous caliber. In view of the downfall of religion and the inevitable relativism of science, art was expected to take upon itself nothing less than the salvation of mankind. Art was important for two reasons: on account of its subjects which dealt with the profoundest problems of humanity, and on account of its own significance as a human pursuit from which the species derived its justification and dignity. It was a remarkable sight, the solemn air with which the great poet or the musical genius appeared before the masses—the air of a prophet and founder of religion, the majestic pose of a statesman responsible for the state of the world.

A present-day artist would be thunderstruck, I suspect, if he were trusted with so enormous a mission and, in consequence, compelled to deal in his work with matters of such scope. To his mind, the kingdom of art commences where the air feels lighter and things, free from formal fetters, begin to cut whimsical capers. In this universal pirouetting he recognizes the best warrant for the existence of the Muses. Were art to redeem man, it could do so only by saving him from the seriousness of life and restoring him to an unexpected boyishness. The symbol of art is seen again in the magic flute of the Great God Pan which makes the young goats frisk at the edge of the grove.

All modern art begins to appear comprehensible and in a way great when it is interpreted as an attempt to instill youthfulness into an ancient world. Other styles must be interpreted in connection with dramatic social or political movements, or with profound religious and philosophical currents. The new style only asks to be linked to the triumph of sports and games. It is of the same kind and origin with them.

In these last few years we have seen almost all caravels of seriousness founder in the tidal wave of sports that floods the newspaper pages. Editorials threaten to be sucked into the abyss of their headlines, and across the surface victoriously sail the yachts of the regattas. Cult of the body is an infallible symptom of a leaning toward youth, for only the young body is lithe and beautiful. Whereas cult of the mind betrays the resolve to accept old age, for the mind reaches plenitude only when the body begins to decline. The triumph of sport marks the victory of the values of youth over the values of age. Note in this context the success of the motion picture, a preeminently corporeal art.

In my generation the manners of old age still enjoyed great prestige. So anxious were boys to cease being boys that they imitated the stoop of their elders. Today children want to prolong their childhood, and boys and girls their youth. No doubt, Europe is entering upon an era of youthfulness.

Nor need this fact surprise us. History moves in long biological rhythms whose chief phases necessarily are brought about not by secondary causes relating to details but by fundamental factors and primary forces of a cosmic nature. It is inconceivable that the major and, as it were, polar differences inherent in the living organism—sex and age—should not decisively mold the profile of the times. Indeed, it can be easily observed that history is rhythmically swinging back and forth between these two poles, stressing the masculine qualities in some epochs and the feminine in others, or exalting now a youthful deportment and then again maturity and old age.

The aspect European existence is taking on in all orders of life points to a time of masculinity and youthfulness. For a while women and old people will have to cede the rule over life to boys; no wonder that the world grows increasingly informal.

All peculiarities of modern art can be summed up in this one feature of its renouncing its importance—a feature which, in its turn, signifies nothing less than that art has changed its position in the hierarchy of human activities and interests. These activities and interests may be represented by a series of concentric circles whose radii measure the dynamic distances from the axis of life where the supreme desires are operating. All human matters—vital and cultural—revolve in their several orbits about the throbbing heart of the system. Art which—like science and politics—used to be very near the axis of enthusiasm, that backbone of our person, has moved toward the outer rings. It has lost none of its attributes, but it has become a minor issue.

The trend toward pure art betrays not arrogance, as is often thought, but modesty. Art that has rid itself of human pathos is a thing without consequence—just art with no other pretenses.

DESIGN AS A CREATIVE PRINCIPLE IN THE ARTS

Northrop Frye is a Canadian literary theorist, critic, and educator of considerable distinction. His most influential work, Anatomy of Criticism *(1957), defines literature as an object rather than a subject of study, and seeks to give criticism a place of its own as a structure of thought and a body of knowledge existing in its own right. Frye has produced scholarly studies of Blake, Milton, and Shakespeare and, most recently,* The Stubborn Structure *(1970), a work concerning society and criticism. In the essay reprinted here, he distinguishes between the appeal of content in a work of literature and the overall design of the work, perhaps mythic in character, which he finds the more powerful element.*

Northrop Frye

There is a time-honored distinction which divides the arts into a major and a minor group, the fine and the useful, but this distinction is rapidly losing all its fineness and most of its usefulness, and is now practically vestigial. It was never in any case a distinction among artists, only among the arts themselves. In reading Cellini's autobiography we can see how the well-trained artist of that day was ready to switch from a commission in the "major" arts to one in the "minor" ones and back again, with no loss of status or feeling of incongruity. We think of Michelangelo as dwelling on the loftiest summits of the major arts, but Michelangelo too had his handyman assignments, such as designing the uniform of the Papal Guards, in which he acquitted himself indifferently but not incompetently. Similar conditions still prevail. In the early years of our marriage, when finances were a bit difficult, my wife assisted the family fortunes by getting a job painting magnolias on coffee trays. She met a sculptress at a party, and approached her with some trepidation, feeling that anyone who practiced so majestic an art might take a dim view of her magnolia project. The sculptress, however, had been living on a private income cut off at the source as a result of the war, and she was making her living painting roses on babies' chamber pots.

One of the primitive functions of art is the production of luxury goods for a ruling class: armor for the warrior, vestments for the priest, jewellery and regalia for the king. Eventually the same kind of social demand produces temples, cathedrals, castles and palaces, with all their contained treasures. Such art is often characterized by great complexity and ingenious skill, a skill sometimes regarded with superstitious awe by contemporaries who do not possess it. One thinks of the legends of the mysterious smiths and forgers of weapons like Weyland and Hephaestus, of the long series of enchanted spears, magic swords and helmets of invisibility in romance, of the deities begotten by the Greek veneration for such work, the Cabeiroi and Dactyls and Cyclops and Telchines, of the many elaborate descriptions of works of "minor" art from Homer's shield of Achilles onward. The *Beowulf* poet's favorite aesthetic judgement is "curiously wrought," a phrase he usually applies to armor.

In our own day we notice how often an unsophisticated eye falls with particular delight on elaborate embroideries or Chinese ivory carvings, the delight being expressed in some such formula as "look at all the work in that." As a ruling class becomes less primitive, the work done for it begins to look more and more like unusually expensive and elaborate toys, as we can see in Fabergé, for example. It is understandable that Yeats should associate his nostalgia for aristocracy with "many ingenious lovely things" of this sort, including the toy bird in *Sailing to Byzantium.* At the same time, as an ascendant class gets more and more of a monopoly of the art produced in its society, it extends its ownership over the "major" arts too, especially of painting and sculpture, which, unlike works of literature, may become the exclusive possession of their purchaser. And although patronage normally restricts such works of art to a small minority, other patrons, such as the Church, may in the stained glass and frescoes of its cathedrals make them to some degree a genuinely public art. I say to some degree, as the old cliché about the art of cathedrals being a "Bible of the poor" could apply only to those of the poor who had exceedingly long-range vision.

Sheer elaboration, as an aesthetic form of conspicuous consumption, still exists, or did until recently. My own city of Toronto possesses an extraordinary example: a palace of an exuberant millionaire known as "Casa Loma," one wing of which is bastard French Renaissance and the other wing bastard Spanish Renaissance, like Siamese twins born out of wedlock. But the rise of democracy (in contrast to the oligarchy of which Casa Loma is an expression) gives a functional cast to public art, and thereby to public taste generally, and the industrial revolution has transferred the "curiously wrought" arts from craftsmanship to mechanism. This aesthetic area is now mainly the area represented by the housewife with a new garbage disposal unit or the teenager with his attention absorbed by the viscera of a motorcycle. Such things of course belong to the useful rather than the fine arts, but so did their ancestors: even the most useless of aristocratic toys still had the social role of dramatizing a certain standard of living.

As a result the "creative" arts have tended increasingly to form a united front, with the "major" and "minor" distinction becoming of less account. We can see this tendency starting in William Morris. For Morris there were two forms of production, the creative and the mechanical. The former is genuine work and in Morris's thought work is identified with the creative act. Genuine work is true "manufacture," in the original sense of something made by a brain-directed hand, and it tends towards social freedom as surely as mechanical production leads toward exploitation and mass slavery. Morris thus assigns a revolutionary social role to the creative arts, but what he sees as essentially creative in the creative arts is design, and design is something that fine and useful arts have in common. Because of his interest in the social role of art, Morris found his centre of gravity in the "minor" arts and when he practised painting and poetry he treated them as "minor" arts. In doing so he threw down a challenge to the theory of criticism. Is not what we consider "major" about the major arts simply their association with the luxury goods of a ruling class? Even literature has always regarded the most major forms of its art as being connected, like epic and tragedy, with the portrayal of ruling-class figures.

Any exhibition of abstract or nonobjective art today will illustrate how far we have gone in the direction of emphasizing design in painting and sculpture. And if we compare such an exhibition with one of handcrafts or industrial design, we can see that the real relation between them now is not that of major to minor art, but of theory to practice, the disinterested to the applied forms of the same constructive principles. The kind of modern building which seems the result of an armaments race between the makers of glass and the makers of curtains shows similar tendencies. It seems almost as though in the visual arts there is now only one art, the art of design, and what used to be different arts are variations of it in different media. This is naturally a considerable overstatement, though it may have some value at that.

Painting and sculpture differ from the applied arts most markedly in the extent of their capacity for representation. Hence representationalism tends to separate the major from the minor visual arts, and formalism tends to unify them. We notice that the more successful nations show a matter-of-fact realism in their arts, but that many aspects of such realism seem to have little creative staying power. Roman art is a good example of the way in which a realistic approach to art tends to become, first derivative, then pedestrian, and finally insipid, while the real creative energy of the culture goes into engineering. Something similar has happened in the totalitarian societies of our time, and there are strong tendencies toward it in the democracies. The reason is that what representational public art represents is mainly a society's idealized picture of itself. A Roman goddess, say the Barberini Juno, suggests, not awe or veneration or majesty, but the impressiveness of a well-to-do Roman matron. "Beauty" in the human form tends to mean, in such an art, the representing of youth, good looks and physical health. One feels of the wax mannequins in a modern shop window that any girl who succeeded in being as haughty and aloof as they look would be in an advanced stage of narcissism, and ought to see a psychiatrist before going out of business entirely. But the abstracted gaze of these models is directly descended from the placid idols of earlier cultures who mirror their own society's dream of realizable pleasure.

Realism in a healthy condition is another form of socially revolutionary art: it explores society, shows compassion with misery, brings strange gleams of beauty out of suffering, and ridicules absurdity and pomposity, especially in those with authority. In an unhealthy condition it expresses the will of the ascendant social group to preserve its status quo, and when it does this it seeks the facile idealizing which is what the word "beauty" so often means. Marxist criticism in Russia is now struggling to work out the paradox of a "social realism" which works properly in a genuinely revolutionary context, but can only turn sickly and parasitic when designed to support the party which achieved its revolution and has now the role of a ruling class. Realism is often associated with, and often rationalized as, a scientific view of the world, but the impetus behind realistic art, good or bad, is of social and not scientific origin. There is a curious law of art, seen in Van Gogh and in some of the surrealists, that even the attempt to reproduce the act of seeing, when carried out with sufficient energy, tends to lose its realism and take on the unnatural glittering intensity of hallucination.

There are two aspects of contemporary art in the democracies which are of particular importance as indicating that democracy is a genuinely revolutionary society, neither about to be revolutionized nor trying to retain its present structure, but mature enough to provide for both change and stability. One of these is realism doing its proper job of social criticism; the other is experimentalism in pure or abstract form. It is, quite consistently, an essential part of Marxist theory to attack "formalism" as the essence of the bourgeois in art. Both of the democratic tendencies are signs of a society that regards its social order as expendable and created for its convenience, the order being made for the sake of man and not man for the sake of the order.

We said that with the growth of democracy and industry the production of luxury goods for a small minority gradually extends itself over a greater part of society. In proportion as it does this, it tends to extinguish another form of art: the popular creation of the minor arts. The immediate production of domestic arts, from pottery to household fetishes, and from peasants' blouses to the weather-vanes and bowsprits of American folk museums, can lead only the most furtive existence in our society, for what we call handcraft follows a different tradition, as we have just seen. Folk art is both popular and primitive, two words which mean much the same thing in the arts. These terms ordinarily mean that representation is subordinated to more geometrical and abstract forms of expression, sometimes merely through incompetence in drawing, sometimes through a naive but genuinely simple wisdom. But despite the pleasure with which we seize on any sign of such creativity, especially when it reaches into the major arts, as it does with painting by Grandma Moses and others, this current of creative energy in our society is now largely diverted into more expert and sophisticated channels (or canals, which mixes the metaphor less). It is still active and influential as a tradition, but hardly as a source of production in its own right.

In contrast to the luxury goods spoken of earlier, which are produced for the centralizing forces in society, the aristocracy and the church, the popular arts are decentralized. William Morris's conception of the social role of art takes off from here. Morris's association of the minor arts with social freedom and stability is anarchist rather than communist, and assumes as its goal a decentralizing of society. For Morris the state, and *a fortiori* the huge industrial empire, is a crude form of human community, the genuine form of which he restores and depicts in his *News from Nowhere*. If we realize that we associate the minor arts today mainly with the smaller countries, and think most readily of Swedish furniture, Swiss watches, Irish linen, or (until recently) Czechoslovakian glass, we can see some force in his idea. *News from Nowhere* is, however, an application of a more general principle that all culture, including the major arts, demands the decentralizing of society. Shelley's preface to *Prometheus Unbound* proposes to break down England into a group of small communities, in which anonymous masses would become identifiable people, so that each community could follow in its own way the tradition of the small-town cultures of Periclean Athens, Renaissance Florence, or Elizabethan London. T. S. Eliot's *Notes Toward a Definition of Culture* is preoccupied with Welsh nationalism, the encouraging of local peculiarities of all kinds, and with the advisability, for most people, of never leaving the place where they were born. But whatever the merits of the art produced in our time, it will certainly be an international art, and decentralizing theories seem at present to be a hopeless anachronism. I am a Canadian intellectual, and therefore (in Canada it is a therefore) I am a cultural regionalist, but the extent to which Canadian culture can grow out of the Canadian soil I realize in advance to be an exceedingly limited one.

The present organization of educational media in the universities, the museums, the art galleries, seems almost deliberately designed to bring about a change from decentralized to international culture. For the contemporary artist, all the arts of all traditions and epochs are available for comparative study, the primitive and the historical, the barbaric and the sophisticated. The basis for comparison, when any is made, is obviously design. The contemporary artist is as free to follow the influences of Benin bronzes as of Rodin, of Etruscan cave paintings as of Cézanne. The enormous expansion of technical resources has united the artist more closely with the educational media, so closely in fact that an "arts" course can be a preparation for the understanding of contemporary art in a way that it could hardly have been a century ago. At the same time most of the expansion, as compared with the cultural traditions of a century ago, has been in the area of the popular and primitive arts.

If these somewhat random remarks about the visual arts have any cogency, is it possible to see analogies between the visual arts and literature which will throw any light on the situation of literature and its criticism today? Analogies are tricky things, and even striking analogies may be specious. Some of the phenomena noted above have no genuine literary analogues at all. If the visual arts have many practitioners who, like Cellini, can tackle either a statue or a salt cellar, one might expect the same situation in literature. The poet or novelist could well be a verbal handyman, able to turn out a piece of advertising copy or a newspaper report or ghost-write a politician's speech as part of his professional competence with words. This is by no means the rule, because the applied verbal arts, especially journalism and advertising, are imprisoned in conventions so rigid that no one who has learned them is fit for anything else unless he starts all over again. Those who followed in *The New Yorker* the record of Miss Marianne Moore's struggles to make her poetic talents useful to the Ford Motor Company in its search for a name for its new car (it was finally called "Edsel") will understand that the gap between the poet and society is one that the poet cannot do much to bridge.

In the production of luxury goods, again, the role of literature is not always easy to trace. One can see that in literature, as elsewhere, what is designed as a toy or plaything is mechanically complex: detective stories are more ingenious than serious novels, and light verse is more deliberately contrived than heavy verse. There has of course been a constant demand for the services of the poet in congratulatory odes, masques, and the kind of work associated with the office of poet laureate. The masque, however, as Ben Jonson, the first official poet laureate, discovered, follows the general rule of drama that the more spectacular the conception of the drama is, the less important the poet's role. The re-

marks above on the importance of experimentalism in a democratic society and of keeping realism to its proper critical role would
apply to literature equally with the other arts. But there are two
features of literature which make all analogies with visual arts
difficult. One is the way in which literature is decentralized by the
barriers of language. The other is the fact that no art of words
can ever be wholly abstract, in the way that painting and sculpture and music can be. There must always be an identifiable content, which corresponds to representation in painting and sculpture. Content, unlike design, demands some knowledge of the
cultural background of the work. Hence the presence of a representational core, along with a specific language to learn, helps to
slow down the internationalizing of literature. Perhaps it is a good
thing that it is slowed down, but it is reasonable to expect that
literature will to some degree follow the tendencies of the other
arts, and, if so, its criticism needs to be prepared for such tendencies. The real problem for our analogy is this: what are the principles of design in literature which enable us to take something
of the same perspective towards it that we can take toward the
visual arts and music?

We notice that one form of literature seems to make its way
easily across all barriers of language and culture, and this is the
folk tale. The reason for its ability to travel is clearly that it is
pure verbal design. It is made up of a number of stock themes
that can be counted and indexed; its plot belongs to an identifiable
type; there is hardly any content beyond the plot, and therefore
the plot can be readily abstracted from the language in which
it is expressed. There is little of the feeling, which every translator
of a fully developed work of literature has, that some elements
are so bound up with the conventions of a specific culture that
they are hard to convey, and that other elements are so bound up
with the features of a specific language that they cannot be conveyed at all. It is, then, the *mythos*, Aristotle's word for plot or
narrative, which is the element of design in literature. It has been
an established principle in literary criticism ever since Aristotle
that the poetic, as distinct from the historical, narrative presents
the typical or universal event rather than the specific and particular one.

If we keep the plot in mind as the principle of design in any
work of literature which contains a fiction, we can see a host of
family likenesses which ought to make "comparative literature"

as comprehensible and systematic a study as the comparative study of folk tales. What begins to emerge from the chaos of literature are certain recurring principles of verbal design, embodied in such conventions and genres as comedy, romance and tragedy, which link Shakespeare with Kalidasa, Melville with the Old Testament, Proust with Lady Murasaki. This is a less myopic approach to the study of comparative literature than the one employed at present, but one which promises more fruitful results. Such typical plots (*mythoi*) show also a clear line of descent from the myths of early mythologies, and illustrate the place of literary fiction and drama as a cultural descendant of mythology.

Plot is a clear and simple example of overall verbal design; but, apart from the fact that not all works of literature have plots, we need to isolate also an example of a *unit* of design. Poetic language is associative rather than descriptive language, and the primitive function of poetry, a function it never loses and frequently returns to, seems to have something to do with identifying the human and the nonhuman worlds. We see this function clearly in the kind of mythology out of which a great deal of literature grows: stories of gods who are human in conception and character and yet are identified with aspects of nature, and are sun-gods or tree-gods or sky-gods. The unit of identity, where two things are said to be the same thing and yet preserve a twofold aspect, appears in poetry as metaphor, and this I take to be the fundamental unit of verbal design in literature. Here again the actual process of identification is one that does not depend either on language (through of course there may be linguistic identifications, as in puns), or on the peculiarities of a specific culture. When an Italian and a Chinese poet both employ metaphor, it makes for very little difficulty if one chooses a rose and the other a lotus.

The tendency of contemporary poets, and many novelists and dramatists as well, to be attracted toward myth and metaphor, rather than toward a realistic emphasis on content, is thus a cultural tendency parallel to the emphasis on abstract design in the visual arts. It exhibits also the same paradox, or seeming paradox: it is usually a highly sophisticated, even erudite and academic, approach to the art, yet the features of the art which are most interesting to it are primitive and popular features. Dylan Thomas seems more complex and baffling than Theodore Dreiser, yet it is easier for me to imagine Dylan Thomas genuinely popular than to imagine Dreiser, for all his obvious and considerable merits, genuinely popular. This is not to suggest a preference between two utterly incomparable things, but to suggest that writers who concentrate on literary design rather than content, despite their superficial difficulties, are the writers most likely to reach the widest public most quickly. The principles of literary design are also the readiest means by which literature can be effectively taught, at any level from kindergarten to graduate school. And as myth and metaphor are habits of mind and not merely artificial devices, such teaching should lead us, not simply to admire works of literature more, but to transfer something of their imaginative energy to our own lives. It is that transfer of imaginative energy which is the aim of all education in the arts, and to the possibility of which the arts themselves bear witness.

At the present time it should be clear to every responsible observer that the popular arts are very much an integral part of the American scene; furthermore, in America, the acceptance or the rejection of these arts at either the level of production or consumption will not soon be a matter of enforceable legislation. It follows, therefore, that an understanding of the nature of the popular arts can be a valuable part of every student's education. It is appropriate that a professional philosopher—and Professor Kaplan is a specialist in the methodology for behavioral science at the University of Michigan—should suggest certain larger issues of the popular arts. First delivered as a paper before the American Philosophical Association in 1964, this essay has been especially edited for inclusion here. The essay is not so much a departure for Abraham Kaplan as it might seem to those who know him best as co-author of Power and Society *and writer of numerous pieces in that area. The pages devoted to art in his* New World of Philosophy *are, like this piece, sympathetic, informed, and clearly based on a wide experience of the arts.*

THE AESTHETICS OF THE POPULAR ARTS

Abraham Kaplan

Aesthetics is so largely occupied with the good in art that it has little to say about what is merely better or worse, and especially about what is worse. Unremitting talk about the good, however, is not only boring but usually inconsequential as well. The study of *dis*-values may have much to offer both aesthetics and criticism for the same reasons that the physiologist looks to disease and the priest becomes learned in sin. Artistic taste and understanding might better be served by a museum of horribilia, presented as such. It is from this standpoint that I invite attention to the aesthetics of the popular arts.

I

By the popular arts I do not mean what has recently come to be known as pop art. This, like junk art and some of the theater of the absurd, is the present generation's version of dada. In some measure, no doubt, it serves as a device for enlarging the range of artistic possibilities, exploring the beauty in what is conventionally dismissed as meaningless and ugly, as well as the ugliness in what is conventionally extolled as beautiful. Basically, it is a revolt against the artistic establishment, a reaction against the oppressiveness of the academic and familiar. As such, it is derivative as though to say, "You call *this* junk?" If it is lacking in artistic virtue, its vice is like that of watching a voyeur—the sins of another are presupposed. It is what pop art presupposes that I am calling *popular art*.

Second, I do not mean simply *bad art*, neither the downright failures nor those that fall just short of some set of critical requirements. It is a question of *how* they fail and, even more, to what sort of success they aspire. Popular art may be bad art, but the converse is not necessarily true. It is a particular species of the unaesthetic that I want to isolate.

Similarly, I set aside what may be deprecated as merely minor art. Its products are likely to be more popular, in the straightforward sense, than those which have greatness. The *Rubaiyat* may be more widely read than *De rerum natura*, and *The Hound of the Baskervilles* more than *Crime and Punishment*, but each is excellent after its own kind. A work of minor art is not necessarily a minor work. Greatness, that is to say, is a distinctive aesthetic attribute—a matter of scope or depth and so forth; the word is not just a designation for the highest degree of artistic value. The lack of greatness may be a necessary condition for popular art, but most surely it is not a sufficient condition.

The *kind* of taste that the popular arts satisfy, and not how widespread that taste is, is what distinguishes them. On this basis, I provisionally identify my subject as *midbrow art*, to be contrasted with what appeals to either highbrow or lowbrow tastes. Popular art is what is found neither in the literary reviews nor in the pulp magazines, but in the slicks; neither in gallery paintings nor on calendars, but on Christmas cards and billboards; neither in serious music nor in jazz, but in Tin Pan Alley. The popular arts may very well appeal to a mass audience, but they have characteristics that distinguish them from other varieties of mass art, and distinctive contexts and patterns of presentation. A work of popular art may be a best seller, but it is not assigned in freshman English nor reprinted as a comic. It may win an Academy Award, but it will be shown neither at the local Art Cinema nor on the late, late show.

Many social scientists think that these symptoms—for they are no more than that—provide an etiology of the disease. Midbrow art, they say, is more properly designated *middle-class art*. It is a product of the characteristic features of modern society: capitalism, democracy, and technology. Capitalism has made art a commodity, and provided the means to satisfy the ever widening demands for the refinements of life that earlier periods reserved to a small elite. Democracy, with its apotheosis of majorities and of public opinion, has inevitably reduced the level of taste to that of the lowest common denominator. The technology of the mass media precludes the care and craftsmanship that alone can create works of art. For a time it was fashionable to lay these charges particularly at American doors, to view the popular arts as the distinctive feature of American culture; but by now, I think, most of those who take this line see popular art more generally, if not more generously, as only "the sickness of the age."

My thesis is this: that popular art is not the degradation of taste but its immaturity, not the product of external social forces but produced by a dynamic intrinsic to the aesthetic experience itself. Modern society, like all others, has its own style, and leaves its imprint on all it embraces. But this is only to say that our popular art is *ours*, not that it is our sole possession. Popular art is usually said to stem from about the beginning of the eighteenth century, but in its essence it is not, I think, a particularity of our time and place. It is as universal as art itself.

II

We might characterize popular art first, as is most often done, with respect to its *form*. Popular art is said to be simple and unsophisticated, aesthetically deficient because of its artlessness. It lacks quality because it makes no qualifications to its flat state-

ment. Everything is straightforward, with no place for complications. And it is standardized as well as simplified: one product
is much like another. But it is just the deadly routine that is so
popular. Confronted with that, we know just where we are,
know what we are being offered, and what is expected of us in
return. We can respond with mechanical routines ourselves, and
what could be simpler and more reliably satisfying?

Yet this account of the matter is itself too simple to be satisfactory. For why should simplicity be unaesthetic? Art always
strips away what is unessential, and purity has always been
recognized as a virtue. Put the adjective *classic* before it and
simplicity becomes a term of high regard. What is simple is not
therefore simple-minded. Art always concentrates, indeed it owes
its force to the power of interests that have been secured against
distraction and dissipation. Art, we may say, does away with
unnecessary complications. We can condemn popular art for
treating as expendable the *necessary* complications, but nothing
has been added to our aesthetic understanding till we have been
given some specification of what complexity is necessary and
what is not.

There is a similar lack in the condemnation of popular art as
being standardized. One Egyptian statue is much like another,
after all, just as there are marked resemblances among Elizabethan
tragedies or among Italian operas. Such works are not for that
reason assigned the status of popular art. The standardization of
popular art does not mean that forms are stylized but that they
are *stereotyped*. The failing does not lie in the recurrence of the
forms but in deficiencies even in the first occurrence. The characters and situations of the usual movie, words and music of
popular songs, the scenes and sentiments of magazine illustrations are all very much of a piece, each after its own kind. What
makes them stereotypes is not that each instance of the type so
closely resembles all the others, but that the type as a whole so
little resembles anything outside it.

The stereotype presents us with the blueprint of a form, rather
than the form itself. Where the simplifications of great art show
us human nature in its nakedness, the stereotypes of popular
art strip away even the flesh, and the still, sad music of humanity
is reduced to the rattle of dry bones. It is not simplification but
schematization that is achieved; what is put before us is not the
substance of the text but a reader's digest. All art selects what is

significant and suppresses the trivial. But for popular art the criteria of significance are fixed by the needs of the standardization, by the editor of the digest and not by the author of the reality to be grasped. Popular art is never a discovery, only a reaffirmation. Both producer and consumer of popular art confine themselves to what fits into their own schemes, rather than omitting only what is unnecessary to the grasp of the scheme of things. The world of popular art is bounded by the limited horizons of what we think we know already; it is two-dimensional because we are determined to view it without budging a step from where we stand.

The simplification characteristic of popular art amounts to this, that we restrict ourselves to what *already* comes within our grasp. Every stereotype is the crystallization of a prejudice—that is, a prejudgment. Even the inanimate materials of its medium have been type-cast.

Popular art is dominated throughout by the star system, not only in its actors but in all its elements, whatever the medium. Every work of art, to be sure, has its dominant elements, to which the rest are subordinate. But in popular art it is the dominant ones alone that are the objects of interest, the ground of its satisfaction. By contrast, great art is in this sense pointless; everything in it is significant, everything makes its own contribution to the aesthetic substance. The domain of popular art is, paradoxically, an aristocracy, as it were: some few elements are singled out as the carriers of whatever meaning the work has while the rest are merged into an anonymous mass. The life of the country is reduced to the mannered gestures of its king. It is this that gives the effect of simplification and standardization. The elements of the schema, of course, need not be characters in the strict sense; action, color, texture, melody, or rhythm may all be simplified and standardized in just this way.

What popular art schematizes it also abstracts from a fully aesthetic context. Such an abstraction is what we call a *formula;* in formula art the schema is called upon to do the work of the full-bodied original, as though a newspaper consisted entirely of headlines. The abstraction can always be made, as is implied in the very concept of style, and of specific stylistic traits. We can always apply formulas to art; the point is that popular art gives us the formula but nothing to apply it to. Popular art uses formulas, not for analysis but for the experience itself. Such sub-

stance as it has is only the disordered residue of other more or less aesthetic experiences, themselves well on the way towards schematization. Popular art is thus doubly derivative: art first becomes academic and then it becomes popular; as art achieves style it provides the seeds of its own destruction.

Thus popular art may be marked by a great emphasis on its newness—it is first-run, the latest thing. Prior exposure diminishes whatever satisfactions it can provide. Alternatively, it may be endlessly repeated: familiarity gives the illusion of intimacy. Most often, popular art is characterized by a combination of novelty and repetition: the same beloved star appears in what can be described as a new role. The novelty whips up a flagging interest. At the same time the repetition minimizes the demands made on us: we can see at a glance what is going on, and we know already how it will all turn out. Curiosity is easily satisfied, but suspense may be intolerable if we must join in the work of its resolution. We are really safe on the old, familiar ground. Popular art tosses baby in the air a very little way, and quickly catches him again.

In sum, what is unaesthetic about popular art is its formlessness. It does not invite or even permit the sustained effort necessary to the creation of an artistic form. But it provides us with an illusion of achievement while in fact we remain passive.

More specifically, there is work undone on both perceptual and psychodynamic levels.

As to the first, aesthetic *perception* is replaced by mere *recognition*. Perceptual discrimination is cut off, as in most nonaesthetic contexts, at the point where we have seen enough to know what we are looking at. Moreover, the perception is faithful, not to the perceptual materials actually presented, but to the stereotyped expectations that are operative. We perceive popular art only so as to recognize it for what it is, and the object of perception consists of no more than its marks of recognition. This is what is conveyed by the designation *kitch:* an object is kitch when it bears the label *Art* (with a capital "A"), so disposed that we see and respond only to the label.

On the psychodynamic level, the aesthetic *response* is replaced by a mere *reaction*. The difference between them is this: a reaction, in the sense I intend it, is almost wholly determined by the initial stimulus, antecedently and externally fixed, while a response follows a course that is not laid out beforehand but is

significantly shaped by a process of self-stimulation occurring then and there. Spontaneity and imagination come into play; in the aesthetic experience we do not simply react to signals but engage in a creative interpretation of symbols. The response to an art object shares in the work of its creation, and only thereby is a work of art produced. But in popular art everything has already been done. Thus the background music for the popular movie signalizes the birth of love with melodious strings and the approach of death by chords on the organ; contrast these signals with the demanding substance of, say, Prokofieff's music for Eisenstein's *Alexander Nevsky*. To vary the metaphor, popular art is a dictatorship forever organizing spontaneous demonstrations and forever congratulating itself on its freedoms.

In the taste for popular art there is a marked intolerance of ambiguity. It is not just that we shrink from doing that much work—the work, that is, of creative interpretation. At bottom, aesthetic ambiguity is frightening. Popular art is a device for remaining in the same old world and assuring ourselves that we like it, because we are afraid to change it.

At best, popular art replaces ambiguity by some degree of complexity. This is most clearly demonstrated by the so-called *adult Western*, which has moved beyond the infantilism of "good guys" and "bad guys," by assigning virtues and vices to both heroes and villains. But the moral qualities themselves remain unambiguous in both sign and substance. The genre, for the most part, is still far from the insight into the nature of good and evil invited, say, by Melville's Captain Ahab or, even more, by his Billy Budd. Yet, *High Noon* is undeniably a far cry from *The Lone Ranger*.

In short, popular art is simple basically in the sense of easy. It contrasts with art in the markedly lesser demands that it makes for creative endeavor on the part of its audience. An artistic form, like a life form, is a creation, and like the living thing again, one which demands a cooperative effort, in this case between artist and audience. We cannot look to popular art for a fresh vision, turn to it for new direction out of the constraints of convention. Unexplored meanings call for their own language, which must be fashioned by a community with the courage and energy of pioneers. But for a new language there must be something new to say; what the pioneer can never do without is—a frontier.

III

Quite another approach to the analysis of popular art is by way of feeling rather than form. Popular art may be characterized by the kinds of emotions involved in it, or by its means of evoking or expressing them.

Thus there is a common view that popular art is merely *entertainment*, in a pejorative sense. It does not instruct, does not answer to any interests other than those aroused then and there; it is just interesting in itself. Popular art offers us something with which to fill our empty lives; we turn to it always in quiet desperation. It is a specific against boredom, and is thus an inevitable concomitant of the industrial civilization that simultaneously gives us leisure and alienates us from anything that might make our leisure meaningful.

Whatever merits this view may have as sociology, as aesthetics I do not find it very helpful. That the interests satisfied by popular art are self-contained is hardly distinctive of the type. All art has inherent value, independent of its direct contributions to extra-aesthetic concerns. And all art has a certain intrinsic value, affording delight in the form and color of the aesthetic surface, independent of depth meaning. That something is entertaining, that it gives joy to the beholder without regard to more serious interests, so-called, is scarcely a reason therefore, for refusing it artistic status. It is surely no more than snobbery or a perverted puritanism to disparage entertainment value, or to deny it to art.

The question still remains, What makes popular art entertaining? To invoke a contrast with boredom is not of much help, for that is a descriptive category, not an explanatory one; as well say that work is an antidote to laziness. Indeed, I think the claim might be more defensible that popular art, far from countering boredom, perpetuates and intensifies it. It does not arouse new interests but reinforces old ones. Such satisfaction as it affords stems from the evocation in memory of past satisfactions, or even from remembered fantasies of fulfillment. What we enjoy is not the work of popular art but what it brings to mind. There is a nostalgia characteristic of the experience of popular art, not because the work as a form is familiar but because its very substance is familiarity.

The skill of the artist is not in providing an experience but in providing occasions for reliving one. In the experience of popular art we lose ourselves, not in a work of art but in the pools of memory stirred up. Poetry becomes a congeries of poetic symbols which now only signalize feeling, as in the lyrics of popular songs; drama presents dramatic materials but does not dramatize them—brain surgery, or landing the crippled airliner; painting becomes illustration or didactic narrative from Jean Greuze to Norman Rockwell.

Conventions are, to be sure, at work; the associations aroused are not wholly adventitious and idiosyncratic. But *convention* is one thing and *style* is another. One is extrinsic to the materials, giving them shape; the other is the very substance of their form. The difference is like that between a railroad track and a satellite's orbit: convention is laid down beforehand, guiding reactions along a fixed path, while style has no existence antecedent to and independent of the ongoing response itself. For this reason popular art so easily becomes dated, as society changes its conventional associations; see today, [the melodramatic play] *A Father's Curse* surely evokes laughter rather than pity or fear. On the other hand, a work of art may become popular as its expressive substance is replaced by associations—Whistler's "*Mother*" is a case in point.

Popular art wallows in emotion while art transcends it, giving us understanding and thereby mastery of our feelings. For popular art, feelings themselves are the ultimate subject matter; they are not present as a quality of the experience of something objectified, but are only stimulated by the object. The addiction to such stimuli is like the frenzied and forever frustrated pursuit of happiness by those lost souls who have never learned that happiness accrues only when the object of pursuit has its own substance. Popular art ministers to this misery, panders to it, we may say. What popular art has in common with prostitution is not that it is commercialized; art also claims its price, and the price is often a high one. The point is that here we are being offered consummations without fulfillment, invited to perform the gestures of love on condition that they remain without meaning. We are not drawn out of ourselves but are driven deeper into loneliness. Emotion is not a monopoly of popular art, as Dickens, Tschaikovsky, or Turner might testify; but these artists do not traffic in emotion. Popular art, on the contrary, deals in

nothing else. That is why it is so commonly judged by its impact.
To say truly that it is sensational would be high praise; what we
usually get is an anaesthetic.

IV

There is yet another reason for questioning whether popular art
provides relief from boredom, bringing color into grey lives.
The popular audience may be chronically bored, but this is not
to say that it is without feeling. On the contrary, it is feeling
above all that the audience contributes to the aesthetic situation
and that the popular artist then exploits. Popular art does not supply a missing ingredient in our lives, but cooks up a savory mess
from the ingredients at hand. In a word, feelings are usually
lacking in *depth,* whatever their intensity. Popular art is correspondingly shallow.

Superficial, affected, spurious—this is the dictionary meaning
of *sentimental.* So far as feeling goes, it is sentimentality that is
most distinctive of popular art. There is a sense, I suppose, in
which we could say that all feeling starts as sentiment: however
deep down you go you must begin at the surface. The point is
that popular art leaves our feelings as it finds them, formless and
immature. The objects of sentiment are of genuine worth—
cynicism has its own immaturity. But the feelings called forth
spring up too quickly and easily to acquire substance and depth.
They are so lightly triggered that there is no chance to build
up a significant emotional discharge. Sentimentality is a mark
always of a certain deficiency of feeling; it is always just words,
a promise that scarcely begins to move toward fulfillment.

Yet it is only an excess of a special kind that is in question
here. We must distinguish sentimentality from sensibility, that
is, a ready responsiveness to demands on our feelings. Art has no
purchase at all on insensibility. Unless a man is capable of being
moved, and moved deeply, in circumstances where his antecedent
interests are not engaged, art has nothing for him. Sensibility becomes sentimental when there is some disproportion between the
response and its object, when the response is indiscriminate and
uncontrolled. Emotion, Beethoven once said, is for women, and
I think we all understand him; but we are to keep in mind the
difference between such women as Elizabeth Bennett and her
mother.

It is this difference that we want to get at. Dewey comes very near the mark, I believe, in characterizing sentimentality as "excess of receptivity without perception of meaning." It is this lack of meaning, and not intensity of feeling, that makes the receptivity excessive. Popular art is not sentimental because it evokes so much feeling, but because it calls for so much more feeling than either its artist or audience can handle. The trouble is not too much feeling but too little understanding; there is too little to be understood.

Sentimentality, then, moves in a closed circle around the self. The emotions released by a stimulus to sentiment satisfy a proprietary interest, and one which is directed inward. The important thing is that they are *my* feelings, and what is more, feelings about *me*. The prototype of sentimentality is self-pity. Popular art provides subjects and situations that make it easy to see ourselves in its materials. Narcissus, W. H. Auden conjectured, was probably a hydrocephalic idiot, who stared into the pool and concluded, "On me it looks good!" The self-centeredness of popular art is the measure of our own diminishing.

V

Perhaps the most common characterization of popular art is that it is *escapist*. There is no doubt that it can produce a kind of narcosis, a state of insensibility arresting thought and feeling as well as action—in a word, a trance. We do not look at popular art, we stare into it, as we would into flames or moving waters. I think it not accidental that the most popular media, movies and television, are viewed in the dark. The medium is such stuff as dreams are made on.

Popular art seeks to escape ugliness, not to transform it. There is nothing like a pretty face to help you forget your troubles, and popular art can prettify everything, even—and perhaps especially—the face of death. It provides an escape first, therefore, by shutting out the reality, glossing over it.

But popular art is said to do more; it seems to provide an escape not only *from* something but also *to* something else, shuts out the real world by opening the door to another. We do not just forget our troubles but are reminded of them to enjoy the fantasy of overcoming them. Popular art is as likely to relieve anxiety as boredom.

The world of popular art is unreal not just in the sense that it consists of symbols rather than realities—"it's only a movie." Science, too, replaces things by abstract representations of them, but it is not for that reason derogated as an escape from reality. But what makes it science, after all, is that it is capable of bringing us back to the realities, however far from them it detours in its abstractions. Whether symbols are essentially an escape depends at bottom on what they symbolize. Popular art is unreal, not as being sign rather than substance, but because what it signifies is unreal. All art is illusion, inducing us as we experience it to take art for life. But some of it is true to life, illusory without being deceptive. Popular art is a tissue of falsehoods.

Popular art depicts the world, not as it is, nor even as it might be, but as we would have it. Everything in it is selected and placed in our interest. It is a world exhausted in a single perspective—our own—and it is peopled by cardboard figures that disappear when viewed edgewise. We are not to ask whether the rescued maiden can cook, nor do we see the gallant knight through the eyes of the dragon, who is after all only wondering where his next meal will come from. In real drama, said [the nineteenth-century German dramatist] Friedrich Hebbel, all the characters must be in the right. That is how God sees them, which is to say, how they are. Art, like science, raises us up to divine objectivity; popular art is all too human.

It must be admitted that popular art is more sophisticated today than it was a generation or so ago. But often its realism is only another romantic pose. In popular art, it is a matter of taking over the shapes of realism but not the forms. The modern hero of popular art is given a generous admixture of human failings; but no one is really fooled—he is only superman in disguise. Indeed, the disguise is so transparent that it can be discarded: we have come full circle from Nick Carter through Sam Spade to James Bond.

Yet, is not all art fantasy, not the symbolic replication of reality but the fulfillment of a wish? To be sure! But what is wish-fulfilling is the art itself, and not the world it depicts.

For this reason popular art could as well be said to suffer from too little fantasy as too much: it does not do enough with its materials. Its imagination is reproductive rather than creative. When it comes to breaking out of the constraints of reality, what better examples are there than *Midsummer Night's Dream* and

The Tempest, the paintings of Hieronymous Bosch, or the sculpture of the Hindu pantheon? But popular art is so bound to reality it gives us nowhere to escape *to*, save deeper within a self that is already painfully constricted. The eighteenth century usefully distinguished between fancy and imagination, according to whether fantasy has worked far enough to confer reality on its own products. Popular art is all fancy. If it sees the world as a prison, it contents itself with painting on the walls an open door.

Though all art is fantasy, there is a mature as well as an infantile process. Art may be produced for children—Lewis Carroll and Robert Louis Stevenson—or with a childlike quality—Paul Klee and Joan Miro—but it is not therefore childish. It is this childishness, however, that characterizes popular art: the fairy tale is retold for adult consumption, but stripped of just those qualities of creative imagination in which lies the artistry of the original.

In mature fantasy both the reality principle and the pleasure principle are at work. Popular art is concerned only with the pleasure, and for just this reason it can provide only immature satisfactions. In responding to popular art we do not escape from reality—we have not yet attained to the reality. Beneath the pleasure in popular art is the pathos of the note lying outside the orphanage wall: "Whoever finds this, I love you!"

VI

Now, after all, what makes popular art so popular? The usual reply follows the account that conceives of popular art in terms of distinctive features of modern society. The major premise is the alienation and deracination of modern man; the minor premise is that popular art serves to counter these forces, providing a basis for at least an ersatz community. Popular art reaches out to the lowest common denominator of society; it provides the touch of nature that makes all men kin, or, at least, all men who share the conventions of a common culture.

In so far as the function of popular art today is to be explained in terms of social conditions rather than psychic processes, the situation seems to be the reverse of what the previous account relies on. It is not man who is alienated and uprooted, but art. In our time art has become increasingly dissociated from the cultural concerns with which it has been so intimately involved throughout most of its history—religion, love, war, politics, and the struggle for subsistence. Art today is, in Dewey's brilliant phrase, "the beauty-parlor of civilization." Popular art at least pretends to a social relevance, and is not only willing but eager to find a place for itself outside the museum.

Popular art today is neither worse nor more common than it always has been. There is a wider audience today for art of every kind: the mass of the Athenian population were slaves, and not much more than that in Renaissance Italy or Elizabethan England. There may be more poor stuff produced today because there are more people to consume it, but this is even more true, proportionately, for the superior product. Nor do I sympathize with the view that ours is an age of barbarism to be defined, according to Ortega y Gasset, as "the absence of standards to which appeal can be made." What is absent, to my mind, is only a cultural elite that sets forth and enforces the standards; and I say, so much the better! It is ironic that popular art is taken as a sign of barbarism; every real development in the history of art, and not only the modern movement, was first greeted as a repudiation of aesthetic standards. My objection to popular art is just the contrary, that it is too rigidly bound to the standards of the academy. Kitch is the homage paid by popular art to those standards: Oscar and Emmy are avatars of the muse.

Art is too often talked about with a breathless solemnity, and viewed with a kind of religious awe; if high art needs its high priests, I hope that aesthetics will leave that office to the critics. To put it plainly, there is much snobbery in the aesthetic domain, and especially in the contempt for popular art on no other basis than its popularity. We speak of popular art in terms of its media (paperbacks, movies, television) as though to say, "Can any good come out of Nazareth?"; or else by the popular genres (western, mystery, love story, science fiction) as though they can be condemned wholesale. For audiences, art is more of a status symbol than ever; its appearance in the mass media is marked by a flourish of trumpets, as befits its status; the sponsor may even go so far as to omit his commercials. Even where popular art vulgarizes yesterday's art, it might anticipate tomorrow's—baroque once meant something like kitch. I am willing to prophesy that even television has art in its future.

But if not, what then? Aesthetic judgment is one thing and personal taste another. The values of art, like all else aesthetic, can only be analyzed contextually. There is a time and a place even for popular art. Champagne and Napoleon brandy are admittedly the best of beverages; but on a Sunday afternoon in the ballpark we want a coke, or maybe a glass of beer. "Even if we have all the virtues," Zarathustra reminds us, "there is still one thing needful: to send the virtues themselves to sleep at the right time." If popular art gives us pleasant dreams, we can only be grateful —when we have wakened.

THE
WAY
OF
MUSIC

This crisp piece of wrting is a chapter from
Poetics of Music, *by Igor Feodorovich Stravinsky
(1882–1971). Originally written in French and
delivered in that language as one of Stravinsky's
Norton lectures at Harvard University, it has
Stravinsky's flair for blunt statement that challenges
as well as reveals something about the nature of
his art and our response to it. "To explain myself
to you is also to explain myself to myself," he says
elsewhere in the* Poetics, *"and to be obliged to
clear up matters that are distorted or betrayed by
the ignorance and malevolence that one always
finds united by some mysterious bond in most
of the judgments that are passed upon the arts."
Stravinsky's judgments of critics have often
been harsh, but their resentment has not been
easily or frequently translated into correspondingly
harsh judgments of his music. Stravinsky was
clearly a titan of twentieth-century music, a
composer who excelled in the modes of impressionism, neoclassicism, and the serial, or twelve-tone,
idiom. A history of music in this century could be
constructed simply on the basis of his compositions.
Any honest history of modern music must give
central consideration to such works of his as*
The Fire Bird, Le Sacre du Printemps, Petrouchka,
L'Histoire du Soldat, The Symphony of Psalms, The
Rake's Progress, Orpheus, Threni, *and his late work,*
Requiem Canticles, *which was performed at his
funeral service in Venice.*

THE PERFORMANCE OF MUSIC

*Igor
Stravinsky*

It is necessary to distinguish two moments, or
rather two states of music: potential music and
actual music. Having been fixed on paper or retained in the memory, music exists already prior
to its actual performance, differing in this respect from all the other arts, just as it differs
from them ... in the categories that determine
its perception.

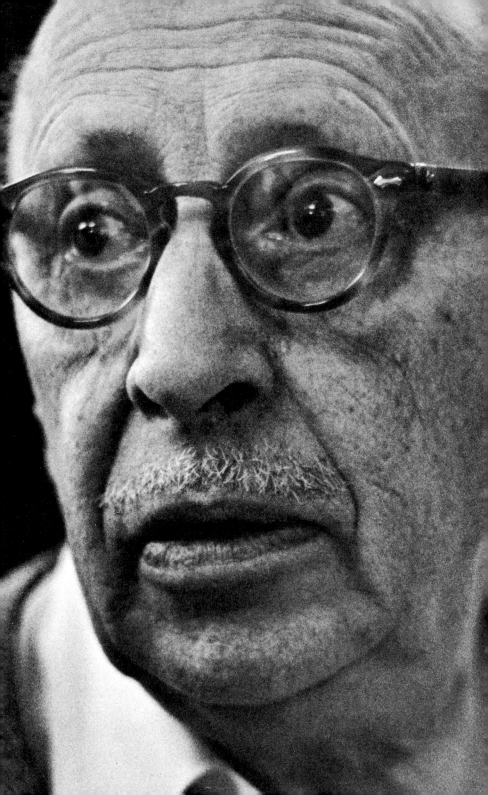

The musical entity thus presents the remarkable singularity of embodying two aspects, of existing successively and distinctly in two forms separated from each other by the hiatus of silence. This peculiar nature of music determines its very life as well as its repercussions in the social world, since it presupposes two kinds of musicians: the creator and the performer.

Let us note in passing that the art of the theater which requires the composition of a text and its translation into oral and visual terms, poses a similar, if not absolutely identical, problem; for there is a distinction that cannot be ignored: the theater appeals to our understanding by addressing itself simultaneously to sight and hearing. Now of all our senses sight is the most closely allied to the intellect, and hearing is appealed to in this case through articulated language, the vehicle for images and concepts. So the reader of a dramatic work can more easily imagine what its actual presentation would be like than the reader of a musical score can imagine how the actual instrumental playing of the score would sound. And it is easy to see why there are far fewer readers of orchestral scores than there are readers of books about music.

In addition, the language of music is strictly limited by its notation. The dramatic actor thus finds he has much more latitude in regard to *chronos* and intonation than does the singer who is tightly bound to *tempo* and *melos*.

This subjection, that is often so trying to the exhibitionism of certain soloists, is at the very heart of the question that we propose to take up now: the question of the executant and the interpreter.

The idea of interpretation implies the limitations imposed upon the performer or those which the performer imposes upon himself in his proper function, which is to transmit music to the listener.

The idea of execution implies the strict putting into effect of an explicit will that contains nothing beyond what it specifically commands.

It is the conflict of these two principles—execution and interpretation—that is at the root of all the errors, all the sins, all the misunderstandings that interpose themselves between the musical work and the listener and prevent a faithful transmission of its message.

Every interpreter is also of necessity an executant. The reverse is not true. Following the order of succession rather than of precedence, we shall first consider the executant.

It is taken for granted that I place before the performer written music wherein the composer's will is explicit and easily discernible from a correctly established text. But no matter how scrupulously a piece of music may be notated, no matter how carefully it may be insured against every possible ambiguity through the indications of *tempo*, shading, phrasing, accentuation, and so on, it always contains hidden elements that defy definition, because verbal dialectic is powerless to define musical dialectic in its totality. The realization of these elements is thus a matter of experience and intuition, in a word, of the talent of the person who is called upon to present the music.

Thus, in contrast to the craftsman of the plastic arts, whose finished work is presented to the public eye in an always identical form, the composer runs a perilous risk every time his music is played, since the competent presentation of his work each time depends on the unforeseeable and imponderable factors that go to make up the virtues of fidelity and sympathy, without which the work will be unrecognizable on one occasion, inert on another, and in any case betrayed.

Between the executant pure and simple and the interpreter in the strict sense of the word, there exists a difference in make-up that is of an ethical rather than of an aesthetic order, a difference that presents a point of conscience: theoretically, one can only require of the executant the translation into sound of his musical part, which he may do willingly or grudgingly, whereas one has the right to seek from the interpreter, in addition to the perfection of this translation into sound, a loving care—which does not mean, be it surreptitious or openly affirmed, a recomposition.

The sin against the spirit of the work always begins with a sin against its letter and leads to the endless follies which an ever-flourishing literature in the worst taste does its best to sanction. Thus it follows that a *crescendo*, as we all know, is always accompanied by a speeding up of movement, while a slowing down never fails to accompany a *diminuendo*. The superfluous is refined upon; a *piano, piano pianissimo* is delicately sought after; great pride is taken in perfecting useless nuances—a concern that usually goes hand in hand with inaccurate rhythm. . . .

These are just so many practices dear to superficial minds for-

ever avid for, and satisfied with, an immediate and facile success
that flatters the vanity of the person who obtains it and perverts
the taste of those who applaud it. How many remunerative
careers have been launched by such practices! How many times
have I been the victim of these misdirected attentions from ab-
stractors of quintessences who waste time splitting hairs over a
pianissimo, without so much as noticing egregious blunders of
rendition! Exceptions, you may say. Bad interpreters should not
make us forget the good ones. I agree—noting, however, that the
bad ones are in the majority and that the virtuosos who serve
music faithfully and loyally are much rarer than those who, in
order to get settled in the comfortable berth of a career, make
music serve them.

The widespread principles that govern the interpretation of
the romantic masters in particular, make these composers the
predestined victims of the criminal assaults we are speaking
about. The interpretation of their works is governed by extra-
musical considerations based on the loves and misfortunes of the
victim. The title of a piece becomes an excuse for gratuitous
hindthought. If the piece has none, a title is thrust upon it for
wildly fanciful reasons. I am thinking of the Beethoven sonata
that is never designated otherwise than by the title of "The
Moonlight Sonata" without anyone ever knowing why; of the
waltz in which it is mandatory to find Frederick Chopin's "Fare-
well."

Obviously, it is not without a reason that the worst interpreters usually tackle the Romantics. The musically extraneous
elements that are strewn throughout their works invite betrayal,
whereas a page in which music seeks to express nothing outside
of itself better resists attempts at literary deformation. It is
not easy to conceive how a pianist could establish his reputation
by taking Haydn as his war-horse. That is undoubtedly the
reason why that great musician has not won a renown among
our interpreters that is in keeping with his true worth.

In regard to interpretation, the last century left us in its
ponderous heritage a curious and peculiar species of soloist without precedent in the distant past—a soloist called the orchestra
leader.

It was romantic music that unduly inflated the personality of
the *Kapellmeister* [concert master] even to the point of conferring upon him—along with the prestige that he today enjoys

on his podium, which in itself concentrates attention upon him—
the discretionary power that he exerts over the music committed
to his care. Perched on his sibylline tripod, he imposes his own
movements, his own particular shadings upon the compositions
he conducts, and he even reaches the point of talking with a
naïve impudence of his specialities, of *his* fifth, of *his* seventh,
the way a chef boasts of a dish of his own concoction. Hearing
him speak, one thinks of the billboards that recommend eating
places to automobilists: "At so-and-so's restaurant, his wines, his
special dishes."

There was never anything like it in the past, in times that
nevertheless already knew as well as our time go-getting and
tyrannical virtuosos, whether instrumentalists or prima donnas.
But those times did not yet suffer from the competition and
plethora of conductors who almost to a man aspire to set up a
dictatorship over music.

Do not think I am exaggerating. A quip that was passed on
to me some years ago clearly shows the importance which the
conductor has come to take on in the preoccupations of the
musical world. One day a person who presides over the fortunes
of a big concert agency was being told about the success obtained in Soviet Russia by that famous conductorless orchestra
[which Stravinsky describes elsewhere]: "That doesn't make
much sense," declared the person in question, "and it doesn't
interest me. What I'd really be interested in is not an orchestra
without a conductor, but a conductor without an orchestra."

To speak of an interpreter means to speak of a translator. And
it is not without reason that a well-known Italian proverb, which
takes the form of a play on words, equates translation with betrayal.

Conductors, singers, pianists, all virtuosos should know or
recall that the first condition that must be fulfilled by anyone
who aspires to the imposing title of interpreter, is that he be first
of all a flawless executant. The secret of perfection lies above
all in his consciousness of the law imposed upon him by the work
he is performing. And here we are back at the great principle
of submission that we have so often invoked in the course of our
lessons. This submission demands a flexibility that itself requires,
along with technical mastery, a sense of tradition and, command-
ing the whole, an aristocratic culture that is not merely a question of acquired learning.

This submissiveness and culture that we require of the creator, we should quite justly and naturally require of the interpreter as well. Both will find therein freedom in extreme rigor and, in the final analysis, if not in the first instance, success—true success, the legitimate reward of the interpreters who in the expression of their most brilliant virtuosity preserve that modesty of movement and that sobriety of expression that is the mark of thoroughbred artists.

I said somewhere that it was not enough to hear music, but that it must also be seen. What shall we say of the ill-breeding of those grimacers who too often take it upon themselves to deliver the "inner meaning" of music by disfiguring it with their affected airs? For, I repeat, one sees music. An experienced eye follows and judges, sometimes unconsciously, the performer's least gesture. From this point of view one might conceive the process of performance as the creation of new values that call for the solution of problems similar to those which arise in the realm of choreography. In both cases we give special attention to the control of gestures. The dancer is an orator who speaks a mute language. The instrumentalist is an orator who speaks an unarticulated language. Upon one, just as upon the other, music imposes a strict bearing. For music does not move in the abstract. Its translation into plastic terms requires exactitude and beauty: the exhibitionists know this only too well.

The beautiful presentation that makes the harmony of what is seen correspond to the play of sounds demands not only good musical instruction on the part of the performer, but also requires a complete familiarity on his part, whether singer, instrumentalist, or conductor, with the style of the works that are entrusted to him; a very sure taste for expressive values and for their limitations, a secure sense for that which may be taken for granted—in a word, an education not only of the ear, but of the mind.

Such an education cannot be acquired in the schools of music and the conservatories, for the teaching of fine manners is not their object: very rarely does a violin teacher even point out to his pupils that it is ill-becoming, when playing, to spread one's legs too far apart.

It is nonetheless strange that such an educational program is nowhere put into effect. Whereas all social activities are regulated by rules of etiquette and good breeding, performers are still in most cases entirely unaware of the elementary precepts of

musical civility, that is to say of *musical good breeding*—a matter
of common decency that a child may learn. . . .

The *Saint Matthew's Passion* of Johann Sebastian Bach is written for a chamber-music ensemble. Its first performance in Bach's
lifetime was perfectly realized by a total force of thirty-four
musicians, including soloists and chorus. That is known. And
nevertheless in our day one does not hesitate to present the work,
in complete disregard of the composer's wishes, with hundreds
of performers, sometimes almost a thousand. This lack of understanding of the interpreter's obligations, this arrogant pride in
numbers, this concupiscence of the many, betray a complete lack
of musical education.

The absurdity of such a practice is in point of fact glaring in
every respect, and above all from the acoustic point of view. For
it is not enough that the sound reach the ear of the public; one
must also consider in what condition, in what state the sound is
received. When the music was not conceived for a huge mass of
performers, when its composer did not want to produce massive
dynamic effects, when the frame is all out of proportion to the
dimensions of the work, multiplication of the number of participant performers can produce only disastrous effects.

Sound, exactly like light, acts differently according to the
distance that separates the point of emission from the point of
reception. A mass of performers situated on a platform occupies
a surface that becomes proportionately larger as the mass becomes more sizeable. By increasing the number of points of
emission one increases the distances that separate these points from
one another and from the hearer. So that the more one multiplies
the points of emission, the more blurred will reception be.

In every case the doubling of parts weighs down the music
and constitutes a peril that can be avoided only by proceeding
with infinite tact. Such additions call for a subtle and delicate
proportioning that itself presupposes the surest of tastes and a
discriminating culture.

It is often believed that power can be increased indefinitely by
multiplying the doubling of orchestral parts—a belief that is
completely false: thickening is not strengthening. In a certain
measure and up to a certain point, doubling may give the illusion
of strength by effecting a reaction of a psychological order on
the listener. The sensation of shock stimulates the effect of power
and helps to establish an illusion of balance between the sounding

tonal masses. A good deal might be said in this connection about the balance of forces in the modern orchestra, a balance which is more easily explained by our aural habits than it is justified by exactness of proportions.

It is a positive fact that beyond a certain degree of extension the impression of intensity diminishes instead of increases and succeeds only in dulling the sensation.

Musicians should come to realize that for their art the same holds true as for the art of the billboard: that the blowing-up of sound does not hold the ear's attention—just as the advertising expert knows that letters which are too large do not attract the eye.

A work of art cannot contain itself. Once he has completed his work, the creator necessarily feels the need to share his joy. He quite naturally seeks to establish contact with his fellow man, who in this case becomes his listener. The listener reacts and becomes a partner in the game, initiated by the creator. Nothing less, nothing more. The fact that the partner is free to accept or to refuse participation in the game does not automatically invest him with the authority of a judge.

The judicial function presupposes a code of sanctions which mere opinion does not have at its disposal. And it is quite illicit, to my way of thinking, to set the public up as a jury by entrusting to it the task of rendering a verdict on the value of a work. It is already quite enough that the public is called upon to decide its ultimate fate.

The fate of a work, of course, depends in the final analysis on the public's taste, on the variations of its humor and habits; in a word, on its preferences. But the fate of a work does not depend upon the public's judgment as if it were a sentence without appeal.

I call your attention to this all-important point: consider on the one hand the conscious effort and patient organization that the composing of a work of art requires, and on the other hand the judgment—which is at least hasty and of necessity improvised —that follows the presentation of the work. The disproportion between the duties of the person who composes and the rights of those who judge him is glaring, since the work offered to the public, whatever its value may be, is always the fruit of study, reasoning, and calculation that imply exactly the converse of improvisation.

I have expatiated at some length on this theme in order to make you see more clearly where the true relations between the composer and the public lie, with the performer acting as an intermediary. You will thereby realize more fully the performer's moral responsibility.

For only through the performer is the listener brought in contact with the musical work. In order that the public may know what a work is like and what its value is, the public must first be assured of the merit of the person who presents the work to it and of the conformity of that presentation to the composer's will.

The listener's task becomes especially harrowing where a first hearing is concerned; for the listener in this case has no point of reference and possesses no basis for comparison.

And so it comes about that the first impression, which is so important, the first contact of the newborn work with the public, is completely dependent upon the validity of a presentation that eludes all controls.

Such, then, is our situation before an unpublished work when the quality of the performers before us does not guarantee that the composer will not be betrayed and that we shall not be cheated.

In every period the forming of an elite has given us that advance assurance in matters of social relations which permits us to have full confidence in the unknown performers who appear before us under the aegis of that flawless bearing which education bestows. Lacking a guarantee of this kind, our relations with music would always be unsatisfactory. You will understand, the situation being what it is, why we have stressed at such length the importance of education in musical matters.

We have said previously that the listener was, in a way, called upon to become the composer's partner. This presupposes that the listener's musical instruction and education are sufficiently extensive that he may not only grasp the main features of the work as they emerge, but that he may even follow to some degree the changing aspects of its unfolding.

As a matter of fact, such active participation is an unquestionably rare thing, just as the creator is a rare occurrence in the mass of humanity. This exceptional participation gives the partner such lively pleasure that it unites him in a certain measure with the mind that conceived and realized the work to which he is listening, giving him the illusion of identifying himself with the creator. That is the meaning of Raphael's famous adage: to understand is to equal.

But such understanding is the exception; the ordinary run of listeners, no matter how attentive to the musical process one supposes them to be, enjoy music only in a passive way.

Unfortunately, there exists still another attitude towards music which differs from both that of the listener who gives himself up to the working out of the music—participating in and following it step by step—and from the attitude of the listener who tries docilely to go along with the music: for we must now speak of indifference and apathy. Such is the attitude of snobs, of false enthusiasts who see in a concert or a performance only the opportunity to applaud a great conductor or an acclaimed virtuoso. One has only to look for a moment at those "faces gray with boredom," as Claude Debussy put it, to measure the power music has of inducing a sort of stupidity in those unfortunate persons who listen to it without hearing it. Those of you who have done me the honor of reading the *Chronicles of My Life* perhaps recall that I stress this matter in regard to mechanically reproduced music.

The propagation of music by all possible means is in itself an excellent thing; but by spreading it abroad without taking precautions, by offering it willy-nilly to the general public which is not prepared to hear it, one lays this public open to the most deadly saturation.

The time is no more when Johann Sebastian Bach gladly traveled a long way on foot to hear Buxtehude. Today radio brings music into the home at all hours of the day and night. It relieves the listener of all effort except that of turning a dial. Now the musical sense cannot be acquired or developed without exercise. In music, as in everything else, inactivity leads gradually to the paralysis, to the atrophying of faculties. Understood in this way, music becomes a sort of drug which, far from stimulating the mind, paralyzes and stultifies it. So it comes about that the very undertaking which seeks to make people like music by giving it a wider and wider diffusion, very often only achieves the result of making the very people lose their appetite for music whose interest was to be aroused and whose taste was to be developed.

*No career in American music has been more
distinguished than that of Aaron Copland
(1900–   ), for awards, for the appreciation and
attention of audiences, composers, critics. His
writing for symphony orchestra, for chamber
groups, and for the piano has drawn wide and warm
critical reaction. His scores for the ballet,* Billy the
Kid, Rodeo, *and* Appalachian Spring, *have been
particularly successful with audiences, and his
compositions for films have also won general approval.
He is a particularly lucid explicator of the mysteries
of musical process, insisting that much of the
notorious obscurity of the art can be dissipated by
the development of certain fixed awarenesses on the
part of listeners, even untrained ones. Such
awarenesses indicate what can and cannot be known
about music. Whether or not Copland has
satisfactorily defined certainty and
uncertainty in listening, he has prepared the
way for serious speculation about the nature of the
musical experience by all of us, no matter how little
or how large our previous instruction in
the techniques of music.*

HOW WE LISTEN

**Aaron
Copland**

We all listen to music according to our separate
capacities. But, for the sake of analysis, the
whole listening process may become clearer if
we break it up into its component parts, so to
speak. In a certain sense we all listen to music on
three separate planes. For lack of a better terminology, one might name these: (1) the sensuous
plane, (2) the expressive plane, (3) the sheerly
musical plane. The only advantage to be gained
from mechanically splitting up the listening
process into these hypothetical planes is the
clearer view to be had of the way in which we
listen.

The simplest way of listening to music is to
listen for the sheer pleasure of the musical sound
itself. That is the sensuous plane. It is the plane

on which we hear music without thinking, without considering it in any way. One turns on the radio while doing something else and absentmindedly bathes in the sound. A kind of brainless but attractive state of mind is engendered by the mere sound appeal of the music.

You may be sitting in a room reading this book. Imagine one note struck on the piano. Immediately that one note is enough to change the atmosphere of the room—proving that the sound element in music is a powerful and mysterious agent, which it would be foolish to deride or belittle.

The surprising thing is that many people who consider themselves qualified music lovers abuse that plane in listening. They go to concerts in order to lose themselves. They use music as a consolation or an escape. They enter an ideal world where one doesn't have to think of the realities of everyday life. Of course they aren't thinking about the music either. Music allows them to leave it, and they go off to a place to dream, dreaming because of and apropos of the music yet never quite listening to it.

Yes, the sound appeal of music is a potent and primitive force, but you must not allow it to usurp a disproportionate share of your interest. The sensuous plane is an important one in music, a very important one, but it does not constitute the whole story.

There is no need to digress further on the sensuous plane. Its appeal to every normal human being is self-evident. There is, however, such a thing as becoming more sensitive to the different kinds of sound stuff as used by various composers. For all composers do not use that sound stuff in the same way. Don't get the idea that the value of music is commensurate with its sensuous appeal or that the loveliest sounding music is made by the greatest composer. If that were so, Ravel would be a greater creator than Beethoven. The point is that the sound element varies with each composer, that his usage of sound forms an integral part of his style and must be taken into account when listening. The reader can see, therefore, that a more conscious approach is valuable even on this primary plane of music listening.

The second plane on which music exists is what I have called the expressive one. Here, immediately, we tread on controversial ground. Composers have a way of shying away from any discussion of music's expressive side. Did not Stravinsky himself proclaim that his music was an "object," a "thing," with a life of its own, and with no other meaning than its own purely musical existence? This intransigent attitude of Stravinsky's may be due to the fact that so many people have tried to read different meanings into so many pieces. Heaven knows it is difficult enough to say precisely what it is that a piece of music means, to say it definitely, to say it finally so that everyone is satisfied with your explanation. But that should not lead one to the other extreme of denying to music the right to be "expressive."

My own belief is that all music has an expressive power, some more and some less, but that all music has a certain meaning behind the notes and that that meaning behind the note constitutes, after all, what the piece is saying, what the piece is about. This whole problem can be stated quite simply by asking, "Is there a meaning to music?" My answer to that would be, "Yes." And "Can you state in so many words what the meaning is?" My answer to that would be, "No." Therein lies the difficulty.

Simple-minded souls will never be satisfied with the answer to the second of these questions. They always want music to have a meaning, and the more concrete it is the better they like it. The more the music reminds them of a train, a storm, a funeral, or any other familiar conception the more expressive it appears to be to them. This popular idea of music's meaning—stimulated and abetted by the usual run of musical commentator—should be discouraged wherever and whenever it is met. One timid lady once confessed to me that she suspected something seriously lacking in her appreciation of music because of her inability to connect it with anything definite. That is getting the whole thing backward, of course.

Still, the question remains, How close should the intelligent music lover wish to come to pinning a definite meaning to any particular work? No closer than a general concept, I should say. Music expresses, at different moments, serenity or exuberance, regret or triumph, fury or delight. It expresses each of these moods, and many others, in a numberless variety of subtle shadings and differences. It may even express a state of meaning for which there exists no adequate word in any language. In that case, musicians often like to say that it has only a purely musical meaning. They sometimes go farther and say that *all* music has only a purely musical meaning. What they really mean is that

no appropriate word can be found to express the music's meaning and that, even if it could, they do not feel the need of finding it.

But whatever the professional musician may hold, most musical
novices still search for specific words with which to pin down
their musical reactions. That is why they always find Tchaikovsky easier to "understand" than Beethoven. In the first place, it
is easier to pin a meaning-word on a Tchaikovsky piece than on
a Beethoven one. Much easier. Moreover, with the Russian composer, every time you come back to a piece of his it almost
always says the same thing to you, whereas with Beethoven it is
often quite difficult to put your finger right on what he is saying.
And any musician will tell you that that is why Beethoven is the
greater composer. Because music which always says the same
thing to you will necessarily soon become dull music, but music
whose meaning is slightly different with each hearing has a
greater chance of remaining alive.

Listen, if you can, to the forty-eight fugue themes of Bach's
Well Tempered Clavichord. Listen to each theme, one after
another. You will soon realize that each theme mirrors a different
world of feeling. You will also soon realize that the more beautiful a theme seems to you the harder it is to find any word that
will describe it to your complete satisfaction. Yes, you will certainly know whether it is a gay theme or a sad one. You will be
able, in other words, in your own mind, to draw a frame of
emotional feeling around your theme. Now study the sad one a
little closer. Try to pin down the exact quality of its sadness. Is
it pessimistically sad or resignedly sad; is it fatefully sad or smil-
ingly sad?

Let us suppose that you are fortunate and can describe to your
own satisfaction in so many words the exact meaning of your
chosen theme. There is still no guarantee that anyone else will be
satisfied. Nor need they be. The important thing is that each one
feel for himself the specific expressive quality of a theme or,
similarly, an entire piece of music. And if it is a great work of
art, don't expect it to mean exactly the same thing to you each
time you return to it.

Themes or pieces need not express only one emotion, of
course. Take such a theme as the first main one of the *Ninth
Symphony*, for example. It is clearly made up of different ele-

ments. It does not say only one thing. Yet anyone hearing it immediately gets a feeling of strength, a feeling of power. It isn't a power that comes simply because the theme is played loudly. It is a power inherent in the theme itself. The extraordinary strength and vigor of the theme results in the listener's receiving an impression that a forceful statement has been made. But one should never try to boil it down to "the fateful hammer of life," etc. That is where the trouble begins. The musician, in his exasperation, says it means nothing but the notes themselves, whereas the nonprofessional is only too anxious to hang on to any explanation that gives him the illusion of getting closer to the music's meaning.

Now, perhaps, the reader will know better what I mean when I say that music does have an expressive meaning but that we cannot say in so many words what that meaning is.

The third plane on which music exists is the sheerly musical plane. Besides the pleasurable sound of music and the expressive feeling that it gives off, music does exist in terms of the notes themselves and of their manipulation. Most listeners are not sufficiently conscious of this third plane. . . .

Professional musicians, on the other hand, are, if anything, too conscious of the mere notes themselves. They often fall into the error of becoming so engrossed with their arpeggios and staccatos that they forget the deeper aspects of the music they are performing. But from the layman's standpoint, it is not so much a matter of getting over bad habits on the sheerly musical plane as of increasing one's awareness of what is going on, in so far as the notes are concerned.

When the man in the street listens to the "notes themselves" with any degree of concentration, he is most likely to make some mention of the melody. Either he hears a pretty melody or he does not, and he generally lets it go at that. Rhythm is likely to gain his attention next, particularly if it seems exciting. But harmony and tone color are generally taken for granted, if they are thought of consciously at all. As for music's having a definite form of some kind, that idea seems never to have occurred to him.

It is very important for all of us to become more alive to music on its sheerly musical plane. After all, an actual musical material is being used. The intelligent listener must be prepared to increase his awareness of the musical material and what happens to it. He must hear the melodies, the rhythms, the harmonies, the tone colors in a more conscious fashion. But above all he must, in order to follow the line of the composer's thought, know something of the principles of musical form. Listening to all of these elements is listening on the sheerly musical plane.

Let me repeat that I have split up mechanically the three separate planes on which we listen merely for the sake of greater clarity. Actually, we never listen on one or the other of these planes. What we do is to correlate them—listening in all three ways at the same time. It takes no mental effort, for we do it instinctively.

Perhaps an analogy with what happens to us when we visit the theater will make this instinctive correlation clearer. In the theater, you are aware of the actors and actresses, costumes and sets, sounds and movements. All these give one the sense that the theater is a pleasant place to be in. They constitute the sensuous plane in our theatrical reactions.

The expressive plane in the theater would be derived from the feeling that you get from what is happening on the stage. You are moved to pity, excitement, or gayety. It is this general feeling, generated aside from the particular words being spoken, a certain emotional something which exists on the stage, that is analogous to the expressive quality in music.

The plot and plot development is equivalent to our sheerly musical plane. The playwright creates and develops a character in just the same way that a composer creates and develops a theme. According to the degree of your awareness of the way in which the artist in either field handles his material will you become a more intelligent listener.

It is easy enough to see that the theatergoer never is conscious of any of these elements separately. He is aware of them all at the same time. The same is true of music listening. We simultaneously and without thinking listen on all three planes.

In a sense, the ideal listener is both inside and outside the music at the same moment, judging it and enjoying it, wishing it would go one way and watching it go another—almost like the composer at the moment he composes it; because in order to write his music, the composer must also be inside and outside his music, carried away by it and yet coldly critical of it. A subjective and objective attitude is implied in both creating and listening to music.

What the reader should strive for, then, is a more *active* kind of listening. Whether you listen to Mozart or Duke Ellington, you can deepen your understanding of music only by being a more conscious and aware listener—not someone who is just listening, but someone who is listening *for* something.

THE LISTENER

Roger Sessions

No one is more concerned with the response of the listener to music than the composer. That concern is meticulously expressed here by the American composer Roger Sessions (1896–). Sessions is a distinguished creator in almost all the forms of music—the string quartet, the symphony, the opera, and so on. Very much a man of the twentieth century in style, he is also very much of his own time in his openness to the various ways that listeners approach his art. The mysterious processes of music are made a good deal more understandable in Roger Sessions' detailed and sympathetic examination of the psychology of listening. Fittingly, the language and style are simple and the comparisons to other arts, by which we sometimes are enabled to proceed with greater ease, are frequent.

We are all very much concerned these days, with the listener—the person who neither makes music nor performs it, but simply listens to it. The market is flooded with books of all sorts, fulfilling all sorts of functions for all sorts of listeners, from the child to "the man who enjoys *Hamlet*" and even "the intelligent listener"—analyses to edify him, critical chit-chat to flatter him, and gossip to amuse him. We have grade school, high school, and university courses designed to inform him and, if possible, to educate him in "appreciation," in "intelligent listening," and even "creative listening." On the radio he may find quiz programs, interviews with personalities, broadcast orchestra rehearsals, and spoken program notes, which have been known on occasion to be so long that there is not enough time for the broadcast of the music. Surely we are leaving no stone unturned in the effort to prepare the listener fully for the strenuous task of listening to music.

This is actually a peculiar state of affairs.

Music, and in fact art in general, is not one of the so-called necessities of life, nor does it yield us any of the creature comforts
associated with the standard of living of which we are so proud.
Why then should we be so concerned about the listener? Is not
music available to him, if he wants it? Should we not rather demand simply that the listener be given the best products available?
Should we not rather concern ourselves with the quality of our
music, and with ways of producing the highest quality, with providing the best possible education for our young musicians, and
with creating opportunities for them to function according to
their merits? In truth, should we not rather devote ourselves to
improving the quality of our music, and to seeing that music of
the highest quality is available for all that wish to hear it?

Of course, we have no such choice of alternatives; and the
concern that is felt for the listener today is no chance development but the result of the situation in which music finds itself
in our contemporary world. . . .

When music or any other product is furnished to millions of
individuals, it is bound to become necessary to consider the tastes
of those individuals in relation to the product offered them.
Those who furnish the product are obliged to produce as efficiently and as cheaply as possible the goods which they can
sell to the most people; they are obliged, furthermore, to try to
persuade the people to whom they sell that it is preferable to buy
the goods that are most cheaply produced; it is furthermore
necessary to do everything possible to enhance the value of the
goods sold. If they fail to do these things they are taking foolish
economic risks. The larger the quantities involved, the greater
the potential profits; but while this is true, it is also true that the
risks of possible catastrophic loss are greater. These facts are
elementary; not only do they apply vitally to the situation of
music today, but I believe that an understanding of them is
absolutely indispensable if we are to understand any economic,
political, or social aspects whatever of the contemporary world.

In brief, the "listener" has become, in relation to these facts,
the "consumer," and however unaware we as individuals are of
this, it is nevertheless the basic explanation of our interest in
him. Though neither he nor we have chosen this role for him,
circumstances have made it inevitable. In relation to the same
facts (and please note the phrase carefully, for I shall try to
show later that these are not the only facts), the status of the

artist in our society has undergone a remarkable change. He has become (in relation to the same facts) no longer a cultural citizen, one of the cultural assets of the community with purely cultural responsibilities, but what is sometimes called a cog in the economic machine. He is asked and even in a sense required to justify his existence as a plausible economic risk; to, as we say, "sell" himself as a possible source of economic profit. Then, having done so, he must produce what is required of him in this sense. He, too, has an interest in the listener; it is the listener who buys his wares and therefore justifies his continued existence as an efficient cog. He has to be constantly aware, in fact, of the requirements of the machinery in approximately the terms I have outlined above. For the aims of business are essentially short-range aims, and it is doubtful whether business, as such, can conceivably operate on any other basis. It can allow itself the luxury of the long-range view only to the extent that it builds up enormous surpluses which make risks economically possible, and even then only under circumstances offering reasonable hope of long-range rewards.

Let me say once again that I do not consider this the entire picture of our cultural situation or of our cultural prospects. I shall later try to show why I do not believe it to be so. Furthermore, these remarks are generalizations, and subject to elaboration, with intricate scoring and with many subtleties of nuance. I do not intend to score them for you here. But we cannot understand the listener unless we know who he is in terms of the conditions actually prevalent. We must see him, in other words, not as an abstraction but as an existing and concrete figure in our musical society.

But it is not mainly in his role of consumer that I wish to speak of the listener. The question for us is rather his own experience of music—what hearing and understanding consist in, and, finally, what discrimination involves. What, in other words, is his relationship to music? How can he get the most from it? How can music mean the most to him? In what does his real education consist? Finally, how can he exercise his powers of discrimination in such a way as to promote valid musical experience in others and, so to speak, in the world in general?

I think we can distinguish four stages in the listener's development. First, he must hear; I have already indicated what I mean by this. It is not simply being present when music is performed, nor is it even simply recognizing bits of the music—leit-motifs, or themes, or salient features in a score. It is rather, as it were, opening one's ears to the sounds as they succeed each other, discovering whatever point of contact one can find, and in fact following the music as well as one can in its continuity. We perhaps tend to ignore the fact that listeners are, like composers and performers, variously endowed, and also that they differ very widely in experience. But this initial stage in listening to music is an entirely direct one; the listener brings to the music whatever he can bring, with no other preoccupation than that of hearing. This is of course what is to be desired; it is the condition of his really hearing. He will hear the music only to the extent that he identifies himself with it, establishing a fresh and essentially naïve contact with it, without preconceived ideas and without strained effort.

The second stage is that of enjoyment, or shall we say the primary response. It is perhaps hardly discernible as a "second stage" at all: the listener's reaction is immediate and seems in a sense identical with the act of hearing. Undoubtedly this is what many listeners expect. And yet, on occasion, one may listen to music attentively, without any conscious response to it until afterwards; one's very attention may be so absorbed that a vivid sense of the sound is retained but a sense of communication is experienced only later. It is this sense of communication to which I refer under the term "enjoyment"; obviously, one may not and often does not, in any real sense, "enjoy" what is being communicated. There is certainly some music that we never "enjoy"; experience inevitably fosters discrimination, and there is certainly some truth even in the frequent, seemingly paradoxical, statement that "the more one loves music, the less music one loves." The statement is true in a sense if we understand it as applying to the experience of the individual, and not as a general rule. But if our relation to music is a healthy one—that is to say, a direct and a simple one—our primary and quite spontaneous effort will be to enjoy it. If this effort becomes inhibited it will be by reason of experience and the associations that inevitably follow in its train. We shall in that case have acquired a sense of musical values, and our specific response will be curtailed in deference to the more general response which our musical experience has given us.

The third of the four phases I have spoken of consists in what we call "musical understanding." I must confess that I am not altogether pleased with this term. To speak quite personally if not too seriously, a composer will certainly have every right to feel pleased, but he may not feel entirely flattered, when he is told "I love your music, but of course I have no right to an opinion—I don't really understand it." In what does "musical understanding" consist? The difficulty, I think, comes from the fact that while . . . the instinctive bases of music, the impulses which constitute its raw materials, are essentially of the most primitive sort, yet the organization of these materials, the shaping of them into a means of communication and later into works of art, is, and historically speaking has been, a long and intricate process and one which has few obvious contacts with the world of ordinary experience. The technique of every art has, of course, its esoteric phases; but in the case of visual art even these phases are relatively accessible to the layman, since he can, if he is really interested, grasp them in terms of quite ordinary practical activity. He will have learned early in his life to be aware of the basic facts of size, contour, color, and perspective on very much the same terms as are required for his perception of visual art. He can to a certain extent appreciate the artist's problems in these terms and can define his response, at least on an elementary level, in terms satisfactory to himself. This is even truer in the case of literary art, since he constantly uses words and to a greater or a lesser degree expresses himself by their means. Like Molière's "bourgeois gentleman," he has talked in prose all his life. His feeling for the values of both visual and literary art consists therefore in a high degree of refinement, and an extension, of experiences which are thoroughly familiar to him, through analogies constantly furnished by his ordinary life.

In the case of music there are no such clear analogies. The technical facts which are commonplace to the composer, and even many of those proper to the performer, have no clear analogies in the ordinary experience of the non-musician. The latter finds them quite mysterious and, as I have already pointed out, tends to exaggerate both their uniqueness and their inaccessibility to the layman. And if the latter finds it difficult to conceive of the mere fact of inner hearing and auditory imagination, how much more difficult will he find such a conception as, for instance, tonality, or the musical facts on which the principles of what we call "musical form" are based. He is likely not only to regard music *per se* as a book in principle closed to him, but, through the impressive unfamiliarity of whatever technical jargon he chances to hear, to misunderstand both the nature and the role of musical technique. It is likely to seem to him something of an abstraction, with an existence of its own, to which the sensations and impressions he receives from music are only remotely related, as by-products. How often, for instance, have I been asked whether the study and mastery of music does not involve a knowledge of higher mathematics! The layman is only too likely to react in either one of two ways, or in a combination of both. He is likely, that is, either to regard music as something to which he is essentially a stranger, or else to regard its generally accepted values as arbitrary, pretentious, and academic, and both to give to it and to receive from it far less than his aptitudes warrant.

The surprising thing is that all of these conclusions are based on a mistaken idea as to the real meaning of musical "understanding." Technique is certainly useful, not to say indispensable, to the composer or the performer; a knowledge of musical theory is certainly an advantage to the performer and practically inescapable for the composer. But theory, in the sense of generalization, is not of the least use to the listener; in practice it is a veritable encumbrance if he allows preoccupation with it to interfere with his contact with the music as such. He can certainly derive both interest and help from whatever can be pointed out to him in connection with the specific content of a piece of music; but he will be only misled if he is persuaded to listen in an exploratory rather than a completely receptive spirit. Any effort to help him must be in the direction of liberating, not of conditioning, his ear; and the generalizations of which musical theory consists demonstrably often lead him to strained efforts which are a positive barrier to understanding. The "technique" of a piece of music is essentially the affair of the composer; it is largely even subconscious, and composers frequently are confronted by perfectly real technical facts, present in their music, of which they had no conscious inkling. And do we seriously believe that understanding of Shakespeare, or James Joyce, or William Faulkner has anything to do with the ability to parse the sentences and describe the functions of the various words in *Hamlet* or *Ulysses?*

Of course not. Understanding of music, as relevant for the

listener, means the ability to receive its full message. . . . In the primary sense, the listener's real and ultimate response to music consists not in merely hearing it, but in inwardly reproducing it, and his understanding of music consists in the ability to do this in his imagination. This point cannot be too strongly emphasized. The really "understanding" listener takes the music into his consciousness and remakes it actually or in his imagination, for his own uses. He whistles it on the street, or hums it at his work, or simply "thinks" it to himself. He may even represent it to his consciousness in a more concentrated form—as a condensed memory of sounds heard and felt, reproduced for his memory by a vivid sensation of what I may call character in sound, without specific details but in terms of sensations and impressions remembered.

It is for this reason that I am somewhat skeptical of the helpfulness of the kind of technical tid-bits and quasi-analyses sometimes offered to the listener as aids to understanding. The trouble with them, as so often presented, seems to me that the essential facts of musical technique cannot really be conveyed in this way. To give one instance, musicians talk, for convenience, about what we call the "sonata form." But they know, or should know, that the conception "sonata form" is a rough generalization and that in practice sonatas, at least those written by masters, are individual and that each work has its own form. To speak of "sonata form" without making clear what constitutes "form" in music, as such, is to falsify, not to illuminate. It is to imply that the composer adapts his ideas to a mold into which he then pours the music. It is also to lay far too much emphasis on what are called "themes," to the detriment of the musical flow in its entirety. What the layman needs is not to acquire facts but to cultivate senses: the sense of rhythm, of articulation, of contrast, of accent. He needs to be aware of the progression of the bass as well as the treble line; of a return to the principal or to a subsidiary key, of a far-flung tonal span. He needs to be aware of all these things as events which his ear witnesses and appreciates as a composition unfolds. Whether or not it is a help to have specific instances pointed out to him, it is certain in any case that his main source of understanding will be through hearing music in general, and specific works in particular, repeatedly, and making them his own through familiarity, through memory, and through inner re-elaboration.

I hardly need point out the fact that this is as true in regard to so-called "modern" music as it is to old. Where the music is radically unfamiliar the three processes I have described are slower. It must therefore be heard more often than the older music needs to be heard. At the beginning the impressions will be chaotic—much more chaotic than impressions produced by purely fortuitous sounds. The impression of chaos comes simply from the fact that the sounds and relationships are unfamiliar; their very consistency—since it, too, is based on contexts which are unfamiliar—seems like a denial of logic. As long as this impression prevails the listener has not yet made contact with the music. In connection with contemporary music, I have often observed the first sensations of real contact, while the musical language in question is still essentially unfamiliar but beginning to be intelligible. These first sensations may be acutely pleasurable; the work becomes highly exciting, conveying a kind of superficial excitement which disappears when the stage of real understanding is reached and gives way to an appreciation for the real "message" of the work. Once more, the key to the "understanding" of contemporary music lies in repeated hearing; one must hear it till the sounds are familiar, until one begins to notice false notes if they are played. One can make the effort to retain it in one's head, and one will always find that the accurate memory of sounds heard coincides with the understanding of them. In fact, the power to retain sounds by memory implies that they have been mastered. For the ear by its nature seeks out patterns and relationships, and it is only these patterns that we can remember and that make music significant for us.

The listener's final stage is that of discrimination. It is important that it should be the final stage since real discrimination is possible only with understanding; and both snobbery and immaturity at times foster prejudices which certainly differ from discrimination in any real sense. Actually it is almost impossible not to discriminate if we persist in and deepen our musical experience. We will learn to differentiate between lasting impressions and those which are fleeting, and between the musical experiences which give full satisfaction and those which only partly satisfy us. We will learn to differentiate between our impressions, too, in a qualitative sense. In this way, we cultivate a sense of values to which to refer our later judgment. We will learn that music is unequal in quality; we will possibly learn that instead of speaking of "immortality" in the case of some works and of the ephemeral quality of others, we must conceive of differences in the life span of works—that some works last in our esteem longer than others without necessarily lasting forever. We will learn finally to differentiate in the matter of character, to be aware of the differences between works in ways which have no relation to intrinsic worth. In other words, we will become critics. . . .

Let us phrase the question in more general terms: What does the listener demand from music? The answer will inevitably be that a variety of listeners want a variety of things. But on any level it may be taken for granted that the listener wants vital experience, whether of a deeply stirring, brilliantly stimulating, or simply entertaining type. If we understand this we should understand, too, that the composer can effectively furnish it only on his own terms. He can persuade others to love only what he loves himself, and can convince only by means of what fully convinces him. It is for this reason that the artist must be completely free, that such a question as I have stated here can ultimately have no importance to him. His obligation is to give the best he can give, wherever it may lead, and to do so without compromise and with complete conviction. This is in fact natural to him; if he is a genuine artist he cannot do otherwise. He can be sure that if he fully achieves his artistic goals, he will find listeners, and that if he has something genuine to say, the number of his listeners will increase, however slowly. This, in any case, will never be for him an artistic preoccupation, however much it may prove to be a practical one.

Composers, like poets, are born, not made; but once born, they have to grow. It is in this sense that a culture will, generally speaking, get the music that it demands. The question, once more, is what we demand of the composer. Do we demand always what is easiest, music that is primarily and invariably entertainment, or do we seriously want from him the best that he has to give? In the latter case, are we willing to come to meet him, to make whatever effort is demanded of us as listeners, in order to get from his music what it has to give us? Once more, it is for the listener and not for the composer, as an individual, that the answer is important. On the answer we ultimately give depends the future of music in the United States.

The ironies of John Cage (1912–   ) often distract his listeners and his readers from his seriousness as a composer. That he can mean what he says, as well as something more or something less, is quite clear in the amusing monologue for two voices that follows. Cage is the daring composer of exactly timed silences, designed as musical pieces to illustrate the sounds of a concert-hall: chairs creaking, lungs wheezing, programs crackling, rumps twisting and turning. He has invented a whole repertoire of hardware with which to augment and diminish the sounds of the "prepared" piano, as he calls his rearranged instrument, and he has written a score for radios, with each twirling of the dials marked out for the performers. He is also a thoughtful spokesman for experimentation in contemporary music who regards his contemporaries highly—Christian Wolff, Earle Brown, and especially Morton Feldman who graphs directions to his players rather than using conventional notation. This piece requires close reading as it moves through its witty examination of the nature of experimental music in a technological era to make its points about music and sound in general.

EXPERIMENTAL MUSIC: DOCTRINE

John Cage

Joseph Schillinger (referred to by his last name) is the author of an ambitious attempt to reduce music to its mathematical components, a composer, and a teacher. The I Ching, *or* Book of Changes, *by* Confucius, *is a book of divination by mathematical pattern and precept.*

Objections are sometimes made by composers to the use of the term *experimental* as descriptive of their works, for it is claimed that any experiments that are made precede the steps that are finally taken with determination, and that this determination is knowing, having, in fact, a particular, if unconventional, ordering of the elements used in view. These objections are clearly justifiable, but only where, as among contemporary evidences in serial music, it remains a question of making a thing upon the boundaries, structure, and expression on which attention is focused. Where, on the other hand, attention moves towards the observation and audition of many things at once, including those that are environmental—becomes, that is, inclusive rather than exclusive—no question of making, in the sense of forming understandable structures, can arise (one is a tourist), and here the word "experimental" is apt, providing it is understood not as descriptive of an act to be later judged in terms of success and failure, but simply as of an act the outcome of which is unknown. What has been determined?

For, when, after convincing oneself ignorantly that sound has, as its clearly defined opposite, silence, that since duration is the only characteristic of sound that is measurable in terms of silence, therefore any valid structure involving sounds and silences should .be based, not as occidentally traditional, on frequency, but rightly on duration, one enters an anechoic chamber, as silent as technologically possible in 1951, to discover that one hears two sounds of one's own unintentional making (nerve's systematic operation, blood's circulation), the situation one is clearly in is not objective (sound-silence), but rather subjective (sounds only), those intended and those others (so-called silence) not intended. If, at this point, one says, "Yes! I do not discriminate between intention and non-intention," the splits, subject-object, art-life, etc., disappear, an identification has been made with the material, and actions are then those relevant to its nature, i.e.:

A sound does not view itself as thought, as ought, as needing another sound for its elucidation, as etc.; it has no time for any consideration—it is occupied with the performance of its characteristics: before it has died away it must have made perfectly exact its frequency, its loudness, its length, its overtone structure, the precise morphology of these and of itself.

Urgent, unique, uninformed about history and theory, beyond the imagination, central to a sphere without surface, its becoming is unimpeded, energetically broadcast. There is no escape from its action. It does not exist as one of a series of discrete steps, but as transmission in all directions from the field's center. It is inextricably synchronous with all other, sounds, non-sounds, which latter, received by other sets than the ear, operate in the same manner.

A sound accomplishes nothing; without it life would not last out the instant.

Relevant action is theatrical (music [imaginary separation of hearing from the other senses] does not exist), inclusive and intentionally purposeless. Theatre is continually becoming that it is becoming; each human being is at the best point for reception. Relevant response (getting up in the morning and discovering onself a musician) (action, art) can be made with any number (including none [none and number, like silence and music, are unreal]) of sounds. The automatic minimum (see above) is two.

Are you deaf (by nature, choice, desire) or can you hear (externals, tympani, labyrinths in whack)?

Beyond them (ears) is the power of discrimination which, among other confused actions, weakly pulls apart (abstraction), ineffectually establishes as not to suffer alteration (the "work"), and unskillfully protects from interruption (museum, concert hall) what springs, elastic, spontaneous, back together again with a beyond that power which is fluent (it moves in or out), pregnant (it can appear when- where- as what-ever [rose, nail, constellation, 485.73482 cycles per second, piece of string]), related (it is you yourself in the form you have that instant taken), obscure (you will never be able to give a satisfactory report even to yourself of just what happened).

In view, then, of a totality of possibilities, no knowing action is commensurate, since the character of the knowledge acted upon prohibits all but some eventualities. From a realist position, such action, though cautious, hopeful, and generally entered into, is unsuitable. An *experimental* action, generated by a mind as empty as it was before it became one, thus in accord with the possibility of no matter what, is, on the other hand, practical. It does not move in terms of approximations and errors, as "informed" action by its nature must, for no mental images of what would happen were set up beforehand; it sees things directly as they are: impermanently involved in an infinite play of interpenetrations. Experimental music—

Question: —in the U.S.A., if you please. Be more specific. What do you have to say about rhythm? Let us agree it is no longer a question of pattern, repetition, and variation.

Answer: There is no need for such agreement. Patterns,

repetitions, and variations will arise and disappear. However, rhythm is durations of any length coexisting in any states of succession and synchronicity. The latter is liveliest, most unpredictably changing, when the parts are not fixed by a score but left independent of one another, no two performances yielding the same resultant durations. The former, succession, liveliest when (as in Morton Feldman's *Intersections*) it is not fixed but presented in situation-form, entrances being at any point within a given period of time.—Notation of durations is in space, read as corresponding to time, needing no reading in the case of magnetic tape.

Question: What about several players at once, an orchestra?

Answer: You insist upon their being together? Then use, as Earle Brown suggests, a moving picture of the score, visible to all, a static vertical line as coordinator, past which the notations move. If you have no particular togetherness in mind, there are chronometers. Use them.

Question: I have noticed that you write durations that are beyond the possibility of performance.

Answer: Composing's one thing, performing's another, listening's a third. What can they have to do with one another?

Question: And about pitches?

Answer: It is true. Music is continually going up and down, but no longer only on those stepping stones, five, seven, twelve in number, or the quarter tones. Pitches are not a matter of likes and dislikes (I have told you about the diagram Schillinger had stretched across his wall near the ceiling: all the scales, Oriental and Occidental, that had been in general use, each in its own color plotted against, no one of them identical with, a black one, the latter the scale as it would have been had it been physically based on the overtone series) except for musicians in ruts; in the face of habits, what to do? Magnetic tape opens the door providing one doesn't immediately shut it by inventing a *phonogène*, or otherwise use it to recall or extend known musical possibilities. It introduces the unknown with such sharp clarity that anyone has the opportunity of having his habits blown away like dust.— For this purpose the prepared piano is also useful, especially in its recent forms where, by alterations during a performance, an otherwise static gamut situation becomes changing. Stringed instruments (not string-players) are very instructive, voices too; and sitting still anywhere (the stereophonic, multiple-loud-speaker manner of operation in the everyday production of sounds and noises) listening. . . .

Question: I understand Feldman divides all pitches into high, middle, and low, and simply indicates how many in a given range are to be played, leaving the choice up to the performer.

Answer: Correct. That is to say, he used sometimes to do so; I haven't seen him lately. It is also essential to remember his notation of super- and subsonic vibrations (*Marginal Intersection No. 1*).

Question: That is, there are neither divisions of the "canvas" nor "frame" to be observed?

Answer: On the contrary, you must give the closest attention to everything.

Question: And timbre?

Answer: No wondering what's next. Going lively on "through many a perilous situation." Did you ever listen to a symphony orchestra?

Question: Dynamics?

Answer: These result from what actively happens (physically, mechanically, electronically) in producing a sound. You won't find it in the books. Notate that. As far as too loud goes: "follow the general outlines of the Christian life."

Question: I have asked you about the various characteristics of a sound; how, now, can you make a continuity, as I take it your intention is, without intention? Do not memory, psychology—

Answer: "—never again."

Question: How?

Answer: Christian Wolff introduced space actions in his compositional process at variance with the subsequently performed time actions. Earle Brown devised a composing procedure in which events, following tables of random numbers, are written out of sequence, possibly anywhere in a total time now and possibly anywhere else in the same total time next. I myself use chance operations, some derived from the *I-Ching*, others from the observation of imperfections in the paper upon which I happen to be writing. Your answer: by not giving it a thought.

Question: Is this athematic?

Answer: Who said anything about themes? It is not a question of having something to say.

Question: Then what is the purpose of this "experimental" music?

Answer: No purposes. Sounds.

Question: Why bother, since, as you have pointed out, sounds are continually happening whether you produce them or not?

Answer: What did you say? I'm still—

Question: I mean—But is this *music?*

Answer: Ah! you like sounds after all when they are made up of vowels and consonants. You are slow-witted, for you have never brought your mind to the location of urgency. Do you need me or someone else to hold you up? Why don't you realize as I do that nothing is accomplished by writing, playing, or listening to music? Otherwise, deaf as a doornail, you will never be able to hear anything, even what's well within earshot.

Question: But, seriously, if this is what music is, I could write it as well as you.

Answer: Have I said anything that would lead you to think I thought you were stupid?

Few arts have so successfully resisted definition as jazz. In this examination of the various attempts at definition, one of the editors of this volume offers as well some meditations on the history and development of jazz. These pages make up the first chapter of A History of Jazz in America *(1952), one of four volumes by Barry Ulanov (1918–   ) which are devoted to jazz or jazz musicians. In* The Two Worlds of American Art: The Private and the Popular *(1965), he adds another definition of sorts: "Jazz is an art of feeling. Its performers nurture their feelings with the tenderness of a parent, the tension of a frustrated adolescent, and the violence of a dispossessed adult. To find feelings and to hold them, jazz musicians use every means known to art and some new ones that they themselves have invented. Their procedures are alternately controlled and disorderly, anarchical and academic. They have developed virtuoso playing techniques to fit them. They have established a whole new series of traditions. All are in the service of feeling."*

WHAT IS JAZZ?

*Barry
Ulanov*

In *The American Scene*, Henry James said of American cities, "So there it all is; arrange it as you can. Poor dear bad bold beauty; there must indeed be something about her . . . !" The same can be said of American jazz.

On the surface there is disorder and conflict in jazz. No common definition of this music has been reached. It resists dictionary definition, and its musicians splutter nervously and take refuge in the colorful ambiguities of its argot. Nonetheless, its beauty can be probed; its badness can be separated from its boldness. The process is a difficult one, as it is in any art, and in jazz two arts, the composing and the performing arts, are joined together. But if one goes beneath the surface and does not allow the contradictions and the confusions of appearances to put one off, much becomes clear, and the mystery at the center is seen to be the central mystery of all the arts.

The cortex of jazz consists of several layers, alternately hard and soft, complex in structure, and hard to take apart. It is compounded of the history of the music and of the many styles of jazz. At first the history seems disjointed and the styles contradictory. One marks a confounding series of shifts in place and person and style. One finds a music dominated by Negroes in New Orleans, by white musicians in Chicago, by important but apparently unrelated figures in New York. One discovers a disastrous split in jazz inaugurated by the swing era and intensified during the days of bebop and so-called progressive jazz. But then one looks and listens more closely, and order and continuity appear.

Americans have long been wedded to the boom-and-bust cycle, and their culture reflects that dizzying course. Jazz is not like that; it has no cycles; it doesn't spiral. Whether you adopt the approach of the economic historian, the cultural anthropologist, or the aesthetic philosopher, you will not find an easy reflection of a theory in jazz. While much of America—crises and ecstasies and even a moment or two of exaltation—has found its way into jazz, the history of jazz is a curiously even one, chaotic at any instant, but always moving ahead in what is for an art form almost a straight line.

For most of its history, jazz, rejected in its homeland, has had consciously to seek survival, conscientiously to explain and defend its existence. From its early homes, the Ozark hills, the Louisiana bayous, the Carolina cotton fields, the Virginia plantations, through the New Orleans bordellos and barrelhouses to its latter-day efflorescence it has been alternately condemned and misunderstood. Variously banned and bullied and sometimes cheered beyond its merits, jazz has led a lonely life but a full one. It is still with us and looks to be around for quite a while.

No matter what the fortunes of jazz, its nucleus has remained constant, little touched by extravagances of opinion, sympathetic or unsympathetic. The nucleus of jazz—as differentiated from its cortex—contains its nerve center, its source of life, and here are its mystery and meaning. The nucleus of jazz is made up of melody, harmony, and rhythm, the triune qualities of the art of music which, as everybody knows, can be fairly simply defined. In bare definition, melody is any succession of notes, harmony any simultaneity of tones, rhythm the arithmetic measure of notes or tones. In closer examination, melody appears as a vast variety of things, ranging from so simple a tune as "Yankee Doodle" to the complexity of one of Arnold Schönberg's constructions. In more detailed analysis, harmony shows up as a vertical ordering of a Bach fugue, or a tight structuring based entirely on whole tones in the impressionism of Debussy. But bewildering as the complications of melody and harmony can be, they are easier to analyze and verbalize than rhythm or any of its parts, and rhythm is the most important of the three in jazz.

Before attempting a synoptic definition of jazz as a noun (or discussing the misuse of "jazz" as a verb and "jazzy" as an adjective), and of the various corollary terms that explain the meaning of this music, it might be instructive to examine definitions by musicians themselves. The following definitions were made by jazz musicians in 1935, when their music was undergoing a revival as a result of the then current vogue for the jazz that went by the new name of swing. Benny Goodman was a great success, and jam sessions had become public again. Musicians themselves found it difficult to define "swing," by which of course they merely meant the 1935 version of jazz, which wasn't very different from the 1930 or 1925 music. Let us examine the definitions.

Wingy Manone: "Feeling an increase in tempo though you're still playing at the same tempo."

Marshall Stearns and *John Hammond* (jazz authorities) and *Benny Goodman:* "A band swings when its collective improvisation is rhythmically integrated."

Gene Krupa: "Complete and inspired freedom of rhythmic interpretation."

Jess Stacy: "Syncopated syncopation."

Morton Kahn and *Payson Re:* "Feeling a multitude of subdivisions in each beat and playing or implying the accents that you feel; that is, if the tune is played at the proper tempo, so that when you're playing it, you'll feel it inside."

Glenn Miller: "Something that you have to feel; a sensation that can be conveyed to others."

Frankie Froeba: "A steady tempo, causing lightness and relaxation and a feeling of floating."

Louis Armstrong.
Photograph by Dennis Stock. Magnum.

Terry Shand: "A synthetic cooperation of two or more instruments helping along or giving feeling to the soloist performing."

Ozzie Nelson: "A vague something that you seem to feel pulsating from a danceable orchestra. To me it is a solidity and compactness of attack by which the rhythm instruments combine with the others to create within the listeners the desire to dance."

Chick Webb: "It's like lovin' a gal, and havin' a fight, and then seein' her again."

Louis Armstrong: "My idea of how a tune should go."

Ella Fitzgerald: "Why, er—swing is—well, you sort of feel—uh—uh—I don't know—you just swing!"

These musicians were looking for a new set of terms that would catch the beat so basic to jazz; they were stumped for the words to describe the kind of improvisation necessary to jazz.

In the simple, compressed, sometimes too elliptic vocabulary of the jazz musician, one learns a great deal about the music he plays. One learns that "jazz" is a noun, that it is not American popular music (as it has often been thought to be), that the jazz musician is most interested in the rhythmic connotation of the word and in little else. If you tell him that some say the term comes from the phonetic spelling of the abbreviation of a jazz musician named Charles (Charles, Chas., Jass, Jazz), he is not in the least interested. If you tell him that there is a great deal of substance to the claim that the word comes from the French word *jaser*—to pep up, to exhilarate—he may nod his head with a degree of interest but ask you, "What about the beat?" You will learn from the jazz musician that "swing" is no longer a noun, in spite of the fact that it was first so used in the title of a Duke Ellington recording in 1931, "It Don't Mean a Thing if It Ain't Got That Swing," which gives it a kind of ex cathedra endorsement. You learn that "swing" is a verb, that it is a way of describing the beat, even as Ellington's title for another tune, "Bouncing Buoyancy," is a description of the same beat, even as the term "jump" is, even as "leaps" is, even as the description of jazz as "music that goes" is, even as in the thirties the compliment of "solid" to performer or performance was like "gone," "crazy," "craziest," "the end," and "cool" today. They are descriptions of the beat.

From an examination of jazz musicians' own words, it is possible to glean the subtle, unruly, and almost mystical concept of the jazz spirit, or feeling, or thinking—it is all these things and is so understood by the jazz musician himself. The jazzman has his own way of getting at the center of his music, and thus he formulates his own musical language. Also he converts the musical language into a verbal dialect of his own. In his own set of terms, musical and verbal, he thinks, he feels; he rehearses, he performs; he scores, he improvises; he gets a beat.

To get that elusive beat, a jazzman will do anything. Without it, he cannot do anything. With it, he is playing jazz, and that is a large and satisfying enough accomplishment. When a jazzman picks up a familiar tune, banal or too well-known through much repetition, and alters its rhythmic pattern in favor of a steady if sometimes monotonous beat, and varies its melodies and maybe even changes its chords, he is working freely, easily, and with as much spontaneity as he can bring to his music. That freedom, ease, and spontaneity brought him to jazz; within those determining limits he will find a place for himself or get out, or join one of the bands whose frightening parodies of jazz are so often more popular than the real thing. It is by his formal understanding of certain definite values that the jazz musician has conceived, organized, and developed his art. It has been hot; it has become cool. It has jumped and swung; it has sauntered. It has borrowed; it has originated. It has effected a change, a literal transformation; inherited conventions have gradually been restated, reorganized, and ultimately restructured as a new expression. It may be that jazz musicians have simply rediscovered a controlling factor in music, the improvising performer. Without any awareness of what he has done, the jazzman may have gone back to some of the beginnings of music, tapping once more the creative roots which nourished ancient Greek music, the plain chant, the musical baroque and its immediate successors and predecessors. We know that seventeenth- and eighteenth-century composers were improvisers and that when they brought their scores to other musicians they left the interpretation of parts to the discretion of the performers, even as an arranger for a jazz band does today.

But the jazz musician has brought more than procedures, composing conceptions, and improvisation to his music. Techniques have been developed that have broadened the resources and intensified the disciplines of certain instruments far beyond their use in other music. Colors have been added to solo instruments and to various combinations and numbers of instruments that are utterly unlike any others in music. New textures have emerged from a conception of tonality and of pitch that is not original but is entirely fresh in its application. The improvising jazz musician has a different and more responsible and rewarding position than that of his counterparts in earlier art and folk music. The rhythmic base of music has been reinterpreted, making the central pulse at once more primitive than it has been before in Western music, and more sophisticated in its variety.

This, then, is how one might define jazz: it is a new music of a certain distinct rhythmic and melodic character, one that constantly involves improvisation—of a minor sort in adjusting accents and phrases of the tune at hand, of a major sort in creating music extemporaneously, on the spot. In the course of creating jazz, a melody or its underlying chords may be altered. The rhythmic valuations of notes may be lengthened or shortened according to a regular scheme, syncopated or not, or there may be no consistent pattern of rhythmic variations so long as a steady beat remains implicit or explicit. The beat is usually four quarter-notes to the bar, serving as a solid rhythmic base for the improvisation of soloists or groups playing eight or twelve measures, or some multiple or dividend thereof.

These things are the means. The ends are the ends of all art, the expression of the universal and the particular, the specific and the indirect and the intangible. In its short history, jazz has generally been restricted to short forms and it has often been directed toward the ephemeral and the trivial, but so too has it looked toward the lasting perception and the meaningful conclusion. Much of the time jazz musicians have sought and obtained an unashamed aphrodisiac effect; they have also worshiped in their music, variously devout before the one God and the unnamed gods. Like poets and painters, they are of all faiths, their doctrines are many; but they are united in one conviction, that they have found a creative form for themselves, for their time, for their place.

At the opening of the *Gradus ad Parnassum*, the dialogue offered as a study of counterpoint by Johann Josef Fux in 1725, the music master Aloysius warns the student Josef: "You must try to remember whether or not you felt a strong natural inclination to this art even in childhood." The student answers: "Yes, most deeply. Even before I could reason, I was overcome by the force of this strange enthusiasm and I turned all my thoughts and feelings to music. And now the burning desire to understand it possesses me, drives me almost against my will, and day and night lovely melodies seem to sound around me. Therefore I think I no longer have reason to doubt my inclination. Nor do the difficulties of the work discourage me, and I hope that with the help of good health I shall be able to master it." Several jazz musicians have read Fux, even as Haydn and Beethoven did, though perhaps with less immediate application. They have, however, echoed the pupil's "strange enthusiasm"; that, these jazzmen said, was their experience, their "burning desire." Following the "inclination," jazz musicians have not had much of the help of good health; some of them have flaunted their doggedly unreasonable living habits and suffered the personal and public consequences of the habits and of the flaunting. All this their music has reflected, and sometimes it is noisy and grotesque as a result. More often it has a fullness and richness of expression. Slowly, clearly, the music is maturing, and, for it and with it and by it, so are the musicians.

Few art forms have had as turbulent a history as rock. Few have been so roundly condemned. Few have been so loyally—and royally—supported, as art, as a political movement, as religion, as a way of life. Everybody knows—and has known since the middle 1950s—that rock is loud, so loud, some physicans have insisted, that it has seriously damaged the hearing of some of its listeners. And everybody knows too that rock is much of the time an art of protest. But what rock really is,

ROCK
in terms of art, is not at all so clear. Does its commercial success, almost unparalleled among the mass media, make it a pop art?

AS
Do its rhythms and instruments make it a kind of jazz? Can it be called an offshoot of hillbilly or country music because of its characteristic dialects,

FOLK
diction, and verse forms? Charles Belz offers the case for rock as folk art, and more—as its own reality, neither

ART
symbolic nor allegorical of other worlds, other people, or other events than those which make up its own contents and

Charles Belz
performances. Belz, an art historian at Brandeis University, has put rock in the mainstream of the history of the arts in the second half of the twentieth century.

The underlying contention of this study is that rock is a part of the long tradition of folk art in the United States and throughout the world. However simple or obvious this thesis may seem at first, it nevertheless involves a number of complicated issues concerning the history of art, the relationship between folk art and fine art, and our notions about the creative act in either domain of expression. The fact that rock first emerged, and has since developed, within the area of popular art only complicates its relationship to the folk and fine art traditions. It is to this general question—of the distinction between folk art, fine art, and popular art—that I wish to address these introductory remarks in order to clarify the position of rock in the larger history of art.

Distinguishing between folk, fine, and popular art has become extremely difficult in [our time]. We live in a culture which is determined to question the validity of such distinctions and in which such questioning has provoked some of the best artistic statements since World War II. The complexity of this situation is partly due to the phenomenon of Pop Art, a fine art style which has been directly stimulated by popular or mass culture. Pop paintings and sculptures draw their inspiration from billboards, comic strips, advertising, and supermarkets, and sometimes look deceptively like the original objects in our predominantly man-made environment. Similarly, certain developments of theater—particularly the "living theater," "happenings," and "environments"—encourage the notion that the entire panorama of life can be viewed as a work of art. In the face of all this, drawing lines between art objects and non-art objects, or even distinguishing between different *classes* of art objects, might seem a less important task than describing a seemingly delightful situation in which anything can be art and maybe everything is. For the critic-historian, however, these distinctions are fundamental. Rock has been considered as popular art, folk art, fine art, and even non-art. Which, in fact, is it?

The vast and current interest in rock might be viewed as a feedback from such phenomena as Pop Art. Taking a hint from the fine arts, the adult public has begun to appreciate material which was previously alien and embarrassing to the critics of modern American civilization. Such appreciation, however, is a development of the 1960's. The development of rock particularly during the first decade of its history, took place in the absence of such appreciation. The music emerged in response to a series of changing values and vital needs—not as the result of a sophistication gleaned from art galleries, museums, or periodicals. Its history, moreover, must be seen as a youth movement and as the reflection of a way of life radically different from the one which prevailed before the 1950's. When rock emerged, it spoke to these new values, to this youth, and to this changed way of life. But it did so in its capacity as a voice *of* the people rather than an art which talked *about* them from a detached and self-determined vantage point. On an immediate level as well as in its ultimate significance, the music has been a confrontation with reality rather than a confrontation with art. This distinctiveness of function marks rock as folk art rather than fine art.

The difference between the functions of folk art and fine art cannot be regarded as absolute or necessarily clearcut. All art, it can be argued, arises in response to vital needs and reflects a changing way of life from generation to generation. Further, all art is admittedly concerned with reality. At this level of generalization, folk art and fine art become alike. But folk art and fine art are not so similar when we consider which elements are more or less important in the creation and appeal of each.

In the modern period the most advanced media of the fine arts have become increasingly conscious of their respective and unique identities. Painting, for instance, has consistently involved itself with questions of the intrinsic nature of its expression: its flatness, its shape, its opticality, and so forth. Furthermore, these questions have evolved into an explicit *content*. In other words, the most successful expressions in the medium have tended to force the viewer to recognize that he is looking at a painting, a work of art. Moreover, by recognizing its particular medium in this way, the individual work compels its viewer to recognize that the object of his experience—in this case, the painting—is also distinct from other kinds of realities and from life in general. To put it another way, fine art declares itself as being different in kind from life. This is not to say that fine art ignores life or is irrelevant to the concerns of reality. Rather, any fine art expression confronts life, and has meaning in terms of it, only by engaging in an immediate confrontation with itself. In this sense, fine art is conscious of its own being, and, more generally, conscious of art.

In folk art, "art-consciousness" does not occupy the primary role that it does in fine art. A folk idiom's immediate concern is with issues of life and reality and with an overt expression of those issues. It is not aware of the identities of the separate media that it may employ. In the sense I am trying to define, a folk idiom employs different media unknowingly; it regards the identities of these media as being passive, like entities that need not be confronted in themselves. More simply, the difference between folk art and fine art can be stated in the following way: The work of folk art says of itself, as it were, "this is reality," while the work of fine art says "this is a picture of reality." In no way, of course, does this distinction imply that one type of expression is of a higher quality than the other.

The distinction I have just made must be cautiously applied. It might very well be rejected by the artists themselves. But, however fascinating and enlightening an artist's remarks may be, they constitute a different area of concern, that of autobiography. A given artist—someone, say, whom I consider the producer of fine art objects—may contend that he never thinks about "art" when he is making a picture. Similarly, the Beatles have frequently commented that they do not *intend* all the meanings the critics find in their songs. Such statements are perplexing unless we understand that they belong to the domain of autobiography. The emphasis in the present study is upon neither autobiography nor biography, but upon the works of art themselves and upon their inherent character as experienced objects. Such an emphasis is not simply capricious, nor is it meant to undermine the significance of other types of studies. It merely represents a method for relating works of art in an historical context, and, more important, for understanding the meanings those works compel in our experience of them.

The ways in which rock relates to the fine art-folk art distinction are apparent in various aspects of the music itself, in the fabric of media which has surrounded it, and in the responses it elicits. In the early days of the *American Bandstand* television show, for instance, a panel of three or four teenagers periodically reviewed newly released records. The record was played, the audience danced, and a discussion of the song's merits followed. This discussion invariably contained remarks such as, "It's got a great beat. . . . I'll give it an 80," or, "You can really dance to it. . . . I'll give it an 85." The panelists never talked about the artistic properties of the record: the way the song was structured, the relation between its structure and meaning, its manipulations of the medium, the implications of its content, or any of the kinds of issues that are central to a meaningful statement about a work of fine art.

No one who appreciated or understood the music ever expected such questions to be discussed, for they are not part of the folk response. That response is spontaneous, and it is directed to the thing-as-reality. In other words, the connection between listener and song is an immediate one; no aesthetic distance separates the two, no gap that would provoke art-consciousness. With rock, as with any folk idiom, a consciousness of art is unnecessary for grasping the full impact of a particular work. This fact probably explains why the *Bandstand* panelists, however "uncritical" they

may have appeared, were usually accurate in naming the best—
that is, the most folk-like—of the new records.

The adult audiences and the popular press who condemned
rock in the 1950's did so because they did not understand the
identity of the music they heard. They failed to grasp the essential
difference between folk art and fine art, a difference tenagers
unconsciously took for granted. Adverse critics of the music complained that it was crude and primitive, that it used poor grammar
and improper enunciation, and that its lyrics were literary nonsense. Even in the 1960's, on his *Open End* show, David Susskind
continued the effort to embarrass the music by reading the lyrics
of some typical rock songs as if they were examples of fine art
poetry. This sort of criticism was as futile and irrelevant as an art
historian's criticism that a painting by Henri Rousseau had awkward perspective or that its human figures were out of scale with
the landscape.

Folk art is neither aware of, nor concerned about, the kinds
of manipulations that constitute "proper" effects in the fine arts.
The rock artist's "crude" enunciation sprang naturally from his
spontaneous effort to express something real. Yet, the grammar
of "Doncha jus know it" or "I got a girl named Rama Lama Ding
Dong" does not alone transform a song into folk material. Artists
in the fine arts have used unconventional or slang expressions for
centuries, from Shakespeare to the present day. What distinguishes the folk artist is that he uses such expressions unconsciously rather than for a desired artistic effect. Unaware of the
option at his disposal—between art and reality—the folk artist
plunges naturally, though unknowingly, into the latter.

Just as rock does not "become" folk music simply because it
includes certain kinds of grammar or sentence structures, its folk
character is not assured by the use of particular musical instruments or by a devotion to specific subject matters. A common
misunderstanding concerning these questions arose during the
latter 1950's and continued into the 1960's. Groups like the
Kingston Trio and individual singers like Joan Baez inspired a
popular movement which seemed to equate folk music with songs
telling a story or conveying a moralistic point and accompanied
by the acoustic or solo guitar. To its enthusiastic audience, this
type of music was pure, eschewing the so-called falsifications of
recording-room manipulations. As such, it appeared to offer an
alternative to the crude and primitive style of rock. The artists

and audiences of this new trend failed to realize, however, that folk styles change. The acoustic guitar may have been all that was available to the folk artist of the 1930's, but his counterpart in the 1950's and the 1960's could work with electronics, with echo chambers, and with complicated recording techniques. Folk music could change its cloak—just as folk art changed its materials between the stone carvings of Cycladic culture, the bark paintings of Australia, and the oils of Rousseau.

A dramatic reflection of rock's essentially folk character is apparent in the large number of one-shot successes in the history of the music. A group or individual produces a high quality record on its first effort but fails to repeat that success. Although the group or individual artist generally issues a second or a third record, these follow-ups rarely achieve the special blend of ingredients that gave the initial song its impact. The explanation for this phenomenon—for the fact that the follow-ups are so often artistic failures—is directly connected with folk art's lack of art-consciousness. When the rock group produces its first record, it is not concerned with style or structure, but, rather, with a sense of immediate impact, with what the *Bandstand* panelists call "the great beat." With the second or third record, however, the group seems to become aware of *art*—that is, with the artistic character of the first record. The group tries to duplicate the elements of the first record with only minor or barely perceptible variations. Yet, as they try for artistic consistency, their folk orientation generally betrays them: Not really understanding art, or the complex blend of aesthetic decisions which produced the original sound, they produce an object bearing only superficial resemblance to the first record. In this instance, the folk artist's lack of art-consciousness plays an ironic role in his creative life: At a time when he consciously believes he is making art, he is merely producing reproductions of his own original and unconsciously creative gesture.

Rock history substantiates the notion that the realities in a particular song carry greater significance than the art of that song. This further suggests that the realities exist and are felt on a day-to-day basis. That is, rock's past is generally experienced as being part of the present rather than a part of history. Its history, in other words, is not usually pursued as an end in itself. While many songs may be remembered from the early or middle 1950's, their artists are usually forgotten. In such cases, the very term "artist" has a radically different meaning from the way it is used in the fine arts. In the latter, the artist is regarded as an individual whose significance and responsibility are linked with the production of a number of objects which are vital to our understanding of art. But with folk art, the relevance of the object-as-reality assumes greater importance than the artist who was responsible for its production—as if that artist only *happened* to have created the record. Hence, we cherish and recognize numerous songs in the folk music tradition, but we do not feel compelled to connect them with particular artists. In the fine arts, such a connection is demanded by the works, and scholars labor for years to discover the names of the masters whose art has survived without evidence of authorship.

That the relevance of rock songs is experienced in terms of day-to-day realities is shown by the numerous polls of "all-time favorites" conducted by local radio stations across the country. These polls usually list 300 songs; of that number, however, more than half are examples from the same year as the poll or from the year preceding it. Contrary to what many disk jockeys say, these figures do not prove that rock has improved over the years. Rather, the polls demonstrate that the current songs are simply more *real* than the older ones. The lists of "all-time favorites" reflect only today's memories of realities which existed when the various songs were originally experienced. The albums of "Oldies But Goodies" are similarly folk-like in their stress upon experienced realities: They thrive because they enable listeners to relive the past in the present, not because they inform their audiences about the art of the past.

I have suggested that folk artists, in contrast to their fine art counterparts, tend to be anonymous in relation to the works they produce. Yet, rock has a distinctive style of anonymity. While the artists of still remembered songs are frequently forgotten, the writers of those songs are even more generally nameless. Rock has only recently granted significance to these figures. Through most of its history their names have merely appeared parenthetically beneath the song titles. Moreover, even the groups who are currently most popular remain tinged with folk anonymity. Most listeners know the Rascals, the Hermits, the Doors, and other groups, but I wonder how many listeners know the names of the individuals who compose those groups. Teenage newspapers and magazines seek to combat our ignorance with their feature stories on one or another group and its members. But, as time passes, even these efforts seem futile in the face of the relentless thrust of folk anonymity; and they *are* futile because the experience of a folk music reality is ultimately more pressing and immediate than the name of the artist who produced it.

This anonymity is one of the differences between rock and jazz. Jazz is a music of great individualists. Further, its roots reach far back into the beginnings of the twentieth century, and its stylistic manifestations have been more varied than those of rock: New Orleans jazz, Chicago jazz, swing, be-bop, and modern jazz *each* represent a whole movement, one that is more expansive than the development so far of any of rock's sub-styles. Finally, improvisation has always been far more important in jazz than in rock. Nevertheless, they share a common ancestry in the blues tradition of America, and they share a folk delight in spontaneity of expression.

Perhaps the greatest difficulty in distinguishing rock as a folk idiom lies in the fact that the music is so closely linked to the enormous and complicated commercial music business, whereas generally works of art in the larger folk tradition are not at all closely related to popular art. This has caused the adverse critics of rock to say that the music has been forced upon a gullible public by some mercenary wholesalers of bad taste. In addition, these critics feel that the artists themselves are exclusively interested in financial rewards and are unconcerned about the quality of their music.

Suspicions like these are based on the fallacious assumption that the quality of art and the salability of art are mutually exclusive. Such a point, however, does not immediately dispel the suspicions themselves. Admittedly, many rock artists have earned fortunes through the sales of their records. My question, at the same time, is whether such evidence provides any meaningful explanation of why rock came into being in the first place, or why it has continued to exist. Rock artists have won and lost commercially, but the experience of the music itself has continued to possess vitality. I cannot imagine any artist who would not *enjoy* the benefits of commercial success, but both folk art and fine art can be originated and can survive without it. On the other hand, popular art does depend on commercial success in order to exist. That is, popular art *must* be popular, whereas folk art and fine art need not be, although they *may* be at any given moment. This demand for popularity is linked to the fact that popular art invariably has a product to sell: The product may be a bottle of shampoo or a new automobile, but it may also be non-material, such as diversion or escape, the "look" of reality or even of art. Popular art has many guises, but unlike either folk art or fine art, it is not self-sustaining.

Popular music, the Tin Pan Alley tradition, or *kitsch* music, has the appearance of fine art but fails to engage in the creative or artistic problems of fine art. *Kitsch* feeds parasitically upon fine art, but only after the latter has passed through its experimental and innovative stages. *Kitsch* represents an institutionalizing of the fine arts, and its product is therefore only the "look" of art. These products may be pleasant, enjoyable, and entertaining—the records of Frank Sinatra, Perry Como, and Andy Williams, and other leading exponents of *kitsch* frequently are—but they are not fundamentally concerned with artistic creation. Rather, they adopt the style of a work of art after it has come into being elsewhere, and they refine it and make it palatable for audiences who could not understand it in its original form.

Popular art avoids an encounter with reality just as it avoids an encounter with art. It succeeds by selling the "look" of reality. So although rock emerged in the same domain as popular music, it cannot be classified simply as popular music. Admittedly, the task of separating the two types of music is occasionally problematic, particularly at those points in rock history where an artist's work, Elvis Presley's for instance, undergoes a transformation from folk art to popular art. But generally the distinction is clear.

I have tried to outline some of the qualities of rock which show that it is folk music. In doing so, I am aware of the risks in generalizing about so large a body of material: Many exceptions can no doubt be offered to my central thesis. More important than the exceptions, however, is the undeniable fact that the music has changed considerably since its beginnings in the mid-1950's. Its history reveals dramatic changes in its attitude both to subject matter and to technique. And developments in the late 1960's further suggest that the music may be changing in its relation to the folk art-fine art distinction. It has been folk music through the greater part of its history; but to say that it is folk music today is more difficult. . . .

THE
EYE
OF
MAN

The language and the point of view of the art historian have had a very broad influence on critics and scholars in literature, music, the dance, the film, television, and all the other arts. The art historian is a philosopher upon occasion, a psychologist sometimes, a close inspector of paintings, buildings, and sculpture always. How much he may bring to his scrutinies is handsomely indicated here by Professor Ernst Gombrich (1909–   ), Director of the Warburg Institute of the University of London and author of what many believe to be the clearest and most useful of one-volume art histories, The Story of Art. *In these meditations, the subject is the visual arts, with particular attention to the function of representation. Some difficult ideas and a few specialized terms are to be encountered, but the Vienna-born writer's graceful handling of English makes these engaging rather than upsetting encounters. They offer not only insights into the nature of art but into one's own nature. That ought to be worth an occasional foray into the dictionary or a quick consultation of a footnote at the end.*

MEDITATIONS ON A HOBBY HORSE

OR THE ROOTS OF ARTISTIC FORM

E. H.
Gombrich

The subject of this article is a very ordinary hobby horse. It is neither metaphorical nor purely imaginary, at least not more so than the broomstick on which Swift wrote his meditations. It is usually content with its place in the corner of the nursery and it has no aesthetic ambitions. Indeed it abhors frills. It is satisfied with its broomstick body and its crudely carved head which just marks the upper end and serves as holder for the reins. How should we address it? Should we describe it as an 'image of a horse'? The compilers of the *Pocket Oxford Dictionary* would hardly have agreed. They defined *image* as 'imitation of an object's external form' and the 'external form' of a horse is surely not 'imitated' here. So much the worse, we might say, for the 'external form,' that elusive remnant of the Greek philosophical tradition which has dominated our aesthetic language for so long. Luckily there is another word in the *Dictionary* which might prove more accommodating: *representation*. To *represent*, we read, can be used in the sense of 'call up by description or portrayal or imagination, figure, place likeness of before mind or senses, serve or be meant as likeness of . . . stand for, be specimen of, fill place of, be substitute for.' A portrayal of a horse? Surely not. A substitute for a horse? Yes. That it is. Perhaps there is more in this formula than meets the eye.

I

Let us first ride our wooden steed into battle against a number of ghosts which still haunt the language of art criticism. One of them we even found entrenched in the *Oxford Dictionary*. The implication of its definition of an image is that the artist 'imitates' the 'external form' of the object in front of him, and the beholder, in his turn, recognizes the 'subject' of the work of art by this 'form.' This is what might be called the traditional view of representation. Its corollary is that a work of art will either be a faithful copy, in fact a complete replica, of the object represented, or will involve some degree of 'abstraction.' The artist, we read, abstracts the 'form' from the object he sees. The sculptor usually abstracts the three-dimensional form, and abstracts *from* colour; the painter abstracts contours and colours, and *from* the third dimension. In this context one hears it said that the draughtsman's line is a 'tremendous feat of abstraction' because it does not 'occur in nature.' A modern sculptor of Brancusi's persuasion may be praised or blamed for 'carrying abstraction to its logical extreme.' Finally the label of 'abstract art' for the creation of 'pure' forms carries with it a similar implication. Yet we need only look at our hobby horse to see that the very idea of abstraction as a complicated mental act lands us in curious absurdities. There is an old music hall joke describing a drunkard who politely lifts his hat to every lamp-post he passes. Should we say that the liquor has so increased his power of abstraction that he is now able to isolate the formal quality of uprightness from both lamp-post and the human figure? Our mind, of course, works by differentiation rather than by generalization, and the child will for long call all four-footers of a certain size 'gee-gee' before it learns to distinguish breeds and 'forms'![1]

II

Then there is that age-old problem of universals as applied to art. It has received its classical formulation in the Platonizing theories of the Academicians. 'A history-painter,' says Reynolds, 'paints man in general; a portrait-painter a particular man, and therefore a defective model.'[2] This, of course, is the theory of abstraction applied to one specific problem. The implications are that the portrait, being an exact copy of a man's 'external form' with all 'blemishes' and 'accidents,' refers to the individual person exactly as does the proper name. The painter, however, who wants to 'evaluate his style' disregards the particular and 'generalizes the forms.' Such a picture will no longer represent a particular man but rather the class or concept 'man.' There is a deceptive simplicity in this argument, but it makes at least one unwarranted assumption: that every image of this kind necessarily refers to something outside itself—be it individual or class. But nothing of the kind need be implied when we point to an image and say 'this is a man.' Strictly speaking that statement may be interpreted to mean that the image itself is a member of the class 'man.' Nor is that interpretation as farfetched as it may sound. In fact our hobby horse would submit to no other interpretation. By the logic of Reynolds's reasoning it would have to represent the most generalized idea of horseness. But if the child calls a stick a horse it obviously means nothing of the kind. The stick is neither a sign signifying the concept horse nor is it a portrait of an individual horse. By its capacity to serve as a 'substitute' the stick becomes a horse in its own right, it belongs to the class of 'gee-gees' and may even merit a proper name of its own.

When Pygmalion blocked out a figure from his marble he did not at first represent a 'generalized' human form, and then gradually a particular woman. For as he chipped away and made it more lifelike the block was not turned into a portrait—not even in the unlikely case that he used a live model. So when his prayers were heard and the statue came to life she was Galatea and no one else—and that regardless of whether she had been fashioned in an archaic, idealistic, or naturalistic style. The question of reference, in fact, is totally independent of the degree of differentiation. The witch who made a 'generalized' wax dummy of an enemy may have meant it to refer to someone in particular. She would then pronounce the right spell to establish this link— much as we may write a caption under a generalized picture to do the same. But even those proverbial replicas of nature, Madame Tussaud's effigies, need the same treatment. Those in the galleries which are labelled are 'portraits of the great.' The figure on the staircase made to hoax the visitor simply represents 'an' attendant, one member of a class. It stands there as a 'substitute' for the expected guard—but it is not more 'generalized' in Reynolds's sense.

III

The idea that art is 'creation' rather than 'imitation' is sufficiently familiar. It has been proclaimed in various forms from the time of Leonardo, who insisted that the painter is 'Lord of all Things,'[3] to that of Klee, who wanted to create as Nature does.[4] But the more solemn overtones of metaphysical power disappear when we leave art for toys. The child 'makes' a train either of a few blocks or with pencil on paper. Surrounded as we are by posters and newspapers carrying illustrations of commodities or events, we find it difficult to rid ourselves of the prejudice that all images should be 'read' as referring to some imaginary or actual reality. Only the historian knows how hard it is to look at Pygmalion's work without comparing it with nature. But recently we have been made aware how thoroughly we misunderstand primitive or Egyptian art whenever we make the assumption that the artist 'distorts' his motif or that he even wants us to see in his work the record of any specific experience.[5] In many cases these images 'represent' in the sense of being substitutes. The clay horse or servant, buried in the tomb of the mighty, takes the place of the living. The idol takes the place of the god. The question whether it represents the 'external form' of the particular divinity or, for that matter, of a class of demons is quite inappropriate. The idol serves as the substitute of the God in worship and ritual —it is a man-made god in precisely the sense that the hobby horse is a man-made horse; to question it further means to court deception.[6]

There is another misunderstanding to be guarded against. We often try instinctively to save our idea of 'representation' by shifting it to another plane. Where we cannot refer the image to a motif in the outer world we take it to be a portrayal of a motif in the artist's inner world. Much critical (and uncritical) writing on both primitive and modern art betrays this assumption. But to apply the naturalistic idea of portrayal to dreams and visions—let alone to unconscious images—begs a whole number of questions.[7] The hobby horse does not portray our idea of a horse. The fearsome monster or funny face we may doodle on our blotting pad is not projected out of our mind as paint is 'ex-pressed' out of a paint tube. Of course any image will be in some way symptomatic of its maker, but to think of it as of a photograph of a pre-existing reality is to misunderstand the whole process of image-making.

IV

Can our substitute take us further? Perhaps, if we consider how it could become a substitute. The 'first' hobby horse (to use eighteenth-century language) was probably no image at all. Just a stick which qualified as a horse because one could ride on it. The *tertium comparationis*, the common factor, was function rather than form. Or, more precisely, that formal aspect which fulfilled the minimum requirement for the performance of the function—for any 'ridable' object could serve as a horse. If that is true we may be enabled to cross a boundary which is usually regarded as closed and sealed. For in this sense 'substitutes' reach deep into biological functions that are common to man and animal. The cat runs after the ball as if it were a mouse. The baby sucks its thumb as if it were the breast. In a sense the ball 'represents' a mouse to the cat, the thumb a breast to the baby. But here too 'representation' does not depend on formal similarities, beyond the minimum requirements of function. The ball has nothing in common with the mouse except that it is chasable. The thumb nothing with the breast except that it is suckable. As 'substitutes' they fulfill certain demands of the organism. They are keys which happen to fit into biological or psychological locks, or counterfeit coins which make the machine work when dropped into the slot.

In the language of the nursery the psychological function of

'representation' is still recognized. The child will reject a perfectly naturalistic doll in favour of some monstrously 'abstract'
dummy which is 'cuddly.' It may even dispose of the element of
'form' altogether and take to a blanket or an eiderdown as its
favourite 'comforter'—a substitute on which to bestow its love.
Later in life, as the psychoanalysts tell us, it may bestow this same
love on a worthy or unworthy living substitute. A teacher may
'take the place' of the mother, a dictator or even an enemy may
come to 'represent' the father. Once more the common denominator between the symbol and the thing symbolized is not the
'external form' but the function; the mother symbol would be
lovable, the father-imago fearable, or whatever the case may be.

Now this psychological concept of symbolization seems to
lead so very far away from the more precise meaning which the
word 'representation' has acquired in the figurative arts. Can
there be any gain in throwing all these meanings together? Possibly: for anything seems worth trying, to get the function of
symbolizing out of its isolation.

The 'origin of art' has ceased to be a popular topic. But the
origin of the hobby horse may be a permitted subject for speculation. Let us assume that the owner of the stick on which he
proudly rode through the land decided in a playful or magic
mood—and who could always distinguish between the two?—to
fix 'real' reins and that finally he was even tempted to 'give' it
two eyes near the top end. Some grass could have passed for a
mane. Thus our inventor 'had a horse.' He had made one. Now
there are two things about this fictitious event which have some
bearing on the idea of the figurative arts. One is that, contrary to
what is sometimes said, communication need not come into this
process at all. He may not have wanted to show his horse to
anyone. It just served as a focus for his fantasies as he galloped
along—though more likely than not it fulfilled this same function
for a tribe to which it 'represented' some horse-demon of fer-
tility and power.[8] We may sum up the moral of this 'Just So
Story' by saying that substitution may precede portrayal, and
creation communication. It remains to be seen how such a general
theory can be tested. If it can, it may really throw light on some
concrete questions. Even the origin of language, that notorious
problem of speculative history,[9] might be investigated from this
angle. For what if the 'pow-wow' theory, which sees the root of
language in imitation, and the 'pooh-pooh' theory, which sees it

in emotive interjection, were to be joined by yet another? We might term it the 'niam-niam' theory postulating the primitive hunter lying awake through hungry winter nights and making the sound of eating, not for communication but as a substitute for eating—being joined, perhaps, by a ritualistic chorus trying to conjure up the phantasm of food.

V

There is one sphere in which the investigation of the 'representational' function of forms has made considerable progress of late, that of animal psychology. Pliny, and innumerable writers after him, have regarded it as the greatest triumph of naturalistic art for a painter to have deceived sparrows or horses. The implication of these anecdotes is that a human beholder easily recognizes a bunch of grapes in a painting because for him recognition is an intellectual act. But for the birds to fly at the painting is a sign of a complete 'objective' illusion. It is a plausible idea, but a wrong one. The merest outline of a cow seems sufficient for a tsetse trap, for somehow it sets the apparatus of attraction in motion and 'deceives' the fly. To the fly, we might say, the crude trap has the 'significant' form—biologically significant, that is. It appears that visual stimuli of this kind play an important part in the animal world. By varying the shapes of 'dummies' to which animals were seen to respond, the 'minimum image' that still sufficed to release a specific reaction has been ascertained.[10] Thus little birds will open their beak when they see the feeding parent approaching the nest, but they will also do so when they are shown two darkish roundels of different size, the silhouette of the head and body of the bird 'represented' in its most 'generalized' form. Certain young fishes can even be deceived by two simple dots arranged horizontally, which they take to be the eyes of the mother fish, in whose mouth they are accustomed to shelter against danger. The fame of Zeuxis will have to rest on other achievements than his deception of birds.

An 'image' in this biological sense is not an imitation of an object's external form but an imitation of certain privileged or relevant aspects. It is here that a wide field of investigation would seem to open. For man is not exempt from this type of reaction.[11] The artist who goes out to represent the visible world is not simply faced with a neutral medley of forms he seeks to 'imitate.' Ours is a structured universe whose main lines of force are still bent and fashioned by our biological and psychological needs, however much they may be overlaid by cultural influences. We know that there are certain privileged motifs in our world to which we respond almost too easily. The human face may be outstanding among them. Whether by instinct or by very early training, we are certainly ever disposed to single out the expressive features of a face from the chaos of sensations that surrounds it, and to respond to its slightest variations with fear or joy. Our whole perceptual apparatus is somehow hypersensitized in this direction of physiognomic vision[12] and the merest hint suffices for us to create an expressive physiognomy that 'looks' at us with surprising intensity. In a heightened state of emotion, in the dark, or in a feverish spell, the looseness of this trigger may assume pathological forms. We may see faces in the pattern of a wallpaper, and three apples arranged on a plate may stare at us like two eyes and a clownish nose. What wonder that it is so easy to 'make' a face with two dots and a stroke even though their geometrical constellation may be greatly at variance with the 'external form' of a real head? The well-known graphic joke of the 'reversible face' might well be taken as a model for experiments which could still be made in this direction. It shows to what extent the group of shapes that can be read as a physiognomy has priority over all other readings. It turns the side which is the right way up into a convincing face and disintegrates the one that is upside down into a mere jumble of forms which is accepted as a strange headgear.[13] In good pictures of this kind it needs a real effort to see both faces at the same time, and perhaps we never quite succeed. Our automatic response is stronger than our intellectual awareness.

Seen in the light of the biological examples discussed above there is nothing surprising in this observation. We may venture the guess that this type of automatic recognition is dependent on the two factors of resemblance and biological relevance, and that the two may stand in some kind of inverse ratio. The greater the biological relevance an object has for us the more will we be attuned to its recognition—and the more tolerant will therefore be our standards of formal correspondence. In an erotically charged atmosphere the merest hint of formal similarity with sexual functions creates the desired response and the same is true of the dream symbols investigated by Freud. The hungry man will be similarly attuned to the discovery of food—he will scan the world for the slightest promise of nourishment. The starving may even project food into all sorts of dissimilar objects—as Chaplin does in *Gold Rush* when his huge companion suddenly appears to him as a chicken. Can it have been some such experience which stimulated our 'niam-niam' chanting hunters to see their longed-for prey in the patches and irregular shapes on the dark cave walls? Could they perhaps gradually have sought this experience in the deep mysterious recesses of the rocks, much as Leonardo sought out crumbling walls to aid his visual fantasies? Could they, finally, have been prompted to fill in such 'readable' outlines with coloured earth—to have at least something 'spearable' at hand which might 'represent' the eatable in some magic fashion? There is no way of testing such a theory, but if it is true that cave artists often 'exploited' the natural formations of the rocks,[14] this, together with the 'eidetic' character of their works,[15] would at least not contradict our fantasy. The great naturalism of cave paintings may after all be a very late flower. It may correspond to our late, derivative, and naturalistic hobby horse.

VI

It needed two conditions, then, to turn a stick into our hobby horse: first, that its form made it just possible to ride on it; secondly—and perhaps decisively—that riding mattered. Fortunately it still needs no great effort of the imagination to understand how the horse could become such a focus of desires and aspirations, for our language still carries the metaphors moulded by a feudal past when to be chival-rous was to be horsy. The same stick that had to represent a horse in such a setting would have become the substitute of something else in another. It might have become a sword, sceptre, or—in the context of ancestor worship—a fetish representing a dead chieftain. Seen from the point of view of 'abstraction,' such a convergence of meanings onto one shape offers considerable difficulties, but from that of psychological 'projection' of meanings it becomes more easily intelligible. After all a whole diagnostic technique has been built up on the assumption that the meanings read into identical forms by different people tell us more about the readers than about the forms. In the sphere of art it has been shown that the same triangular shape which is the favourite pattern of many adjoining American Indian tribes is given different meanings reflecting the main preoccupations of the peoples concerned.[16] To the student of styles this discovery that one basic form can be made to represent a variety of objects may still become significant. For while the idea of realistic pictures being deliberately 'stylized' seems hard to swallow, the opposite idea of a limited vocabulary of simple shapes being used for the building up of different representations would fit much better into what we know of primitive art.

VII

Once we get used to the idea of 'representation' as a two-way affair rooted in psychological dispositions we may be able to refine a concept which has proved quite indispensable to the historian of art and which is nevertheless rather unsatisfactory: that of the 'conceptual image.' By this we mean the mode of representation which is more or less common to children's drawings and to various forms of primitive and primitivist art. The remoteness of this type of imagery from any visual experience has often been described.[17] The explanation of this fact which is most usually advanced is that the child (and the primitive) do not draw what they 'see' but what they 'know.' According to this idea the typical children's drawing of a manikin is really a graphic enumeration of those human features the child remembered.[18] It represents the content of the childish 'concept' of man. But to speak of 'knowledge' or 'intellectual realism' (as the French do[19]) brings us dangerously near to the fallacy of 'abstraction.' So back to our hobby horse. Is it quite correct to say that it consists of features which make up the 'concept' of a horse or that it reflects the memory image of horses seen? No—because this formulation omits one factor: the stick. If we keep in mind that representation is originally the creation of substitutes out of given material we may reach safer ground. The greater the wish to ride, the fewer may be the features that will do for a horse. But at a certain stage it must have eyes—for how else could it see? At the most primitive level, then, the conceptual image might be identified with what we have called the minimum image—that minimum, that is, which will make it fit into a psychological lock. The form of the key depends on the material out of which it is fashioned, and on the lock. It would be a dangerous mistake, however, to equate the 'conceptual image' as we find it used in the historical styles with this psychologically grounded minimum image. On the contrary. One has the impression that the presence of these schemata is always felt but that they are as much avoided as exploited.[20] We must reckon with the possibility of a 'style' being a set of conventions born out of complex tensions. The man-made image must be complete. The servant for the grave must have two hands and two feet. But he must not become a double under the artist's hands. Image-making is beset with dangers. One false stroke and the rigid mask of the face may assume an evil leer. Strict adherence to conventions alone can guard against such dangers. And thus primitive art seems often to keep on that narrow ledge that lies between the lifeless and the uncanny. If the hobby horse became too lifelike it might gallop away on its own.[21]

VIII

The contrast between primitive art and 'naturalistic' or 'illusionist' art can easily be overdrawn.[22] All art is 'image-making' and all image-making is rooted in the creation of substitutes. Even the artist of an 'illusionist' persuasion must make the man-made, the 'conceptual' image of convention his starting point. Strange as it may seem he cannot simply 'imitate an object's external form' without having first learned how to construct such a form. If it were otherwise there would be no need for the innumerable books on 'how to draw the human figure' or 'how to draw ships.' Wölfflin once remarked that all pictures owe more to other pictures than they do to nature.[23] It is a point which is familiar to the student of pictorial traditions but which is still insufficiently understood in its psychological implications. Perhaps the reason is that, contrary to the hopeful belief of many artists, the 'innocent eye' which should see the world afresh would not see it at all. It would smart under the painful impact of a chaotic medley of forms and colours.[24] In this sense the conventional vocabulary of basic forms is still indispensable to the artist as a starting point, as a focus of organization.

How, then, should we interpret the great divide which runs through the history of art and sets off the few islands of illusionist styles, of Greece, of China, and of the Renaissance, from the vast ocean of 'conceptual' art?

One difference, undoubtedly, lies in a change of function. In a way the change is implicit in the emergence of the idea of the image as a 'representation' in our modern sense of the word. As soon as it is generally understood that an image need not exist in its own right, that it may refer to something outside itself and therefore be the record of a visual experience rather than the creation of a substitute, the basic rules of primitive art can be transgressed with impunity. No longer is there any need for that completeness of essentials which belongs to the conceptual style, no longer is there the fear of the casual which dominates the archaic conception of art. The picture of a man on a Greek vase no longer needs a hand or a foot in full view. We know it is meant as a shadow, a mere record of what the artist saw or might see, and we are quite ready to join in the game and to supplement with our imagination what the real motif undoubtedly possessed. Once this idea of the picture suggesting something beyond what is really there is accepted in all its implications—and this certainly did not happen overnight—we are indeed forced to let our imagination play around it. We endow it with 'space' around its forms which is only another way of saying that we understand the reality which it evokes as three-dimensional, that the man could move and that even the aspect momentarily hidden 'was there'.[25] When medieval art broke away from that narrative conceptual symbolism into which the formulas of classical art had been frozen, Giotto made particular use of the figure seen from behind which stimulates our 'spatial' imagination by forcing us to imagine the other side.

Thus the idea of the picture as a representation of a reality outside itself leads to an interesting paradox. On the one hand it compels us to refer every figure and every object shown to that imaginary reality which is 'meant'. This mental operation can only be completed if the picture allows us to infer not only the 'external form' of every object represented but also its rela-

tive size and position. It leads us to that 'rationalization of space'
we call scientific perspective by which the picture plane becomes
a window through which we look into the imaginary world the
artist creates there for us. In theory, at least, painting is then
conceived in terms of geometrical projection.[26]

The paradox of the situation is that, once the whole picture
is regarded as the representation of a slice of reality, a new context is created in which the conceptual image plays a different
part. For the first consequence of the 'window' idea is that we
cannot conceive of any spot on the panel which is not 'significant', which does not represent something. The empty patch
thus easily comes to signify light, air, and atmosphere, and the
vague form is interpreted as enveloped by air. It is this confidence
in the representational context which is given by the very convention of the frame, which makes the development of impressionist methods possible. The artists who tried to rid themselves
of their conceptual knowledge, who conscientiously became
beholders of their own work and never ceased matching their
created images against their impressions by stepping back and
comparing the two—these artists could only achieve their aim
by shifting something of the load of creation on to the beholder.
For what else does it mean if we are enjoined to step back in
turn and watch the coloured patches of an impressionist landscape 'spring to life'? It means that the painter relies on our
readiness to take hints, to read contexts, and to call up our conceptual image under his guidance. The blob in the painting by
Manet which stands for a horse is no more an imitation of its
external form than is our hobby horse. But he has so cleverly
contrived it that it evokes the image in us—provided, of course,
we collaborate.

Here there may be another field for independent investigation.
For those 'privileged' objects which play their part in the earliest
layers of image-making recur—as was to be expected—in that of
image-reading. The more vital the feature that is indicated by the
context and yet omitted, the more intense seems to be the process
that is started off. On its lowest level this method of 'suggestive
veiling' is familiar to erotic art. Not, of course, to its Pygmalion
phase, but to its illusionist applications. What is here a crude
exploitation of an obvious biological stimulus may have its paral-

lel, for instance, in the representation of the human face. Leonardo achieved his greatest triumphs of lifelike expression by blurring precisely the features in which the expression resides, thus compelling us to complete the act of creation. Rembrandt could dare to leave the eyes of his moving portraits in the shade because we are thus stimulated to supplement them[27]. The 'evocative' image, like its 'conceptual' counterpart, should be studied against a wider psychological background.

IX

My hobby horse is not art. At best it can claim the attention of iconology, that emerging branch of study which is to art criticism what linguistics is to the criticism of literature. But has not modern art experimented with the primitive image, with the 'creation' of forms, and the exploitation of deep-rooted psychological forces? It has. But whatever the nostalgic wish of their makers, the meaning of these forms can never be the same as that of their primitive models. For that strange precinct we call 'art' is like a hall of mirrors or a whispering gallery. Each form conjures up a thousand memories and after-images. No sooner is an image presented as art than, by this very act, a new frame of reference is created which it cannot escape. It becomes part of an institution as surely as does the toy in the nursery. If—as might be conceivable—a Picasso would turn from pottery to hobby horses and send the products of this whim to an exhibition, we might read them as demonstrations, as satirical symbols, as a declaration of faith in humble things or as self-irony—but one thing would be denied even to the greatest of contemporary artists: he could not make the hobby horse mean to us what it meant to its first creator. That way is barred by the angel with a flaming sword.

NOTES

1. In the sphere of art this process of differentiation rather than abstraction is wittily described by Oliver Wendell Holmes in the essay *'Cacoethes Scribendi'*, from *Over the Teacups* (London: 1890): 'It's just the same thing as my plan . . . for teaching draw-

ing. . . . A man at a certain distance appears as a dark spot—nothing more. Good. Anybody . . . can make a dot. . . . Lesson No. 1. Make a dot; that is, draw your man, a mile off. . . . Now make him come a little nearer. . . . The dot is an oblong figure now. Good. Let your scholar draw an oblong figure. It is as easy as to make a note of admiration. . . . So by degrees the man who serves as a model approaches. A bright pupil will learn to get the outline of a human figure in ten lessons, the model coming five hundred feet nearer each time.'

2. *Discourses on Art* (Everyman Edition, p. 55). I have discussed the historical setting of this idea in 'Icones Symbolicae', *Journal of the Warburg and Courtauld Institutes*, XI (1948), p. 187, and some of its more technical aspects in a review of Charles Morris, *Signs, Language, and Behavior* (New York: 1946) in *The Art Bulletin*, March, 1949. In Morris's terminology these present meditations are concerned with the status and origin of the 'iconic sign'.

3. Leonardo da Vinci, *Paragone*, edited by I. A. Richter (London: 1949), p. 51.

4. Paul Klee, *On Modern Art* (London, 1948). For the history of the idea of *deus artifex* cf. E. Kris and O. Kurz, *Die Legende vom Künstler* (Vienna: 1934).

5. H. A. Groenewegen-Frankfort, *Arrest and Movement: An Essay on Space and Time in the Representational Art of the Ancient Near East* (London: 1951).

6. Perhaps it is only in a setting of realistic art that the problem I have discussed in 'Icones Symbolicae', loc. cit., becomes urgent. Only then the idea can gain ground that the allegorical image of, say, Justice, must be a portrait of Justice as she dwells in heaven.

7. For the history of this misinterpretation and its consequences cf. my article on 'Art and Imagery in the Romantic Period.' . . .

8. This, at least, would be the opinion of Lewis Spence, *Myth and Ritual in Dance, Game, and Rhyme* (London: 1947). And also of Ben Jonson's Busy, the Puritan: 'Thy Hobby-horse is an Idoll, a feirce and rancke Idoll: And thou, the *Nabuchadnezzar* . . . of the *Faire*, that set'st it up, for children to fall downe to, and worship'. (*Bartholomew Fair*, Act. III, Scene 6).

9. Cf. Géza Révész, *Ursprung und Vorgeschichte der Sprache* (Berne: 1946).

10. Cf. Konrad Lorenz, 'Die angeborenen Formen möglicher Erfahrung', *Zeitschrift für Tierpsychologie* V (1943), and the discussion of these experiments in E. Grassi and Th. von Uexküll, *Vom Ursprung und von den Grenzen der Geisteswissenschaften und Naturwissenschaften* (Bern: 1950).

11. K. Lorenz, loc. cit. The citation of this article does not imply sup-

port of the author's moral conclusions. On these more general issues see K. R. Popper, *The Open Society and Its Enemies*, esp., I, pp. 59 ff. and p. 268.

12. F. Sander, 'Experimentelle Ergebnisse der Gestaltpsychologie', *Berichte über den* 10. *Kongress für Experimentelle Psychologie* (Jena: 1928), p. 47, notes experiments that show the distance of two dots is much harder to estimate in its variations when these dots are isolated than when they are made to represent eyes in a schematic face and thus attain physiognomic significance.

13. For a large collection of such faces cf. Laurence Whistler, *Oho! The Drawings of Rex Whistler* (London: 1946).

14. G. H. Luquet, *The Art and Religion of Fossil Man* (London: 1930), pp. 141 f.

15. G. A. S. Snijder, *Kretische Kunst* (Berlin: 1936), pp. 68 f.

16. Franz Boas, *Primitive Art* (Oslo: 1927), pp. 118–28.

17. E.g., E. Löwry, *The Rendering of Nature in Early Greek Art* (London: 1907), H. Schaefer, *Von aegyptischer Kunst* (Leipzig: 1930), M. Verworn, *Ideoplastische Kunst* (Jena: 1914).

18. Karl Bühler, *The Mental Development of the Child* (London: 1930), pp. 113–17, where the connection with the linguistic faculty is stressed. A criticism of this idea was advanced by R. Arnheim, 'Perceptual Abstraction and Art', *Psychological Review*, LVI, 1947

19. G. H. Luquet, *L'Art primitif* (Paris: 1930).

20. The idea of avoidance (of sexual symbols) is stressed by A. Ehrenzweig, *Psycho-Analysis of Artistic Vision and Hearing*, (London: 1953), pp. 22–70.

21. E. Kris and O. Kurz, loc. cit., have collected a number of legends reflecting this age-old fear: thus a famous Chinese master was said never to have put the light into the eyes of his painted dragons lest they would fly away.

22. It was the intellectual fashion in German art history to work with contrasting pairs of concepts such as haptic-optic (Riegl), para-tactic-hypotactic (Coellen), abstraction-empathy (Worringer), idealism-naturalism (Dvořák), physioplastic-ideoplastic (Verworn), multiplicity-unity (Wölfflin), all of which could probably be expressed in terms of 'conceptual' and 'less conceptual' art. While the heuristic value of this method of antithesis is not in doubt it often tends to introduce a false dichotomy. In my book *The Story of Art* (London: 1950) I have attempted to stress the continuity of tradition and the persistent role of the conceptual image.

23. H. Wölfflin, *Principles of Art History* (New York: 1932).

24. The fallacy of a passive idea of perception is discussed in detail by E. Brunswik, *Wahrnehmung und Gegenstandswelt* (Vienna: 1934). In its application to art the writings of K. Fiedler contain many

valuable hints; cf. also A. Ehrenzweig, loc. cit., for an extreme and challenging presentation of this problem.

25. This may be meant in the rather enigmatic passage on the painter Parrhasius in Pliny's *Natural History*, XXXV, 67, where it is said that 'the highest subtlety attainable in painting is to find an outline . . . which should appear to fold back and to enclose the object so as to give assurance of the parts behind, thus clearly suggesting even what it conceals'.

26. Cf. E. Panofsky, 'The Codex Huygens and Leonardo da Vinci's Art Theory', *Studies of the Warburg Institute*, XIII (London: 1940), pp. 90 f.

27. Cf. J. v. Schlosser, 'Gespräch von der Bildniskunst', *Präludien* (Vienna: 1927), where, incidentally, the hobby horse also makes its appearance.

*A few painters in the modern era have been re-
markably articulate about their art in general and
their own aims in particular. One of the most absorbing to read is Wassily Kandinsky (1866–1944),
perhaps the best known Russian painter in this
century, and the close associate of Paul Klee and
Franz Marc in the founding, in 1912, of the group of
painters called* Der Blaue Reiter [The Blue Rider]
*after one of Kandinsky's paintings. The group was
determined to lead the way back to pure form and
pure color in art. The significance of essentials to
Kandinsky, one of the greatest of abstract painters,
is demonstrated in this opening
section of his famous essay on
the "spiritual" in art. His
reading of the "spiritual" is touched on throughout,
but it is given particular clarity in the illuminating
footnote appended to this excellent translation
from the German, which, in spite
of having been worked on by many
hands, retains the flavor of
Kandinsky's thought and style.*

CONCERNING THE SPIRITUAL IN ART

*Wassily
Kandinsky*

Every work of art is the child of its time; often
it is the mother of our emotions. It follows that
each period of culture produces an art of its
own, which cannot be repeated. Efforts to revive
the art principles of the past at best produce
works of art that resemble a stillborn child. For
example, it is impossible for us to live and feel as
did the ancient Greeks. For this reason those who
follow Greek principles in sculpture reach only
a similarity of form, while the work remains for
all time without a soul. Such an imitation resembles the antics of apes: externally a monkey
resembles a human being; he will sit holding a
book in front of his nose, turning over the pages
with a thoughtful air, but his actions have no
real significance.

But among the forms of art there is another
kind of external similarity, which is founded on a

fundamental necessity. When there is, as sometimes happens, a similarity of inner direction in an entire moral and spiritual milieu, a similarity of ideals, at first closely pursued but later lost to sight, a similarity of "inner mood" between one period and another, the logical consequence will be a revival of the external forms which served to express those insights in the earlier age. This may account partially for our sympathy and affinity with and our comprehension of the work of primitives. Like ourselves, these pure artists sought to express only inner[1] and essential feelings in their works; in this process they ignored as a matter of course the fortuitous.

This great point of inner contact is, in spite of its considerable importance, only one point. Only just now awakening after years of materialism, our soul is infected with the despair born of unbelief, of lack of purpose and aim. The nightmare of materialism, which turned life into an evil, senseless game, is not yet passed;

---

[1] A work of art consists of two elements, the inner and the outer.

The inner is the emotion in the soul of the artist; this emotion has the capacity to evoke a similar emotion in the observer.

Being connected with the body, the soul is affected through the medium of the senses—the felt. Emotions are aroused and stirred by what is sensed. Thus the sensed is the bridge, i.e., the physical relation, between the immaterial (which is the artist's emotion) and the material, which results in the production of a work of art. And again, what is sensed is the bridge from the material (the artist and his work) to the immaterial (the emotion in the soul of the observer).

The sequence is: emotion (in the artist) → the sensed → the art-work → the sensed → emotion (in the observer).

The two emotions will be like and equivalent to the extent that the work of art is successful. In this respect painting is in no way different from a song: each is a communication. The successful singer arouses in listeners his emotions; the successful painter should do no less.

The inner element, i.e., emotion, must exist; otherwise the work of art is a sham. The inner element determines the form of the work of art.

In order that the inner element, which at first exists only as an emotion, may develop into a work of art, the second element, i.e., the outer, is used as an embodiment. Emotion is always seeking means of expression, a material form, a form that is able to stir the senses. The determining and vital element is the inner one, which controls the outer form, just as an idea in the mind determines the words we use, and not *vice versa*. The determination of the form of a work of art is therefore determined by the irresistible inner force: this is the only unchanging law in art. A beautiful work is the consequence of an harmonious cooperation of the inner and the outer; i.e., a painting is an intellectual organism which, like every other material organism, consists of many parts. (*This explanation by Kandinsky of the relation between internal and external, or inner and outer, is a slightly revised version of a translation by Arthur Jerome Eddy of part of an article by Kandinsky which appeared in* Der Sturm, Berlin, 1913; cf. Cubists and Post-Impressionists, *A. C. McClurg, Chicago, 1914, pp. 119–20.*)

Right, Vasily Kandinsky, Sign with Accompaniment, *No. 382, 1927.*
From The Solomon R. Guggenheim Museum, New York City.

Below, Vasily Kandinsky, Arrow, *No. 258, 1923.*
From The Solomon R. Guggenheim Museum, New York City.

it still darkens the awakening soul. Only a feeble light glimmers, a tiny point in an immense circle of darkness. This light is but a presentiment; and the mind, seeing it, trembles in doubt over whether the light is a dream and the surrounding darkness indeed reality. This doubt and the oppression of materialism separate us sharply from primitives. Our soul rings cracked when we sound it, like a precious vase, dug out of the earth, which has a flaw. For this reason, the primitive phase through which we are now passing, in its present derivative form, must be short-lived.

The two kinds of resemblance between the forms of art of today and of the past can be easily recognized as diametrically opposed. The first, since it is external, has no future. The second, being internal, contains the seed of the future. After a period of materialist temptation, to which the soul almost succumbed, and which it was able to shake off, the soul is emerging, refined by struggle and suffering. Cruder emotions, like fear, joy and grief, which belonged to this time of trial, will no longer attract the artist. He will attempt to arouse more refined emotions, as yet unnamed. Just as he will live a complicated and subtle life, so his work will give to those observers capable of feeling them emotions subtle beyond words.

The observer of today is seldom capable of feeling such vibrations. He seeks instead an imitation of nature with a practical function (for example, a portrait in the ordinary sense) or an intuition of nature involving a certain interpretation (e.g., "impressionist" painting) or an inner feeling expressed by nature's forms (as we say, a picture of "mood"[2]). When they are true works of art, such forms fulfil their purposes and nourish the spirit. Though this remark applies to the first case, it applies more strongly to the third, in which the spectator hears an answering chord in himself. Such emotional chords cannot be superficial or without value; the feeling of such a picture can indeed deepen and purify the feeling of the spectator. The spirit at least is preserved from coarseness: such pictures tune it up, as a tuning fork does the strings of a musical instrument. But the subtilization and extension of this chord in time and space remained limited, and the potential power of art is not exhausted by it.

[2] Alas, this word, which in the past was used to describe the poetical aspirations of an artist's soul, has been misused and finally ridiculed. Was there ever a great word that the crowd did not try immediately to desecrate?

Imagine a building, large or small, divided into rooms; each room is covered with canvases of various sizes, perhaps thousands of them. They represent bits of nature in color—animals in sunlight or shadow, or drinking, standing in water, or lying on grass; close by, a "Crucifixion," by a painter who does not believe in Christ; then flowers, and human figures, sitting, standing, or walking, and often naked; there are many naked women foreshortened from behind; apples and silver dishes; a portrait of Mister So-and-So; sunsets; a lady in pink; a flying duck; a portrait of Lady X; flying geese; a lady in white; some cattle in shadow, flecked by brilliant sunlight; a portrait of Ambassador Y; a lady in green. All this is carefully reproduced in a book with the name of the artist and the name of the picture. Book in hand, people go from wall to wall, turning pages, reading names. Then they depart, neither richer nor poorer, again absorbed by their affairs, which have nothing to do with art. Why did they come? In every painting a whole life is mysteriously enclosed, a whole life of tortures, doubts, of hours of enthusiasm and inspiration.

What is the direction of that life? What is the cry of the artist's soul, if the soul was involved in the creation? "To send light into the darkness of men's hearts—such is the obligation of the artist," said Schumann. "A painter is a man who can draw and paint everything," said Tolstoi.

Of these two definitions we must choose the second, if we think of the exhibition just described. With more or less skill, virtuosity and vigor, objects are created on a canvas, "painted" either roughly or smoothly. To bring the whole into harmony on the canvas is what leads to a work of art. With cold eye and indifferent mind the public regards the work. Connoisseurs admire "technique," as one might admire a tight-rope walker, or enjoy the "painting quality," as one might enjoy a cake. But hungry souls go hungry away.

The public ambles through the rooms, saying "nice" or "interesting." Those who could speak have said nothing; those who could hear have heard nothing. This condition is called "art for art's sake." This annihilation of internal vibrations that constitute the life of the colors, this dwindling away of artistic force, is called "art for art's sake."

The artist seeks material rewards for his facility, inventiveness and sensitivity. His purpose becomes the satisfaction of ambition and greediness. In place of an intensive cooperation among artists, there is a battle for goods. There is excessive competition, over-production. Hatred, partisanship, cliques, jealousy, intrigues are the natural consequences of an aimless, materialist art.[3]

The public turns away from artists who have higher ideals, who find purpose in an art without purpose.

"Comprehension" is educating the spectator to the point of view of the artist. It has been said that art is the child of its time. But such an art can only repeat artistically what is already clearly realized by the contemporary. Since it is not germinative, but only a child of the age, and unable to become a mother of the future, it is a castrated art. It is transitory; it dies morally the moment the atmosphere that nourished it alters.

---

[3] A few exceptions do not affect the truth of this sad and ominous picture; even the exceptions are chiefly believers in the doctrine of art for art's sake. They serve, therefore, a higher ideal, but one which is ultimately a useless waste of their strength. External beauty is one element in a spiritual milieu. But beyond this positive fact (that what is beautiful is good) lies the weakness of a talent not used to the full (*talent* in the biblical sense).

THE SHAPING FORCES OF THE ARTIST

Paul Klee

It is fitting that the last painter in this section should be Paul Klee (1879–1940). One of the great modern artists, Klee was also one of the most broadly experienced, a musician, a master teacher and maker of teaching theory, a fine writer. His art is full of delicate lines, soft ironies, respect for the primitive and the immediate, reverence for the "moment" and all the imaginative resources any instant may contain. This statement, the last portion of a talk given in Germany in 1924, is a reasoned defense of his own art and much of the art of his time. It has almost all the elements of his drawing and painting in it, all except the ironies. He means exactly what he says. And perhaps much of what he says is what modern art "means."

I should now like to consider the question of the object, and attempt to show why the artist so frequently arrives at an apparently arbitrary "deformation" of the natural form of an object. In the first place he does not attribute to this natural form such crucial importance as do the realists who criticize him. For he does not regard these terminal forms as expressing the essence of nature's creative process. He is more concerned with the shaping forces than with the terminal forms. Perhaps we may say that he is an involuntary philosopher. And although he is not such an optimist as to affirm that this is the best of all possible worlds, neither does he say that this world surrounding us is so bad that he wants to have no part in copying its images. What he does say is the following:

The existing shape of the world is by no means the only possible shape! Therefore the artist directs a searching and penetrating look at the existing forms of nature. The more deeply he looks, the easier he finds it to extend his vision

from the present to the past. Instead of the present shapes of
nature, he more and more sees that the essential image of creation
is genesis. He hazards the bold thought that the process of creation can scarcely be over and done with as yet, and so he extends
the universal creative process both backward and forward, thus
conferring duration upon genesis. He goes still farther. First
lingering in this world, he says to himself: This world looked
different in the past, and in the future it will also look different.
Then, sliding toward otherworldliness, he decides: On other
planets it may well have assumed altogether different forms.

To wander about this way along the natural paths of creation
is good training for the artist. It can stir him to the depths of
his being; and once he has been set in motion he will seek freedom of development along his own creative paths. And when he
has had the benefit of such freedom, we cannot blame him for
deciding that the present state of the phenomenal world, as he
happens to encounter it, is hamstrung, accidentally, temporally
and spatially hamstrung, and much too limited in comparison to
his deeper visions and far-ranging sensibilities.

And isn't it true that if we only take the relatively small step
of glancing into a microscope, we will see images that we would
all call fantastic and exaggerated if we happened to see them in
a painting without realizing the joke? Mr. X, coming across a
reproduction of a microphotograph in a cheap journal, would
exclaim indignantly: Are those supposed to be natural forms?
Why, the man just doesn't know how to draw!

Then does the artist have to deal with microscopy? History?
Palaeontology? Only by way of comparison, only by way of
gaining greater scope, not so that he has to be ready to prove his
fidelity to nature! The main thing is freedom, a freedom which
does not necessarily retrace the course of evolution, or project
what forms nature will some day display, or which we may some
day discover on other planets; rather, a freedom which insists
on its right to be just as inventive as nature in her grandeur is
inventive. The artist must proceed from the type to the prototype!

The artist who soon comes to a halt en route is one who has
pretensions, but no more. The artists with real vocations nowadays are those who travel to within fair distance of that secret
cavern where the primal law is hidden; where the central organ
of all temporal and spatial movement—we may call it the brain or

the heart of creation—makes everything happen. What artist would not wish to dwell there—in the bosom of nature, in the primordial source of creation, where the secret key to everything is kept? But not all are meant to reach it. Everyone must go where his own instinct leads him. Thus the impressionists who today are our polar opposites were in their own time absolutely right to stay with the hair-roots, the ground-cover of everyday phenomena. But our own instinct drives us downward, deep down to the primal source. Whatever emerges from this activity, call it what you will, dream, idea, fantasy, should be taken quite seriously if it combines with proper pictorial elements and is given form. Then curiosities become realities, realities of art, which add something more to life than it usually seems to have. For then we no longer have things seen and reproduced with more or less display of temperament, but we have visionary experiences made visible.

"With proper pictorial elements," I have said. For that tells us whether the result is a painting or something else, and what kind of painting it is to be.

Our age has passed through many confusions and vicissitudes, or so it seems to us, for we may be so close that our judgment is faulty. But one general tendency seems to be gradually winning ground among artists, even among the youngest of them: pure cultivation of these pictorial elements and their pure application. The myth about the childishness of my drawing must have started with those linear structures in which I attempted to combine the idea of an object—a man, say—with pure representation of the linear elements. If I wanted to render a man "just as he is," I would need such a bewildering complex of lines that pure presentation of the elements would be impossible; instead, they would be blurred to the point of being unrecognizable. Moreover, I don't at all want to represent a man as he is, but only as he might be.

Only by such procedures can I succeed in combining philosophy with the pure practice of my art.

These principles hold true for the entire procedure. Blurring must be everywhere avoided, in dealing with colors too. This effort to avoid blurring lies behind what people sneer at as the "false" coloration in modern art.

As I have just suggested in my remark on "childishness," I also deal separately with the various elements of painting. That is, I

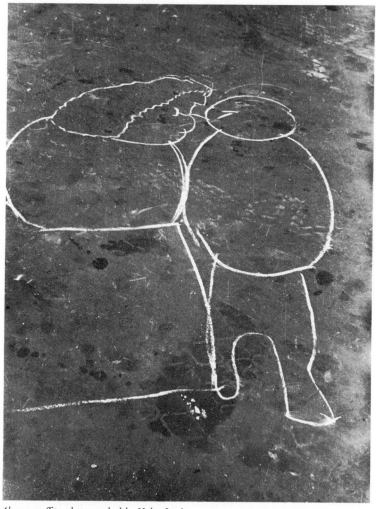

Above, graffito photographed by Helen Levitt.
From A Way of Seeing. *Photographs of New York by Helen Levitt with an essay by James Agee.*
All rights reserved. Reprinted by permission of The Viking Press, Inc.

Right, Paul Klee, The Notorious One, *F. 2, 1929.*
From The Solomon R. Guggenheim Museum, New York City.

am also a draftsman. I have tried pure drawing; I have tried pure chiaroscuro painting; and I have tried all sorts of experiments with color as these arose out of my meditations on the color wheel. Thus I have worked out the various types of colored chiaroscuro painting, complementary color painting, particolored painting and totally colored painting. And in each case I have combined these experiments with the more subconscious dimensions of painting.

Then I have tried all possible syntheses of the two types, combining and recombining, but always trying to keep hold of the pure elements as far as possible. Sometimes I dream of a work of vast expanse which would encompass the whole realm of elements, objects, contents and styles. Doubtless that will remain a dream, but it is good occasionally to imagine this possibility which at present remains a vague one.

Creation cannot be done with undue haste. A thing must grow, must mature, and if the time ever comes for that vast, all-embracing work, so much the better. We must go on seeking. We have found parts of it, but not yet the whole. Nor do we have the strength for it as yet, for we have no public supporting us. But we are seeking a public; we have made a beginning at the Bauhaus. We have begun with a community to which we are giving everything we have to give. More than that we cannot do.

Much of the force of twentieth-century writing about the arts has been sociological in origin and intent. If one follows this approach to the arts, one is directed to economic and social classes, to their various conditions, and to the resultant blunting or (more rarely) sharpening of tastes. Clement Greenberg (1909–   ), in a notable separation of quality from pseudo-quality, defines the aims and achievements of contemporary painting and the values and pretensions of its viewers. The essay, written in 1939 for Partisan Review, *the pre-eminent organ of the sociological esthetic, is a fine example of the work of a tireless spokesman for American abstract painting and painters. It is also a guide, albeit limited, to essential terminology and especially to those two central terms,* avant-garde *and* kitsch.

AVANT-GARDE AND KITSCH

Clement Greenberg

One and the same civilization produces simultaneously two such different things as a poem by T. S. Eliot and a Tin Pan Alley song, or a painting by Braque and a *Saturday Evening Post* cover. All four are on the order of culture, and ostensibly, parts of the same culture and products of the same society. Here, however, their connection seems to end. A poem by Eliot and a poem by Eddie Guest—what perspective of culture is large enough to enable us to situate them in an enlightening relation to each other? Does the fact that a disparity such as this within the frame of a single cultural tradition, is and has been taken for granted—does this fact indicate that the disparity is a part of the natural order of things? Or is it something entirely new, and particular to our age?

The answer involves more than an investigation in aesthetics. It appears to me that it is necessary to examine more closely and with more originality than hitherto the relationship between aesthetic experience as met by the specific—not generalized—individual, and the social and historical contexts in which that experience takes place. What is brought to light will answer, in addition to the question posed above, other and perhaps more important ones.

I

A society, as it becomes less and less able, in the course of its development, to justify the inevitability of its particular forms, breaks up the accepted notions upon which artists and writers must depend in large part for communication with their audiences. It becomes difficult to assume anything. All the verities involved by religion, authority, tradition, style, are thrown into question, and the writer or artist is no longer able to estimate the response of his audience to the symbols and references with which he works. In the past such a state of affairs has usually resolved itself into a motionless Alexandrianism, an academicism in which the really important issues are left untouched because they involve controversy, and in which creative activity dwindles to virtuosity in the small details of form, all larger questions being decided by the precedent of the old masters. The same themes are mechanically varied in a hundred different works, and yet nothing new is produced: Statius, mandarin verse, Roman sculpture, Beaux Arts painting, neo-republican architecture.

It is among the hopeful signs in the midst of the decay of our present society that we—some of us—have been unwilling to accept this last phase for our own culture. In seeking to go beyond Alexandrianism, a part of Western bourgeois society has produced something unheard of heretofore: avant-garde culture. A superior consciousness of history—more precisely, the appearance of a new kind of criticism of society, an historical criticism—made this possible. This criticism has not confronted our present society with timeless utopias, but has soberly examined in the terms of history and of cause and effect the antecedents, justifications, and functions of the forms that lie at the heart of every society. Thus our present bourgeois social order was shown to be, not an eternal, "natural" condition of life, but simply the latest term in a succession of social orders. New perspectives of this kind, becoming a part of the advanced intellectual conscience of the fifth and sixth decades of the nineteenth century, soon were absorbed by artists and poets, even if unconsciously for the most part. It was no accident, therefore, that the birth of the avant-garde coincided chronologically—and geographically too—with the first bold development of scientific revolutionary thought in Europe.

True, the first settlers of bohemia—which was then identical with the avant-garde—turned out soon to be demonstratively uninterested in politics. Nevertheless, without the circulation of revolutionary ideas in the air about them, they would never have been able to isolate their concept of the "bourgeois" in order to define what they were *not*. Nor, without the moral aid of revolutionary political attitudes would they have had the courage to assert themselves as aggressively as they did against the prevailing standards of society. Courage indeed was needed for this, because the avant-garde's emigration from bourgeois society to bohemia meant also an emigration from the markets of capitalism, upon which artists and writers had been thrown by the falling away of aristocratic patronage. (Ostensibly, at least, it meant this—meant starving in a garret—although, as will be shown later, the avant-garde remained attached to bourgeois society precisely because it needed its money.)

Yet it is true that once the avant-garde had succeeded in "detaching" itself from society, it proceeded to turn around and repudiate revolutionary as well as bourgeois politics. The revolution was left inside society, a part of that welter of ideological struggle which art and poetry find so unpropitious as soon as it begins to involve those "precious," axiomatic beliefs upon which culture thus far has had to rest. Hence it was developed that the true and most important function of the avant-garde was not to "experiment," but to find a path along which it would be possible to keep culture *moving* in the midst of ideological confusion and violence. Retiring from the public altogether, the avant-garde poet or artist sought to maintain the high level of his art by both narrowing and raising it to the expression of an absolute in which all relativities and contradictions would be either resolved or beside the point: "Art for art's sake" and "pure poetry" appear, and subject matter or content becomes something to be avoided like a plague.

It has been in search of the absolute that the avant-garde has arrived at "abstract" or "nonobjective" art—and poetry, too. The avant-garde poet or artist tries in effect to imitate God by creating something valid solely on its own terms in the way

nature itself is valid, in the way a landscape—not its picture—
is aesthetically valid; something *given*, increate, independent of
meanings, similars, or originals. Content is to be dissolved so
completely into form that the work of art or literature cannot
be reduced in whole or in part to anything not itself.

But the absolute is absolute, and the poet or artist, being what
he is, cherishes certain relative values more than others. The
very values in the name of which he invokes the absolute are
relative values, the values of aesthetics. And so he turns out to
be imitating, not God—and here I use "imitate" in its Aristotelian
sense—but the disciples and processes of art and literature themselves. This is the genesis of the "abstract."[1] In turning his attention away from subject matter of common experience, the poet
or artist turns it in upon the medium of his own craft. The
nonrepresentational or "abstract," if it is to have aesthetic validity, cannot be arbitrary and accidental, but must stem from
obedience to some worthy constraint or original. This constraint,
once the world of common, extraverted experience has been
renounced, can only be found in the very processes or disciplines
by which art and literature have already imitated the former.
These themselves become the subject matter of art and literature.
If, to continue with Aristotle, all art and literature are imitation,
then what we have here is the imitation of imitat*ing*. To quote
Yeats:

> "Nor is there singing school but studying
> Monuments of its own magnificence."

Picasso, Braque, Mondrian, Miro, Kandinsky, Brancusi, even
Klee, Matisse, and Cézanne, derive their chief inspiration from

---

[1] The example of music, which has long been an abstract art, and which avant-
garde poetry has tried so much to emulate, is interesting. Music, Aristotle said
curiously enough, is the most imitative and vivid of all arts because it imitates its
original—the state of the soul—with the greatest immediacy. Today this strikes
us as the exact opposite of the truth, because no art seems to us to have less reference to something outside itself than music. However, aside from the fact that in a
sense Aristotle may still be right, it must be explained that ancient Greek music
was closely associated with poetry, and depended upon its character as an accessory to verse to make its imitative meaning clear. Plato, speaking of music, says:
"For when there are no words, it is very difficult to recognize the meaning of the
harmony and rhythm, or to see that any worthy object is imitated by them." As
far as we know, all music originally served such an accessory function. Once, however, it was abandoned, music was forced to withdraw into itself to find a constraint
or original. This is found in the various means of its own composition and performance.

the medium they work in.[2] The excitement of their art seems to lie most of all in its pure preoccupation with the invention and arrangement of spaces, surfaces, shapes, colors, etc., to the exclusion of whatever is not necessarily implicated in these factors. The attention of poets like Rimbaud, Mallarmé, Valéry, Eluard, Pound, Hart Crane, Stevens, even Rilke and Yeats, appears to be centered on the effort to create poetry and on the "moments" themselves of poetic conversion rather than on experience to be converted into poetry. Of course, this cannot exclude other preoccupations in their work, for poetry must deal with words, and words must communicate. Certain poets, such as Mallarmé and Valéry,[3] are more radical in this respect than others—leaving aside those poets who have tried to compose poetry in pure sound alone. However, if it were easier to define poetry, modern poetry would be much more "pure" and "abstract." . . . As for the other fields of literature—the definition of avant-garde aesthetics advanced here is no Procrustean bed. But aside from the fact that most of our best contemporary novelists have gone to school with the avant-garde, it is significant that Gide's most ambitious book is a novel about the writing of a novel, and that Joyce's *Ulysses* and *Finnegans Wake* seem to be above all, as one French critic says, the reduction of experience to expression for the sake of expression, the expression mattering more than what is being expressed.

That avant-garde culture is the imitation of imitat*ing*—the fact itself—calls for neither approval nor disapproval. It is true that this culture contains within itself some of the very Alexandrianism it seeks to overcome. The lines quoted from Yeats above referred to Byzantium, which is very close to Alexandria; and in a sense this imitation of imitat*ing* is a superior sort of Alexandrianism. But there is one most important difference: the avant-garde moves, while Alexandrianism stands still. And this, precisely, is what justifies the avant-garde's methods and makes them necessary. The necessity lies in the fact that by no other means is it possible today to create art and literature of a high order. To quarrel with necessity by throwing about terms like "for-

---

2 I owe this formulation to a remark made by Hans Hofmann, the art teacher, in one of his lectures. From the point of view of this formulation surrealism in plastic art is a reactionary tendency which is attempting to restore "outside" subject matter. The chief concern of a painter like Dali is to represent the processes and concepts of his consciousness, not the processes of his medium.

3 See Valéry's remarks about his own poetry.

malism," "purism," "ivory tower," and so forth is either dull or dishonest. This is not to say, however, that it is to the *social* advantage of the avant-garde that it is what it is. Quite the opposite.

The avant-garde's specialization of itself, the fact that its best artists are artists' artists, its best poets, poets' poets, has estranged a great many of those who were capable formerly of enjoying and appreciating ambitious art and literature, but who are now unwilling or unable to acquire an initiation into their craft secrets. The masses have always remained more or less indifferent to culture in the process of development. But today such culture is being abandoned by those to whom it actually belongs—our ruling class. For it is to the latter that the avant-garde belongs. No culture can develop without a social basis, without a source of stable income. And in the case of the avant-garde this was provided by an élite among the ruling class of that society from which it assumed itself to be cut off, but to which it has always remained attached by an umbilical cord of gold. The paradox is real. And now this élite is rapidly shrinking. Since the avant-garde forms the only living culture we now have, the survival in the near future of culture in general is thus threatened.

We must not be deceived by superficial phenomena and local successes. Picasso's shows still draw crowds, and T. S. Eliot is taught in the universities; the dealers in modernist art are still in business, and the publishers still publish some "difficult" poetry. But the avant-garde itself, already sensing the danger, is becoming more and more timid every day that passes. Academicism and commercialism are appearing in the strangest places. This can mean only one thing: that the avant-garde is becoming unsure of the audience it depends on—the rich and the cultivated.

Is it the nature itself of avant-garde culture that is alone responsible for the danger it finds itself in? Or is that only a dangerous liability? Are there other, and perhaps more important, factors involved?

II

Where there is an avant-garde, generally we also find a rearguard. True enough—simultaneously with the entrance of the avant-garde, a second new cultural phenomenon appeared in the

industrial West: that thing to which the Germans give the wonderful name of *Kitsch:* popular, commercial art and literature
with their chromeotypes, magazine covers, illustrations, ads,
slick and pulp fiction, comics, Tin Pan Alley music, tap dancing,
Hollywood movies, etc., etc. For some reason this gigantic
apparition has always been taken for granted. It is time we
looked into its whys and wherefores.

Kitsch is a product of the industrial revolution which urban-
ized the masses of western Europe and America and established
what is called universal literacy.

Previous to this the only market for formal culture, as dis-
tiguished from folk culture, had been among those who in
addition to being able to read and write could command the
leisure and comfort that always goes hand in hand with cultivation of some sort. This until then had been inextricably associated
with literacy. But with the introduction of universal literacy,
the ability to read and write became almost a minor skill like
driving a car, and it no longer served to distinguish an individual's cultural inclinations, since it was no longer the exclusive
concomitant of refined tastes. The peasants who settled in the
cities as proletariat and petty bourgeois learned to read and
write for the sake of efficiency, but they did not win the leisure
and comfort necessary for the enjoyment of the city's traditional
culture. Losing, nevertheless, their taste for the folk culture whose
background was the countryside, and discovering a new capacity
for boredom at the same time, the new urban masses set up a
pressure on society to provide them with a kind of culture fit
for their own consumption. To fill the demand of the new
market a new commodity was devised: ersatz culture, kitsch,
destined for those who, insensible to the values of genuine culture, are hungry nevertheless for the diversion that only culture
of some sort can provide.

Kitsch, using for raw material the debased and academicized
simulacra of genuine culture, welcomes and cultivates this insensibility. It is the source of its profits. Kitsch is mechanical and
operates by formulas. Kitsch is vicarious experience and faked
sensations. Kitsch changes according to style, but remains always
the same. Kitsch is the epitome of all that is spurious in the life
of our times. Kitsch pretends to demand nothing of its customers
except their money—not even their time.

The precondition for kitsch, a condition without which kitsch would be impossible, is the availability close at hand of a fully matured cultural tradition, whose discoveries, acquisitions, and perfected self-consciousness kitsch can take advantage of for its own ends. It borrows from it devices, tricks, stratagems, rules of thumb, themes, converts them into a system, and discards the rest. It draws its life blood, so to speak, from this reservoir of accumulated experience. This is what is really meant when it is said that the popular art and literature of today were once the daring, esoteric art and literature of yesterday. Of course, no such thing is true. What is meant is that when enough time has elapsed the new is looted for new "twists," which are then watered down and served up as kitsch. Self-evidently, all kitsch is academic, and conversely, all that's academic is kitsch. For what is called the academic as such no longer has an independent existence, but has become the stuffed-shirt "front" for kitsch. The methods of industrialism displace the handicrafts.

Because it can be turned out mechanically, kitsch has become an integral part of our productive system in a way in which true culture could never be except accidentally. It has been capitalized at a tremendous investment which must show commensurate returns; it is compelled to extend as well as to keep its markets. While it is essentially its own salesman, a great sales apparatus has nevertheless been created for it, which brings pressure to bear on every member of society. Traps are laid even in those areas, so to speak, that are the preserves of genuine culture. It is not enough today, in a country like ours, to have an inclination toward the latter; one must have a true passion for it that will give him the power to resist the faked article that surrounds and presses in on him from the moment he is old enough to look at the funny papers. Kitsch is deceptive. It has many different levels, and some of them are high enough to be dangerous to the naïve seeker of true light. A magazine like the *New Yorker*, which is fundamentally high-class kitsch for the luxury trade, converts and waters down a great deal of avant-garde material for its own uses. Nor is every single item of kitsch altogether worthless. Now and then it produces something of merit, something that has an authentic folk flavor; and these accidental and isolated instances have fooled people who should know better.

Kitsch's enormous profits are a source of temptation to the avant-garde itself, and its members have not always resisted this temptation. Ambitious writers and artists will modify their work under the pressure of kitsch, if they do not succumb to it entirely. And then those puzzling borderline cases appear, such as the popular novelist, Simenon, in France, and Steinbeck in this country. The net result is always to the detriment of true culture, in any case.

Kitsch has not been confined to the cities in which it was born, but has flowed out over the countryside, wiping out folk culture. Nor has it shown any regard for geographical and national-cultural boundaries. Another mass product of Western industrialism, it has gone on a triumphal tour of the world, crowding out and defacing native cultures in one colonial country after another, so that it is now by way of becoming a universal culture, the first universal culture ever beheld. Today the Chinaman, no less than the South American Indian, the Hindu, no less than the Polynesian, have come to prefer to the products of their native art, magazine covers, rotogravure sections, and calendar girls. How is this virulence of kitsch, this irresistible attractiveness, to be explained? Naturally, machine-made kitsch can undersell the native handmade article, and the prestige of the West also helps, but why is kitsch a so much more profitable export article than Rembrandt? One, after all, can be reproduced as cheaply as the other.

In his article on the Soviet cinema in the *Partisan Review*, Dwight Macdonald points out that kitsch has in the last ten years become the dominant culture in Soviet Russia. For this he blames the political regime—not only for the fact that kitsch is the official culture, but also that it is actually the dominant, most popular culture; and he quotes the following from Kurt London's *The Seven Soviet Arts:* ". . . the attitude of the masses both to the old and new art styles probably remains essentially dependent on the nature of the education afforded them by their respective states." Macdonald goes on to say: "Why after all should ignorant peasants prefer Repin (a leading exponent of Russian academic kitsch in painting) to Picasso, whose abstract technique is at least as relevant to their own primitive folk art as is the former's realistic style? No, if the masses crowd into the Tretyakov (Moscow's museum of contemporary Russian art: kitsch) it is largely because they have been conditioned to shun 'formalism' and to admire 'socialist realism.' "

In the first place it is not a question of a choice between merely the old and merely the new, as London seems to think—but of a choice between the bad, up-to-date old and the genuinely new. The alternative to Picasso is not Michelangelo, but kitsch. In the second place, neither in backward Russia nor in the advanced West do the masses prefer kitsch simply because their governments condition them toward it. Where state educational systems take the trouble to mention art, we are told to respect the old masters, not kitsch; and yet we go and hang Maxfield Parrish or his equivalent on our walls, instead of Rembrandt and Michelangelo. Moreover, as Macdonald himself points out, around 1925 when the Soviet régime was encouraging avant-garde cinema, the Russian masses continued to prefer Hollywood movies. No, "conditioning" does not explain the potency of kitsch. . . .

All values are human values, relative values, in art as well as elsewhere. Yet there does seem to have been more or less of a general agreement among the cultivated of mankind over the ages as to what is good art and what bad. Taste has varied, but not beyond certain limits: contemporary connoisseurs agree with the eighteenth-century Japanese that Hokusai was one of the greatest artists of his time; we even agree with the ancient Egyptians that Third and Fourth Dynasty art was the most worthy of being selected as their paragon by those who came after. We may have come to prefer Giotto to Raphael, but we still do not deny that Raphael was one of the best painters of his *time*. There has been an agreement then, and this agreement rests, I believe, on a fairly constant distinction made between those values only to be found in art and the values which can be found elsewhere. Kitsch, by virtue of rationalized technique that draws on science and industry, has erased this distinction in practice.

Let us see for example what happens when an ignorant Russian peasant such as Macdonald mentions stands with hypothetical freedom of choice before two paintings, one by Picasso, the other by Repin. In the first he sees, let us say, a play of lines, colors, and spaces that represent a woman. The abstract technique—to accept Macdonald's supposition, which I am inclined to doubt—reminds him somewhat of the icons he has left behind him in the village, and he feels the attraction of the familiar. We will even suppose that he faintly surmises some of the great art values the cultivated find in Picasso. He turns next to Repin's picture and sees a battle scene. The technique is not so familiar —as technique. But that weighs very little with the peasant, for he suddenly discovers values in Repin's picture which seem far superior to the values he has been accustomed to finding in icon art; and the unfamiliar technique itself is one of the sources of those values: the values of the vividly recognizable, the miraculous, and the sympathetic. In Repin's picture the peasant recognizes and sees things in the way in which he recognizes and sees things outside of pictures—there is no discontinuity between art and life, no need to accept a convention and say to oneself, that icon represents Jesus because it intends to represent Jesus, even if it does not remind me very much of a man. That Repin can paint so realistically that identifications are self-evident immediately and without any effort on the part of the spectator— that is miraculous. The peasant is also pleased by the wealth of self-evident meanings which he finds in the picture: "it tells a story." Picasso and the icons are so austere and barren in comparison. What is more, Repin heightens reality and makes it dramatic: sunset, exploding shells, running and falling men. There is no longer any question of Picasso or icons. Repin is what the peasant wants, and nothing else but Repin. It is lucky, however, for Repin that the peasant is protected from the products of American capitalism, for he would not stand a chance next to a *Saturday Evening Post* cover by Norman Rockwell.

Ultimately, it can be said that the cultivated spectator derives the same values from Picasso that the peasant gets from Repin, since what the latter enjoys in Repin is somehow art too, on however low a scale, and he is sent to look at pictures by the same instincts that send the cultivated spectator. But the ultimate values which the cultivated spectator derives from Picasso are derived at a second remove, as the result of reflection upon the immediate impression left by the plastic values. It is only then that the recognizable, the miraculous, and the sympathetic enter. They are not immediately or externally present in Picasso's painting, but must be projected into it by the spectator sensitive enough to react sufficiently to plastic qualities. They belong to the "reflected" effect. In Repin, on the other hand, the "reflected" effect has already been included in the picture, ready for the spectator's unreflective enjoyment.[4] Where Picasso paints

---

[4] T. S. Eliot said something to the same effect in accounting for the shortcomings of English Romantic poetry. Indeed the Romantics can be considered the original sinners whose guilt kitsch inherited. They showed kitsch how. What does Keats write about mainly, if not the effect of poetry upon himself?

cause, Repin paints *effect*. Repin pre-digests art for the spectator and spares him effort, provides him with a short cut to the pleasure of art that detours what is necessarily difficult in genuine art. Repin, or kitsch, is synthetic art.

The same point can be made with respect to kitsch literature: it provides vicarious experience for the insensitive with far greater immediacy than serious fiction can hope to do. And Eddie Guest and the *Indian Love Lyrics* are more poetic than T. S. Eliot and Shakespeare.

III

If the avant-garde imitates the processes of art, kitsch, we now see, imitates its effects. The neatness of this antithesis is more than contrived; it corresponds to and defines the tremendous interval that separates from each other two such simultaneous cultural phenomena as the avant-garde and kitsch. This interval, too great to be closed by all the infinite gradations of popularized "modernism" and "modernistic" kitsch, corresponds in turn to a social interval, a social interval that has always existed in formal culture as elsewhere in civilized society, and whose two termini converge and diverge in fixed relation to the increasing or decreasing stability of the given society. There has always been on one side the minority of the powerful—and therefore the cultivated—and on the other the great mass of the exploited and poor —and therefore the ignorant. Formal culture has always belonged to the first, while the last have had to content themselves with folk or rudimentary culture, or kitsch.

In a stable society which functions well enough to hold in solution the contradictions between its classes the cultural dichotomy becomes somewhat blurred. The axioms of the few are shared by the many; the latter believe superstitiously what the former believe soberly. And at such moments in history the masses are able to feel wonder and admiration for the culture, on no matter how high a plane, of its masters. This applies at least to plastic culture, which is accessible to all.

In the Middle Ages the plastic artist paid lip service at least to the lowest common denominators of experience. This even remained true to some extent until the seventeenth century. There was available for imitation a universally valid conceptual reality, whose order the artist could not tamper with. The subject matter of art was prescribed by those who commissioned works of art, which were not created, as in bourgeois society, on speculation. Precisely because his content was determined in advance, the artist was free to concentrate on his medium. He needed not to be philosopher, or visionary, but simply artificer. As long as there was general agreement as to what were the worthiest subjects for art, the artist was relieved of the necessity to be original and inventive in his "matter" and could devote all his energy to formal problems. For him the medium became, privately, professionally, the content of his art, even as today his medium is the public content of the abstract painter's art—with that difference, however, that the medieval artist had to suppress his professional preoccupation in public—had always to suppress and subordinate the personal and professional in the finished, official work of art. If, as an ordinary member of the Christian community, he felt some personal emotion about his subject matter, this only contributed to the enrichment of the work's public meaning. Only with the Renaissance do the inflections of the personal become legitimate, still to be kept, however, within the limits of the simply and universally recognizable. And only with Rembrandt do "lonely" artists begin to appear, lonely in their art.

But even during the Renaissance, and as long as Western art was endeavoring to perfect its technique, victories in this realm could only be signalized by success in realistic imitation, since there was no other objective criterion at hand. Thus the masses could still find in the art of their masters objects of admiration and wonder. Even the bird who pecked at the fruit in Zeuxis' picture could applaud.

It is a platitude that art becomes caviar to the general when the reality it imitates no longer corresponds even roughly to the reality recognized by the general. Even then, however, the resentment the common man may feel is silenced by the awe in which he stands of the patrons of this art. Only when he becomes dissatisfied with the social order they administer does he begin to criticize their culture. Then the plebeian finds courage for the first time to voice his opinions openly. Every man, from the Tammany alderman to the Austrian house-painter, finds that he is entitled to his opinion. Most often this resentment toward culture is to be found where the dissatisfaction with society is a reactionary dissatisfaction which expresses itself in revivalism and puritanism, and latest of all, in fascism. Here revolvers and torches begin to be mentioned in the same breath as culture. In the name of godliness or the blood's health, in the name of simple ways and solid virtues, the statue-smashing commences.

IV

Returning to our Russian peasant for the moment, let us suppose that after he has chosen Repin in preference to Picasso, the state's educational apparatus comes along and tells him that he is wrong, that he should have chosen Picasso—and shows him why. It is quite possible for the Soviet state to do this. But things being as they are in Russia—and everywhere else—the peasant soon finds that the necessity of working hard all day for his living and the rude, uncomfortable circumstances in which he lives do not allow him enough leisure, energy, and comfort to train for the enjoyment of Picasso. This needs, after all, a considerable amount of "conditioning." Superior culture is one of the most artificial of all human creations, and the peasant finds no "natural" urgency within himself that will drive him toward Picasso in spite of all difficulties. In the end the peasant will go back to kitsch when he feels like looking at pictures, for he can enjoy kitsch without effort. The state is helpless in this matter and remains so as long as the problems of production have not been solved in a socialist sense. The same holds true, of course, for capitalist countries and makes all talk of art for the masses there nothing but demagogy.[5]

[5] It will be objected that such art for the masses as folk art was developed under rudimentary conditions of production—and that a good deal of folk art is on a high level. Yes, it is—but folk art is not Athene, and it's Athene whom we want: formal culture with its infinity of aspects, its luxuriance, its large comprehension. Besides, we are now told that most of what we consider good in folk culture is the static survival of dead, formal, artistocratic, cultures. Our old English ballads, for instance, were not created by the "folk," but by the postfeudal squirearchy of the English countryside, to survive in the mouths of the folk long after those for whom the ballads were composed had gone on to other forms of literature. . . . Unfortunately, until the machine-age culture was the exclusive prerogative of a society that lived by the labor of serfs or slaves. They were the real symbols of culture. For one man to spend time and energy creating or listening to poetry meant that another man had to produce enough to keep himself alive and the former in comfort. In Africa today we find that the culture of slave-owning tribes is generally much superior to that of the tribes which possess no slaves.

Where today a political regime establishes an official cultural policy, it is for the sake of demagogy. If kitsch is the official tendency of culture in Germany, Italy, and Russia, it is not because their respective governments are controlled by Philistines, but because kitsch is the culture of the masses in these countries, as it is everywhere else. The encouragement of kitsch is merely another of the inexpensive ways in which totalitarian régimes seek to ingratiate themselves with their subjects. Since these régimes cannot raise the cultural level of the masses—even if they wanted to—by anything short of a surrender to international socialism, they will flatter the masses by bringing all culture down to their level. It is for this reason that the avant-garde is outlawed, and not so much because a superior culture is inherently a more critical culture. (Whether or not the avant-garde could possibly flourish under a totalitarian régime is not pertinent to the question at this point.) As a matter of fact, the main trouble with avant-garde art and literature, from the point of view of fascists and Stalinists, is not that they are too critical, but that they are too "innocent," that it is too difficult to inject effective propaganda into them, that kitsch is more pliable to this end. Kitsch keeps a dictator in closer contact with the "soul" of the people. Should the official culture be one superior to the general mass-level, there would be a danger of isolation.

Nevertheless, if the masses were conceivably to ask for avant-garde art and literature, Hitler, Mussolini and Stalin would not hesitate long in attempting to satisfy such a demand. Hitler is a bitter enemy of the avant-garde, both on doctrinal and personal grounds, yet this did not prevent Goebbels in 1932–1933 from strenuously courting avant-garde artists and writers. When Gottfried Benn, an Expressionist poet, came over to the Nazis he was welcomed with a great fanfare, although at that very moment Hitler was denouncing Expressionism as *Kulturbolschewismus*. This was at a time when the Nazis felt that the prestige which the avant-garde enjoyed among the cultivated German public could be of advantage to them, and practical considerations of this nature, the Nazis being the skillful politicians they are, have always taken precedence over Hitler's personal inclinations. Later the Nazis realized that it was more practical to accede to the wishes of the masses in matters of culture than to those of their paymasters; the latter, when it came to a question of preserving power, were as willing to sacrifice their culture as they were their moral principles, while the former, precisely because power was being withheld from them, had to be cozened in every other way possible. It was necessary to promote in a much more grandiose style than in the democracies the illusion that the masses actually rule. The literature and art they enjoy and understand were to be proclaimed the only true art and literature and any other kind was to be suppressed. Under these circumstances people like Gottfried Benn, no matter how ardently they support Hitler, become a liability; and we hear no more of them in Nazi Germany.

We can see then that although from one point of view the personal Philistinism of Hitler and Stalin is not accidental to the political roles they play, from another point of view it is only an incidentally contributory factor in determining the cultural policies of their respective régimes. Their personal Philistinişm simply adds brutality and double-darkness to policies they would be forced to support anyhow by the pressure of all their other policies—even were they, personally, devotees of avant-garde culture. What the acceptance of the isolation of the Russian Revolution forces Stalin to do, Hitler is compelled to do by his acceptance of the contradictions of capitalism and his efforts to freeze them. As for Mussolini—his case is a perfect example of the *disponibilité* of a realist in these matters. For years he bent a benevolent eye on the Futurists and built modernistic railroad stations and government-owned apartment houses. One can still see in the suburbs of Rome more modernistic apartments than almost anywhere else in the world. Perhaps Fascism wanted to show its up-to-dateness, to conceal the fact that it was a retrogression; perhaps it wanted to conform to the tastes of the wealthy élite it served. At any rate Mussolini seems to have realized lately that it would be more useful to him to please the cultural tastes of the Italian masses than those of their masters. The masses must be provided with objects of admiration and wonder; the latter can dispense with them. And so we find Mussolini announcing a "new Imperial style." Marinetti, Chirico, et al. are sent into the outer darkness, and the new railroad station in Rome will not be modernistic. That Mussolini was late in coming to this only illustrates again the relative hesitancy with which Italian Fascism has drawn the necessary implications of its role. . . .

Capitalism in decline finds that whatever of quality it is still capable of producing becomes almost invariably a threat to its own existence. Advances in culture no less than advances in science and industry corrode the very society under whose aegis they are made possible. Here, as in every other question today, it becomes necessary to quote Marx word for word. Today we no longer look towards socialism for a new culture—as inevitably as one will appear, once we do have socialism. Today we look to socialism *simply* for the preservation of whatever living culture we have right now.

Like Igor Stravinsky or Wallace Stevens,
Pablo Picasso could never be dull when he talked
about his art. The most casual conversation with
Picasso about painting or sculpture was always
bound to be rewarding, whether it moved about one
or two central issues or jumped around, like this
one with Christian Zervos, which occurred when
Picasso was fifty-four years old. Inevitably, he moves
between autobiographical confessions and
epigrammatic obiter dicta *about the nature of art*
and the duty of the artist. Here he commands,
defines, cajoles, and implores, while saying a
great deal about the nature of the modern visual arts.
His pronouncements about abstract and figurative

STATEMENT:

1935

Pablo
Picasso

art, about beauty and
the meaning of a
work of art, speak not
only for himself but for most of the major
artists in the major schools of painting
in this century. Here he asserts the definitive
role of the artist's "being"—of his nature as a man—
in shaping the meaning and quality of his work
by a scathing comparison between the person of
Cézanne and that of a Parisian portraitist and man
of letters, Jacques Emile Blanche, whose tastes were
much too catholic and bland for one of such
revolutionary ardors as Pablo Picasso.

... It would be very interesting to preserve photographically, not the stages, but the metamor-
phoses of a picture. Possibly one might then
discover the path followed by the brain in ma-
terializing a dream. But there is one very odd
thing—to notice that basically a picture doesn't
change, that the first "vision" remains almost intact, in spite of appearances. I often ponder on
a light and a dark when I have put them into a
picture; I try hard to break them up by inter-
polating a color that will create a different effect.
When the work is photographed, I note that
what I put in to correct my first vision has dis-

appeared, and that, after all, the photographic image corresponds with my first vision before the transformation I insisted on.

A picture is not thought out and settled beforehand. While it is being done it changes as one's thoughts change. And when it is finished, it still goes on changing, according to the state of mind of whoever is looking at it. A picture lives a life like a living creature, undergoing the changes imposed on us by our life from day to day. This is natural enough, as the picture lives only through the man who is looking at it.

At the actual time that I am painting a picture I may think of white and put down white. But I can't go on working all the time thinking of white and painting it. Colors, like features, follow the changes of the emotions. You've seen the sketch I did for a picture with all the colors indicated on it. What is left of them? Certainly the white I thought of and the green I thought of are there in the picture, but not in the places I intended, nor in the same quantities. Of course, you can paint pictures by matching up different parts of them so that they go quite nicely together, but they'll lack any kind of drama.

I want to get to the stage where nobody can tell how a picture of mine is done. What's the point of that? Simply that I want nothing but emotion to be given off by it.

Work is a necessity for man.

A horse does not go between the shafts of its own accord.

Man invented the alarm clock.

When I begin a picture, there is somebody who works with me. Toward the end, I get the impression that I have been working alone—without a collaborator.

When you begin a picture, you often make some pretty discoveries. You must be on guard against these. Destroy the thing, do it over several times. In each destroying of a beautiful discovery, the artist does not really suppress it, but rather transforms it, condenses it, makes it more substantial. What comes out in the end is the result of discarded finds. Otherwise, you become your own connoisseur. I sell myself nothing.

Actually, you work with few colors. But they seem like a lot more when each one is in the right place.

Abstract art is only painting. What about drama?

There is no abstract art. You must always start with something. Afterward you can remove all traces of reality. There's no danger then, anyway, because the idea of the object will have left an indelible mark. It is what started the artist off, excited his ideas, and stirred up his emotions. Ideas and emotions will in the end be prisoners in his work. Whatever they do, they can't escape from the picture. They form an integral part of it, even when their presence is no longer discernible. Whether he likes it or not, man is the instrument of nature. It forces on him its character and appearance. In my Dinard pictures and in my Pourville pictures I expressed very much the same vision. However, you yourself have noticed how different the atmosphere of those painted in Brittany is from those painted in Normandy, because you recognized the light of the Dieppe cliffs. I didn't *copy* this light nor did I pay it any special attention. I was simply soaked in it. My eyes saw it and my subconscious registered what they saw: my hand fixed the impression. One cannot go against nature. It is stronger than the strongest man. It is pretty much to our interest to be on good terms with it. We may allow ourselves certain liberties, but only in details.

Nor is there any "figurative" and "non-figurative" art. Everything appears to us in the guise of a "figure." Even in metaphysics ideas are expressed by means of symbolic "figures." See how ridiculous it is then to think of painting without "figuration." A person, an object, a circle are all "figures"; they react on us more or less intensely. Some are nearer our sensations and produce emotions that touch our affective faculties; others appeal more directly to the intellect. They all should be allowed a place because I find my spirit has quite as much need of emotion as my senses. Do you think it concerns me that a particular picture of mine represents two people? Though these two people once existed for me, they exist no longer. The "vision" of them gave me a preliminary emotion; then little by little their actual presences became blurred; they developed into a fiction and then disappeared altogether, or rather they were transformed into all kinds of problems. They are no longer two people, you see, but forms and colors: forms and colors that have taken on, meanwhile, the *idea* of two people and preserve the vibration of their life. . . .

Academic training in beauty is a sham. We have been deceived, but so well deceived that we can scarcely get back even a shadow of the truth. The beauties of the Parthenon, Venuses, Nymphs, Narcissuses, are so many lies. Art is not the application of a canon of beauty but what the instinct and the brain can conceive beyond any canon. When we love a woman we don't start measuring her limbs. We love with our desires—although everything has been done to try and apply a canon even to love. The Parthenon is really only a farmyard over which someone put a roof; colonnades and sculptures were added because there were people in Athens who happened to be working, and wanted to express themselves. It's not what the artist *does* that counts, but what he *is*. Cézanne would never have interested me a bit if he had lived and thought like Jacques Emile Blanche, even if the apple he painted had been ten times as beautiful. What forces our interest is Cézanne's anxiety—that's Cézanne's lesson; the torments of van Gogh—that is the actual drama of the man. The rest is a sham.

Everyone wants to understand art. Why not try to understand the songs of a bird? Why does one love the night, flowers, everything around one, without trying to understand them? But in the case of a painting people have to *understand*. If only they would realize above all that an artist works of necessity, that he himself is only a trifling bit of the world, and that no more importance should be attached to him than to plenty of other things which please us in the world, though we can't explain them. People who try to explain pictures are usually barking up the wrong tree. Gertrude Stein joyfully announced to me the other day that she had at last understood what my picture of the three musicians was meant to be. It was a still life!

How can you expect an onlooker to live a picture of mine as I lived it? A picture comes to me from miles away: who is to say from how far away I sensed it, saw it, painted it; and yet the next day I can't see what I've done myself. How can anyone enter into my dreams, my instincts, my desires, my thoughts, which have taken a long time to mature and to come out into the daylight, and above all grasp from them what I have been about—perhaps against my own will?

With the exception of a few painters who are opening new horizons to painting, young painters today don't know which way to go. Instead of taking up our researches in order to react clearly against us, they are absorbed with bringing the past back to life—when truly the whole world is open before us, everything waiting to be done, not just redone. Why cling desperately to everything that has already fulfilled its promise? There are miles of painting "in the manner of"; but it is rare to find a young man working in his own way.

Does he wish to believe that man can't repeat himself? To repeat is to run counter to spiritual laws; essentially escapism.

I'm no pessimist, I don't loathe art, because I couldn't live without devoting all my time to it. I love it as the only end of my life. Everything I do connected with it gives me intense pleasure. But still, I don't see why the whole world should be taken up with art, demand its credentials, and on that subject give free rein to its own stupidity. Museums are just a lot of lies, and the people who make art their business are mostly imposters. I can't understand why revolutionary countries should have more prejudices about art than out-of-date countries! We have infected the pictures in museums with all our stupidities, all our mistakes, all our poverty of spirit. We have turned them into petty and ridiculous things. We have been tied up to a fiction, instead of trying to sense what inner life there was in the men who painted them. There ought to be an absolute dictatorship . . . a dictatorship of painters . . . a dictatorship of one painter . . . to suppress all those who have betrayed us, to suppress the cheaters, to suppress the tricks, to suppress mannerisms, to suppress charms, to suppress history, to suppress a heap of other things. But common sense always gets away with it. Above all, let's have a revolution against that! The true dictator will always be conquered by the dictatorship of common sense . . . and maybe not!

Some of the force of Hans Hofmann (1880–1966)
as a teacher comes through in this conversation,
one of the last recorded statements of the highly
influential painter. One can understand a little
better, perhaps, after reading Hofmann on
Kandinsky's notion of "spirituality," on teaching
painting, on titling painting, and on his "push-pull"
theory of art, why the leading figures of the
New York school of painting, the so-called Abstract
Expressionists, were so eager to study with
him and felt so complimented when they
were exhibited with him. Out of his
experience as a
painter and as a
teacher—which
really was, as he suggests, without
equal in modern art—he developed
the extraordinarily direct and
complete involvement with the painting
process which as much as anything else
was responsible for producing the
massive canvases of Abstract
Expressionism. In a sense, not
only his own great swooping
attacks on color, texture, and form, but the works of
Jackson Pollock, Willem de Kooning, Franz Kline,
Adolph Gottlieb, and Mark Rothko—to mention
only the best-known names—are a monument to
his ideas about painting. Irma B. Jaffe is
Chairman of the Department of Fine Arts at
Fordham University.

A CONVERSATION WITH HANS HOFMANN

Irma B.
Jaffe

Kandinsky speaks of the nightmare of materialism
in which man has been living and still lives, and
he speaks of the crude emotions, like fear, joy
and grief, that belong to this materialist environ-
ment. The artist of the future, on a higher spirit-
ual plane, according to Kandinsky, will not be
concerned with these crudities, but will attempt
to arouse more refined emotions. Do you agree
with this evaluation of emotion? Are fear, joy
and grief spiritual crudities? Do you, too, believe

in the possibility, in some future time, of human beings having souls so spiritually refined that they will experience emotions we've never been aware of?

Well, I will tell you, I have quite a different standpoint in relationship to the whole thing. I believe in spirituality, yes, but I have to explain it in a very, very different way. First of all, what is spirituality? *Geistigkeit*—this is a German word; in English, spirituality. It is the result of a sixth sense, the sense of sensibility, the ability to see or look into things in depth, to discover the inner life. We see only the surface of things, but our sensibility explores the inner life of everything and has the capacity to feel every new relationship within this inner life. This is naturally an extremely complicated process. And that is the reason that it is extremely difficult to explain and bring out. You have to have certain experiences before you can understand what I speak about here.

If it is fear—whatever it might be—if it is something rough or smooth or beautiful—everything must in the end come to expression through spirituality. It is not merely the surface that counts. An artist never can be an imitator. He must be a creator, and as a creator he can be nothing else but a spiritual personality. Lacking this his art will be only academic and have no interest whatsoever.

You have to reorder things—what you have experienced—into the sense of the material through which you express yourself.

This material has inner laws, and that is my greatest discovery. On the basis of these inner laws, you create. You need not know these laws, but you must—every artist when he has temperament—he senses and feels these inner laws.

It's not really *what* you say, see; it's always *how* you say what you have to say. If you write, if you just write poetry, if you dance, if you paint, it is all the same thing. It's not merely what you show. It's the process which is inherited in the created work that makes it a work of art. In other words, it reflects the artist in his full capacity of sensing, of feeling, in his capacity of thinking, of ordering, of feeling, and sensing things which only he senses.

William Seitz wrote about your work that sometimes it might suggest soft winds, the feel of soft winds, or the sound of a storm . . .

When I paint, I paint under the dictate of feeling or sensing, and the outcome all the time is supposed to say something. And that is most often my sense of nature . . . especially in relation to . . . it might suggest landscape and might only suggest certain moods, and so on but this must be expressed in pictorial means, according to the inner laws of these means. Only this is acceptable as art.

Then, it would be fair, as regards your intentions, for a viewer looking at your abstract picture to respond as if it were quite specific imagery . . . ?

Sure. Let him take his own pleasure [laughter]. Maybe he has an analytical mind, he wants to understand, he wants to make sense. He wants actually to understand it. But this understanding of what is really creation cannot be philosophical. This is an inner process, and how *I* say, is based on a sixth sense. We have not only five senses. And this sixth sense is sensibility, sensing and feeling. Either we have it or we have it not. When we have it not, well, then we are just a little closer to the animal. When we have it, then, we are above the horizon.

You would feel, then, that an artist is born—you can't learn to be an artist.

Never. See, I as a teacher . . . It's a tremendous experience, teaching . . . I think there is not another man in this world who has the experience as a teacher that I have. So as a result of my long, long period of teaching, I have come to the conclusion that you cannot actually teach art; *you cannot.* You can let everyone paint, let him have his enjoyment, but you cannot teach him the sixth sense. You cannot. Everyone, more or less, has talent, a little bit. It then depends on the teacher *how* the talent is developed. It must develop through work, not through a teacher, not through influences from the outside. You cannot help it, you belong to a certain time. You are yourself the result of this time. You are also the creator of this time. That all goes hand in hand to make your work significant.

The child is really an artist, and the artist should be like a child, but he should not stay a child. He must become an artist. That

means he cannot permit himself to become sentimental or something like that. He must know what he is doing. A child knows
nothing. A child has tried color. He tasted art. He spits on it.
[Laughter.] And so he goes, through a thousand and then ten
thousand steps until the artist in his full maturity has developed,
until his . . . Titian took 99 years to paint the greatest picture in
the world, *The Flagellation of Christ.*

Would you discuss your ideas about the role of accident in art?

The accident, it's very important. There is absolutely no objection against it because through accident you discover. You discover not through calculations. You discover through destructions. When you want to build a house you must tear something
down so the house can be built.

You have seen this every day—a slum is destroyed, and half an
hour later you see a new city, see. That is only possible on the
basis of the machine that had the capacity to destroy a hundred
times more than it could do in earlier times . . . In every gesture
there is an accident.

*What is the relationship between the titles of your paintings
and the paintings themselves?*

I start out with no preconception from the very start. I let
things develop according to my sensing and feeling, to my moods,
especially those in which I find myself when I get up in the
morning.

Sometimes I'm in extremely gay moods, sometimes I'm not so
gay. When that's already come to expression on the first spot I
see on my canvas, from then on, it goes on and on and the painting—my paintings—I say it once more—my paintings go through
tens of thousands of developments, tens of thousands of developments in which the different values have been brought up to the
creation of an immense volume with the expression of universality,
with space, and so on.

That is not accident. That is all created. That is also the control
from a certain momentum, see? But at the same time there develops in me a relationship to my own paintings, and this is mostly

a poetic relationship, because my painting itself is poetry. I consider this poetry expressed in color, and according to the outcome, I give my title.

I see. The meaning grows out of your relationship to the painting.

That's what I *wanted*, see. This was *all the time* just what I wanted.

The titles are often extremely difficult to give because the title is very significant. It is not only significant but it often expresses itself as . . . the signature in a painting which is part of the painting, too, you see. The signature can destroy a whole painting.

(Mrs. H: It can make and break it.)

It can destroy the whole meaning of a painting. In a good painting every point counts, even when it is only a millimeter point. I very often send pictures to framers, and accidental things on which I have counted through the whole development of the picture that this should not be destroyed, they think it is dirt and . . . [Laughter.]

Do you work on a painting over a period of days or weeks or months or hours?

I work very different. I work spontaneously and very rapidly, and I take extreme pains until I bring my picture to full—to full expression, how I want to have it. I mean, it must have the richness, let's say, of music of an organ, like an organ. You can use color in a thousand different ways, see, and I know color in all its possibilities.

Is it possible to see op art in terms of your push-pull theory?

Push and pull is not so simple as people think it is. It is actually the secret of three dimensionality, of a flat surface . . . creating space, deep, deep space without destroying the surface, without drilling a hole in the surface. That's my great discovery, which I discovered through my very rich teachings here.

It is all wrong with Italian perspective—it has only one direction in the depth, but nothing comes back. But in my pictures it goes back and comes—it goes in and it comes back, but comes not *this* back what I have *done*. Something's added to the surface. But I have not touched. This comes back.

You mention the Renaissance, and mathematical perspective. I believe it's fair to say the Renaissance artists were also aware of these abstract qualities in painting.

Yes, this has nothing to do. That is what hinders . . . it is not abstract quality—just the opposite. You see, on the basis of this comes the great simplification. What we all want now in art is to say the most with the least, not the least with the most.

Henry Moore (1898–   ) was for many years a teacher at the Royal College of Art in London and then at the Chelsea School of Art. He organizes his writing like a teacher, systematically; one can almost see the term's work taking shape in these "notes," putting general ideas next to special applications, and setting all in the frame of the history of modern culture. He composes his sculpture with the same systematic precision. Everything is in the service of a full three dimensions. Flatness is out. To make these dimensions clear, he developed a style that is characterized by piercings of his figures and by roundings of their edges that carry the viewer's eye well beyond the surfaces first presented. Moore is a sculptor in depth and a thinker about sculpture in the same dimension.

NOTES ON SCULPTURE

Henry Moore

It is a mistake for a sculptor or a painter to speak or write very often about his job. It releases tension needed for his work. By trying to express his aims with rounded-off logical exactness, he can easily become a theorist whose actual work is only a caged-in exposition of conceptions evolved in terms of logic and words.

But though the nonlogical, instinctive, subconscious part of the mind must play its part in his work, he also has a conscious mind which is not inactive. The artist works with a concentration of his whole personality, and the conscious part of it resolves conflicts, organizes memories, and prevents him from trying to walk in two directions at the same time.

It is likely, then, that a sculptor can give, from his own conscious experience, *clues* which will help others in their approach to sculpture, and this article tries to do this, and no more. It is not a general survey of sculpture, or of my own development, but a few notes on some of the problems that have concerned me from time to time.

THREE DIMENSIONS

Appreciation of sculpture depends upon the ability to respond to form in three dimensions. That is, perhaps, why sculpture has been described as the most difficult of all arts; certainly it is more difficult than the arts which involve appreciation of flat forms, shape in only two dimensions. Many more people are 'form-blind' than colour-blind. The child learning to see first distinguishes only two-dimensional shape; it cannot judge distances, depths. Later, for its personal safety and practical needs, it has to develop (partly by means of touch) the ability to judge roughly three-dimensional distances. But having satisfied the requirements of practical necessity most people go no further. Though they may attain considerable accuracy in the perception of flat form, they do not make the further intellectual and emotional effort needed to comprehend form in its full spatial existence.

This is what the sculptor must do. He must strive continually to think of and use form in its full spatial completeness. He gets the solid shape, as it were, inside his head—he thinks of it, whatever its size, as if he were holding it completely enclosed in the hollow of his hand. He mentally visualizes a complex form *from all round itself:* he knows while he looks at one side what the other side is like; he identifies himself with its centre of gravity, its mass, its weight; he realizes its volume, as the space that the shape displaces in the air.

And the sensitive observer of sculpture must also learn to feel shape simply as shape, not as description or reminiscence. He must, for example, perceive an egg as a simple single solid shape, quite apart from its significance as food, or from the literary idea that it will become a bird. And so with solids such as a shell, a nut, a plum, a pear, a tadpole, a mushroom, a mountain peak, a kidney, a carrot, a tree-trunk, a bird, a bud, a lark, a ladybird, a bullrush, a bone. From these he can go on to appreciate more complex forms or combinations of several forms.

Brancusi

Since Gothic, European sculpture had become overgrown with moss, weeds—all sorts of surface excrescences which completely concealed shape. It has been Brancusi's special mission to get rid of this overgrowth, and to make us once more shape-conscious.

To do this he has had to concentrate on very simple direct shapes, to keep his sculpture, as it were, one-cylindered, to refine and polish a single shape to a degree almost too precious. Brancusi's work apart from its individual value has been of great historical importance in the development of contemporary sculpture. But it may now be no longer necessary to close down and restrict sculpture to the single (static) form unit. We can now begin to open out. To relate and combine together several forms of varied sizes, sections and direction, into one organic whole.

SHELLS AND PEBBLES—

BEING CONDITIONED TO RESPOND TO SHAPES

Although it is the human figure which interests me most deeply, I have always paid great attention to natural forms, such as bones, shells, pebbles, etc. Sometimes, for several years running, I have been to the same part of the sea-shore—but each year a new shape of pebble has caught my eye, which the year before, though it was there in hundreds, I never saw. Out of the millions of pebbles passed in walking along the shore, I choose out to see with excitement only those which fit in with my existing form interest at the time. A different thing happens if I sit down and examine a handful one by one. I may then extend my form experience more by giving my mind time to become conditioned to a new shape.

There are universal shapes to which everybody is subconsciously conditioned and to which they can respond if their conscious control does not shut them off.

HOLES IN SCULPTURE

Pebbles show Nature's way of working stone. Some of the pebbles I pick up have holes right through them.

When first working direct in a hard and brittle material like stone, the lack of experience and great respect for the material, the fear of ill-treating it, too often result in relief surface carving, with no sculptural power.

But with more experience the completed work in stone can be

kept within the limitations of its material, that is, not be weakened beyond its natural constructive build, and yet be turned from an inert mass into a composition which has a full form existence, with masses of varied sizes and sections working together in spatial relationship.

A piece of stone can have a hole through it and not be weakened—if the hole is of a studied size, shape and direction. On the principle of the arch it can remain just as strong.

The first hole made through a piece of stone is a revelation.

The hole connects one side to the other, making it immediately more three-dimensional.

A hole can itself have as much shape-meaning as a solid mass.

Sculpture in air is possible, where the stone contains only the hole, which is the intended and considered form.

The mystery of the hole—the mysterious fascination of caves in hillsides and cliffs.

SIZES AND SCALE

There is a right physical size for every idea.

Pieces of good stone have stood about my studio for long periods, because, though I've had ideas which would fit their proportions and materials perfectly, their size was wrong.

There is a side to scale not to do with its actual physical size, its measurement in feet and inches—but connected with vision.

A carving might be several times over life size and yet be petty and small in feeling—and a small carving only a few inches in height can give the feeling of huge size and monumental grandeur, because the vision behind it is big. Example: Michelangelo's drawings or a Masaccio madonna—and the Albert Memorial.

Yet actual physical size has an emotional meaning. We relate everything to our own size, and our emotional response to size is controlled by the fact that men on the average are between five and six feet high.

An exact model to one-tenth scale of Stonehenge, where the stones would be less than us, would lose all its impressiveness.

Sculpture is more affected by actual size considerations than painting. A painting is isolated by a frame from its surroundings (unless it serves just a decorative purpose), and so retains more easily its own imaginary scale.

If practical considerations allowed me (cost of material, of transport, etc.) I should like to work on large carvings more often than I do. The average in-between size does not disconnect an idea enough from prosaic everyday life. The very small or the very large take on an added size emotion.

Recently I have been working in the country, where, carving in the open air, I find sculpture more natural than in a London studio, but it needs bigger dimensions. A large piece of stone or wood placed almost anywhere at random in a field, orchard or garden, immediately looks right and inspiring.

DRAWING AND SCULPTURE

My drawings are done mainly as a help towards making sculpture —as a means of generating ideas for sculpture, tapping oneself for the initial idea; and as a way of sorting out ideas and developing them.

Also, sculpture compared with drawing is a slow means of expression, and I find drawing a useful outlet for ideas which there is not time enough to realize as sculpture. And I use drawing as a method of study and observation of natural form (drawings from life, drawings of bones, shells, etc.)

And I sometimes draw just for its own enjoyment.

Experience, though, has taught me that the difference there is between drawing and sculpture should not be forgotten. A sculptural idea which may be satisfactory as a drawing always needs some alteration when translated into sculpture.

At one time whenever I made drawings for sculpture I tried to give them as much the illusion of real sculpture as I could—that is, I drew by the method of illusion, of light falling on a solid object. But now I find that carrying a drawing so far that it becomes a substitute for the sculpture either weakens the desire to do the sculpture, or is likely to make the sculpture only a dead realization of the drawing.

I now leave a wider latitude in the interpretation of the drawings I make for sculpture, and draw often in line and flat tones without the light and shade illusion of three dimensions; but this

Above, photograph by George W. Martin.

Right, photograph by Bob Barrett, ASMP.

does not mean that the vision behind the drawing is only two-dimensional.

ABSTRACTION AND SURREALISM

The violent quarrel between the abstractionists and the surrealists seems to me quite unnecessary. All good art has contained both abstract and surrealist elements, just as it has contained both classical and romantic elements—order and surprise, intellect and imagination, conscious and unconscious. Both sides of the artist's personality must play their part. And I think the first inception of a painting or a sculpture may begin from either end. As far as my own experience is concerned, I sometimes begin a drawing with no preconceived problem to solve, with only the desire to use pencil on paper, and make lines, tones and shapes with no conscious aim; but as my mind takes in what is so produced a point arrives where some idea becomes conscious and crystallizes, and then a control and ordering begins to take place.

Or sometimes I start with a set subject, or to solve, in a block of stone of known dimensions, a sculptural problem I've given myself, and then consciously attempt to build an ordered relationship of forms, which shall express my idea. But if the work is to be more than just a sculptural exercise, unexplainable jumps in the process of thought occur; and the imagination plays its part.

It might seem from what I have said of shape and form that I regard them as ends in themselves. Far from it. I am very much aware that associational, psychological factors play a large part in sculpture. The meaning and significance of form itself probably depends on the countless associations of man's history. For example, rounded forms convey an idea of fruitfulness, maturity, probably because the earth, women's breasts, and most fruits are rounded, and these shapes are important because they have this background in our habits of perception. I think the humanist organic element will always be for me of fundamental importance in sculpture, giving sculpture its vitality. Each particular carving I make takes on in my mind a human, or occasionally animal, character and personality, and this personality controls its design and formal qualities, and makes me satisfied or dissatisfied with the work as it develops.

My own aim and direction seems to be consistent with these beliefs, though it does not depend upon them. My sculpture is becoming less representational, less an outward visual copy, and so what some people would call more abstract; but only because I believe that in this way I can present the human psychological content of my work with the greatest directness and intensity.

THE WORD ARTS:

The Novel

THE FUTURE OF THE NOVEL

Henry James (1843–1916) was the most distin-guished American novelist (The Portrait of a Lady, The Turn of the Screw, *and* The Ambassadors *are some of his most famous novels) of his time, an age notable for the high development of the novel as an art form. Possibly above all other American men of letters, James's lifelong interest lay in literary theory, and he was an influential reviewer and critic of prose fiction. In this essay, James clearly defines the conflict between the values of mass distribution and mass readership and those of high quality work designed for a discerning taste. In addition to suggesting the obligations of both novelist and reader, James also voices his lofty expectations for the novel. Even a close reading, however, may not reveal James's final estimate of the "future" of the novel, an art form to which so much of his life was devoted.*

Henry James

Beginnings, as we all know, are usually small things, but continuations are not always strik-ingly great ones, and the place occupied in the world by the prolonged prose fable has become, in our time, among the incidents of literature, the most surprising example to be named of swift and extravagant growth, a development beyond the measure of every early appearance. It is a form that has had a fortune so little to have been foretold at its cradle. The germ of the comprehensive epic was more recognizable in the first barbaric chant than that of the novel as we know it today in the first anecdote retailed to amuse. It arrived, in truth, the novel, late at self-consciousness; but it has done its utmost ever since to make up for lost opportunities. The flood at present swells and swells, threatening the whole field of letters, as would often seem, with submersion. It plays, in what may be called the passive consciousness of many persons, a part that directly marches with the rapid increase of the multitude able to possess itself in one way and another of the *book*. The book, in the Anglo-Saxon world, is almost everywhere, and it is in the form of the voluminous prose fable that we see it penetrate easiest and farthest. Penetration appears really to be directly aided by mere mass and bulk. There is an immense public, if public be the name, inarticulate, but abysmally absorbent, for which, at its hours of ease, the printed volume has no other association. This public—the public that subscribes, borrows, lends, that picks up in one way and another, sometimes even by purchase—grows and grows each year, and nothing is thus more apparent than that of all the recruits it brings to the book the most numerous by far are those that it brings to the "story."

This number has gained, in our time, an augmentation from three sources in particular, the first of which, indeed, is perhaps but a comprehensive name for the two others. The diffusion of the rudiments, the multiplication of common schools, has had more and more the effect of making readers of women and of the very young. Nothing is so striking in a survey of this field, and nothing to be so much borne in mind, as that the larger part of the great multitude that sustains the teller and the publisher of tales is constituted by boys and girls; by girls in especial, if we apply the term to the later stages of the life of the innumerable women who, under modern arrangements, increasingly fail to marry—fail, apparently, even, largely, to desire to. It is not too much to say of many of these that they live in a great measure by the immediate aid of the novel—confining the question, for the moment, to the fact of consumption alone. The literature, as it may be called for convenience, of children is an industry that occupies by itself a very considerable quarter of the scene. Great fortunes, if not great reputations, are made, we learn, by writing for schoolboys, and the period during which they consume the compound artfully prepared for them appears—as they begin earlier and continue later—to add to itself at both ends. This helps to account for the fact that public libraries, especially those that are private and money-making enterprises, put into circulation more volumes of "stories" than of all other things together of which volumes can be made. The published statistics are extraordinary, and of a sort to engender many kinds of uneasiness. The sort of taste that used to be called "good" has nothing to do with the matter: we are so demonstrably in the presence of millions for whom taste is but an obscure, confused, immediate instinct. In the flare of railway bookstalls, in the shop-fronts of most booksellers, especially the provincial, in the advertisements of the weekly newspapers, and in fifty places besides, this testimony to the general preference triumphs, yielding a good-natured corner at most to a bunch of treatises on athletics or sport, or a patch of theology old and new.

The case is so marked, however, that illustrations easily overflow, and there is no need of forcing doors that stand wide open. What remains is the interesting oddity or mystery—the anomaly that fairly dignifies the whole circumstance with its strangeness: the wonder, in short, that men, women, and children *should* have so much attention to spare for improvisations mainly so arbitrary and frequently so loose. That, at the first blush, fairly leaves us gaping. This great fortune then, since fortune it seems, has been reserved for mere unsupported and unguaranteed history, the *inexpensive* thing, written in the air, the record of what, in any particular case, has *not* been, the account that remains responsible, at best, to "documents" with which we are practically unable to collate it. This is the side of the whole business of fiction on which it can always be challenged, and to that degree that if the general venture had not become in such a manner the admiration of the world it might but too easily have become the derision. It has in truth, I think, never philosophically met the challenge, never found a formula to inscribe on its shield, never defended its position by any better argument than the frank, straight blow: "Why am I not so unprofitable as to be preposterous? Because I can do *that*. There!" And it throws up from time to time some purely practical masterpiece. There is nevertheless an admirable minority of intelligent persons who care not even for the masterpieces, nor see any pressing point in them, for whom the very form itself has, equally at its best and at its worst, been ever a vanity and a mockery. This class, it should be added, is beginning to be visibly augmented by a different circle altogether, the group of the formerly subject, but now estranged, the deceived and bored, those for whom the whole movement too decidedly fails to live up to its possibilities. There are people who have loved the novel, but who actually find themselves drowned in its verbiage, and for whom, even in some of its approved manifestations, it has become a terror they exert every ingenuity, every hypocrisy, to evade. The indifferent and the

Henry James.
Photograph by E. O. Hoppe, Biblioteque Nationale, Paris. Courtesy of
The New York Public Library.

alienated testify, at any rate, almost as much as the omnivorous, to the reign of the great ambiguity, the enjoyment of which rests, evidently, on a primary need of the mind. The novelist can only fall back on that—on his recognition that man's constant demand for what he has to offer is simply man's general appetite for a *picture*. The novel is of all pictures the most comprehensive and the most elastic. It will stretch anywhere—it will take in absolutely anything. All it needs is a subject and a painter. But for its subject, magnificently, it has the whole human consciousness. And if we are pushed a step farther backward, and asked why the representation should be required when the object represented is itself mostly so accessible, the answer to that appears to be that man combines with his eternal desire for more experience an infinite cunning as to getting his experience as cheaply as possible. He will steal it whenever he can. He likes to live the life of others, yet is well aware of the points at which it may too intolerably resemble his own. The vivid fable, more than anything else, gives him this satisfaction on easy terms, gives him knowledge abundant yet vicarious. It enables him to select, to take and to leave; so that to feel he can afford to neglect it he must have a rare faculty, or great opportunities, for the extension of experience—by thought, by emotion, by energy— at first hand.

Yet it is doubtless not this cause alone that contributes to the contemporary deluge; other circumstances operate, and one of them is probably, in truth, if looked into, something of an abatement of the great fortune we have been called upon to admire. The high prosperity of fiction has marched, very directly, with another "sign of the times," the demoralization, the vulgarization of literature in general, the increasing familiarity of all such methods of communication, the making itself supremely felt, as it were, of the presence of the ladies and children—by whom I mean, in other words, the reader irreflective and uncritical. If the novel, in fine, has found itself, socially speaking, at such a rate, the book *par excellence*, so on the other hand the book has in the same degree found itself a thing of small ceremony. So many ways of producing it easily have been discovered that it is by no means the occasional prodigy, for good or for evil, that it was taken for in simpler days, and has therefore suffered a proportionate discredit. Almost any variety is thrown off and taken up, handled, admired, ignored by too many people, and this, precisely, is the point at which the question of its future becomes one with that of the future of the total swarm. How are the generations to face, at all, the monstrous multiplications? Any speculation on the further development of a particular variety is subject to the reserve that the generations may at no distant day be obliged formally to decree, and to execute, great clearings of the deck, great periodical effacements and destructions. It fills, in fact, at moments the expectant ear, as we watch the progress of the ship of civilization—the huge splash that must mark the response to many an imperative, unanimous "Overboard!" What at least is already very plain is that practically the great majority of volumes printed within a year cease to exist as the hour passes, and give up by that circumstance all claim to a career, to being accounted or provided for. In speaking of the future of the novel we must of course, therefore, be taken as limiting the inquiry to those types that have, for criticism, a present and a past. And it is only superficially that confusion seems here to reign. The fact that in England and in the United States every specimen that sees the light may look for a "review" testifies merely to the point to which, in these countries, literary criticism has sunk. The review is in nine cases out of ten an effort of intelligence as undeveloped as the ineptitude over which it fumbles, and the critical spirit, which knows where it is concerned and where not, is not touched, is still less compromised, by the incident. There are too many reasons why newspapers must live.

So, as regards the tangible type, the end is that in its un-defended, its positively exposed state, we continue to accept it, conscious even of a peculiar beauty in an appeal made from a footing so precarious. It throws itself wholly on our generosity, and very often indeed gives us, by the reception it meets, a use-ful measure of the quality, of the delicacy, of many minds. There is to my sense no work of literary, or of any other, art, that any human being is under the smallest positive obligation to "like." There is no woman—no matter of what loveliness—in the presence of whom it is anything but a man's unchallengeably *own* affair that he is "in love" or out of it. It is not a question of manners; vast is the margin left to individual freedom; and the trap set by the artist occupies no different ground—Robert Louis Stevenson has admirably expressed the analogy—from the offer of her charms by the lady. There only remain infatuations that we envy and emulate. When we do respond to the appeal, when we *are* caught in the trap, we are held and played upon; so that how in the world can there *not* still be a future, however late in the day, for a contrivance possessed of this precious secret? The more we consider it the more we feel that the prose picture can never be at the end of its tether until it loses the sense of what it can do. It can do simply everything, and that is its strength and its life. Its plasticity, its elasticity are infinite; there is no color, no extension it may not take from the nature of its subject or the temper of its craftsman. It has the extraordinary advantage—a piece of luck scarcely credible—that, while capable of giving an impression of the highest perfection and the rarest finish, it moves in a luxurious independence of rules and restrictions. Think as we may, there is nothing we can mention as a consideration outside itself with which it must square, nothing we can name as one of its peculiar obligations or interdictions. It must, of course, hold our attention and reward it, it must not appeal on false pretenses; but these necessities, with which, obviously, disgust and displeasure interfere, are not peculiar to it—all works of art have them in common. For the rest it has so clear a field that if it perishes this will surely be by its fault—by its superficiality, in other words, or its timidity. One almost, for the very love of it, likes to think of its appearing threatened with some such fate, in order to figure the dramatic stroke of its revival under the touch of a life-giving master. The temperament of the artist can do so much for it that our desire for some exemplary felicity fairly demands even the vision of that supreme proof. If we were to linger on this vision long enough, we should doubtless, in fact, be brought to wondering—and still for very loyalty to the form itself—whether our own prospective conditions may not before too long appear to many critics to call for some such happy *coup* on the part of a great artist yet to come.

There would at least be this excuse for such a reverie: that speculation is vain unless we confuse it, and that for ourselves the most convenient branch of the question is the state of the industry that makes its appeal to readers of English. From any attempt to measure the career still open to the novel in France I may be excused, in so narrow a compass, for shrinking. The French, as a result of having ridden their horse much harder than we, are at a different stage of the journey, and we have doubtless many of their stretches and baiting-places yet to traverse. But if the range grows shorter from the moment we drop to inductions drawn only from English and American material, I am not sure that the answer comes sooner. I should have at all events—a formidably large order—to plunge into the particulars of the question of the present. If the day *is* approaching when the respite of execution for almost any book is but a matter of mercy, does the English novel of commerce tend to strike us as a production more and more equipped by its high qualities for braving the danger? It would be impossible, I think, to make one's attempt at an answer to that riddle really interesting without bringing into the field many illustrations drawn from individuals—without pointing the moral with names both conspicuous and obscure. Such a freedom would carry us, here, quite too far, and would moreover only encumber the path. There is nothing to prevent our taking for granted all sorts of happy symptoms and splendid promises—so long, of course, I mean, as we keep before us the general truth that the future of fiction is intimately bound up with the future of the society that produces and consumes it. In a society with a great and diffused literary sense the talent at play can only be a less negligible thing than in a society with a literary sense barely discernible. In a world in which criticism is acute and mature such talent will find itself trained, in order successfully to assert itself, to many more kinds of precautionary expertness than in a society in which the art I have named holds an inferior place or makes a sorry figure. A community addicted to reflection and fond of ideas will try experiments with the "story" that will be left untried in a community mainly devoted to traveling and shooting, to pushing trade and playing football. There are many judges, doubtless, who hold that experiments—queer and uncanny things at best—are not necessary to it, that its face has been, once for all, turned in one way, and that it has only to go straight before it. If that is what it is actually doing in England and America the main thing to say about its future would appear to be that this future will in very truth more and more define itself as negligible. For all the while the immense variety of life will stretch away to right and to left, and all the while there may be, on such lines, perpetuation of its great mistake of failing of intelligence. That mistake will be, ever, for the admirable art, the only one really inexcusable, because of being a mistake about, as we may say, its own soul. The form of novel that is

stupid on the general question of its freedom is the single form
that may, *a priori*, be unhesitatingly pronounced wrong.

The most interesting thing today, therefore, among ourselves
is the degree in which we may count on seeing a sense of that
freedom cultivated and bearing fruit. What else is this, indeed,
but one of the most attaching elements in the great drama of
our wide English-speaking life! As a novel is at any moment the
most immediate and, as it were, admirably *treacherous* picture
of actual manners—indirectly as well as directly, and by what it
does not touch as well as by what it does—so its present situation, where we are most concerned with it, is exactly a reflection
of our social changes and chances, of the signs and portents that
lay most traps for most observers, and make up in general what
is most "amusing" in the spectacle we offer. Nothing, I may say,
for instance, strikes me more as meeting this description than the
predicament finally arrived at, for the fictive energy, in consequence of our long and most respectable tradition of making it
defer supremely, in the treatment, say, of a delicate case, to the
inexperience of the young. The particular knot the coming
novelist who shall prefer not simply to beg the question will
have here to untie may represent assuredly the essence of his
outlook. By what it shall decide to do in respect to the "young"
the great prose fable will, from any serious point of view, practically see itself stand or fall. What is clear is that it has, among us,
veritably never chosen—it has, mainly, always obeyed an un-
reasoning instinct of avoidance in which there has often been
much that was felicitous. While society was frank, was free
about the incidents and accidents of the human constitution, the
novel took the same robust ease as society. The young then were
so very young that they were not table-high. But they began to
grow, and from the moment their little chins rested on the
mahogany, Richardson and Fielding began to go under it. There
came into being a mistrust of any but the most guarded treatment
of the great relation between men and women, the constant
world-renewal, which was the conspicuous sign that whatever
the prose picture of life was prepared to take upon itself, it was
not prepared to take upon itself not to be superficial. Its position
became very much: "There are other things, don't you know?
For heaven's sake let *that* one pass!" And to this wonderful
propriety of letting it pass the business has been for these so many
years—with the consequences we see today—largely devoted.

These consequences are of many sorts, not a few altogether charming. One of them has been that there is an immense omission in our fiction—which, though many critics will always judge that it has vitiated the whole, others will continue to speak of as signifying but a trifle. One can only talk for one's self, and of the English and American novelists of whom I am fond, I am so superlatively fond that I positively prefer to take them as they are. I cannot so much as imagine Dickens and Scott *without* the *"love-making"* left, as the phrase is, out. They were, to my perception, absolutely right—from the moment their attention to it could only be perfunctory—practically not to deal with it. In all their work it is, in spite of the number of pleasant sketches of affection gratified or crossed, the element that matters least. Why not therefore assume, it may accordingly be asked, that discriminations which have served their purpose so well in the past will continue not less successfully to meet the case? What will you have better than Scott and Dickens?

Nothing certainly *can* be, it may at least as promptly be replied, and I can imagine no more comfortable prospect than jogging along perpetually with a renewal of such blessings. The difficulty lies in the fact that two of the great conditions have changed. The novel is older, and so are the young. It would seem that everything the young can possibly do for us in the matter has been successfully done. They have kept out one thing after the other, yet there is still a certain completeness we lack, and the curious thing is that it appears to be they themselves who are making the grave discovery. "You have kindly taken," they seem to say to the fiction-mongers, "our education off the hands of our parents and pastors, and that, doubtless, has been very convenient for *them*, and left them free to amuse themselves. But what, all the while, pray, if it is a question of education, have you done with your own? These are directions in which you seem dreadfully untrained, and in which *can* it be as vain as it appears to apply to you for information?" The point is whether, from the moment it is a question of averting discredit, the novel can afford to take things quite so easily as it has, for a good while now, settled down into the way of doing. There are too many sources of interest neglected—whole categories of manners, whole corpuscular classes and provinces, museums of character and condition, unvisited; while it is on the other hand mistakenly taken for granted that safety lies in all the loose and thin material that keeps reappearing in forms at once ready-made and sadly the worse for wear. The simple themselves may finally turn against our simplifications; so that we need not, after all, be more royalist than the king or more childish than the children. It is certain that there is no real health for any art—I am not speaking, of course, of any mere industry—that does not move a step in advance of its farthest follower. It would be curious—really a great comedy—if the renewal were to spring just from the satiety of the very readers for whom the sacrifices have hitherto been supposed to be made. It bears on this that as nothing is more salient in English life today, to fresh eyes, than the revolution taking place in the position and outlook of women—and taking place much more deeply in the quiet than even the noise on the surface demonstrates—so we may very well yet see the female elbow itself, kept in increasing activity by the play of the pen, smash with final resonance the window all this time most superstitiously closed. The particular draught that has been most deprecated will in that case take care of the question of freshness. It is the opinion of some observers that when women do obtain a free hand they will not repay their long debt to the precautionary attitude of men by unlimited consideration for the natural delicacy of the latter.

To admit, then, that the great anodyne can ever totally fail to work, is to imply, in short, that this will only be for some grave fault in some high quarter. Man rejoices in an incomparable faculty for presently mutilating and disfiguring any plaything that has helped create for him the illusion of leisure; nevertheless, so long as life retains its power of projecting itself upon his imagination, he will find the novel works off the impression better than anything he knows. Anything better for the purpose has assuredly yet to be discovered. He will give it up only when life itself too thoroughly disagrees with him. Even then, indeed, may fiction not find a second wind, or a fiftieth, in the very portrayal of that collapse? Till the world is an unpeopled void there will be an image in the mirror. What need more immediately concern us, therefore, is the care of seeing that the image shall continue various and vivid. There is much, frankly, to be said for those who, in spite of all brave pleas, feel it to be considerably menaced, for very little reflection will help to show us how the prospect strikes them. They see the whole business too divorced on the one side from observation and perception, and on the other from the art and taste. They get too little of the first-hand impression, the effort to penetrate—that effort for which the French have the admirable expression to *fouiller*—and still less, if possible, of any science of composition, any architecture, distribution, proportion. It is not a trifle, though indeed it is the concomitant of an edged force, that "mystery" should, to so many of the sharper eyes, have disappeared from the craft, and a facile flatness be, in place of it, in acclaimed possession. But these are, at the worst, even for such of the disconcerted, signs that the novelist, not that the novel, has dropped. So long as there is a subject to be treated, so long will it depend wholly on the treatment to rekindle the fire. Only the ministrant must really approach the altar; for if the novel *is* the treatment, it is the treatment that is essentially what I have called the anodyne.

A prolific novelist of exceptional range—his best known trilogy consists of Herself Surprised, To Be a Pilgrim, *and* The Horse's Mouth—*Joyce Cary (1888–1957) here suggests the broad relationship which obtains between the artist and the society in which he happens to live. Understandably this relationship is an uneasy one, partaking (at least in Cary's works) of the comic, the absurd, the pathetic. This essay suggests that the world is a very real place and that the artist must do what he can to transcend imperfect conditions not only in the extensional world, but in himself as well.*

THE ARTIST AND THE WORLD

Joyce Cary

This is an attempt to examine the relation of the artist with the world as it seems to him, and to see what he does with it. That is to say, on the one side with what is called the artist's intuition, on the other with his production, or the work of art.

My only title to discuss the matter is some practical knowledge of two arts. I know very little about aesthetic philosophy, so I shall try, as far as possible, to speak from practical experience.

It is quite true that the artist, painter, writer or composer starts always with an experience that is a kind of discovery. He comes upon it with the sense of a discovery; in fact, it is truer to say that it comes upon *him* as a discovery. It surprises him. This is what is usually called an intuition or an inspiration. It carries with it always the feeling of directness. For instance, you go walking in the fields and all at once they strike you in quite a new aspect: you find it extraordinary that they should be like that. This is what happened to Monet as a young man. He suddenly saw the fields, not as solid flat objects covered with grass or useful crops and dotted with trees, but as colour in astonishing variety and subtlety of gradation. And this gave him a

delightful and quite new pleasure. It was a most exciting discovery, especially as it was a discovery of something real. I mean,
by that, something independent of Monet himself. That, of
course, was half the pleasure. Monet has discovered a truth about
the actual world.

This delight in discovery of something new in or about the
world is a natural and primitive thing. All children have it. And
it often continues until the age of twenty or twenty-five, *even*
throughout life.

Children's pleasure in exploring the world, long before they
can speak, is very obvious. They spend almost all their time at
it. We don't speak of their intuition, but it is the same thing as
the intuition of the artist. That is to say, it is direct knowledge
of the world as it is, direct acquaintance with things, with characters, with appearance, and this is the primary knowledge of
the artist and writer. This joy of discovery is his starting point.

Croce, probably the most interesting of the aesthetic philosophers, says that art is simply intuition. But he says, too, that
intuition and expression are the same thing. His idea is that we
can't know what we have intuited until we have named it, or
given it a formal character, and this action is essentially the
work of art.

But this is not at all the way it seems to an artist or a writer.
To him, the intuition is quite a different thing from the work of
art. For the essential thing about the work of art is that it is
work, and very hard work too. To go back to the painter. He
has had his intuition, he has made his discovery, he is eager to
explore it, to reveal it, to fix it down. For, at least in a grown,
an educated man, intuitions are highly evanescent. This is what
Wordsworth meant when he wrote of their fading into the light
of common day.

I said the joy of discovery often dies away after twenty years
or so. And this is simply a truth of observation; we know it from
our own experience. The magic object that started up before our
eyes on a spring day in its own individual shape, is apt, in the
same instant, to turn into simply another cherry tree, an ordinary
specimen of a common class. We have seen it and named it
pretty often already. But Housman, as poet, fixed his vision of
the cherry tree before it had changed into just another tree in
blossom.

Housman fixed it for himself and us, but not by an immediate act, indistinguishable from the intuition. He had to go to work and find words, images, rhyme, which embodied his feeling about the tree, which fixed down its meaning for him, so that he could have it again when he wanted it, and also give it to us. He made a work of art, but he made it by work.

So for the painter, when he has his new, his magic landscape in front of him; he has to fix it down. And at once he is up against enormous difficulties. He has only his paints and brushes, and a flat piece of canvas with which to convey a sensation, a feeling, about a three-dimensional world. He has somehow to translate an intuition from real objects into a formal and ideal arrangement of colours and shapes, which will still, mysteriously, fix and convey his sense of the unique quality, the magic of these objects in their own private existence. That is to say, he has a job that requires thought, skill, and a lot of experience.

As for the novelist, his case is even worse. He starts also with his intuition, his discovery; as when Conrad, in an Eastern port, saw a young officer come out from a trial in which he had been found guilty of a cowardly desertion of his ship and its passengers after a collision. The young man had lost his honour and Conrad realised all at once what that meant to him, and he wrote *Lord Jim* to fix and communicate that discovery in its full force.

For that he had to invent characters, descriptions, a plot. All these details, as with the painter, had to enforce the impression, the feeling that he wanted to convey. The reader had to *feel*, at the end of the tale, 'That is important, that is true'. It's no good if he says, 'I suppose that is true, but I've heard it before'. In that case Conrad has failed, at least with that reader. For his object was to give the reader the same discovery, to make him feel what it meant to that young man to lose his honour, and how important honour is to men.

And to get this sharp and strong feeling, the reader must not be confused by side issues. All the scenes and characters, all the events in the book, must contribute to the total effect, the total meaning. The book must give the sense of an actual world with real characters. Otherwise they won't engage the reader's sympathy, his feelings will never be concerned at all.

But actual life is not like that, it doesn't have a total meaning, it is simply a wild confusion of events from which we have to select what we think significant for ourselves. Look at any morning paper. It makes no sense at all—it means nothing but chaos. We read only what we think important; that is to say, we provide our own sense to the news. We have to do so because otherwise it wouldn't be there. To do this, we have to have some standard of valuation, we have to know whether the political event is more important than a murder, or a divorce than the stock market, or the stock market than who won the Derby.

The writer, in short, has to find some meaning in life before he gives it to us in a book. And his subject-matter is much more confused than that of a painter. Of course, in this respect, everyone is in the same boat. Everyone, not only the writer, is presented with the same chaos, and is obliged to form his own idea of the world, of what matters and what doesn't matter. He has to do it, from earliest childhood, for his own safety. And if he gets it wrong, if his idea does not accord with reality, he will suffer for it. A friend of mine, as a child, thought he could fly, and jumped off the roof. Luckily he came down in a flower-bed and only broke a leg.

This seems to contradict what I said just now about the chaos which stands before us every morning. For the boy who failed to fly did not suffer only from bad luck. He affronted a law of gravity, a permanent part of a reality objective to him. As we know very well, underneath the chaos of events, there are laws, or if you like consistencies, both of fact and feeling. What science calls matter, that is to say, certain fixed characteristics of being, presents us with a whole framework of reality which we defy at our peril. Wrong ideas about gravity or the wholesomeness of prussic acid are always fatal.

So, too, human nature and its social relations present certain constants. Asylums and gaols are full of people who have forgotten or ignored them. On the other hand, we can still comprehend and enjoy palaeolithic art and Homer. Homer's heroes had the same kind of nature as our own.

These human constants are also a part of reality objective to us, that is, a permanent character of the world as we know it. So we have a reality consisting of permanent and highly obstinate facts, and permanent and highly obstinate human nature. And human nature is always in conflict with material facts, although men are themselves most curious combinations of fact and feeling, and actually require the machinery of their organism to realise their emotions, their desires and ambitions. Though the ghost could not exist without the machine which is at once its material form, its servant, its limitation, its perfection and its traitor, it is always trying to get more power over it, to change it.

Men have in fact obtained more power over matter, but to change it is impossible. It may be said that all works of art, all ideas of life, all philosophies are 'As if', but I am suggesting that they can be checked with an objective reality. They might be called propositions for truth and their truth can be decided by their correspondence with the real. Man can't change the elemental characters. If you could, the world would probably vanish into nothing. But because of their very permanence, you can assemble them into new forms. You can build new houses with the bricks they used for the oldest Rome, because they are still bricks. For bricks that could stop being bricks at will would be no good to the architect. And a heart that stopped beating at its own will would be no good to the artist. The creative soul needs the machine, as the living world needs a fixed character, or it could not exist at all. It would be merely an idea. But by a paradox we have to accept, part of this fixed character is the free mind, the creative imagination, in everlasting conflict with facts, including its own machinery, its own tools.

*This essay by Andrew Hook of the University of
Edinburgh explores the generally gray area of a
writer's commitment (or lack of it) to society, to
politics, to reform, to propaganda—this last,
perhaps, in behalf of his own country, Scotland.
Many writers have placed their gifts in the service
of some "higher" cause; the social concerns of Dos
Passos and Steinbeck are peculiarly American
examples. In another way, Tolstoy used his literary
talent to dramatize his version of a Christian ethic;
by contrast, some writers in the U.S.S.R. today
see themselves as "engineers of the human mind." In
America, the writer's concept of his commitment to*

COMMITMENT

*society is largely a matter
of individual conscience,
but most writers*

AND

*understand very well that this delicate issue may
affect the acceptance of their work.*

REALITY

*Andrew
Hook*

While his *Crack-Up* articles, which tried to account for an overwhelming sense of personal frustration and failure, were appearing in *Esquire*, Scott Fitzgerald received a letter from his friend Dos Passos of which this is part:

I've been wanting to see you, naturally, to argue about your *Esquire* articles.—Christ man, how do you find time in the middle of the general conflagration to worry about all that stuff? . . . After all not many people write as well as you do. Here you've gone and spent forty years in perfecting an elegant and complicated piece of machinery (tool I was going to say) and the next forty years is the time to use it—or as long as the murderous forces of history will let you.

The date is 1936 and this is the letter of a committed writer to one he regards as uncommitted. Dos Passos cannot understand why at this critical moment of time Fitzgerald should allow himself to be so taken up with personal, individ-

ual problems and concerns. As an artist he should be preoccupied
not with the cracking-up of his own life, but with what Dos
Passos recognises as the imminent dissolution and disintegration
of the society and the world of which he is part. For Dos
Passos the duty of the writer is not to look inward, to the
exploration of the individual consciousness, but outward to society at large, to the broader forces and movements which
mould and control man's destiny. The final confrontation is not
that of man and his deepest, truest, thinking and feeling self,
but that of man and 'the murderous forces of history.' Just such
an argument as this over the necessary priority of either the
inner, psychological reality, or the outer, social reality lies behind every debate on commitment.

Dos Passos' last phrase, however—the murderous forces of
history—provides us with a clue to the origins of commitment
as an ideal for the writer. Commitment, as it is generally understood—the acceptance by the writer of an extra-artistic, usually
political, programme of action and belief which lies behind his
creative endeavours—depends essentially on a Romantic view of
society, of what society stands for. In the eighteenth century in
England, writers such as Pope and Swift were just as much
committed, committed to a dream, a vision of the ideal society,
as any of the English or French or American writers of the nine-
teen-thirties. But their dream was the dream of all of their society; their vision was a vision to which all reasonable men gave
their consent—hence the power with which they assailed the
non-ideal elements in their society. This typical Augustan situation, however, in which individual values reflected social values,
in which the individual found the values in which he believed
endorsed and upheld by the society of which he was part, was
not an enduring one. Whether it had ever in fact been more than
a literary reality may be open to question. But the point is that
the development of Romanticism meant it ceased even to be that.
One of the manifold meanings of Romanticism is precisely a new
interest in the individual as individual rather than as member of
society, a turning away from society to the individual as the focus
of interest, the centre of consciousness. The consequence was that
social and individual values tended to diverge. And for the Romantic artist, as for a great many other artists and writers down
to the present day, society came to be seen not as the institution-
alised defender and protector of humane values, of 'the good life,'

but as a vast, imponderable, unregenerate mass, destructive of everything the good life embodies.

Where the Augustan artist is typically the spokesman for, the defender of, the ideals of his society, the Romantic artist is again and again the defender of ideals to which he feels his society is hostile. Seeing society in this light, as something by definition destructive of individual values, how could the post-Augustan writer respond? How could he preserve and defend those values in which he believed? One method was that of strategic withdrawal. The artist embraced his alienation from society, defined himself as artist precisely by that alienation, and proclaimed the absolute autonomy of art and artistic values. The other was the method of counter-attack, by which the artist provided society with images of its own repressiveness and destructiveness, and by so doing implicitly or explicitly pointed the way to social reformation.

It has already been noted that Romanticism involved a new interest in the individual—in the individual and his personal response to experience; a cultivation then of the feelings, of the individual sensibility. But the question of the relationship between the individual response and the established, impersonal, social realities, between what might be called the private and public visions of reality, is at once problematical. The artist who pursues the first of the methods mentioned above—the method that may produce the doctrine of art for art's sake—unhesitatingly follows his private vision to the total disregard of any kind of public reality. He is committed, in other words, to the cultivation of the self, the individual sensibility. The artist who follows the second way—the prototype of what we understand by the committed writer—also pursues a private vision; only to realise it he becomes preoccupied with the external, social reality. Neither method, that is, successfully overcomes the difficulty of relating the private and public worlds, the inner world of private sensibility and the outer world of social reality.

Jane Austen was probably the last English writer for whom these two worlds could be readily reconciled—and of course Jane Austen looks back to the eighteenth century rather than on to the nineteenth. Certainly the work of her contemporaries and successors manifests no such harmonious reconciliation; rather have private sensibility and public reality remained firmly opposed to each other. Once the personal response to experience was allowed superior validity, perhaps such an opposition followed inevitably; certainly once the artistic effort itself came to be identified wholly with the cultivation of the individual sensibility, once the private vision came to be equated with the life of the imagination, then reconciliation was problematical indeed.

But for the majority of Victorian writers an unheeding pursuit of the private vision, at the expense of the surrounding social reality, was never even a possibility. Most of the Victorians were all too aware of that social reality with its orthodoxies of conduct and beliefs, established and sanctioned by custom, tradition, and even religion. For most of the Victorians society represented a reality that could not be denied or ignored, towards which the artist as man, and probably as artist too, owed certain responsibilities, certain duties. It is, in fact, the recognition and acceptance of these duties and responsibilities which create the 'divided self' of the typical Victorian artist, drawn by both the public and private worlds. The Victorian artist comes more and more to identify the sources of his creative inspiration with something that is private and individual, something entirely detached from the normal, social world, something which may even be inimical to that everyday world of moral choices and responsibilities. Carried to an extreme, this identification of the sources of creative inspiration with something dangerously private and non-moral, brings the artist to a basic mistrust of the imagination itself, to the belief that the palace of art may be a lotos island, a seduction from the real world of essential moral responsibility. Wordsworth, Tennyson, Arnold, Charlotte Brontë, George Eliot, George Meredith—all of them were aware of such a danger. And surely it is feelings of a similar kind about the status of the imaginative process which underlie most of the modern arguments in favour of commitment.

But 'duty'—the escape route from the self—which we may fairly see as the Victorian version of 'commitment', did not prove itself a powerful, creative stimulus. The careers of, say, Wordsworth and Tennyson rather suggest the reverse. 'Duty', seen as something opposed to the cultivation, or indulgence, of the individual sensibility, seems to have had a deadening effect upon that sensibility, that is, upon the springs of creative expression. Only when the conflict between the private and public

worlds was raised to the level of a dialogue between 'duty' and
the 'self' did any kind of imaginative release follow—as novels
such as *Jane Eyre, The Mill on the Floss,* and *The Ordeal of
Richard Feverel* suggest.

The doctrine of the essentially private and individual nature
of the aesthetic response to experience, and of the autonomy of
that response, was one that survived unscathed in the literary
revolution that occurred early in this century. Hence the choice
for the modern writer between commitment and non-commit-
ment is essentially the same choice as his Victorian predecessor
made between duty and the self. No doubt, of course, the choice
is often not a fully conscious one, and no doubt, too, most writers
would be unwilling to accept either of the extreme positions ad-
vocated by its partisans. Certainly few of the great writers of the
twentieth century have been prepared to accept the logic of art
for art's sake; but few too, it seems to me, have been prepared
to accept engagement with the external, social reality as the
only kind of engagement that matters. To do so would amount
to a denial of the validity of the individual, feeling response
—which remains identified with the sources of the creative
process itself.

The example of those writers who have accepted the ideal of
commitment certainly does not suggest that commitment necessarily produces any kind of creative sterility. But commitment
does tend in practice to mean the rejection of whole areas of
human experience—areas accessible only through the exercise of
the individual sensibility. If over-cultivation of the private
sensibility leads to narrowness, limitation, and finally to a self-
indulgent turning away from the external world altogether,
commitment can lead to undesirable limitations of a different kind
—limitations in kinds of subject-matter and in methods of rendering experience. The committed writer tends to over-simplify; to
see human experience only in terms of the pattern to which he
is committed. This is perhaps the greatest weakness of all committed, social realist writing; the individual is seen as the helpless
victim of the murderous forces of history and society, and as
such he ceases to be an individual. In *The Grapes of Wrath,* for
example, the members of the Joad family are intended to be
representative of an underprivileged and exploited section of
American society. But their representative nature—the sense in

which they illustrate the pattern—seems in some typical way to act against their full imaginative realisation.

But the work of John Dos Passos himself provides us with a perfect symbol of the basic difficulty confronting the writer preoccupied with the nature of the external, social reality. *USA*, Dos Passos' trilogy about American society, greatly underrated by current fashions, is of course in the main dedicated to that reality. But Dos Passos is impelled to admit into this public world, the other private, passional world of the individual sensibility: hence the recurring device of the Camera Eye which renders the individual response to experience.

Dos Passos' instinct that the private and public visions of the individual and society must be combined is clearly a sound one. And one may go on believing that some kind of reconciliation can be obtained irrespective of whether one begins with Dos Passos' 'murderous forces of history' or with Fitzgerald's exploration of the individual consciousness.

THE
END
OF
THE
NOVEL

Leslie
Fiedler

Novelist, poet, critic, Leslie A. Fiedler (1917–)
is the unusual combination of gifted teacher and
incisive social critic. After some years as a professor of
English and Director of the Humanities Program
at Montana State University, he has taken up
residence at the State University of New York
(Buffalo). A linguist of unusual gifts, he speaks
several languages, including Japanese, and has
been a Fulbright Fellow and Lecturer in Rome
and Paris. To date his most sustained, penetrating
book is Love and Death in the American Novel
(1960). The essay which follows invites
comparison and contrast with the article of
similar theme and intent, "Decline of the Novel,"
by Ortega y Gasset. Surely it is the achieve-
ment of both essays to make us consider
what we really cherish in the novel, and want,
against any odds, to preserve in literature.

And what is there for Burroughs to do with the
novel in his present future, his anticipation of
non-human times? Nothing, of course, but to
destroy it; or rather, to make clear that it has
already destroyed itself; for it is a form which
realized itself in the mid-eighteenth century, precisely at the moment that men become conscious
of their unconscious minds and resolved to redeem them. And it is hard to see how it can outlive the faith of the first novelists in the power of
reason to know even the irrational. There are
various ways to declare the death of the novel: to
mock it while seeming to emulate it, like Nabokov, or John Barth; to reify it into a collection of
objects like Robbe-Grillet; or to *explode* it, like
William Burroughs, to leave only twisted fragments of experience and the miasma of death. The
latter seems, alas, the American way; and it is
certainly the way which has haunted Burroughs,
whose recent work has been impregnated with
the image of the Nova, the flare-up of an explod-

ing planet, which blends into, on the one hand, the glare and
terror of the atom bomb, and, on the other, the spatter and release
of orgasm. "A new mythology," Burroughs comments, explain-
ing this very image like the good science-fictionist he is, "is possible in the space age."

But what form will emerge to embody that mythology? Surely
nothing Burroughs himself has been able to contrive; for since he
has been thrown back on his own largely mechanical and magical
devices; since, that is to say, Ginsberg last put the semblance of a
book together for him, he has seemed repetitious, dull, and long-
winded. The nausea of the end has an intrinsic appeal as strong as
that of pornography itself; but for a long time Burroughs has
lived simply on the basis of that appeal. Only the belated discovery of his early work has given him now the reputation of a
new and currently rewarding writer.

Perhaps, though, we do not have to believe Burroughs, who has
a special stake in declaring the end of everything. Perhaps, after
all, the novel still flourishes in the United States in forms too
conventional to be noticed by those determined to pretend that
we have still, or at last, an avant-garde. Are not many of our
recent novels major efforts by major or immensely promising
writers? Do we not have big books by James Baldwin and Philip
Roth, Bernard Malamud, Robert Penn Warren and Mary Mc-
Carthy? Was there not a last book from Faulkner, as well as another by Nabokov, and even the twenty-years-promised-and-
delayed magnum opus of Katherine Anne Porter? Indeed, in
prospect, even those who know that fewer and fewer people buy
novels these days, and who for a long time have had a prevision
of the year in which every adult in the United States would write
a novel which no one else would read—even such professional
ironists have not been able to prevent a tremor of excitement
from unsettling their tranquil sense of doom.

But how every one of these books (except the anti-novel of
Nabokov) cheated our hopes: the Malamud slight and inconclu-
sive; the Roth morally obtuse and ill-organized; the Baldwin shrill
and unconvincing; the McCarthy intolerably "female" in the
worst sense; the Porter appallingly obvious and dull. Surely there
has never been so large a cluster of egregious flops in the span of
a couple of years; and surely it is not merely that, for quite different reasons unconnected with each other or with the general
cultural situation, so large a number of promising writers have

betrayed not only their extravagant promises but even our quite modest expectations. Is there no relationship at all between so general a failure and the fact, reported by publishers and known to every writer, that at the moment, in our country of 180,000,-000 people, a good first novel, prominently and favorably reviewed, may sell as few as 600 copies?

Yet any suggestion that the novel, after its brief two hundred years of existence, may be about to disappear, in the United States at least, lose its pre-eminence, its status as the reigning literary genre, is greeted by howls of dismay and hoots of contempt. Such predictions are received not with the pious lack of interest or mild concern common to literary statements, but with the sort of agitation more appropriate to a surmise that the United States may be approaching its final days as a significant power, or that the Church of Rome has outlived its last accommodation. To many earnest types I meet and read, forecasts of the death of the novel seem even *more* unnerving than comments on the death of the Republic or of God, the end of the family, or the overthrow of the male sex.

This must be, it occurs to me, because we cannot imagine anything after the novel that is still literature, cannot conceive of an alternative form which will provide all the satisfactions of the novel, including the exercise of those prestigeful skills we call "reading." Such a failure does not, I think, reflect the weakness of our imaginations, but rather our appreciation of the fact that the novel is the last narrative art-form invented, or capable of being invented, for *literates*. Beyond it, we sense, lie only those forms to which we who read cannot help condescending a little: comic books, movies, television, etc. Most of us find it personally upsetting to confess, even to ourselves, that the reigning narrative art of the not-so-distant future may well be one appropriate to a post-literate culture; and this despite our realization that it becomes more and more difficult to write what most people mean when they say a "book," a recognizable novel.

Still, we tell ourselves, there will always be the novels which have survived; even if no one ever writes another *Moby Dick*, someone will be around to read the first one. And surely it will have been preserved to be read by an interested élite, however marginal literacy may become. That novels like *Moby Dick* will survive, I cannot doubt; and it pleases me to envision a tiny few gathering in that world, perhaps half-secretly, to discuss with each other the remaining great books, the reading of which has become an art as learned and abstruse, and suspect, as deciphering heiroglyphics. Meanwhile everyone else will be acquiring only the simple skills required to follow the pidgin used in the sub-titles of foreign movies or to consult the schedule of the day's television programs.

If the novel disappears, then, it will have disappeared for two quite different reasons: First because the artistic faith that sustained its writers is dead, and second because the audience-need it was invented to satisfy is being better satisfied otherwise. From the consumer's point of view, the novel came into existence at the paradoxical insistence of a hitherto illiterate middle-class audi-ence that everyone be given the skills necessary for deciphering words on a page, and yet that no one be required to practice those skills against his will. The demand for the extension of literacy and the reservation of the right to reject literacy were thus bound up together from the first, and no literary form extant at the moment of their formulation seemed capable of satisfying both at once. What history required (and what those who stood in its vanguard were willing to pay for) was a new genre which made possible symbolic, or perhaps better, demon-stration literacy. This represents a typical demand and a typical solution of the modern world, of mass industrial society, which has gone on to demand and get, along similar lines, demonstration trials (the Reichstag trial, the Moscow trials) and demonstration voting—either in the form of the two-party-choice, much ad-mired in the democracies, or of the single-party-plebiscite favored in totalitarian regimes.

From any traditional point of view, then, from the standpoint, say, of those still pledged in the eighteenth century to writing epics in verse, the novel seemed already anti-literature, even post-literature; that is, it appeared then precisely what we take tele-vision or comic books to be now. In the jargon of our own day, the novel represents the beginnings of popular culture, of that machine-made, mass-produced, mass-distributed *ersatz* which, un-like either traditional high art or folk art, *does not know its place*; since, while pretending to meet the formal standards of literature, it is actually engaged in smuggling into the republic of letters extra-literary satisfactions. It not merely instructs and delights and moves, but also embodies the myths of a society, serves as the scriptures of an underground religion; and these latter functions, unlike the former ones, depend not at all on any particular form, but can be indifferently discharged by stained-glass windows, comic strips, ballads, and movies.

Yet it is precisely this cultural *ambiguity* of the novel which made it for so long so popular on so many levels, at the same time creating those tensions and contradictions by virtue of which it is presently dying. From the first, there have been, certainly, two kinds of novel, not always clearly distinguished from each other (sometimes because of the blessed un-self-consciousness of their writers; sometimes because of their deviousness): the bestseller, ill-written and scriptural, and at home in the world of mass culture; and the art novel, a hybrid form into which men of talent and the highest ambitions have poured certain insights and perceptions no longer viable in traditional forms—including basic criticisms of mass culture itself. It is for this reason that the serious artist has had to *fight* for the attention of the audience which invented the genre he exploits and resents his attempt to use that genre against its own values and aspirations. But in modern times there has been no other audience.

The serious novelist has, then, tended simultaneously to woo and to war on the bourgeois world; which in turn has both wooed and warred on him by adapting to its own uses (i.e., by turning into stereotypes) the very devices he has used to mock it. Pornography, horror, the merciless documentation of the sordid which we call "naturalism," even the attack on mass culture itself, have been assimilated into mass culture; just as the favorite refuges of the artist, his bohemias and places of exile, have been transformed into tourist attractions; and his very vices, from tobacco to marijuana, have become country-club diversions.

The only unredeemable offense against middlebrow culture in the power of the novelist is to consider his work as absolute art: a form which aspires to the condition of poetry, and which refuses the weary reader any possibility of forgetting that he is reading *words*, dealing not with archetypes only, but with nuances of language, and the strategies of form. The perpetrators of that ultimate offense have already been immortalized in scandal; and the names of Proust, Mann, Joyce, and Kafka, for instance, stir still in some quarters the uneasy grimace and the embarrassed snicker. In the United States, however, there has never been an unequivocal avant-gardist among the novelists of first rank. What experimentalism there has been in our fiction has been imported and, at the moment of importation, accommodated to middlebrow demands. Think, for instance, of how the example of Joyce's *Portrait of the Artist as a Young Man* is modified in Thomas Wolfe's *Look Homeward, Angel.*

As early as the twenties, certain of our writers had learned from the example of the European avant-garde simply to do otherwise: Scott Fitzgerald, for instance, Glenway Wescott and, after a brief period of indecision, Kay Boyle. Others took longer to accommodate themselves, like Katherine Anne Porter, who only in the past few years has clearly exposed herself as having gone over to ladies'-magazine fiction; while Hemingway's and Faulkner's final apostasy to art is revealed only in their last works, and, especially, in the works of their followers. There is, in the American grain, an implicit anti-intellectualism, a contempt for mere art (of which Mark Twain is a chief source) which threatens always to turn our writers against their fellows and to deliver them into the hands of their enemies. However, so long as the counter-tendency to avant-gardism ran strong in the Western world in general, this native American know-nothingism cast a valuable counterbalance, protecting our novelists against becoming academicians of the new.

There is now, however, nothing to stem a world-wide drift toward middlebrow art except the sterile and academic nostalgia for yesterday's avant-garde on the part of such European writers as Alain Robbe-Grillet. Everywhere else there are signs of a great revolt against the aspirations of the novel to art, a turning on the part of novelists themselves—without outside pressure—toward the mass audience. Included in this great middlebrow revolt are writers as different from each other as Yael Dayan in Israel, Françoise Sagan in France, Kingsley Amis and John Wain in England; and in America, Jack Kerouac, J. D. Salinger, Truman Capote, Herbert Gold, Vance Bourjaily, perhaps even Philip Roth.

Some of these writers, in America, at least, are harder to recognize as Philistines than, say, Irwin Shaw or James Gould Cozzens because, to begin with, they are younger, and because there attaches to them, for one reason or another, a certain avant-garde cachet. They are likely to appear in magazines, with avant-garde pretensions or an avant-garde past (the *Evergreen Review*, for instance, or *Partisan Review*); and they may even lead lives more like those once led by avant-garde artists than by most of the readers to whom they actually appeal. Moreover, they have failed to develop a new or notable Philistine style, writing, whether ill or well, in manners associated not so long ago with experimental writers of the first rank. And finally, they may not even know they write for the great audience, since, in fact, they often don't get its attention. Certain writers of the school of Saul Bellow (not including Bellow himself), Herbert Gold, for instance, could in this regard cry out in all truth, "How can I be as bad as the critics say I am, when I'm not even popular?"

The disconcerting fact suggested by such cases is this: at the moment when a considerable wave of semi-serious writers find themselves, deliberately or not, wooing the mass audience for the novel, that audience has begun to detach itself from the novel completely. After all, what does the largest sub-literate public need fiction for? What documentary realism once promised to give them in novel form, non-fiction provides more efficiently, more painlessly. And the mythical reassurances they have long sought in books (boy gets girl, good man kills bad, etc.) the non-literary arts of television and film provide more vividly and at less intellectual cost. At the same moment, those non-literary arts satisfy more fully, less hypocritically than the hybrid novel form ever could, the revulsion of the great audience from the very act of reading, their half-secret, shamefaced hatred of the literacy which once they had found it politically expedient to demand.

In the end, what the neo-middlebrow movements succeed in doing is not (as some exponents of that movement may fondly hope) to raise the level of the mass audience, but to substitute, for the former élite, a pseudo-élite conditioned to *kitsch*, corn, and self-congratulation. The rejection of literacy by the mass audience and the betrayal of standards by the semi-artist combine with the onslaught against the novel form by the exponents of the alteration of consciousness to doom that genre, or at least to make the possibility of that doom a leading item on the agenda of contemporary criticism. I, myself, though I practice the art of the novel ironically and desperately in a world which provides me no assurances about the nature, or even existence, of such an audience as I dream, am inclined to believe that the history of the genre is approaching its end.

I do not mean, of course, that I have lost faith in the survival of the art of fiction, for I cannot conceive a human situation in which stories are not somehow told, and I do not myself foresee the end of man. Perhaps narrative will not continue much longer to be entrusted to print and bound between hard covers. But this does not especially dismay me, since I have no special affection for the novel as such: that fat, solid commodity invented by the bourgeoisie for the ends of commerce and culture-climbing. There is always the screen, if the page proves no longer viable: the neighborhood movie, the drive-in, or the parlor television set. And I presume that if cinema eventually becomes a lost art, too, there will be some of us scratching pictographs on the walls of caves, or telling each other stories over bonfires made of the last historical romance hailed as the novel of the year in the last book review section of the last *New York Times*.

As a philosopher and aesthetician, José Ortega y Gasset (1883–1955) brings uncommon weight and sensibility to bear on the possible future of the novel. Nevertheless, the author's implied assumptions concerning the nature of the artist's

DECLINE

OF

THE

NOVEL

imagination, the possible variety of human emotion, character, and motive, the nature of literary "materials" all demand close inspection. For example, if it were once true that novels did not "sell well" as he says in his opening statement, that is hardly the case today. Does this discrepancy, in itself, either refute or substantiate the argument on that point?

*José Ortega
y Gasset*

Publishers complain that novels do not sell well, and it is true that the reading public buys fewer novels while the demand for books of a theoretical character is relatively increasing. This statistical fact, even if there were no more intrinsic reasons, would suffice to make us suspect that something is amiss with the literary genre of the novel. When I hear a friend, particularly if he is a young writer, calmly announce that he is working on a novel I am appalled, and I feel that in his case I should be trembling in my boots. Perhaps I am wrong, but I cannot help scenting behind such an equanimity an alarming dose of incomprehension. To produce a good novel has always been a difficult thing. But while, before, it was enough to have talent the difficulty has now grown immeasurably, for to be a gifted novelist is no longer a guaranty for producing a good novel.

Unawareness of this fact is one component of the aforementioned incomprehension. Anyone who gives a little thought to the conditions of a work of art must admit that a literary genre may wear out. One cannot dismiss the subject by comfortably assuming that artistic creation depends on nothing but the artist's personal power called inspiration or talent—in which case decadence of a genre would be due exclusively to an accidental lack of talents, and the sudden appearance of a man of genius would at any time automatically turn the tide. Better beware of notions like genius and inspiration; they are a sort of magic wand and should be used sparingly by anybody who wants to see things clearly. Imagine a woodsman, the strongest of woodsmen, in the Sahara desert. What good are his bulging muscles and his sharp ax? A woodsman without woods is an abstraction. And the same applies to artists. Talent is but a subjective disposition that is brought to bear upon a certain material. The material is independent of individual gifts; and when it is lacking genius and skill are of no avail.

Just as every animal belongs to a species, every literary work belongs to a genre. (The theory of Benedetto Croce who denies the existence of literary forms in this sense has left no trace in aesthetics.) A literary genre, the same as a zoological species, means a certain stock of possibilities; and since in art only those possibilities count which are different enough not to be considered replicas of one another, the resources of a literary genre are definitely limited. It is erroneous to think of the novel—and I refer to the modern novel in particular—as of an endless field capable of rendering ever new forms. Rather it may be compared to a vast but finite quarry. There exist a definite number of possible themes for the novel. The workmen of the primal hour had no trouble finding new blocks—new characters, new themes. But present-day writers face the fact that only narrow and concealed veins are left them.

With this stock of objective possibilities, which is the genre, the artistic talent works, and when the quarry is worked out, talent, however great, can achieve nothing. Whether a genre is altogether done for can, of course, never be decided with mathematical rigor; but it can at times be decided with sufficient practical approximation. At least, that the material is getting scarce may appear frankly evident.

This, I believe, is now happening to the novel. It has become practically impossible to find new subjects. Here we come upon the first cause of the enormous difficulty, an objective not a personal difficulty, of writing an acceptable novel at this advanced stage.

During a certain period novels could thrive on the mere

novelty of their subjects which gratuitously added an induced current, as it were, to the value proper of the material. Thus many novels seemed readable which we now think a bore. It is not for nothing that the novel is called "novel." The difficulty of finding new subjects is accompanied by another, perhaps more serious, dilemma. As the store of possible subjects is more and more depleted the sensibility of the reading public becomes subtler and more fastidious. Works that yesterday would still have passed, today are deemed insipid. Not only is the difficulty of finding new subjects steadily growing, but ever "newer" and more extraordinary ones are needed to impress the reader. This is the second cause of the difficulty with which the genre as such is faced in our time.

Proof that the present decline is due to more fundamental causes than a possibly inferior quality of contemporary novels is given by the fact that, as it becomes more difficult to write novels, the famous old or classical ones appear less good. Only a very few have escaped drowning in the reader's boredom.

This development is inevitable and need not dishearten the novelists. On the contrary; for they themselves are bringing it about. Little by little they train their public by sharpening the perception, and refining the taste, of their readers. Each work that is better than a previous one is detrimental to this and all others of the same level. Triumph cannot help being cruel. As the victor wins the battle at the cost of smashing the foe, thus the superior work automatically becomes the undoing of scores of other works that used to be highly thought of.

In short, I believe that the genre of the novel, if it is not yet irretrievably exhausted, has certainly entered its last phase, the scarcity of possible subjects being such that writers must make up for it by the exquisite quality of the other elements that compose the body of a novel.

Michel Butor (1926–   ), born near Lille, was taken
to Paris at age three, and after university studies
became a teacher. After posts in Upper Egypt,
Salonica, and Geneva, Butor came to Bryn Mawr
as a visiting professor; presently he resides, for
the most part, in France. Butor came to the novel
by studying philosophy and poetry, most notably
the English contemporary poets and the surrealists.
His novels combine an
interest in the phenome-
nological domain and the
didactic, epic possibilities of poetry. For
further reading of his experimental, extreme
fiction, which contributed a very great deal
to the French school
of the "new novel,"
see La Modification
(A Change of Heart,
1959) and Degrés
(Degrees, 1961).
In the essay below,
Butor brings
uncommon analytical
powers to bear on the well-established, popular
genre of science fiction.

THE CRISIS IN THE GROWTH OF SCIENCE FICTION

Michel
Butor

I

If the genre science fiction is rather difficult to
define—disputes among the experts afford super-
abundant proof of that—it is, at least, one of the
easiest to designate. It is enough to say "You
know, those stories that are always mentioning
interplanetary rockets" for the least-prepared in-
terlocutor to understand immediately what you
mean. This does not imply that any such apparatus occurs in every SF story; it may be replaced
by other accessories which will perform a comparable role. But it is the most usual, the typical,
example, like the magic wand in fairy tales.

Two remarks are immediately relevant:

1) There exists for the moment no interplanetary rocket. If there ever has been one, or if there

is one now, the ordinary reader knows nothing about it. A narrative in which a device of this kind occurs is therefore a narrative of fantasy.

2) But we all believe quite firmly that such devices will soon exist, that the question is no more than one of time—a few years of development. The apparatus is possible. This notion is fundamental, and requires some explanation.

It might be claimed that for the Arab storytellers, who believed in the power of magicians, flying carpets were also "possible." But for most of us, the possibility of rockets is of an altogether different order. It is guaranteed by what we might call, by and large, modern science, a sum of doctrines whose validity no serious Occidental dares question.

If the author of a narrative has taken the trouble to introduce such a device, it is because he chooses to depart from reality only to a certain degree, he wants to prolong or extend reality, but not to be separated from it. He wants to give us an impression of realism, he wants to insert the imaginary into the real, anticipating results already achieved. Such a narrative naturally situates its action in the future.

We can imagine, taking modern science in its broadest acceptance, not only other devices but technologies of all kinds—psychological, pedagogical, social, etc. This scientific guarantee may become increasingly loose, but it nonetheless constitutes the specificity of SF which we can define: a literature which explores the range of the possible, as science permits us to envision it.

It is, then, a fantasy framed by a realism.

The work of Jules Verne is the best example of SF to the first degree, which is justified by the results achieved and which uniquely anticipates certain applications. Wells inaugurates a SF to the second degree, much more audacious but much less convincing, which anticipates the results themselves. He lets us assume behind Cavor's machine, which will take the first men to the moon, an explanation of a scientific type, one that conforms to a possible science which will develop from the science of his time.

II

The SF tourist agencies offer their customers three main types of spectacles which we can group under the following rubrics: life in the future, unknown worlds, unexpected visitors.

1) *Life in the Future*

We start from the world as we know it, from the society which surrounds us. We introduce a certain number of changes whose consequences we attempt to foresee. By a projection into the future, we open up the complexity of the present, we develop certain still-larval aspects. SF of this type is a remarkable instrument of investigation in the tradition of Swift. It readily assumes a satiric aspect. We shall find excellent examples in the works of Huxley (*Brave New World*), Orwell (*1984*), Werfel (*Star of the Unborn*), Hesse (*Magister Ludi*), Bradbury, etc.

2) *Unknown Worlds*

It suffices to mention the name Ray Bradbury, whose best-known work is called *The Martian Chronicles*, to see that an altogether different element occurs here, almost of necessity.

Technological progress has for its goal not only the transformation of our daily life but also the satisfaction of our curiosity. New instruments, new sciences, must allow us to discover domains of reality which are hidden from us today. Within the scientific representation of the world, there are enormous districts which our imagination is free to populate with strange beings and landscapes according to its whim, subject to several very broad restrictions. Here we can project our dreams.

This aspect of SF links up with a very respectable tradition. Dante, when he locates his inferno inside the globe, his purgatory at the antipodes and his paradise in the stars, is merely projecting his theology, and a good deal more, into the empty spaces which medieval cosmology reserved.

Thus Verne scrupulously inventoried the lacunae of the geography of his age and filled them with myths inscribed within the extension of the known facts, achieving a synthesis which strikes us as naïve but which by its breadth and harmony outstrips anything his successors have attempted.

When an author of the eighteenth century wanted to give his story some appearance of reality, he had a ready-made site in which to locate it: the islands of the Pacific. (Cf. Diderot: *Supplément au Voyage de Bougainville*.) Today, when the exploration of the earth's surface is quite advanced, we prefer to locate our islands in the sky. But if we once knew nothing, of course, of the archipelagos which had not yet been discovered, we were at least quite sure that apart from certain remarkable peculiarities they could not be very different from those we knew already. We were still on the same Earth, with the same general conditions.

On the other hand, the little we know today about the islands of the sky proves to us that everything must be very different there. We know that gravity is more powerful on Venus, less powerful on Mars, than on Earth, etc. These several elements oblige the writer who respects them to make an enormous effort of imagination, force him to invent something truly new. Unfortunately, the creation of another "nature," even when based on elementary information, is a task so arduous that no author, so far, has undertaken it methodically.

In order not to acknowledge ourselves vanquished, we raise our sights: instead of describing what might happen on Mars and Venus, we leap at once to the third planet of the epsilon system of Cygnus, or else, since in fact there is nothing to stop us once we have started on this path, planet n of star n in galaxy n. At first the reader is impressed by these cascades of light years; the solar system was certainly a wretched little village; here we are launched into the universe at large. But he soon realizes that these ultra-remote planets resemble the earth much more than they do its neighbors. Out of the immense number of stars which populate space, it is always permissible to imagine one on which the conditions of life are very close to those we know. The authors have rediscovered the islands of the eighteenth century. They employ a vaguely scientific jargon and decorate the sky with charming fantasies; the trick is turned.

This infinite freedom is a false freedom. If we flee infinitely far into space or time, we shall find ourselves in a region where everything is possible, where the imagination will no longer even need to make an effort of coordination. The result will be an impoverished duplication of everyday reality. We are told of an enormous war between galactic civilizations, but we see at once that the league of the democratic planets strangely resembles the UN, the empire of the Nebula of Andromeda stands for the Soviet Union as a subscriber to the *Reader's Digest* might conceive that nation, and so on. The author has merely translated into SF language a newspaper article he read the night before. Had he remained on Mars, he would have been obliged to invent something.

At its best moments, the SF that describes unknown worlds becomes an instrument of an extreme flexibility, thanks to which all kinds of political and moral fables, of fairy tales, of myths, can be transposed and adapted to modern readers. Anticipation has created a language by whose aid we can in principle examine everything.

3) *Unexpected Visitors*

The description of unknown worlds, in SF, necessarily becomes part of our anticipation, however rudimentary it may be; it is natural that it should affect that anticipation. It is not so much by the improvement of commercial relations that the invention of the compass transformed the Old World, but by the discovery of America. The description of unknown worlds and beings involves the description of their intervention in the future history of humanity.

We can easily imagine that the inhabitants of other planets have a civilization in advance of our own, hence that they have a realm of action superior to our own, that they are ahead of us in discovery.

All of space becomes threatening; strange beings may intervene even before we know of their existence. Most of the pre-Columbians had no expectation that a deadly invasion would come out of the East.

It is in Wells's *War of the Worlds* that we encounter this theme for the first time, and his countless imitators have not added much to it. It is a profoundly modern theme (it never occurred to anyone in the sixteenth century that Europe might be discovered in its turn) and an extremely powerful one (as several memorable radio broadcasts have demonstrated).

Thanks to this notion of intervention, SF can assimilate those aspects of the fantastic which at first seem most opposed to it: all that we might classify under the heading: "Superstitions."

In the *Divine Comedy*, Beatrice transports Dante from planet to planet; in Father Kircher's *Iter Ecstaticum*, an angel does the job; we are not yet in SF, which implies that the journey is made as a result of a technology developed by man. But this technology will allow us to enter into contact with beings to whom we can attribute knowledge we do not possess, technologies we do not understand. It might, of course, occur to one of them to come to Earth, to carry one of us off and transport him elsewhere by

means which there is no longer any need to explain. The difference between such a being and Kircher's angel becomes infinites-
imal; only the language has changed. As a matter of fact, in order
to gain a sufficient suspension of disbelief, today it is necessary
that the being be described in the same way as a being that man
might have discovered on another planet. Thus we could unite
within SF all the narratives of phantoms and demons, all the old
myths which speak of superior beings that intervene in the life
of men. Certain tales by H. P. Lovecraft illustrate this possibility.

C. S. Lewis begins his curious antimodern trilogy with a novel
which has all of SF's characteristics: *Out of the Silent Planet.*
Two wicked scientists transport a young philologist to Mars by
means of a spaceship furnished with every modern convenience.
In the second volume, *Perelandra*, the author drops his mask: it is
an angel who transports the philologist to Venus; as for the
scientists, they are Satan's henchmen.

III

We see that all kinds of merchandise can be sold under the label
SF; and that all kinds of merchandise seek to be packaged under
this label. Hence it seems that SF represents the normal form of
mythology in our time: a form which is not only capable of revealing profoundly new themes, but also capable of integrating
all the themes of the old literature.

Despite several splendid successes, we cannot help thinking that
SF is keeping very few of its promises.

This is because SF, by extending itself, is denaturing itself; it
is gradually losing its specificity. It furnishes a very particular
element of credibility; this element is increasingly weakened when
it is utilized without discernment. SF is fragile, and the enormous
circulation it has achieved in recent years merely renders it
more so.

We have already noted that the flight to ultra-distant planets
and epochs, which seems at first glance a conquest, actually masks
the authors' incapacity to imagine in a coherent fashion, in conformity with the requirements of "science," the planets or the
epochs which are closer at hand. Similarly the divination of a
future science affords, surely, a great freedom, but we soon discover that it is above all a revenge of the authors against their incapacity to master the entire range of contemporary science.

The day is long past when an Aristotle could be the first researcher of his age in every domain, and the day when a Pico could claim to defend a thesis *De omni re scibili*; but the day is also past when a Verne could easily handle the notions implied in all the technological applications achieved in his age, and anticipate other applications while remaining perfectly clear to the secondary-school students who formed his public.

Today the notions implied in devices as common as a radio set or an atomic bomb exceed by a good deal the average reader's level of scientific culture. He uses without understanding; he accepts without asking explanations; and the author takes advantage of this situation, which frequently causes him to multiply his blunders—for he too generally lacks a sufficient knowledge of the notions he is obliged to use—or causes him to seem backward, a grave accusation when one is claiming to reveal the mysteries of 200,000 years hence.

As a result SF, which should derive the greatest part of its prestige from its precision, remains vague. The story does not truly manage to take shape. And when the scientists themselves begin writing, they quite often prove their ignorance of disciplines unfamiliar to them and their difficulty in vulgarizing their specialty.

SF is distinguished from the other genres of the fantastic by the special kind of plausibility it introduces. This plausibility is in direct proportion to the solid scientific elements the author introduces. If they fail, SF becomes a dead form, a stereotype.

IV

Hence we understand why few authors risk specifying the details of their image of a transformed world. It is an undertaking, indeed, which supposes not only a scientific culture far above the average, but also a knowledge of present reality comparable to that supposed by a novel of the realistic type, and finally an enormous effort of coordination. The author is generally content to evoke a future world "in general," one which might just as well be located in 1975 as in 19750, a world characterized by the widespread use of plastic substances, of television, and of atomic-powered rockets. It is within this setting that he will briefly develop what is often a highly ingenious idea. In another tale, he will use this same background in order to develop another idea, without taking the trouble to coordinate them. The result is an infinity of variously sketched futures, all independent of one another and generally contradictory. We shall have, in the same way, an infinity of Venuses, each of which diminishes the plausibility of the rest.

This dispersion has monotony as its direct consequence, for the authors, since they renounce constructing systematically, can describe only in a rudimentary fashion and depart only slightly from banality.

It appears that SF has begun with the cake. It had things too much its own way: it was once enough to mention Martians to enthrall the reader. But the time has come when the reader will notice that most of these monsters, despite their crests, their tentacles, their scales, are much less different from the average American than an ordinary Mexican. SF has cut the grass under its own feet, has spoiled thousands of ideas. The doors have been thrown open to start on a great quest, and we discover we are still walking round and round the house. If the authors scamp their texts, it is because they realize that an effort to improve them would lead to an impasse.

The SF narratives derive their power from a great collective dream we are having, but for the moment they are incapable of giving it a unified form. It is a mythology in tatters, impotent, unable to orient our action in any precise way.

v

But the last word has not been said, and it is certainly possible that SF will surmount this crisis in its growth.

It has the power to solicit our belief in an entirely new way, and it is capable of affording, in its description of the possible, a marvelous precision. But to realize its full power, it must undergo a revolution, it must succeed in unifying itself. It must become a collective work, like the science which is its indispensable basis.

We all dream of clean, well-lighted cities, so that when an author situates a narrative in such a place, he is certain of striking a sympathetic note. But we find ourselves, in the present state of SF, facing an enormous choice of barely sketched future cities among which the imagination hesitates, unsatisfied.

Everyone knows Heraclitus' famous fragment: "Those who

are awakened are in the same world, but those who sleep are each in a separate world." Our dreamers' worlds are simultaneously without communication and very much like one another. The classical mythologies united the common elements of these dreams into unique and public myths.

Now, let us imagine that a certain number of authors, instead of describing at random and quite rapidly certain more or less interchangeable cities, were to take as the setting of their stories a single city, named and situated with some precision in space and in future time; that each author were to take into account the descriptions given by the others in order to introduce his own new ideas. This city would become a common possession to the same degree as an ancient city that has vanished; gradually, all readers would give its name to the city of their dreams and would model that city in its image.

SF, if it could limit and unify itself, would be capable of acquiring over the individual imagination a constraining power comparable to that of any classical mythology. Soon all authors would be obliged to take this predicted city into account, readers would organize their actions in relation to its imminent existence, ultimately they would find themselves obliged to build it. Then SF would be veracious, to the very degree that it realized itself.

It is easy to see what a prodigious instrument of liberation or oppression it could become.

This is a closely reasoned, densely written essay by a critic and theorist who has become the literary voice of structuralism, that central movement in modern French thought. The difficulties of the essay are worth struggling with, for Barthes says a great deal about the elusive subject of structuralist methodology and in effect defines the methodology by his use of it. More important, he offers a defense for literature which altogether rescues it from functioning in the service of other disciplines. Unlike the scientist who stands outside his work when he talks about it, the writer of literature "can practise language in its totality." Literature, as Barthes sees it, makes no facile distinctions between subject and object. What a writer says and the way he says it are one and the same thing, or rather, are all the same things: "The literary word is at once a cultural reference, a rhetorical model, a deliberately ambiguous utterance and a simple indicative unit...."

SCIENCE VERSUS LITERATURE

Roland Barthes

These terms may seem to echo the special interests and "codes"—to use a basic structuralist word—of such leading representatives of structuralist procedure as the anthropologist Claude Lévi-Strauss and the psychologist Jean Piaget, turning literature once again in the direction of science. In fact, Barthes ends his essay by stressing the high place of pleasure in literature—"of what might be called the Eros of language"—and by attempting to turn science in the direction of literature.

French university departments keep an official list of the social and human sciences recognized as being taught, and are thus restricted to awarding degrees in specific subjects; it is possible to become a doctor of aesthetics, psychology or sociology, but not of heraldry, semantics or victimology. It is thus the institution which directly determines the nature of human knowledge, by imposing its own modes of division and classification on it, in exactly the same way that a language, with its "compulsory headings" (and not only its exclusions), obliges us to think in a certain way. In other words, science (this word will henceforth be taken here to mean the social and human sciences as a whole) is defined not by its content (often ill-determined and labile) nor by its method (this varies from science to science: what do historical science and experimental psychology have in common?) nor by its ethic (science is not alone in being serious-minded and rigorous) nor by its mode of communication (science is printed in books, like everything else), but simply by its *status*, that is its determination by society: the subject-matter of science is everything that society deems worthy of being handed on. In short, science is what is taught.

Literature has all the secondary characteristics of science, that is, all those attributes which do not define it. Its contents are exactly the same as those of science; there is certainly not a single scientific topic that has not been dealt with at some point in the world's literature. The world of the literary work is a total one, in which all knowledge, social, psychological or historical, has a place, with the result that for us literature has that great cosmogonic unity which the ancient Greeks enjoyed but which we are denied today by the fragmented state of our sciences. Moreover, like science, literature has its methods; it has its programmes of research, which vary from school to school and age to age (again like those of science), its rules of investigation and sometimes even its pretensions to experiment. Like science, literature also has its ethic, a certain way of extracting the rules governing its practice from the view it takes of its own nature and, consequently, of submitting its projects to a certain sense of the absolute.

There is one last feature which not only unites science and literature but also divides them more surely than any other of their differences: they are both discursive (the ancient idea of the *logos* expressed this very well). But science and literature do not assume or, if one prefers, profess the language which constitutes both of them in the same way. As far as science is concerned language is simply an instrument, which it profits it to make as transparent and neutral as possible: it is subordinate to the matter of science (workings, hypotheses, results) which, so it is said, exists outside language and precedes it. On the one hand and *first* there is the content of the scientific message, which is everything; on the other hand and *next*, the verbal form responsible for expressing that content, which is nothing. It is no coincidence that, from the sixteenth century onwards, the corporate blossoming of empiricism, rationalism and an evidential religion (with the Reformation), that is, of the scientific spirit in the widest sense of the term, should have been accompanied by a regression in the autonomy of language, henceforth relegated to the rank of instrument or "fine style," whereas in the Middle Ages human culture had shared out the secrets of speech and nature almost equally, under the headings of the Seven Liberal Arts.

For literature, on the other hand, or at any rate that literature which has freed itself from classicism and humanism, language can no longer be the convenient instrument or the superfluous backcloth of a social, emotional or poetic "reality" which pre-exists it, and which it is language's subsidiary responsibility to express, by means of submitting itself to a number of stylistic rules. Language is literature's Being, its very world; the whole of literature is contained in the act of writing, and no longer in those of "thinking," "portraying," "telling" or "feeling." Technically, as Roman Jakobson has defined it, the "poetic" (i.e., the literary) refers to that type of message which takes as its object not its content but its own form. Ethically, it is only by its passage through language that literature can continue to shake loose the essential concepts of our culture, one of the chief among which is the "real." Politically, it is by professing and illustrating that no language is innocent, by practising what might be called "integral language" that literature is revolutionary. Thus today literature finds itself bearing unaided the entire responsibility for language, for although science has a certain need of language it is not, like literature, *in* language. The one is taught, that is, expressed and exhibited, the other is fulfilled rather than transmitted (only its history being taught). Science is spoken, literature written, the one is led by the voice, the other follows the hand; they do not both have the same physical body and hence the same desire behind them.

Since it turns essentially on a certain way of taking language, conjured away into thin air in one case and assumed in the other, the opposition between science and literature is of particular importance for structuralism. Agreed that this word, most often imposed from outside, is today applied to projects that are very

diverse, sometimes divergent and sometimes even antagonistic, and
no one can arrogate the right to speak in its name. The present
writer does not claim to be doing so, but retains contemporary
"structuralism" only in its most specialized and consequently most
relevant version, using it to mean a certain mode of analysis of
cultural artefacts, in so far as this mode originates in the methods
of contemporary linguistics. This is to say that structuralism, itself
developed from a linguistic model, finds in literature, which is
the work of language, an object that has much more than an
affinity with it; the two are homogeneous. Their coincidence
does not exclude a certain confusion or even cleavage, according
to whether structuralism sets out to maintain a scientific distance
between itself and its object or whether, on the oher hand, it
agrees to compromise and abandon the analysis of which it is the
bearer in that infinitude of language that today passes through
literature; in short, whether it elects to be science or writing.

As a science, structuralism can be said to "find itself" at each
level of the literary work. First, at the level of the content or, to
be more exact, of the form of the content, since it seeks to establish the "language" of the stories that are told, their articulation,
their units and the logic which links these together; in short, the
general mythology in which each literary work shares. Secondly,
at the level of the forms of discourse. By virtue of its method
structuralism gives special attention to classification, hierarchies
and arrangements; its essential object is the taxonomy or distribu-
tive model which every human creation, be it institution or book,
inevitably establishes, since there can be no culture without classification. Now the discourse, or the complex of words superior to
the phrase, has its own forms of organization; it too is a classification and a classification which signifies. In this respect structuralism has an august forebear whose historical role has generally been
underestimated or discredited for ideological reasons: Rhetoric,
that impressive attempt by a whole culture to analyse and classify
the forms of speech, and to make the world of language intelligible. And, finally, at the level of the words. The phrase does not
only have a literal or indicative sense, it is crammed with additional meanings. The literary word is at once a cultural reference,
a rhetorical model, a deliberately ambiguous utterance and a simple indicative unit; it has three dimensions, within which lies the
field of structural analysis, whose aims are much wider than those
of the old stylistics, based as they were on an erroneous idea of

"expressivity." At every level, therefore, be it that of the argument, the discourse or the words, the literary work offers structuralism the picture of a structure perfectly homological (present-day research is tending to prove this) with that of language itself. Structuralism has emerged from linguistics and in literature it finds an object which has itself emerged from language. We can understand then why structuralism should want to found a science of literature or, to be more exact, a linguistics of discourse, whose object is the "language" of literary forms, grasped on many levels. This aim is a comparatively new one, since until now literature has only been approached "scientifically" in a very marginal way, through the history of literary works, their authors, the schools they belong to, or the texts themselves (philology).

But although it may be a new aim it is not a satisfactory, or at least not a sufficient, one. It does nothing to solve the dilemma we spoke of at the beginning and which is suggested allegorically by the opposition between science and literature, in so far as the latter assumes its language under the name of writing, whereas the former evades it, by pretending to believe that this language is merely instrumental. In short, structuralism will be just one more "science" (several are born each century, some of them only ephemeral) if it does not manage to place the actual subversion of scientific language at the centre of its programme, that is, to "write itself." How could it fail to question the very language it uses in order to know language? The logical continuation of structuralism can only be to rejoin literature, no longer as an "object" of analysis but as the activity of writing, to do away with the distinction derived from logic which turns the work itself into a language-object and science into a meta-language, and thus to forgo that illusory privilege which science attaches to the possession of a captive language.

It remains therefore for the structuralist to turn himself into a "writer," certainly not in order to profess or practise "fine style," but in order to rediscover the crucial problems involved in every utterance, once it is no longer wrapped in the beneficent cloud of strictly *realist* illusions, which see language simply as the medium of thought. This transformation, still pretty theoretical it must be admitted, requires that certain things should be made clear or recognized. In the first place, the relationship between subjectivity and objectivity or, if one prefers, the place of the subject in his own work, can no longer be thought of as in the halcyon days of positivist science. Objectivity and rigour, those attributes of the scientist which are still used as a stick to beat us with, are essentially preparatory qualities necessary at the time of starting out on the work, and as such there is no cause to suspect or abandon them. But they are not qualities that can be transferred to the discourse itself, except by a sort of sleight-of-hand, a purely metonymical procedure which confuses *precaution* with its end-product in discourse. Every utterance implies its own subject, whether this subject be expressed in an apparently direct fashion, by the use of "I," or indirectly, by being referred to as "he," or avoided altogether by means of impersonal constructions. These are purely grammatical decoys, which do no more than vary the way in which the subject is constituted within the discourse, that is, the way he gives himself to others, theatrically or as a phantasm; they all refer therefore to forms of the imaginary. The most specious of these forms is the privative, the very one normally practised in scientific discourse, from which the scientist excludes himself because of his concern for objectivity. What is excluded, however, is always only the "person," psychological, emotional or biographical, certainly not the subject. It could be said more-over that this subject is heavy with the spectacular exclusion it has imposed on its person, so that, on the discursive level—one, be it remembered, which cannot be avoided—objectivity is as imaginary as anything else. In point of fact, only an integral formalization of scientific discourse (that of the human sciences, of course, since this has largely been achieved in the others) can preserve science from the risks of the imaginary, unless, naturally, it agrees to practise that imaginary *in the full awareness of what it is doing*, a knowledge that can only be attained by writing; only writing has a hope of removing the bad faith attaching to any language which is ignorant of itself.

Only writing, again, and this is a first step towards defining it, can practise language in its totality. To resort to scientific dis-course as if to an instrument of thought is to postulate that there exists a neutral state of language, from which a certain number of specialized languages, the literary or poetic languages for exam-ple, have derived, as so many deviants or embellishments. It is held that this neutral state would be the referential code for all the "ex-centric" languages, which themselves would be merely its subcodes. By identifying itself with this referential code, as the basis of all normality, scientific discourse is arrogating to itself a right which it is writing's duty precisely to contest. The notion of "writing" implies indeed that language is a vast system, none of whose codes is privileged or, if one prefers, central, and whose various departments are related in a "fluctuating hierarchy." Scientific discourse believes itself to be a superior code; writing aims at being a total code, including its own forces of destruction. It follows that writing alone can smash the theological idol set up by a paternalistic science, refuse to be terror-stricken by what is wrongly thought of as the "truth" of the content and of reasoning, and open up all three dimensions of language to research, with its subversions of logic, its mixing of codes, its shifts of meaning, dialogues and parodies. Only writing can oppose the self-assurance of the scientist, in so far as he "expresses" his science, with what Lautréamont called the "modesty" of the writer.

There is, finally, between science and literature, a third margin which science must reconquer, that of pleasure. In a civilization entirely brought up by monotheism to the idea of sin, where every value is attained through suffering, the word "pleasure" has an unfortunate ring; there is something frivolous, trivial and incomplete about it. Coleridge said: "A poem is that species of composition which is opposed to works of science by purposing for its immediate object, pleasure, not truth"; an ambiguous statement, for although it assumes the nature of the poem (or of literature) to be in some degree erotic, our civilization continues to assign it to a special reserve where it can keep an eye on it, so to speak, distinct from the more important territory of truth. Yet "pleasure," as we are readier to admit these days, implies an experience much vaster and more meaningful than the mere satisfaction of a "taste." Now the pleasure of language has never been seriously measured, although, in its way, the ancient Rhetoric had the right idea when it established a special class of discourse, devoted to spectacle and admiration, the epideictic. But classical art wrapped the "pleasurable," which it claimed to have made its law (Racine: "La première règle est de plaire . . .") in all the constraints of the "natural." Only the baroque, a literary experiment which has never been more than tolerated by our society, at least in France, has dared to explore to some extent what might be called the Eros of language. Scientific discourse is far from doing so, for if it accepted this idea it would have to give up all those privileges with which society as instituted surrounds it, and agree to return to that "literary life" which, Baudelaire tells us in connection with Edgar Allan Poe, is "le seul élément où puissent respirer certains êtres declassés."

What we must perhaps ask for today is a mutation in the consciousness, the structure and the objectives of scientific discourse, at a time, however, when the human sciences, now firmly established and flourishing, seem to be leaving less and less room for a literature commonly charged with being unreal and inhuman. To be precise: the role of literature is actively to *represent* to the scientific establishment what the latter denies, to wit the sovereignty of language. And structuralism ought to be in a strong position to cause such a scandal because, being acutely aware of the linguistic nature of human artefacts, it alone today can reopen the question of the linguistic status of science. Its subject-matter being language—all languages—it has come to define itself very quickly as the meta-language of our culture. But this stage must be transcended, because the opposition of language-objects and their meta-languages is still subject in the end to the paternalistic model of a science without a language. The task confronting structuralist discourse is to make itself entirely homogeneous with its object. There are two ways in which this task can be successfully tackled, both equally radical: by an exhaustive formalization or else by "integral writing." In the second of these hypotheses, the one we are defending here, science will become literature, to the same extent as literature, growingly subject as it is to an overturning of the traditional genres of poetry, narrative, criticism and essay, already is and always has been a science. What the human sciences are discovering today, in whatever field it may be, sociological, psychological, psychiatric, linguistic, etc., literature has always known. The only difference is that literature has not *said* it, but *written* it. In contrast to the integral truth of literature, the human sciences, belatedly formulated in the wake of bourgeois positivism, appear as the technical alibis proffered by our society in order to maintain within itself the faction of a theological truth proudly, and improperly, freed from language.

A composer of serious music (symphonies performed in London) and a linguistic scholar (specializing in Slavic studies and Russian), Anthony Burgess (1917–   ) is the author of at least a dozen novels and a growing body of commentary and criticism. As a serious novelist Burgess is "attempting to extend the range of subject matter available to fiction," and also to be a "practitioner who is anxious to exploit words much as a poet does." His work of greatest scope is Malayan Triology *(1964); his most extreme fiction to date is a brilliant* shorter novel, A Clockwork Orange *(1962). In* the essay which follows Burgess brings a combination of learning, good humor, and insight to the issue of pornographic materials and literature.

OUR BEDFELLOW, THE MARQUIS DE SADE

Anthony Burgess

Only two writers in the whole of world literature have, solely on the strength of the philosophies they preached, been elevated into monstrous figures of evil. The first was Niccolò Machiavelli, whose book on statecraft, *Il Principe* (The Prince), was not well understood by his chief traducers, the Elizabethan English. The popular view of "Old Nick" (yes, that's where the diabolic sobriquet comes from) was of a bogeyman dedicated to the subversion of good, the liquidation of religion, and the promotion of death and violence for their own sake. A close reading of *Il Principe* shows that Machiavelli went, in fact, nowhere near so far: he was concerned with a very laudable end—that of maintaining order in a community threatened by enemies without and traitors within. What earned him such extravagent odium was his lack of scruple about the means by which that end should be fulfilled. Every state, even the most liberal and democratic, has in time of emergency had to use Machiavellian devices: yet mention the term, or preferably whisper it ("Machiavellian!"), and the response is a shuddering one. The word has been loaded for centuries.

The second of these writers is the Marquis de Sade, and till recently, the term sadism has not carried the full load of horror available to it. The most popular joke that admits the perversion and its complement is about the sadist and the masochist who share adjoining beds in a psychiatric ward. "Beat me, beat me!" cries the masochist. "No," says the sadist. But that is not it at all: there is nothing negative in sadism. And the small torturer, the boy who pulls wings off flies, the husband who drops burning brown paper on his wife's bare body—these don't go far enough. The extravagance of evil falsely attributed to Machiavelli should, by rights, be transferred to the Marquis. But few people have read his works, and few imaginations are capable of teaching the ingenuities of his fancies. It is only fairly recently that this devil has been given his due.

The world that George Orwell presents in *Nineteen Eighty-Four* owes a great deal to Sade. The ruling oligarchy knows what it is doing: it wants power, and it intends, behind the immortal, because mythical, facade of Big Brother, to keep power till the end of time. This power is the ultimate pleasure, the final human fulfillment. Its image is of a jackboot poised voluptuously over a terrified human face. The exercise of power means the exercise of cruelty, for it is only through cruelty that you can show your victim the extent of your total domination over him.

Sade's actions and, more patently, Sade's literary fantasies represented power as an aspect of the sexual impulse. The sexual act is shown not as a reciprocity of pleasure giving, but as the enforcing of strange desires on an unwilling victim. To share pleasure, said Sade, is to weaken it. The victim (like Winston Smith in *Nineteen Eighty-Four*) must be impotent to strike back and must be of a preordained persecutable type. In the sexual field it is women who are made for persecution: physiologically they are natural victims. Sade's major work, the unfinished *120 Days of Sodom*, is a detailed catalogue of sexual perversions, all of which involve torture and some of them death. The form of the book is fictional. The setting is a castle in the Black Forest, totally impregnable, and in it four debauchées from Paris—a banker, a

bishop, a duke, and a judge—spend seventeen weeks in perverse
pleasures that are graduated from the merely revolting to the
ineffably and transcendently evil. It was Sade's intention to describe six hundred perversions, but he only managed to get
through the first thirty days—though he made very detailed notes
for the other ninety. Thus the seventy-ninth perversion in the
"Third Class of Criminal Passions" entails strapping a naked girl
face down to a table and having "a piping hot omelette served
upon her buttocks." The eater "uses an exceedingly sharp fork."
This is comparatively mild. The ultimate horror has fifteen girls
(none older than seventeen) all tortured simultaneously in fifteen
different ways, while the *grand seigneur* who arranges this elaborate *grand guignol* watches and waits for orgasm. It does not
come easily, despite the monstrous stimulus: it has to be effected
through masturbation and the exhibition of two male bottoms.

It is evident that Sade, in conceiving these nightmares (nightmares to us; delicious dreams to him), was in a state of sexual
frustration so intense that it drove him to a kind of clearheaded
mania. The deprivations of prison life were an obvious factor, but
they must be only a small part of the story. For Sade's dreams are
essentially dreams of impotence, just as the recorded orgies on
which some of the dreams are based are attempts to find satisfaction when the normal means have failed. The situation is not all
that unusual. Eighteenth-century France was notable for its lech-
erous aristocracy, and Sade's youthful roistering was not more
spectacular than that of many of his peers and superiors. But the
normal sexual vein was overworked; the palate demanded sharper
sauces. Or put it another way: the familiar intoxication could
only, as with drug takers, be attained by stimulants that grew
stronger and stronger.

The first stimulant was sodomy—one that has never been as
rare as the law, which represses it mercilessly, would have us
believe. Heterosexual sodomy (read the *Kamasutra* on this) is a
regular age-old practice among Tamils, and it carries little flavor
of the perverse. But sodomy is selfish, and it can also be cruel.
Sade was fascinated by it, and he is led through it to a genuinely
nauseating preoccupation with the anus: he plays with feces like
an infant.

When what may be termed pure sodomy fails to bring satisfaction, the next stage of cruelty is reached: the imposition of pain
unconnected with coition and not necessarily centered on the

erogenous zones. To inflict suffering is enough, by whatever
means. But the more elementary forms—burning the flesh, cutting,
flaying, even poisoning—must pall sooner or later, and then the
sadist is led on to the more ingenious tortures, most of them
slowly lethal. Where is the limit? The limit is reached, it would
seem, when heterosexual fantasies are swallowed up in apocalyptic
visions of mass destruction—Hitlerian visions whose sexual content
is not immediately apparent. Sade's destructive fantasies are curiously modern—the blasting of whole towns, a sort of fête in
which "children are blown up by rockets and bombs." Edmund
Wilson, to whose long essay on the Sade documents I am deeply
indebted, says apropos of this: "How gratified Sade would have
been if he could have foreseen the scale on which we were later
to indulge in this pastime! Or would he perhaps have been appalled, as he was by the Terror?"

Sade was capable of being appalled; his sadism was not so
thoroughgoing as, for total philosophical consistency, it ought to
have been. But once you divide the world into victims and
persecutors, you are faced with the problem of a frontier where
roles may change: sadism tends to embrace its opposite, masoch-
ism. Leopold von Sacher-Masoch was born twenty-two years
after Sade's death, but his stories about the pleasure of being hurt,
degraded, dominated, are to some extent anticipated in the older
master. While in prison at Vincennes, Sade regularly flagellated
himself. The girls involved in the Marseilles orgy testified that the
inflictions of cruelty were not all onesided. Nowadays, informed
by the sexologist of whom Sade was the true forerunner, we
recognize in ourselves the dichotomy of our response to one of
these magazine photographs we're always seeing—a girl in top
boots with a whip or gun. "Kinky," we say, and shudder with
two kinds of anticipatory pleasure: we identify with the torturer;
we see ourselves as the victim.

That the sadomasochistic impulse is in all of us we no longer
doubt. There is some obscure neural liaison in the brain between
the sexual urge and the desire for domination—and the latter
phrase I have deliberately left ambiguous. We are, quite rightly,
scared of letting the sadomasochistic get out of hand: it is all too
easy. We're all pretty bad inside; it's what we do outside that
counts.

Sade, in his actions, and even more in his books, extrapolated
on a Wagnerian scale what society insists on keeping locked in

the crypts of the mind. Though vicious and perhaps demented, he does not belong to a race very different from our own. That is why he fascinates. But the fascination does not long survive the actual opening of one of his books. Nauseated by his anal fixations, we soon become bored with his ingenuities. Nobody is real; he seems to be playing with automata. He was interested in the art of the novel, and he wanted to contribute to the pornographic branch of it (in this he was merely one among many); but he was not sufficiently interested in people as people. There is no give and take, none of the dialectic of character that we find in competent fiction; there is only the wearying but unwearied catalogue of atrocities. The people who publish extracts from Sade in paperback are misrepresenting him: they are picking out the plums and putting in the wastebasket the dollops of farinaceous inedibility. Sade has to be given us entire, so that we may yawn over the long pages of eighteenth-century moralizing and become irritated by the self-contradictions. The public ought not to be titillated by half-censorship: the works of the Marquis de Sade ought to be freely available, and that would cure the smut hounds.

Has he any value in the history of literature or philosophy? His literary interest is slight though not entirely negligible. His philosophy of Nature is untenable but stimulating. Where he has to be taken seriously is in his role as pioneer sexologist. He was the first modern Western man to list the varieties of erotic perversion, and the list is pretty well exhaustive. Moreover, his view of sex is not limited to the European ethos. He was something of an anthropologist and argued that there was not one sexual practice regarded as perverse by the West that was not accepted as normal in some remoter society. Most important of all, he saw with terrible clarity the sexual springs of cruelty, no matter how cruelty was disguised as a device of politics or of ecclesiastical discipline. Even in his recognition of the sexual elements that lie below family relationships and manifest themselves long before the age of puberty, he anticipated the Viennese school of psychology. He knew what we have taken a long time to learn— that sex is not just something that happens in a bedroom.

His profound misanthropy, while justified by the events of European history through which he lived, was not in conformity with the optimistic philosophies of his time. The chains of man could be broken, said Rousseau; reason could triumph, said the Encyclopedists. Sade never expected anything but the worst from

mankind, so he could never be disappointed. He did not over-
estimate the rational capacities of man; however—following the
custom of the age—he did invoke reason in his writings. Nowadays there are millions of people who find cause, far better cause
than Sade had, to despair of the human race. Sade merely dreamed
of chemists who could blow up whole cities; we have seen the
reality of conventional high explosives and the thermonuclear
bomb. His visions, like those of science fiction in our own day,
were ahead of their time.

It is sourly amusing to observe where his true influence lies.
The great dictators, bemused by dreams of national glory, have
found him abhorrent (Napoleon was the first to be shocked).
Schoolmasters with canes and parents with flat, hard hands have
scarcely thought about him. It is the popular writers who have
diluted his message and made it palatable to suburban minds.
Ian Fleming, for instance:

". . . I can tell you that the entire population of Fort Knox will be
dead or incapacitated by midnight. . . . The substance that will be
inserted in the water supply, outside the filter plant, will be a highly
concentrated form of GB."

"You're mad! You don't really mean you're going to kill sixty
thousand people!"

"Why not? American motorists do it every two years."

Bond stared into Goldfinger's face in fascinated horror. It couldn't
be true! He couldn't mean it! He said tersely, "What's this GB?"

"GB is the most powerful of the Trilone group of nerve poisons. It
was perfected by the Wehrmacht in 1943, but never used for fear of
reprisals. In fact, it is a more effective instrument of destruction than
the hydrogen bomb. . . . Introduction through the water supply is an
ideal method of applying it to a densely populated area."

How the Marquis de Sade would have reveled in the technological
triumphs that now, in literature, merely serve the end of a popular frisson.

In literature less popular, the misanthropy of Sade has become
totally acceptable. I'm thinking particularly of William Golding's
novel *The Inheritors*, where Homo sapiens, supervening on the
gentle Neanderthals, destroys a worthier race because it is in his
nature to destroy. Evil, Golding seems to say, is built into man.
What do we do about that: acquiesce in it, as Sade did, or seek,
however hopelessly, some form of regeneration? Mankind is not

doing very well at the moment, but mankind has never done very well. Always expect the worst, and then you can never be depressed by your morning paper. As for action, note that history has a few lonely figures who did good or, fearing to do evil, did nothing. The impulses we share with the diabolic Marquis are best left to him, to be worked out in fantasy. We can never rid ourselves of these impulses by merely banning the books that most thoroughly express them. They are merely a spectacular symptom of one of the big human diseases. Whether the disease is curable is something we have still to find out.

THE
WORD
ARTS:

Poetry

PURE POETRY: NOTES FOR A LECTURE

A poet of major stature in France, Paul Valéry (1871–1945) has been a widely influential commentator on the nature of poetry and the implied roles of the poet. The following "notes" formed the basis of a lecture delivered in late 1927; since that time, the phrase "pure poetry" has passed into the vocabulary of criticism and poetic theory. Among other things, this essay is notable for an analytic approach, combined with a rare speculative turn of mind, the whole being a particularly "French" statement on the problem central to all the word arts: the paradox that language which is necessarily used by all men, is equally necessarily the vehicle of artistic expression when it is exploited by the professional poet. Valéry's resolution of this problem and others invites comparison with the statements of I. A. Richards, in the essay that follows this one.

*Paul
Valéry*

Today there is a good deal of excitement in the world (I mean in the world of the most precious and most useless things) over these two words: *pure poetry*. I am somewhat responsible for this excitement. A few years ago, in a preface to a friend's book of poems, I happened to express these words without attaching any extreme importance to them and without foreseeing the conclusions that various persons concerned with poetry would draw from them. I knew quite well what I meant by those words, but I did not know that they would give rise to such reverberations and reactions among lovers of literature. I merely wanted to draw attention to a fact, and certainly not to set forth a theory or, worse yet, establish a doctrine and regard as heretics those who would not share it.

To my mind, every written work, every product of language, contains certain fragments or recognizable elements endowed with properties that we will examine and which I will provisionally call *poetic*. Whenever speech exhibits *a certain deviation* from the most direct expression—that is, the most *insensible* expression of thought; whenever these deviations make us aware in some way of a world of relationships distinct from purely practical reality, we conceive more or less clearly of the possibility of enlarging this exceptional area, and we have the sensation of seizing the fragment of a noble and living substance which is perhaps capable of development and cultivation; and which, once developed and used, constitutes poetry in its artistic effect.

Whether it is possible to make a work of art consisting wholly of these recognizable elements, so fully distinct from those of the language I have called *insensible*—whether it is possible, consequently, in a work written in verse or otherwise, to give the impression of a complete system of *reciprocal* relations between our images and ideas on the one hand and our means of expression on the other, a system which would correspond especially to the creation of an emotive state of mind—this, on the whole, is the problem of pure poetry. I mean *pure* in the way in which the doctor speaks of pure water. I mean that the question is to know if we can bring about a work which would be *pure* of elements that are not poetic. I have always held, and still do, that this is an unattainable object, and that poetry is always an effort to approach this purely ideal condition. In sum, what we call a *poem* is made up in practice of fragments of *pure poetry* inserted into the substance of a discourse. A very beautiful line is a very pure element of poetry. The banal comparison of a beautiful line to a diamond makes it clear that the feeling of this quality of purity is in every mind.

The inconvenience of this phrase, *pure poetry*, is that it makes one think of a moral purity which is not the issue here, for the idea of pure poetry is for me, quite the contrary, an essentially analytic idea. Pure poetry is, in sum, a fiction deduced from observation which should help us make precise our idea of poems in general and guide us in the difficult and important study of the diverse and multiform relations of language to the effects it produces on men. It would, perhaps, be much better instead of *pure poetry* to say *absolute poetry*, and we should then have to understand it as a search for the effects resulting from the relationships of words, or rather of the interrelations of their resonances, which suggests, in sum, *an exploration of the whole domain of the sensibility that is governed by language.* This exploration might be made gropingly, for such is the way it is generally done. But it is not impossible that it may one day be carried out systematically.

I have tried to construct and I am trying to give a clear idea of the poetic problem or, at least, what I believe to be a *clearer* idea of this problem. It is remarkable that these questions should today arouse a widespread interest. Never, it seems, has so large a public been concerned. We can be present at discussions, we can see experiments that are not restricted, as in times past, to narrow cliques and to a very small number of amateurs and experimenters; but more wonderful yet, in our age we see even in the public at large a kind of interest, sometimes impassioned, attach itself to these almost theological discussions. (What can be more theological than to debate, for example, on inspiration and labor, on the value of intuition and of the artifices of art? Have we not here problems altogether comparable to the famous theological problem of grace and works? Likewise, there are problems in poetry which, opposing the rules that have been determined and fixed by tradition and the immediate data of personal experience or of personal meaning, are absolutely analogous to the problems that are similarly found in the domain of theology, between the personal meaning, the direct knowledge of divine things, and the teachings of various religions, the texts of the Scriptures and dogmatic forms. . . .)

But I come to the subject now with the firm intention of saying nothing that is a matter of sheer assertion or the result of light speculation. Let us go back to this word, "poetry," and let us observe first of all that this beautiful name engenders two distinct orders of concepts. We speak of "poetry" and we speak of "a poem." We say of a scene, a situation, and sometimes of a person, that they are *poetic;* on the other hand, we also speak of *the art of poetry* and we say: "This poem is beautiful." But in the first case we are concerned with the evidence of a certain kind of feeling; everyone is familiar with this peculiar trembling comparable to our condition when we feel ourselves excited, enchanted, by the effect of certain events. This condition is entirely independent of any determinate work of art and results naturally and spontaneously from a certain accord between our inner disposition, physical and psychic, and the circumstances (real or ideal) which act on us. But on the other hand, when we say *the art of poetry* or when we speak of *a poem* we are concerned clearly with the means of bringing about a condition analogous to the preceding condition, of artificially producing this kind of feeling. And this is not all. The means which serve to bring about this condition must be those which belong to the properties and the mechanism of articulate language. The feeling which I spoke of can be brought about by things. It can also be brought about by means quite different from those of language, such as architecture, music, etc., but poetry properly named has as its essence the use of the devices of language. As for independent poetic feeling, let us observe that it is distinguished from other human feelings by a singular character, an admirable property: that it tends to give us the sense of an illusion or the illusion of a world (of a *world* in which events, images, beings, things, if they do resemble those which inhabit the ordinary world, are, on the other hand, inexplicably but intimately related to the whole of our sensibility). Known objects and beings are thus in some way —forgive the expression—*musicalized;* they have become harmonious and resonant, and as if *in tune* with our sensibility. Poetic experience defined in this way bears great similarities to the dream state, or at least to the condition produced in certain dreams. Dream, when we return to it through memory, makes us understand that our consciousness can be awakened or filled, and satisfied, by a whole range of productions that differ noticeably in their laws from ordinary productions of perception. But this emotive world that we can know at times through dream can not be entered or left at will. *It is enclosed in us and we are enclosed in it,* which means that we have no way of acting on it in order to modify it and that, on the other hand, it can not coexist with our great power of action over the external world. It appears and disappears capriciously, but man has done for it what he has done or tried to do for everything precious and perishable: he has sought for and has found the means of recreating this condition at will, of regaining it when he wishes, and finally, of artificially developing these natural products of his sentient being. In some sort of way he has managed to extract from nature and redeem from the blind movement of time these formations or constructions that are so uncertain; in this design he makes use of several devices which I have already mentioned. Now, among these means of producing a poetic world, of reproducing and enriching it, perhaps the most venerable and also the most complex and the most difficult to use is language.

At this point I must make you feel or understand to what extent the task of the poet in the modern age is a delicate one, and how many difficulties (of which, happily, he is not always aware) the poet encounters in his task. Language is a common and practical element; it is thereby necessarily a coarse instrument, for everyone handles and appropriates it according to his needs and tends to deform it according to his personality. Language, no matter how personal it may be or how close the way of thinking in words may be to our spirit, is nevertheless *of statistical origin* and has *purely practical ends.* Now the poet's problem must be *to derive from this practical instrument the means of creating a work essentially not practical.* As I have already told you, it is a matter, for him, of creating a world or an order of things, a system of relations, without any relationship to the practical order.

To make you understand all the difficulties of this task, I am going to *compare the poet's gifts with those of the musician.* How fortunate is the musician! The evolution of his art has given him an altogether privileged position for centuries. What does music consist of? The sense of hearing gives us *the universe of noises.* Our ear admits an infinite number of sensations that it receives in some kind of order and of which it can single out four distinct qualities. Now ancient observations and very old experiments have made it possible to deduce, from *the universe of noises,* the system or *the universe of sounds*—which are particularly simple and recognizable noises, particularly prone to form combinations, associations, whose structure, sequence, differences or resemblances are perceived by the ear, or rather by the understanding, as soon as they are produced. These elements are pure or are composed of pure—that is to say, recognizable—elements. They are sharply defined and—a very important point—the way has been found to produce them in a constant and identical manner by means of instruments which are, basically, true instruments of measure. A musical instrument is one that can be gauged and used in such a way that from given actions a given result can be uniformly obtained. And here we see the remarkable result of this organization of the province of hearing: as the world of sounds is quite separate from that of noises, and as our ear is also accustomed to distinguishing them clearly, it follows that *if a pure sound*—that is, a relatively exceptional sound—*happens to be heard, at once a particular atmosphere is created, a particular state of expectation is produced in our senses, and this expectation tends,* to some degree, *to give rise to sensations of the same kind, of the same purity, as the sensation produced.* If a pure sound is produced in a concert hall, *everything is changed within us;* we await the production of music. If, on the contrary, the reverse is tried; if during the performance of a composition in a concert hall a noise should be heard (a falling chair, the voice or cough of a listener), at once we feel that something inside us has been broken, there has been a violation of some sort of substance or law of association; *a universe is shattered,* a charm is wiped out.

Thus for the musician, before he has begun his work, all is in readiness so that the operation of his creative spirit may find, right from the start, the appropriate matter and means, without any possibility of error. He will not have to make this matter and means submit to any modification; he need only assemble elements which are clearly defined and ready-made.

But in how different a situation is the poet! Before him is ordinary language, this aggregate of means which are not suited to his purpose, not made for him. There have not been physicians to determine the relationships of these means for him; there have not been constructors of scales; no diapason, no metronome, no certitude of this kind. He has nothing but the coarse instrument of the dictionary and the grammar. Moreover, he must address himself not to a special and unique sense like *hearing,* which the musician bends to his will, and which is, besides, the organ *par excellence* of expectation and attention; but rather to a general and diffused expectation, and he does so through a language which is a very odd mixture of incoherent *stimuli.* Nothing is more complex, more difficult to make out, than the strange combination of qualities that exists in language. Everyone knows quite well how rare indeed are the agreements *of sound and sense;* and moreover, we all know that a discourse can develop qualities altogether different. A discourse can be logical and completely void of harmony; it can be harmonious and insignificant: it can be clear and lacking in any sort of beauty; it can be prose or poetry; and it is enough, to sum up all of these independent modes, to mention the various sciences which have been created to exploit this diversity of language and to study it under different aspects. Language is subject, in turn, to *phonetics*, along with *metrics* and *rhythm;* it has a *logical* aspect and a *semantic* aspect; it includes *rhetoric* and *syntax.* We know that all these diverse disciplines can be brought to bear on the same text in many mutually exclusive ways. . . . Here we have the poet come to grips with this ensemble so diverse and so rich in initial capacities; too rich, in sum, not to be confused. It is from it that he must draw his *art object,* the contrivance to produce poetic emotion—that is, he must force the practical instrument, the coarse instrument created by anyone at all, the instrument of every moment, used for immediate needs and modified at every instant by the living, to become, for the time that his attention gives to the poem, the substance of a selected emotive condition, quite distinct from all of the accidental conditions of indeterminate length which make up ordinary sensory or psychic existence. We can say without exaggeration that the common language is the fruit of the disorder of common life, because men of every sort, subject to an innumerable quantity of conditions and needs, receive it and make use of it as best they can for their desires and their interests so as to make possible relations between them; while the language of the poet, although he necessarily makes use of the elements furnished by this statistical disorder, constitutes, on the contrary, *an effort of man in isolation* to create an artificial and ideal order by means of a substance of vulgar origin.

If this paradoxical problem could be wholly resolved; that is, if the poet could manage to construct works where nothing that partakes of prose would be present—poems where the musical continuity would never be interrupted, where the relationships of meanings would be themselves forever like harmonica relations, *where the transmutation of thoughts from one into the other would be more important than any thought,* where the play of figures would contain the reality of the Subject—then we could talk about *pure poetry* as though it existed. Such is not the case: the practical or pragmatic part of language, the logical habits and forms and, as I have indicated, the disorder, the irrationality that we find in the vocabulary (because of infinitely various derivations from very different ages in which the elements of the language were introduced) make the existence of these creations of absolute poetry impossible; but it is easy to conceive that the notion of such an ideal or imaginary condition is very precious for the appreciation of all observable poetry.

The conception of pure poetry is one of an inaccessible kind, of an ideal limit of the desires, the efforts, and the powers of the poet. . . .

Although E. E. Cummings (1894–1962) was one of the most unconventional poets ever to achieve worldwide recognition, his antecedents are classically of New England, of America. Born in Cambridge, Massachusetts, where his father was the pastor of a well-established church, Cummings attended Harvard (M.A., 1916); after service in the Ambulance Corp in France he attended art school in Paris. After winning the Dial Prize (1925) he continued to write lyric, experimental, and satiric poetry, while gaining a reputation as a painter of considerable merit as well. In the realm of prose his best-known work is The Enormous Room *(1922),*

THREE STATEMENTS

E. E. Cummings

a short novel describing his three-month term in a French concentration camp during World War I. The prose statements which follow were introductions to books and an answer to a letter written to the poet by a student.

FOREWORD

On the assumption that my technique is either complicated or original or both, the publishers have politely requested me to write an introduction to this book.[1]

At least my theory of technique, if I have one, is very far from original; nor is it complicated. I can express it in fifteen words, by quoting The Eternal Question And Immortal Answer of burlesk, viz., "Would you hit a woman with a child? —No, I'd hit her with a brick." Like the burlesk comedian, I am abnormally fond of that precision which creates movement.

If a poet is anybody, he is somebody to whom things made matter very little—somebody who is obsessed by Making. Like all obsessions, the Making obsession has disadvantages; for instance, my only interest in making money would be to make

[1] *is 5* (1926).

it. Fortunately, however, I should prefer to make almost anything else, including locomotives and roses. It is with roses and locomotives (not to mention acrobats Spring electricity Coney Island the 4th of July the eyes of mice and Niagara Falls) that my "poems" are competing.

They are also competing with each other, with elephants, and with El Greco.

Ineluctable preoccupation with The Verb gives a poet one priceless advantage: whereas nonmakers must content themselves with the merely undeniable fact that two times two is four, he rejoices in a purely irresistible truth (to be found, in abbreviated costume, upon the title page of the present volume).

INTRODUCTION [2]

The poems to come are for you and for me and are not for mostpeople
    —it's no use trying to pretend that mostpeople and ourselves are alike. Mostpeople have less in common with ourselves than the squarerootofminusone. You and I are human beings; mostpeople are snobs.

Take the matter of being born. What does being born mean to mostpeople? Catastrophe unmitigated. Socialrevolution. The cultured aristocrat yanked out of his hyperexclusively ultravoluptuous superpalazzo, and dumped into an incredibly vulgar detentioncamp swarming with every conceivable species of undesirable organism. Mostpeople fancy a guaranteed birthproof safetysuit of nondestructible selflessness. If mostpeople were to be born twice they'd improbably call it dying—
    you and I are not snobs. We can never be born enough. We are human beings; for whom birth is a supremely welcome mystery, the mystery of growing: the mystery which happens only and whenever we are faithful to ourselves. You and I wear the dangerous looseness of doom and find it becoming. Life, for eternal us,is now;and now is much too busy being a little more than everything to seem anything,catastrophic included.

Life, for mostpeople,simply isn't. Take the socalled standard-ofliving. What do mostpeople mean by "living"? They don't mean living. They mean the latest and closest plural approximation to singular prenatal passivity which science,in its finite but unbounded wisdom, has succeeded in selling their wives. If science could fail,a mountain's a mammal. Mostpeople's wives can spot a genuine delusion of embryonic omnipotence immediately and will accept no substitutes

—luckily for us,a mountain is a mammal. The plusorminus movie to end moving,the strictly scientific parlourgame of real unreality,the tyranny conceived in misconception and dedicated to the proposition that every man is a woman and any woman a king,hasn't a wheel to stand on. What their most synthetic not to mention transparent majesty,mrsandmr collective foetus,would improbably call a ghost is walking. He isn't an undream of anaesthetized impersons,or a cosmic comfortstation,or a transcendentally sterilized lookiesoundiefeelietastiesmellie. He is a healthily complex, a naturally homogeneous,citizen of immortality. The now of his each pitying free imperfect gesture,his any birth or breathing,insults perfected inframortally millenniums of slavishness. He is a little more than everything, he is democracy;he is alive:he is ourselves.

Miracles are to come. With you I leave a remembrance of miracles: they are by somebody who can love and who shall be continually reborn,a human being;somebody who said to those near him,when his fingers would not hold a brush "tie it into my hand"—

nothing proving or sick or partial. Nothing false,nothing difficult or easy or small or colossal. Nothing ordinary or extraordinary,nothing emptied or filled,real or unreal;nothing feeble and known or clumsy and guessed. Everywhere tints childrening,innocent spontaneous,true. Nowhere possibly what flesh and impossibly such a garden,but actually flowers which breasts are among the very mouths of light. Nothing believed or doubted;brain over heart, surface:nowhere hating or to fear;shadow,mind without soul. Only how measureless cool flames of making;only each other building always distinct selves of mutual entirely opening;only alive. Never the murdered finalities of wherewhen and yesno, impotent nongames of wrongright and rightwrong;never to gain or pause,never the soft adventure of undoom,greedy anguishes and cringing ecstasies of inexistence;never to rest and never to have:only to grow.

Always the beautiful answer who asks a more beautiful question

A POET'S ADVICE [3]

A poet is somebody who feels, and who expresses his feeling through words.

This may sound easy. It isn't.

A lot of people think or believe or know they feel—but that's thinking or believing or knowing; not feeling. And poetry is feeling—not knowing or believing or thinking.

Almost anybody can learn to think or believe or know, but not a single human being can be taught to feel. Why? Because whenever you think or you believe or you know, you're a lot of other people: but the moment you feel, you're nobody-but-yourself.

To be nobody-but-yourself—in a world which is doing its best, night and day, to make you everybody else—means to fight the hardest battle which any human being can fight; and never stop fighting.

As for expressing nobody-but-yourself in words, that means working just a little harder than anybody who isn't a poet can possibly imagine. Why? Because nothing is quite as easy as using words like somebody else. We all of us do exactly this nearly all of the time—and whenever we do it, we're not poets.

If, at the end of your first ten or fifteen years of fighting and working and feeling, you find you've written one line of one poem, you'll be very lucky indeed.

And so my advice to all young people who wish to become poets is: do something easy, like learning how to blow up the world—unless you're not only willing, but glad, to feel and work and fight till you die.

Does this sound dismal? It isn't.

It's the most wonderful life on earth.

Or so I feel.

---

[3] Reply to a letter from a high school editor; published in Ottawa Hills (Grand Rapids, Mich.) High School *Spectator*, Oct. 26, 1955.

W. H. Auden (1907–) came to prominence as one of a group of new writers at Oxford University in the early 1930s. Now a widely honored professional poet, Auden is an American citizen and a long-time resident of New York City. The essay which follows is highly personal but, by intention, also suggests a kind of allegory on the literary and social processes that help bring a poetic talent to maturity. In this connection, it is interesting to speculate on the nature and the function of the "Censor" which is mentioned several times in the text. The student who might himself wish to write will find cogent, witty advice on the matters of apprenticeship, imitation, and the kinds of reading best calculated to help the emerging poet.

MAKING, KNOWING, AND JUDGING

W. H. Auden

I began writing poetry myself because one Sunday afternoon in March 1922, a friend suggested that I should: the thought had never occurred to me. I scarcely knew any poems —*The English Hymnal*, the *Psalms*, *Struwwelpeter* and the mnemonic rhymes in *Kennedy's Shorter Latin Primer* are about all I remember— and I took little interest in what is called Imaginative Literature. Most of my reading had been related to a private world of Sacred Objects. Aside from a few stories like George MacDonald's *The Princess and the Goblin* and Jules Verne's *The Child of the Cavern*, the subjects of which touched upon my obsessions, my favourite books bore such titles as *Underground Life, Machinery for Metalliferous Mines, Lead and Zinc Ores of Northumberland and Alston Moor*, and my conscious purpose in reading them had been to gain information about my sacred objects. At the time, therefore, the suggestion that I write poetry seemed like a revelation from heaven for which nothing in my past could account.

Looking back, however, I now realize that I had read the technological prose of my favourite books in a peculiar way. A word like *pyrites*, for example, was for me, not simply an indicative sign; it was the Proper Name of a Sacred Being, so that, when I heard an aunt pronounce it *pirrits*, I was shocked. Here pronunciation was more than wrong, it was ugly. Ignorance was impiety.

It was Edward Lear, I believe, who said that the true test of imagination is the ability to name a cat, and we are told in the first chapter of *Genesis* that the Lord brought to unfallen Adam all the creatures that he might name them and whatsoever Adam called every living creature, that was the name thereof, which is to say, its Proper Name. Here Adam plays the role of the Proto-poet, not the Proto-prosewriter. A Proper Name must not only refer, it must refer aptly and this aptness must be publicly recognizable. It is curious to observe, for instance, that when a person has been christened inaptly, he and his friends instinctively call him by some other name. Like a line of poetry, a Proper Name is untranslatable. Language is prosaic to the degree that 'It does not matter what particular word is associated with an idea, provided the association once made is permanent.'[1] Language is poetic to the degree that it does matter.

The power of verse [writes Valéry] is derived from an indefinable harmony between what it *says* and what it *is*. Indefinable is essential to the definition. The harmony ought not to be definable, when it can be defined it is imitative harmony and that is not good. The impossibility of defining the relation, together with the impossibility of denying it, constitutes the essence of the poetic line.[2]

The poet is someone, says Mallarmé, who 'de plusieurs vocables refait un mot total'[3] and the most poetical of all scholastic disciplines is, surely, Philology, the study of language in abstraction from its uses so that words become, as it were, little lyrics about themselves.

Since Proper Names in the grammatical sense refer to unique objects, we cannot judge their aptness without personal acquaintance with what they name. To know whether *Old Foss* was an

[1] George Boole, *An Investigation of the Laws of Thought.*
[2] *Tel Quel,* ii.
[3] *Divagations,* Crise de Vers.

apt name for Lear's cat, we should have had to have known them both. A line of poetry like

A drop of water in the breaking gulf[4]

is a name for an experience we all know so that we can judge its aptness, and it names, as a Proper Name cannot, relations and actions as well as things. But Shakespeare and Lear are both using language in the same way and, I believe, for the same motive, but into that I shall go later. My present point is that, if my friend's suggestion met with such an unexpected response, the reason may have been that, without knowing it, I had been enjoying the poetic use of language for a long time.

A beginner's efforts cannot be called bad or imitative. They are imaginary. A bad poem has this or that fault which 'can be pointed out; an imitative poem is a recognizable imitation of this or that poem, this or that poet. But about an imaginary poem no criticism can be made since it is an imitation of poetry-in-general. Never again will a poet feel so inspired, so certain of genius, as he feels in these first days as his pencil flies across the page. Yet something is being learned even now. As he scribbles on he is beginning to get the habit of noticing metrical quantities, to see that any two-syllable word in isolation must be either a *ti-tum*, a *tum-ti* or, occasionally, a *tum-tum*, but that when associated with other words it can sometimes become a *ti-ti;* when he discovers a rhyme he has not thought of before, he stores it away in his memory, a habit which an Italian poet may not need to acquire but which an English poet will find useful.

And, though as yet he can only scribble, he has started reading real poems for pleasure and on purpose. Many things can be said against anthologies, but for an adolescent to whom even the names of most of the poets are unknown, a good one can be an invaluable instructor. I had the extraordinary good fortune to be presented one Christmas with the De La Mare anthology *Come Hither*. This had, for my purposes, two great virtues. Firstly, its good taste. Reading it today, I find very few poems which I should have omitted and none which I should think it bad taste to admire. Secondly, its catholic taste. Given the youthful audience for which it was designed, there were certain kinds of poetry which it did not represent, but within those

4 *Comedy of Errors*, II. 2.

limits the variety was extraordinary. Particularly valuable was
its lack of literary class-consciousness, its juxtaposition on terms
of equality of unofficial poetry, such as counting-out rhymes,
and official poetry such as the odes of Keats. It taught me at the
start that poetry does not have to be great or even serious to be
good, and that one does not have to be ashamed of moods in
which one feels no desire whatsoever to read *The Divine Comedy*
and a great desire to read

> When other ladies to the shades go down,
> Still Flavia, Chloris, Celia stay in town.
> These Ghosts of Beauty ling'ring there abide,
> And haunt the places where their Honour died.[5]

Matthew Arnold's notion of Touchstones by which to measure
all poems has always struck me as a doubtful one, likely to turn
readers into snobs and to ruin talented poets by tempting them
to imitate what is beyond their powers.

A poet who wishes to improve himself should certainly keep
good company, but for his profit as well as for his comfort the
company should not be too far above his station. It is by no
means clear that the poetry which influenced Shakespeare's development most fruitfully was the greatest poetry with which
he was acquainted. Even for readers, when one thinks of the
attention that a great poem demands, there is something frivolous
about the notion of spending every day with one. Masterpieces
should be kept for High Holidays of the Spirit.

I am not trying to defend the aesthetic heresy that one subject
is no more important than any other, or that a poem has no
subject or that there is no difference between a great poem
and a good one—a heresy which seems to me contrary to human
feeling and common sense—but I can understand why it exists.
Nothing is worse than a bad poem which was intended to be
great.

So a would-be poet begins to learn that poetry is more various
than he imagined and that he can like and dislike different poems
for different reasons. His Censor, however, has still not yet been
born. Before he can give birth to him, he has to pretend to be
somebody else; he has to get a literary transference upon some
poet in particular.

---

[5] Alexander Pope, *Epigram*.

If poetry were in great public demand so that there were over-worked professional poets, I can imagine a system under which an established poet would take on a small number of apprentices who would begin by changing his blotting paper, advance to typing his manuscripts and end up by ghost-writing poems for him which he was too busy to start or finish. The apprentices might really learn something for, knowing that he would get the blame as well as the credit for their work, the Master would be extremely choosey about his apprentices and do his best to teach them all he knew.

In fact, of course, a would-be poet serves his apprenticeship in a library. This has its advantages. Though the Master is deaf and dumb and gives neither instruction nor criticism, the apprentice can choose any Master he likes, living or dead, the Master is available at any hour of the day or night, lessons are all for free, and his passionate admiration of his Master will ensure that he work hard to please him.

To please means to imitate and it is impossible to do a recognizable imitation of a poet without attending to every detail of his diction, rhythms and habits of sensibility. In imitating his Master, the apprentice acquires a Censor for he learns that, no matter how he finds it, by inspiration, by potluck or after hours of laborious search, there is only one word or rhythm or form that is the *right* one. The right one is still not yet the *real* one, for the apprentice is ventriloquizing but he has got away from poetry-in-general; he is learning how *a* poem is written. Later in life, incidentally, he will realize how important is the art of imitation, for he will not infrequently be called upon to imitate himself.

My first Master was Thomas Hardy, and I think I was very lucky in my choice. He was a good poet, perhaps a great one, but not *too* good. Much as I loved him, even I could see that his diction was often clumsy and forced and that a lot of his poems were plain bad. This gave me hope where a flawless poet might have made me despair. He was modern without being too modern. His world and sensibility were close enough to mine— curiously enough his face bore a striking resemblance to my father's—so that, in imitating him, I was being led towards not away from myself, but they were not so close as to obliterate my identity. If I looked through his spectacles, at least I was conscious of a certain eye-strain. Lastly, his metrical variety, his fondness for complicated stanza forms, were an invaluable training in the craft of making. I am also thankful that my first Master did not write in free verse or I might then have been tempted to believe that free verse is easier to write than stricter forms, whereas I know it is infinitely more difficult.

Presently the curtain rises on a scene rather like the finale to Act II of *Die Meistersinger*, the setting of which in my own memories is geographically close to this afternoon. Let us call it The Gathering of the Apprentices. The apprentices gather together from all over and discover that they are a new generation; somebody shouts the word 'modern' and the riot is on. The New Iconoclastic Poets and Critics are discovered—when I was an undergraduate a critic could still describe Mr. T. S. Eliot, O.M., as 'a drunken helot'—the poetry which these new authorities recommend becomes the Canon, that on which they frown is thrown out of the window. There are gods whom it is blasphemy to criticize and devils whose names may not be mentioned without execrations. The apprentices have seen a great light while their tutors sit in darkness and the shadow of death.

Really, how do the dons stand it, for I'm sure this scene repeats itself year after year. When I recall the kindness of our tutors, the patience with which they listened, the courtesy with which they hid their boredom, I am overwhelmed by their sheer goodness. I suppose that, having got there, they knew that the road of excess can lead to the palace of Wisdom, though it frequently does not.

An apprentice discovers that there is a significant relation between the statement 'Today I am nineteen' and the statement 'Today is February the twenty-first, 1926'. If the discovery goes to his head, it is, nevertheless, a discovery he must make for, until he realizes that all the poems he has read, however different they may be, have one common characteristic, they have all been written, his own writing will never cease to be imitative. He will never know what he himself *can write* until he has a general sense of what *needs to be written*. And this is the one thing his elders cannot teach him, just because they are his elders; he can only learn it from his fellow apprentices with whom he shares one thing in common, they are contemporaries.

The discovery is not wholly pleasant. If the young speak of

the past as a burden it is a joy to throw off, behind their words
may often lie a resentment and fright at realizing that the past
will not carry them on its back.

The critical statements of the Censor are always polemical
advice to his poet, meant not as objective truths but as pointers,
and in youth which is trying to discover its own identity, the
exasperation at not having yet succeeded naturally tends to express itself in violence and exaggeration.

If an undergraduate announces to his tutor one morning that
Gertrude Stein is the greatest writer who ever lived or that
Shakespeare is no good, he is really only saying something like
this: 'I don't know what to write yet or how, but yesterday
while reading Gertrude Stein, I thought I saw a clue' or 'Reading Shakespeare yesterday, I realized that one of the faults in
what I write is a tendency to rhetorical bombast'.

Fashion and snobbery are also valuable as a defence against
literary indigestion. Regardless of their quality, it is always better
to read a few books carefully than skim through many, and,
short of a personal taste which cannot be formed overnight,
snobbery is as good a principle of limitation as any other.

I am eternally grateful, for example, to the musical fashion
of my youth which prevented me from listening to Italian Opera
until I was over thirty, by which age I was capable of really
appreciating a world so beautiful and so challenging to my own
cultural heritage.

The apprentices do each other a further mutual service which
no older and sounder critic could do. They read each other's
manuscripts. At this age a fellow apprentice has two great virtues
as a critic. When he reads your poem, he may grossly over-
estimate it, but if he does, he really believes what he is saying;
he never flatters or praises merely to encourage. Secondly, he
reads your poem with that passionate attention which grown-up
critics only give to masterpieces and grown-up poets only to
themselves. When he finds fault, his criticisms are intended to
help you to improve. He really wants your poem to be better.

It is just this kind of personal criticism which, in later life
when the band of apprentices have dispersed, a writer often
finds it so hard to get. The verdicts of reviewers, however just,
are seldom of any use to him. Why should they be? A critic
is dealing with a published work, not a manuscript. His job is

to tell the public what that work is, not tell its author what he should and could have written instead. Yet this is the only kind of criticism from which an author can benefit. Those who could do it for him are generally, like himself, too elsewhere, too busy, too married, too selfish.

We must assume that our apprentice does succeed in becoming a poet, that, sooner or later, a day arrives when his Censor is able to say truthfully and for the first time: 'All the words are right, and all are yours.'

His thrill at hearing this does not last long, however, for a moment later comes the thought: 'Will it ever happen again?' Whatever his future life as a wage-earner, a citizen, a family man may be, to the end of his days his life as a poet will be without anticipation. He will never be able to say: 'Tomorrow I will write a poem and, thanks to my training and experience, I already know I shall do a good job.' In the eyes of others a man is a poet if he has written one good poem. In his own he is only a poet at the moment when he is making his last revision to a new poem. The moment before, he was still only a potential poet: the moment after he is a man who has ceased to write poetry, perhaps for ever.

NOTES ON THE ART OF POETRY

Dylan Thomas

At Laugharne, in the summer of 1951, Dylan Thomas (1914–1953) wrote the following replies to questions posed by a student. If the questions are very general, they elicit a response of unusual candor; if the impression is strong that the poet often proceeded largely by indirection—or chance—there is something of this quality in some of his best works. At the same time, however, he enjoys the reputation of an exceedingly conscientious craftsman. In any event, his statement that "the joy and function of poetry is . . . the celebration of man, which is also the celebration of God" suggests a lofty concept of poetry and the poet's function. Thomas's death at the age of thirty-nine was apparently the result of unresolvable inner conflicts—and alcoholism—in about equal proportions.

You want to know why and how I just began to write poetry, and which poets or kinds of poetry I was first moved and influenced by.

To answer the first part of this question, I should say I wanted to write poetry in the beginning because I had fallen in love with words. The first poems I knew were nursery rhymes, and before I could read them for myself I had come to love just the words of them, the words alone. What the words stood for, symbolised, or meant, was of very secondary importance. What mattered was the *sound* of them as I heard them for the first time on the lips of the remote and incomprehensible grown-ups who seemed, for some reason, to be living in my world. And these words were, to me, as the notes of bells, the sounds of musical instruments, the noises of wind, sea, and rain, the rattle of milkcarts, the clopping of hooves on cobbles, the fingering of branches on a window pane, might be to someone, deaf from birth, who has miraculously found his hearing. I did not care what the

words said, overmuch, nor what happened to Jack and Jill and the
Mother Goose rest of them; I cared for the shapes of sound that
their names, and the words describing their actions, made in my
ears; I cared for the colours the words cast on my eyes. I realise
that I may be, as I think back all that way, romanticising my reactions to the simple and beautiful words of those pure poems; but
that is all I can honestly remember, however much time might
have falsified my memory. I fell in love—that is the only expression I can think of—at once, and am still at the mercy of words,
though sometimes now, knowing a little of their behaviour very
well, I think I can influence them slightly and have even learned
to beat them now and then, which they appear to enjoy. I tumbled
for words at once. And, when I began to read the nursery rhymes
for myself, and, later, to read other verses and ballads, I knew
that I had discovered the most important things, to me, that
could be ever. There they were, seemingly lifeless, made only of
black and white, but out of them, out of their own being, came
love and terror and pity and pain and wonder and all the other
vague abstractions that make our ephemeral lives dangerous,
great, and bearable. Out of them came the gusts and grunts and
hiccups and heehaws of the common fun of the earth; and though
what the words meant was, in its own way, often deliciously
funny enough, so much funnier seemed to me, at that almost
forgotten time, the shape and shade and size and noise of the
words as they hummed, strummed, jugged and galloped along.
That was the time of innocence; words burst upon me, un-
encumbered by trivial or portentous association; words were
their spring-like selves, fresh with Eden's dew, as they flew out
of the air. They made their own original associations as they
sprang and shone. The words, "Ride a cock-horse to Banbury
Cross," were as haunting to me, who did not know then what a
cock-horse was nor cared a damn where Banbury Cross might
be, as, much later, were such lines as John Donne's, "Go and
catch a falling star, Get with child a mandrake root," which
also I could not understand when I first read them. And as I read
more and more, and it was not all verse, by any means, my love
for the real life of words increased until I knew that I must live
with them and *in* them always. I knew, in fact, that I must be
a writer of words, and nothing else. The first thing was to feel
and know their sound and substance; what I was going to do with
those words, what use I was going to make of them, what I was

going to *say* through them, would come later. I knew I had to
know them most intimately in all their forms and moods, their
ups and downs, their chops and changes, their needs and demands.
(Here, I am afraid, I am beginning to talk too vaguely. I do not
like writing *about* words, because then I often use bad and wrong
and stale and wooly words. What I like to do is to treat words
as a craftsman does his wood or stone or what-have-you, to hew,
carve, mould, coil, polish and plane them into patterns, sequences,
sculptures, fugues of sound expressing some lyrical impulse, some
spiritual doubt or conviction, some dimly-realised truth I must
try to reach and realise). It was when I was very young, and
just at school, that, in my father's study, before homework that
was never done, I began to know one kind of writing from another, one kind of goodness, one kind of badness. My first, and
greatest, liberty was that of being able to read everything and
anything I cared to. I read indiscriminately, and with my eyes
hanging out. I could never have dreamt that there were such
goings-on in the world between the covers of books, such sand-
storms and ice-blasts of words, such slashing of humbug, and
humbug too, such staggering peace, such enormous laughter,
such and so many blinding bright lights breaking across the
just-awaking wits and splashing all over the pages in a million
bits and pieces all of which were words, words, words, and each
of which was alive forever in its own delight and glory and
oddity and light (I must try not to make these supposedly helpful
notes as confusing as my poems themselves.) I wrote endless
imitations, though I never thought them to be imitations but,
rather, wonderfully original things, like eggs laid by tigers. They
were imitations of anything I happened to be reading at the time:
Sir Thomas Browne, de Quincey, Henry Newbolt, the Ballads,
Blake, Baroness Orczy, Marlowe, Chums, the Imagists, the Bible,
Poe, Keats, Lawrence, Anon., and Shakespeare. A mixed lot, as
you see, and randomly remembered. I tried my callow hand at
almost every poetical form. How could I learn the tricks of a
trade unless I tried to do them myself? I learned that the bad
tricks come easily; and the good ones, which help you to say
what you think you wish to say in the most meaningful, moving
way, I am still learning. (But in earnest company you must call
these tricks by other names, such as technical devices, prosodic
experiments, etc.)

The writers, then, who influenced my earliest poems and

stories were, quite simply and truthfully, all the writers I was reading at the time, and, as you see from a specimen list higher up the page, they ranged from writers of schoolboy adventure yarns to incomparable and inimitable masters like Blake. That is, when I began, bad writing had as much influence on my stuff as good. The bad influences I tried to remove and renounce bit by bit, shadow by shadow, echo by echo, through trial and error, through delight and disgust and misgiving, as I came to love words more and to hate the heavy hands that knocked them about, the thick tongues that [had] no feel for their multitudinous tastes, the dull and botching hacks who flattened them out into a colourless and insipid paste, the pedants who made them moribund and pompous as themselves. Let me say that the things that first made me love language and want to work *in* it and *for* it were nursery rhymes and folk tales, the Scottish Ballads, a few lines of hymns, the most famous Bible stories and the rhythms of the Bible, Blake's "Songs of Innocence," and the quite incomprehensible magical majesty and nonsense of Shakespeare heard, read, and near-murdered in the first forms of my school.

You ask me, next, if it is true that three of the dominant influences on my published prose and poetry are Joyce, the Bible, and Freud. (I purposely say my 'published' prose and poetry, as in the preceding pages I have been talking about the primary influences upon my very first and forever unpublishable juvenilia.) I cannot say that I have been 'influenced' by Joyce, whom I enormously admire and whose "Ulysses," and earlier stories I have read a great deal. I think this Joyce question arose because somebody once, in print, remarked on the closeness of the title of my book of short stories, "Portrait of the Artist As a Young Dog" to Joyce's title, "Portrait of the Artist as a Young Man." As you know, the name given to innumerable portrait paintings by their artists is, "Portrait of the Artist as a Young Man"—a perfectly straightforward title. Joyce used the painting-title for the first time as the title of a literary work. I myself made a bit of doggish fun of the *painting*-title and, of course, intended no possible reference to Joyce. I do not think that Joyce has had any hand at all in my writing; certainly, his "Ulysses" has not. On the other hand, I cannot deny that the shaping of some of my "Portrait" stories might owe something to Joyce's stories in the volume "Dubliners." But then, "Dubliners" was a pioneering work in the world of the short story, and no good storywriter since can have failed, in some way, however little, to have benefited by it.

The Bible, I have referred to in attempting to answer your first question. Its great stories, of Noah, Jonah, Lot, Moses, Jacob, David, Solomon and a thousand more, I had, of course, known from very early youth; the great rhythms had rolled over me from the Welsh pulpits; and I read, for myself, from Job and Ecclesiastes; and the story of the New Testament is part of my life. But I have never sat down and studied the Bible, never consciously echoed its language, and am, in reality, as ignorant of it as most brought-up Christians. All of the Bible that I use in my work is remembered from childhood, and is the common property of all who were brought up in English-speaking communities. Nowhere, indeed, in all my writing, do I use any knowledge which is not commonplace to any literate person. I *have* used a few difficult words in early poems, but they are easily looked-up and were, in any case, thrown into the poems in a kind of adolescent showing-off which I hope I have now discarded.

And that leads me to the third 'dominant influence': Sigmund Freud. My only acquaintance with the theories and discoveries of Dr. Freud has been through the work of novelists who have been excited by his case-book histories, of popular newspaper scientific-potboilers who have, I imagine, vulgarised his work beyond recognition, and of a few modern poets, including Auden, who have attempted to use psychoanalytical phraseology and theory in some of their poems. I have read only one book of Freud's, "The Interpretation of Dreams," and do not recall having been influenced by it in any way. Again, no honest writer today can possibly avoid being influenced by Freud through his pioneering work into the Unconscious and by the influence of those discoveries on the scientific, philosophic, and artistic work of his contemporaries: but not, by any means, necessarily through Freud's own writing.

To your third question—Do I deliberately utilise devices of rhyme, rhythm, and word-formation in my writing—I must, of course, answer with an immediate Yes. I am a painstaking, conscientious, involved, and devious craftsman in words, however unsuccessful the result so often appears, and to whatever wrong uses I may apply my technical paraphernalia. I use everything and anything to make my poems work and move in the direction

I want them to: old tricks, new tricks, puns, portmanteau-words, paradox, allusion, paronomasia, paragram, catachresis, slang, assonantal rhymes, vowel rhymes, sprung rhythm. Every device there is in language is there to be used if you will. Poets have got to enjoy themselves sometimes, and the twisting and convolutions of words, the inventions and contrivances, are all part of the joy that is part of the painful, voluntary work.

Your next question asks whether my use of combinations of words to create something new, "in the Surrealist way," is according to a set formula or is spontaneous.

There is a confusion here, for the Surrealists' set formula *was* to juxtapose the unpremeditated.

Let me make it clearer if I can. The Surrealists—(that is, super-realists, or those who work *above* realism)—were a coterie of painters and writers in Paris, in the nineteen twenties, who did not believe in the conscious selection of images. To put it in another way: They were artists who were dissatisfied with both the realists—(roughly speaking, those who tried to put down in paint and words an actual representation of what they imagined to be the real world in which they lived)—and the impressionists who, roughly speaking again, were those who tried to give an impression of what they imagined to be the real world. The Surrealists wanted to dive into the subconscious mind, the mind below the conscious surface, and dig up their images from there without the aid of logic of reason, and put them down, illogically and unreasonably, in paint and words. The Surrealists affirmed that, as three quarters of the mind was submerged, it was the function of the artist to gather his material from the greatest, submerged mass of the mind rather than from that quarter of the mind which, like the tip of an iceberg, protruded from the subconscious sea. One method the Surrealists used in their poetry was to juxtapose words and images that had no rational relationship; and out of this they hoped to achieve a kind of subconscious, or dream, poetry that would be truer to the real, imaginative world of the mind, mostly submerged, than is the poetry of the conscious mind that relies upon the rational and logical relationship of ideas, objects, and images.

This is, very crudely, the credo of the Surrealists, and one with which I profoundly disagree. I do not mind from where the images of a poem are dragged up; drag them up, if you like, from the nethermost sea of the hidden self; but, before they reach paper, they must go through all the rational processes of the intellect. The Surrealists, on the other hand, put their words down together on paper exactly as they emerge from chaos; they do not shape these words or put them in order; to them, chaos *is* the shape and order. This seems to me to be exceedingly presumptuous; the Surrealists imagine that whatever they dredge from their subconscious selves and put down in paint or in words must essentially be of some interest or value. I deny this. One of the arts of the poet is to make comprehensible and articulate what might emerge from subconscious sources; one of the great main uses of the intellect is to *select*, from the amorphous mass of subconscious images those that will best further his imaginative purpose, which is to write the best poem he can.

And question five is, God help us, what is my definition of Poetry?

I myself, do not read poetry for anything but pleasure. I read only the poems I like. This means, of course, that I have to read a lot of poems I don't like before I find the ones I do, but, when I *do* find the ones I do, then all I can say is "Here they are," and read them to myself for pleasure.

Read the poems you like reading. Don't bother whether they're important, or if they'll live. What does it matter what poetry *is*, after all? If you want a definition of poetry, say: "Poetry's what makes me laugh or cry or yawn, what makes my toenails twinkle, what makes me want to do this or that or nothing," and let it go at that. All that matters about poetry is the enjoyment of it, however tragic it may be. All that matters is the eternal movement behind it, the vast undercurrent of human grief, folly, pretension, exaltation, or ignorance, however unlofty the intention of the poem.

You can tear a poem apart to see what makes it technically tick, and say to yourself, when the works are laid out before you, the vowels, the consonants, the rhymes and rhythms. "Yes, this is *it*. This is why the poem moves me so. It is because of the craftsmanship." But you're back again where you began. You're back with the mystery of having been moved by words. The best craftsmanship always leaves holes and gaps in the works of the poem so that something that is *not* in the poem can creep, crawl, flash, or thunder in.

The joy and function of poetry is, and was, the celebration of man, which is also the celebration of God.

A lawyer by training and a successful executive for an insurance company, Wallace Stevens (1879–1955) was one of America's most accomplished poets of the present century. His intense, life-long involvement with French culture, most notably poetry and painting, found expression in prose works which speculate not only on the nature and function of poetry, but on poetry's relationship with the other arts as well. In the present essay, from The Necessary Angel, *Stevens comes to terms with the delicate area where poetry and painting may intersect. It is typical of Stevens's thought that he should see both poetry and painting as functions of the imagination and of the "miraculous reason" as common to the imaginations of all artists. The present essay is rich in referential materials and cogent in its discourse; in addition to being one of the most valuable essays of its kind in this collection, it is doubtless the most difficult. Nevertheless, as with all of Stevens' work, it nobly repays close study.*

THE RELATIONS BETWEEN POETRY AND PAINTING

Wallace Stevens

I

Roger Fry concluded a note on Claude by saying that "few of us live so strenuously as never to feel a sense of nostalgia for that Saturnian reign to which Virgil and Claude can waft us." He spoke in that same note of Corot and Whistler and Chinese landscape and certainly he might just as well have spoken, in relation to Claude, of many poets, as, for example, Chénier or Wordsworth. This is simply the analogy between two different forms of poetry. It might be better to say that it is the identity of poetry revealed as between poetry in words and poetry in paint.

Poetry, however, is not limited to Virgilian landscape, nor painting to Claude. We find the poetry of mankind in the figures of the old men of Shakespeare, say, and the old men of Rembrandt; or in the figures of Biblical women, on the one hand, and of the madonnas of all Europe, on the other; and it is easy to wonder whether the poetry of children has not been created by the poetry of the Child, until one stops to think how much of the poetry of the whole world is the poetry of children, both as they are and as they have been written of and painted, as if they were the creatures of a dimension in which life and poetry are one. The poetry of humanity is, of course, to be found everywhere.

There is a universal poetry that is reflected in everything. This remark approaches the idea of Baudelaire that there exists an unascertained and fundamental aesthetic, or order, of which poetry and painting are manifestations, but of which, for that matter, sculpture or music or any other aesthetic realization would equally be a manifestation. Generalizations as expansive as these: that there is a universal poetry that is reflected in everything or that there may be a fundamental aesthetic of which poetry and painting are related but dissimilar manifestations, are speculative. One is better satisfied by particulars.

No poet can have failed to recognize how often a detail or remark, apropos in respect to painting, applies also to poetry. The truth is that there seems to exist a corpus of remarks in respect to painting, most often the remarks of painters themselves, which are as significant to poets as to painters. All of these details, to the extent that they have meaning for poets as well as for painters, are specific instances of relations between poetry and painting. I suppose, therefore, that it would be possible to study poetry by studying painting or that one could become a painter after one had become a poet, not to speak of carrying on in both métiers at once, with the economy of genius, as Blake did. Let me illustrate this point of the double value (and one might well call it the multifold value) of sayings for painters that mean as much for poets because they are, after all, sayings about art. Does not the saying of Picasso that a picture is a horde of destructions also say that a poem is a horde of destructions? When Braque says "The senses deform, the mind forms," he is speaking to poet, painter, musician and sculptor. Just as poets can be affected by the sayings of painters, so can painters be affected by the sayings of poets and so can both be affected by sayings addressed to neither. For many examples, see Miss Sitwell's *Poet's Note-Book*. These details come together so subtly and so minutely that the existence of relations is lost sight of. This, is turn, dissipates the idea of their existence.

II

We may regard the subject, then, from two points of view, the first from the point of view of the man whose center is painting, whether or not he is a painter, the second from the point of view of the man whose center is poetry, whether or not he is a poet. To make use of the point of view of the man whose center is painting let me refer to the chapter in Leo Stein's *Appreciation* entitled "On Reading Poetry and Seeing Pictures." He says that, when he was a child, he became aware of composition in nature and gradually realized that art and composition are one. He began to experiment as follows:

I put on the table . . . an earthenware plate . . . and this I looked at every day for minutes or for hours. I had in mind to see it as a picture, and waited for it to become one. In time it did. The change came suddenly when the plate as an inventorial object . . . a certain shape, certain colors applied to it . . . went over into a composition to which all these elements were merely contributory. The painted composition on the plate ceased to be *on* it but became a part of a larger composition which was the plate as a whole. I had made a beginning to seeing pictorially.

What had been begun was carried out in all directions. I wanted to be able to see anything *as* a composition and found that it was possible to do this.

He improvised a definition of art: that it is nature seen in the light of its significance, and recognizing that this significance was one of forms, he added "formal" to "significance."

Turning to education in hearing, he observed that there is nothing comparable to the practice in composition that the visible world offers. By composition he meant the compositional use of words: the use of their existential meanings. Composition was his passion. He considered that a formally complete picture is one in which all the parts are so related to one another that they all imply each other. Finally he said, "an excellent illustration is the line from Wordsworth's 'Michael' . . . 'And never lifted up a single stone.' " One might say of a lazy workman, "He's been out there, just loafing, for an hour and never lifted up a single stone," and no one would think this great poetry. . . . These lines would have no existential value; they would simply call attention to the lazy workman. But the compositional use by Wordsworth of his line makes it something entirely different. These simple words become weighted with the tragedy of the old shepherd, and are saturated with poetry. Their referential importance is slight, for the importance of the action to which they refer is not in the action itself, but in the meaning; and that meaning is borne by the words. Therefore this is a line of great poetry.

The selection of composition as a common denominator of poetry and painting is the selection of a technical characteristic by a man whose center was painting, even granting that he was not a man whom one thinks of as a technician. Poetry and painting alike create through composition.

Now, a poet looking for an analogy between poetry and painting and trying to take the point of view of a man whose center is poetry begins with a sense that the technical pervades painting to such a degree that the two are identified. This is untrue, since, if painting was purely technical, that conception of it would exclude the artist as a person. I want to say something, therefore, based on the sensibility of the poet and of the painter. I am not quite sure that I know what is meant by sensibility. I suppose that it means feeling or, as we say, the feelings. I know what is meant by nervous sensibility, as, when at a concert, the auditors, having composed themselves and resting there attentively, hear suddenly an outburst on the trumpets from which they shrink by way of a nervous reaction. The satisfaction that we have when we look out and find that it is a fine day or when we are looking at one of the limpid vistas of Corot in the *pays de Corot* seems to be something else. It is commonly said that the origins of poetry are to be found in the sensibility. We began with the conjunction of Claude and Virgil, noting how one evoked the other. Such evocations are attributable to similarities of sensibility. If, in Claude, we find ourselves in the realm of Saturn, the ruler of the world in a golden age of innocence and plenty, and if, in Virgil, we find ourselves in the same realm, we recognize that there is, as between Claude and Virgil, an identity of sensibility. Yet if one questions the dogma that the origins of poetry are to be found in the sensibility and if one says that a fortunate poem or a fortunate painting is a synthesis of exceptional concentration (that

degree of concentration that has a lucidity of its own, in which
we see clearly what we want to do and do it instantly and perfectly), we find that the operative force within us does not, in
fact, seem to be the sensibility, that is to say, the feelings. It
seems to be a constructive faculty, that derives its energy more
from the imagination than from the sensibility. I have spoken
of questioning, not of denying. The mind retains experience, so
that long after the experience, long after the winter clearness of
a January morning, long after the limpid vistas of Corot, that
faculty within us of which I have spoken makes its own constructions out of that experience. If it merely reconstructed the
experience or repeated for us our sensations in the face of it, it
would be the memory. What it really does is to use it as material
with which it does whatever it wills. This is the typical function
of the imagination which always makes use of the familiar to
produce the unfamiliar. What these remarks seem to involve is
the substitution for the idea of inspiration of the idea of an
effort of the mind not dependent on the vicissitudes of the
sensibility. It is so completely possible to sit at one's table and
without the help of the agitation of the feelings to write plays
of incomparable enhancement that that is precisely what Shakespeare did. He was not dependent on the fortuities of inspiration.
It is not the least part of his glory that one can say of him, the
greater the thinker the greater the poet. It would come nearer the
mark to say the greater the mind the greater the poet, because
the evil of thinking as poetry is not the same thing as the good
of thinking in poetry. The point is that the poet does his job by
virtue of an effort of the mind. In doing so, he is in rapport with
the painter, who does his job, with respect to the problems of
form and color, which confront him incessantly, not by inspiration, but by imagination or by the miraculous kind of reason
that the imagination sometimes promotes. In short, these two
arts, poetry and painting, have in common a laborious element,
which, when it is exercised, is not only a labor but a consumma-
tion as well. For proof of this let me set side by side the poetry
in the prose of Proust, taken from his vast novel, and the painting,
by chance, of Jacques Villon. As to Proust, I quote a paragraph
from Professor Saurat:

Another province he has added to literature is the description of those
eternal moments in which we are lifted out of the drab world. . . .

The madeleine dipped in tea, the steeples of Martinville, some trees on a road, a perfume of wild flowers, a vision of light and shade on trees, a spoon clinking on a plate that is like a railway man's hammer on the wheels of the train from which the trees were seen, a stiff napkin in an hotel, an inequality in two stones in Venice and the disjointment in the yard of the Guermantes' town house. . . .

As to Villon: shortly before I began to write these notes I dropped into the Carré Gallery in New York to see an exhibition of paintings which included about a dozen works by him. I was immediately conscious of the presence of the enchantments of intelligence in all his prismatic material. A woman lying in a hammock was transformed into a complex of planes and tones, radiant, vaporous, exact. A tea-pot and a cup or two took their place in a reality composed wholly of things unreal. These works were *deliciae* of the spirit as distinguished from *delectationes* of the senses and this was so because one found in them the labor of calculation, the appetite for perfection.

III

One of the characteristics of modern art is that it is uncompromising. In this it resembles modern politics, and perhaps it would appear on study, including a study of the rights of man and of women's hats and dresses, that everything modern, or possibly merely new, is, in the nature of things, uncompromising. It is especially uncompromising in respect to precinct. One of the De Goncourts said that nothing in the world hears as many silly things said as a picture in a museum; and in thinking about that remark one has to bear in mind that in the days of the De Goncourts there was no such thing as a museum of modern art. A really modern definition of modern art, instead of making concessions, fixes limits which grow smaller and smaller as time passes and more often than not come to include one man alone, just as if there should be scrawled across the façade of the building in which we now are, the words *Cézanne delineavit*. Another characteristic of modern art is that it is plausible. It has a reason for everything. Even the lack of a reason becomes a reason. Picasso expresses surprise that people should ask what a picture means and says that pictures are not intended to have meanings. This explains everything. Still another characteristic of modern art is that it is bigoted. Every painter who can be defined as a modern painter becomes, by virtue of that definition, a freeman of the world of art and hence the equal of any other modern painter. We recognize that they differ one from another but in any event they are not to be judged except by other modern painters.

We have this inability (not mere unwillingness) to compromise, this same plausibility and bigotry in modern poetry. To exhibit this, let me divide modern poetry into two classes, one that is modern in respect to what it says, the other that is modern in respect to form. The first kind is not interested primarily in form. The second is. The first kind is interested in form but it accepts a banality of form as incidental to its language. Its justification is that in expressing thought or feeling in poetry, the purpose of the poet must be to subordinate the mode of expression, that, while the value of the poem as a poem depends on expression, it depends primarily on what is expressed. Whether the poet is modern or ancient, living or dead, is, in the last analysis, a question of what he is talking about, whether of things modern or ancient, living or dead. The counterpart of Villon in poetry, writing as he paints, would concern himself with like things (but not necessarily confining himself to them), creating the same sense of aesthetic certainty, the same sense of exquisite realization and the same sense of being modern and living. One sees a good deal of poetry, thanks, perhaps, to Mallarmé's *Un Coup de Dés*, in which the exploitation of form involves nothing more than the use of small letters for capitals, eccentric line-endings, too little or too much punctuation and similar aberrations. These have nothing to do with being alive. They have nothing to do with the conflict between the poet and that of which his poems are made. They are neither "bonne soupe" nor "beau langage."

What I have said of both classes of modern poetry is inadequate as to both. As to the first, which permits a banality of form, it is even harmful, as suggesting that it possesses less of the artifice of the poet than the second. Each of these two classes is intransigent as to the other. If one is disposed to think well of the class that stands on what it has to say, one has only to think of Gide's remark, "Without the unequaled beauty of his prose, who would continue to interest himself in Bossuet?" The division between the two classes, the division, say, between Valéry

and Apollinaire, is the same division into factions that we find
everywhere in modern painting. But aesthetic creeds, like other
creeds, are the certain evidences of exertions to find the truth.
I have tried to say no more than was necessary to evince the
relations, in which we are interested, as they exist in the manifestations of today. What, when all is said and done, is the
significance of the existence of such relations? Or is it enough
to note them? The question is not the same as the question of the
significance of art. We do not have to be told of the significance
of art. "It is art," said Henry James, "which makes life, makes
interest, makes importance . . . and I know of no substitute whatever for the force and beauty of its process." The world about
us would be desolate except for the world within us. There is
the same interchange between these two worlds that there is
between one art and another, migratory passings to and fro,
quickenings, Promethean liberations and discoveries.

Yet it may be that just as the senses are no respecters of reality,
so the faculties are no respecters of the arts. On the other hand,
it may be that we are dealing with something that has no significance, something that is the result of imitation. Quatremère de
Quincy distinguished between the poet and the painter as between two imitators, one moral, the other physical. There are
imitations within imitations and the relations between poetry
and painting may present nothing more. This idea makes it possible, at least, to see more than one side of the subject.

IV

All of the relations of which I have spoken are themselves related in the deduction that the *vis poetica*, the power of poetry,
leaves its mark on whatever it touches. The mark of poetry
creates the resemblance of poetry as between the most disparate
things and unites them all in its recognizable virtue. There is one
relation between poetry and painting which does not participate
in the common mark of common origin. It is the paramount
relation that exists between poetry and people in general and between painting and people in general. I have not overlooked the
possibility that, when this evening's subject was suggested, it was
intended that the discussion should be limited to the relations
between modern poetry and modern painting. This would have

involved much tinkling of familiar cymbals. In so far as it would have called for a comparison of this poet and that painter, this school and that school, it would have been fragmentary and beyond my competence. It seems to me that the subject of modern relations is best to be approached as a whole. The paramount relation between poetry and painting today, between modern man and modern art is simply this: that in an age in which disbelief is so profoundly prevalent or, if not disbelief, indifference to questions of belief, poetry and painting, and the arts in general, are, in their measure, a compensation for what has been lost. Men feel that the imagination is the next greatest power to faith: the reigning prince. Consequently their interest in the imagination and its work is to be regarded not as a phase of humanism but as a vital self-assertion in a world in which nothing but the self remains, if that remains. So regarded, the study of the imagination and the study of reality come to appear to be purified, aggrandized, fateful. How much stature, even vatic stature, this conception gives the poet! He need not exercise this dignity in vatic works. How much authenticity, even orphic authenticity, it gives to the painter! He need not display this authenticity in orphic works. It should be enough for him that that to which he has given his life should be so enriched by such an access of value. Poet and painter alike live and work in the midst of a generation that is experiencing essential poverty in spite of fortune. The extension of the mind beyond the range of the mind, the projection of reality beyond reality, the determination to cover the ground, whatever it may be, the determination not to be confined, the recapture of excitement and intensity of interest, the enlargement of the spirit at every time, in every way, these are the unities, the relations, to be summarized as paramount now. It is not material whether these relations exist consciously or unconsciously. One goes back to the coercing influences of time and place. It is possible to be subjected to a lofty purpose and not to know it. But I think that most men of any degree of sophistication, most poets, most painters know it.

When we look back at the period of French classicism in the seventeenth century, we have no difficulty in seeing it as a whole. It is not so easy to see one's own time that way. Pretty much all of the seventeenth century, in France, at least, can be summed up in that one word: classicism. The paintings of Poussin, Claude's contemporary, are the inevitable paintings of the generation of Racine. If it had been a time when dramatists used the detailed scene directions that we expect today, the directions of Racine would have left one wondering whether one was reading the description of a scene or the description of one of Poussin's works. The practice confined them to the briefest generalization. Thus, after the list of persons in *King Lear*, Shakespeare added only two words: "Scene: Britain." Yet even so, the directions of Racine, for all their brevity, suggest Poussin. That a common quality is to be detected in such simple things exhibits the extent of the interpenetration persuasively. The direction for *Britannicus* is "The scene is at Rome, in a chamber of the palace of Nero"; for *Iphigénie en Aulide*, "The scene is at Aulis, before the tent of Agamemnon"; for *Phèdre*, "The scene is at Trézène, a town of the Peloponnesus"; for *Esther*, "The scene is at Susa, in the palais of Assuérus"; and for *Athalie*, "The scene is in the temple of Jerusalem, in a vestibule of the apartment of the grand priest."

Our own time, and by this I mean the last two or three generations, including our own, can be summed up in a way that brings into unity an immense number of details by saying of it that it is a time in which the search for the supreme truth has been a search in reality or through reality or even a search for some supremely acceptable fiction. Juan Gris began some notes on his painting by saying: "The world from which I extract the elements of reality is not visual but imaginative." The history of this attitude in literature and particularly in poetry, in France, has been traced by Marcel Raymond in his *From Baudelaire to Surrealism*. I say particularly in poetry because there are associated with it the names of Baudelaire, Rimbaud, Mallarmé and Valéry. In painting, its history is the history of modern painting. Moreover, I say in France because, in France, the theory of poetry is not abstract as it so often is with us, when we have any theory at all, but is a normal activity of the poet's mind in surroundings where he must engage in such activity or be extirpated. Thus necessity develops an awareness and a sense of fatality which give to poetry values not to be reproduced by indifference and chance. To the man who is seeking the sanction of life in poetry, the namby-pamby is an intolerable dissipation. The theory of poetry, that is to say, the total of the theories of poetry, often seems to become in time a mystical theology or, more simply, a mystique. The reason for this must by now be clear.

The reason is the same reason why the pictures in a museum of modern art often seem to become in time a mystical aesthetic, a prodigious search of appearance, as if to find a way of saying and of establishing that all things, whether below or above appearance, are one and that it is only through reality, in which they are reflected or, it may be, joined together, that we can reach them. Under such stress, reality changes from substance to subtlety, a subtlety in which it was natural for Cézanne to say: "I see planes bestriding each other and sometimes straight lines seem to me to fall" or "Planes in color. . . . The colored area where shimmer the souls of the planes, in the blaze of the kindled prism, the meeting of planes in the sunlight." The conversion of our *Lumpenwelt* went far beyond this. It was from the point of view of another subtlety that Klee could write: "But he is one chosen that today comes near to the secret places where original law fosters all evolution. And what artist would not establish himself there where the organic center of all movement in time and space—which he calls the mind or heart of creation —determines every function." Conceding that this sounds a bit like sacerdotal jargon, that is not too much to allow to those that have helped to create a new reality, a modern reality, since what has been created is nothing less.

This reality is, also, the momentous world of poetry. Its instantaneities are the familiar intelligence of poets, although it has been the intelligence of another ambiance. Simone Weil in *La Pesanteur et La Grâce* has a chapter on what she calls decreation. She says that decreation is making pass from the created to the uncreated, but that destruction is making pass from the created to nothingness. Modern reality is a reality of decreation, in which our revelations are not the revelations of belief, but the precious portents of our own powers. The greatest truth we could hope to discover, in whatever field we discovered it, is that man's truth is the final resolution of everything. Poets and painters alike today make that assumption and this is what gives them the validity and serious dignity that become them as among those that seek wisdom, seek understanding. I am elevating this a little, because I am trying to generalize and because it is incredible that one should speak of the aspirations of the last two or three generations without a degree of elevation. Sometimes it seems the other way. Sometimes we hear it said that in the eighteenth century there were no poets and that the painters—

Chardin, Fragonard, Watteau—were élégants and nothing more; that in the nineteenth century the last great poet was the man that looked most like one and that the whole Pierian sodality had better have been fed to the dogs. It occasionally seems like that today. It must seem as it may. In the logic of events, the only wrong would be to attempt to falsify the logic, to be disloyal to the truth. It would be tragic not to realize the extent of man's dependence on the arts. The kind of world that might result from too exclusive a dependence on them has been questioned, as if the discipline of the arts was in no sense a moral discipline. We have not to discuss that here. It is enough to have brought poetry and painting into relation as sources of our present conception of reality, without asserting that they are the sole sources, and as supports of a kind of life, which it seems to be worth living, with their support, even if doing so is only a stage in the endless study of an existence, which is the heroic subject of all study.

A major figure in American poetry, Theodore Roethke (1908–1963) wrote and taught in several universities, most notably at the University of Washington, Seattle, from 1948 until his death in 1963. The Waking (1953) won the Pulitzer Prize; in 1958 Words for the Wind won seven awards, including the Bollingen Prize and the National Book Award. The Far Field, published posthumously in 1964, won a second National Book Award. Roethke portrayed a wide variety of subject matter: human excitement at natural events, identity emerging from death or separation, the haunting nature of childhood memories, the world of the plant struggling for life—these number among his recurring themes. His classically oriented style is as varied as the content it shaped, for Roethke acknowledged the seventeenth-century poets as well as Blake, Clare, Stevens, and Yeats as his greatest influences. The essay which follows (in response to readers' letters) indicates certain of Roethke's convictions on the spiritual nature of the world.

ON "IDENTITY"

Theodore
Roethke

I remember the late E. E. Cummings once answered a questionnaire—from *New Verse*, the English magazine of the thirties: answered it by quotations from his own work. At the time, being a fierce, youngish man, I thought this a bit exhibitionistic: but now I'm beginning to see the point. One has said a thing as best one can in the poem—in usually a dramatic context: why debase it or water it down to a didactic prose for a lazy modern audience. But this is not a lazy audience, but a young, idealistic, and deeply serious audience: I can judge by its letters, its questions, indeed, I have been astonished at the pertinence, the relevance of the general subjects; and even more astonished by the fact that, I judge from Mr. Payson Wilde's letter, all this has official credence and sanction. It would seem you have administrators who read—even books.

I take it that we are faced with at least four principal themes: (1) The multiplicity, the chaos of modern life; (2) The way, the means of establishing a personal identity, a self in the face of that chaos; (3) The nature of creation, that faculty for producing order out of disorder in the arts, particularly in poetry; and (4) The nature of God Himself.

I take it as the poet, the intuitive man, I am entitled to, am expected to, throw out what suggestions, what hints I can from my own work, from my own life. I think of this life as an instrument, as an example; and I am perfectly willing to appear ridiculous, absurd, if a real point can be established, a real dent can be made.

I had reason to be delighted with Mr. Bracken's letter: after all he quoted from my work four times. An all-time record. "Nice young man," I thought; "either going to go far, or go entirely mad." Besides, his prose was better than mine. I felt that, in Kierkegaardian terms, we had reached the true state of education in one bound: the student was teaching the teacher. Behind his letter and the various statements I received, one could sense a real hunger for a reality more than the immediate: a desire not only for a finality, for a consciousness beyond the mundane, but a desire for quietude, a desire for joy. Now this desire is what the drunkard, the saint, the mystic hankers for in varying ways:—a purity, a final innocence—the phrase is Mr. Spender's. I think we Americans are very wistful about it. Yet we continue to make a fetish of "thing-hood," we surround ourselves with junk, ugly objects endlessly repeated in an economy dedicated to waste. Hence the possible relevance of my quotation from "Dolor," which I repeat in part:

> I have known the inexorable sadness of pencils,
> Neat in their boxes, dolor of pad and paper-weight, . . .
> And I have seen dust from the walls of institutions,
> Finer than flour, alive, more dangerous than silica,
> Sift, almost invisible, through long afternoons of tedium,
> Dropping a fine film on nails and delicate eyebrows,
> Glazing the pale hair, the duplicate gray standard faces.

This poem is an exposition of one of the modern hells: the institution that overwhelms the individual man. The "order," the trivia of the institution, is, in human terms, a disorder, and as such, must be resisted. It's truly a sign of psychic health that the young are already aware of this. How far-reaching all this is, how subtle its ramifications, how disastrous to the human psyche—to worship bigness, the firm, the university; numbers, even, let me say, the organized team effort.

The human problem is to find out what one really *is*: whether one exists, whether existence is possible. But how? "Am I but nothing, leaning toward a thing?" I think of what I wrote and felt nearly thirty years ago in a period of ill-health and economic terror—the first poem in my first book. The middle stanza says:

> My truths are all foreknown,
> This anguish self-revealed,
> I'm naked to the bone,
> With nakedness my shield.
> Myself is what I wear:
> I keep the spirit spare.

The last stanza was personally prophetic:

> The anger will endure,
> The deed will speak the truth
> In language strict and pure.
> I stop the lying mouth:
> Rage warps my clearest cry
> To witless agony.

All this has been said before, in Thoreau, in Rilke.

I was going through, though I didn't realize it at the time, a stage that all contemplative men must go through. This poem is a clumsy, innocent, desperate asseveration. I am not speaking of the empirical self, the flesh-bound ego; it's a single word: *myself*, the aggregate of the several selves, if you will. The spirit or soul—should we say the self, once perceived, *becomes* the soul?—this I was keeping "spare" in my desire for the essential. But the spirit need not be spare: it can grow gracefully and beautifully like a tendril, like a flower. I did not know this at the time. This sense I tried later to describe, metaphorically, many times:

> The spirit moves,
> Yet stays:
> Stirs as a blossom stirs,

Still wet from its bud-sheath,
Slowly unfolding,
Turning in the light with its tendrils;
Plays as a minnow plays,
Tethered to a limp weed, swinging,
Tail around, nosing in and out of the current,
Its shadows loose, a watery finger;
Moves, like the snail,
Still inward,
Taking and embracing its surroundings,
Never wishing itself away,
Unafraid of what it is,
A music in a hood,
A small thing,
Singing.

Nor need this final self, or spirit, be a foulness, a disgusting thing from which we should be delivered. A stanza from Stanley Kunitz says:

Father, the darkness of the self goes out
And spreads contagion in the flowing air.
I walk obscurely in a cloud of dark:
Yea, when I kneeled, the dark kneeled down with me.
Touch me: my folds and my defenses fall;
I stand within myself, myself my shield.

This is far more complex than my little stanza, with a great line: "Yea, when I kneeled, the dark kneeled down with me." But this sense of contamination, the "my taste was me," is *not* a necessity: we need *not* be guilt-ridden—if we are pure in heart. It may, of course, as in the Kunitz stanza, be a prelude to a real psychic purgation.

But the young often do have an acute sense of defilement, a hatred of the body. Thus I remember marking this feeling in a violent little poem:

I hate my epidermal dress,
The savage blood's obscenity,
The rags of my anatomy,
And willingly would I dispense
With false accouterments of sense,

> To sleep immodestly, a most
> Incarnadine and carnal ghost.

Hyperbole, of course, but behind it is still the same desire for a reality of the spirit. Again I was wrong. For the body should be cherished: a temple of God, some Christians say.

In any quest for identity today—or any day—we run up inevitably against this problem: What to do with our ancestors? I mean it as an ambiguity: both the literal or blood, and the spiritual ancestors. Both, as we know, can overwhelm us. The devouring mother, the furious papa. And if we're trying to write, the Supreme Masters. In this same harried period, I wrote, in a not very good poem:

> Corruption reaps the young. You dread
> The menace of ancestral eyes
> Recoiling from the serpent head
> Of fate, you blubber in surprise. . . .

And so on . . . in the last stanza,

> You meditate upon the nerves,
> Inflame with hate. This ancient feud
> Is seldom won. The spirit starves
> Until the dead have been subdued.

I remember the late John Peale Bishop, that fine neglected poet, reading this and saying, "You're impassioned, but wrong. The dead can help us." And he was right; but it took me some years to learn that.

Let me say boldly, now, that the extent to which the great dead can be evoked, or can come to us, can be eerie, and astonishing. Let me, at the risk of seeming odd, recite a personal incident.

I was in that particular hell of the poet: a longish dry period. It was 1952, I was 44, and I thought I was done. I was living alone in a biggish house in Edmonds, Washington. I had been reading— and re-reading—not Yeats, but Ralegh and Sir John Davies. I had been teaching the five-beat line for weeks—I knew quite a bit about it, but write it myself?—*no*: so I felt myself a fraud.

Suddenly, in the early evening, the poem "The Dance" started, and finished itself in a very short time—say thirty minutes, maybe in the greater part of an hour, it was all done. I felt, I *knew*, I had hit it. I walked around, and I wept; and I knelt down—I always do after I've written what I know is a good piece. But at the same time I had, as God is my witness, the actual sense of a Presence— as if Yeats himself were *in* that room. The experience was in a way terrifying, for it lasted at least half an hour. That house, I repeat, was charged with a psychic presence: the very walls seemed to shimmer. I wept for joy. At last I was somebody again. He, they—the poets dead—were with me.

Now I know there are any number of cynical explanations for this phenomenon: auto-suggestion, the unconscious playing an elaborate trick, and so on, but I accept none of them. It was one of the most profound experiences of my life.

If the dead can come to our aid in a quest for identity, so can the living—and I mean *all* living things, including the sub-human. This is not so much a naïve as a primitive attitude: animistic, maybe. Why not? Everything that lives is holy: I call upon these holy forms of life. One could even put this theologically: St. Thomas says, "God is above all things by the excellence of His nature; nevertheless, He is in all things as causing the being of all things." Therefore, in calling upon the snail, I am calling, in a sense, upon God:

> Snail, snail, glister me forward,
> Bird, soft-sigh me home.
> Worm, be with me.
> This is my hard time.

Or again, in a passage Mr. Bracken mentions:

> I could watch! I could watch!
> I saw the separateness of all things!
> My heart lifted up with the great grasses;
> The weeds believed me, and the nesting birds.

It is paradoxical that a very sharp sense of the being, the identity of some other being—and in some instances, even an inanimate thing—brings a corresponding heightening and awareness of one's own self, *and*, even more mysteriously, in some instances, a feeling of the oneness of the universe. Both feelings are not always present, I'm aware, but either can be an occasion for gratitude. And *both* can be induced. The first simply by intensity in the seeing. To look at a thing so long that you are a part of it and it is a part of you—Rilke gazing at his tiger for eight hours, for instance. If you can effect this, then you are by way of getting somewhere: knowing you will break from self-involvement, from I to Otherwise, or maybe even to Thee.

True, I'm speaking in these lines of a heightened consciousness. In the early part of that poem, nature was "dead," ambiguous, ominous. But the "angel," an emissary of the "other," was invoked; there was some kind of ritualistic, even penitential, act: "Was it dust I was kissing? . . . Alone, I kissed the skin of a stone."—the inanimate itself becomes alive before the final euphoria of this piece.

The second part of this feeling, the "oneness," is, of course, the first stage in mystical illumination, an experience many men have had, and still have: the sense that all is one and one is all. This is inevitably accompanied by a loss of the "I," the purely human ego, to another center, a sense of the absurdity of death, a return to a state of innocency.

This experience has come to me so many times, in so many varying circumstances, that I cannot suspect its validity: it is *not* one of the devil's traps, an hallucination, a voice, a snare. I can't claim that the soul, my soul, was absorbed in God. No, God for me still remains someone to be confronted, to be dueled with: that is perhaps my error, my sin of pride. But the oneness, Yes!

But let us return to the more homely but related form of exaltation: creativity itself. Can we say this: that the self can be found in love, in human, mutual love, in work that one loves—not in *arbeit* in the German sense? Think of what happened to them and is still happening. The novel, that secondary form, can teach us how to act; the poem, and music, how to feel: and the feeling is vastly more important. And the "creativity" may be vicarious. Once we feel deeply, to paraphrase Marianne Moore, we begin to behave.

And of all the instruments for verbal creativity close at hand today, the supreme example seems to me the short lyric.

When I was young, to make something in language, a poem that was all of a piece, a poem that could stand for what I was at the time—that seemed to be the most miraculous thing in the world. Most scholarship seemed irrelevant rubbish; most teachers seemed lacking in wisdom, in knowledge they had proved on their pulses. Certain writers called out to me: I believed them implicitly. I still do.

"We think by feeling. What is there to know?" This, in its essence, is a description of the metaphysical poet who thinks with his body: an idea for him can be as real as the smell of a flower or a blow on the head. And those so lucky as to bring their whole sensory equipment to bear on the process of thought grow faster, jump more frequently from one plateau to another more often.

And it is one of the ways man at least approaches the divine—in this comprehensive human act, the really good poem.

For there *is* a God, and He's here, immediate, accessible. I don't hold with those thinkers that believe in this time He is farther away—that in the Middle Ages, for instance, He was closer. He is equally accessible now, not only in works of art or in the glories of a particular religious service, or in the light, the aftermath that follows the dark night of the soul, but in the lowest forms of life, He moves and has His being. Nobody has killed off the snails. Is this a new thought? Hardly. But it needs some practicing in Western society. Could Reinhold Niebuhr love a worm? I doubt it. But I—we—can.

THEATRE
AND
DANCE

No one in the modern theater is a more eloquent defender of the social drama than George Bernard Shaw (1856–1950). His plays exemplify the drama that deals with social problems at its most engaging, if not necessarily at its most profound. In his prefaces to his plays, Shaw explained what he was doing, always with charm, and often with a crackling, crusading zeal for social, political, and economic justice that continues to be moving even in areas where justice has long since had its due in almost precisely the terms that Shaw demanded. A learned, witty, and persuasive theater critic and theorist, he is never better than when his crusade for justice in society is joined to his crisp criticism of those playwrights either too dull or too timid to crusade for justice in their own works. In this short statement, full of crackle and crusade, Shaw sums up, in effect, his own achievement in the social drama as well as Henrik Ibsen's. He not only asserts his principles, but does so with such clarity and logic that even the most dogged opponent of the drama of social consciousness must pause long and think hard before rejecting any part of the argument, the principle, or the drama.

THE PROBLEM PLAY—

A SYMPOSIUM

George Bernard Shaw

Should social problems be freely dealt with in the Drama?

The Humanitarian VI, May, 1895

I do not know who has asked the question, Should social problems be freely dealt with in the drama?—some very thoughtless person evidently. Pray what social questions and what sort of drama? Suppose I say yes, then, vaccination being a social question, and the Wagnerian music drama being the one complete form of drama in the opinion of its admirers, it will follow that I am in favor of the production of a Jennerian tetralogy at Bayreuth.[1] If I say no, then, marriage being a social question, and also the theme of Ibsen's *Doll's House*, I shall be held to contemn that work as a violation of the canons of art. I therefore reply to the propounder that I am not prepared to waste my own time and that of the public in answering maladroit conundrums. What I am prepared to do is to say what I can with the object of bringing some sort of order into the intellectual confusion which has expressed itself in the conundrum.

Social questions are produced by the conflict of human institutions with human feeling. For instance, we have certain institutions regulating the lives of women. To the women whose feelings are entirely in harmony with these institutions there is no Woman Question. But during the present century, from the time of Mary Wollstonecraft [English feminist, 1759–1797, mother by William Godwin of Shelley's wife Mary] onwards, women have been developing feelings, and consequently opinions, which clash with these institutions. The institutions assumed that it was natural to a woman to allow her husband to own her property and person, and to represent her in politics as a father represents his infant child. The moment that seemed no longer natural to some women, it became grievously oppressive to them. Immediately there was a Woman Question, which has produced Married Women's Property Acts, Divorce Acts, Woman's Suffrage in local elections, and the curious deadlock to which the Weldon and Jackson cases have led our courts in the matter of conjugal rights. When we have achieved reforms enough to bring our institutions as far into harmony with the feelings of women as they now are with the feelings of men, there will no longer be a Woman Question. No conflict, no question.

Now the material of the dramatist is always some conflict of human feeling with circumstances; so that, since institutions are circumstances, every social question furnishes material for drama. But every drama does not involve a social question, because human feeling may be in conflict with circumstances which are not institutions, which raise no question at all, which are part of human destiny. To illustrate, take Mr. Pinero's *Second Mrs. Tanqueray* [most famous of the characters of the English play-

---

[1] Shaw's fanciful set of plays, designed for performance at Wagner's festival city of Bayreuth, is based on the achievement of Dr. Edward Jenner (1749–1823), the English physician who discovered vaccination.

wright Sir Arthur Wing Pinero, 1855–1934, in the play of the
same name]. The heroine's feelings are in conflict with the
human institutions which condemn to ostracism both herself and
the man who marries her. So far, the play deals with a social
question. But in one very effective scene the conflict is between
that flaw in the woman's nature which makes her dependent for
affection wholly on the attraction of her beauty, and the stealthy
advance of age and decay to take her beauty away from her.
Here there is no social question: age, like love, death, accident,
and personal character, lies outside all institutions; and this gives
it a permanent and universal interest which makes the drama that
deals with it independent of period and place. Abnormal greatness of character, abnormal baseness of character, love, and
death: with these alone you can, if you are a sufficiently great
dramatic poet, make a drama that will keep your language alive
long after it has passed out of common use. Whereas a drama
with a social question for the motive cannot outlive the solution
of that question. It is true that we can in some cases imaginatively
reconstruct an obsolete institution and sympathize with the
tragedy it has produced: for instance, the very dramatic story of
Abraham commanded to sacrifice his son, with the interposition
of the angel to make a happy ending; or the condemnation of
Antonio to lose a pound of flesh, and his rescue by Portia at the
last moment, have not completely lost their effect nowadays—
though it has been much modified—through the obsolescence of
sacrificial rites, belief in miracles, and the conception that a
debtor's person belongs to his creditors. It is enough that we still
have paternal love, death, malice, moneylenders, and the tragedies
of criminal law. But when a play depends entirely on a social
question—when the struggle in it is between man and a purely
legal institution—nothing can prolong its life beyond that of the
institution. For example, Mr. Grundy's *Slaves of the Ring* [a
play of the utmost inconsequence by a sentimental and melodramatic playwright (Sydney Grundy, 1848–1914) of the same
merit], in which the tragedy is produced solely by the conflict
between the individual and the institution of indissoluble marriage, will not survive a rational law of divorce, and actually fails
even now to grip an English audience because the solution has
by this time become so very obvious. And that irrepressibly
popular play *It's Never Too Late to Mend* will hardly survive
our abominable criminal system. Thus we see that the drama

which deals with the natural factors in human destiny, though not necessarily better than the drama which deals with the political factors, is likely to last longer.

It has been observed that the greatest dramatists show a prefer- ence for the non-political drama, the greatest dramas of all being almost elementarily natural. But so, though for a different reason, do the minor dramatists. The minor dramatist leads the literary life, and dwells in the world of imagination instead of in the world of politics, business, law, and the platform agitations by which social questions are ventilated. He therefore remains, as a rule, astonishingly ignorant of real life. He may be clever, imagi- native, sympathetic, humorous, and observant of such manners as he has any clue to; but he has hardly any wit or knowledge of the world. Compare his work with that of Sheridan, and you feel the deficiency at once. Indeed, you need not go so far as Sheridan: Mr. Gilbert's *Trial by Jury* is unique among the works of living English playwrights, solely because it, too, is the work of a wit and a man of the world. Incidentally, it answers the inquiry as to whether social questions make good theatrical material; for though it is pointless, and, in fact, unintelligible except as a satire on a social institution (the breach-of-promise suit), it is highly entertaining, and has made the fortune of the author and his musical collaborator. *The School for Scandal*, the most popular of all modern comedies, is a dramatic sermon, just as *Never Too Late to Mend*, the most popular of modern melo- dramas, is a dramatic pamphlet: Charles Reade [1814–1884, author of *Never Too Late to Mend*, an English novelist who moved his own works and others' (such as Tennyson's *Dora* and Zola's *L'Assommoir*) onto the stage with some box-office and critical success but little theatrical skill] being another example of the distinction which the accomplished man of the world at- tains in the theatre as compared to the mere professional dramatist. In fact, it is so apparent that the best and most popular plays are dramatized sermons, pamphlets, satires, or bluebooks, that we find our popular authors, even when they have made a safe posi- tion for themselves by their success in purely imaginative drama, bidding for the laurels and the percentages of the sociologist dramatist. Mr. Henry Arthur Jones [1851–1929, along with Shaw and Pinero, one of the top English playwrights at the turn of the century; admired by Shaw as a social portraitist in the theater] takes a position as the author of *The Middleman* and *The Cru-*

saders, which *The Silver King,* enormously popular as it was, never could have gained him; and Mr. Pinero, the author of *The Second Mrs. Tanqueray* and *The Notorious Mrs. Ebbsmith,* is a much more important person, and a much richer one, than the author of *Sweet Lavender* [a highly sentimental play by Pinero]. Of course, the sociology in some of these dramas is as imaginary as the names and addresses of the characters; but the imitation sociology testifies to the attractiveness of the real article.

We may take it then that the ordinary dramatist only neglects social questions because he knows nothing about them, and that he loses in popularity, standing, and money by his ignorance. With the great dramatic poet it is otherwise. Shakespear and Goethe do not belong to the order which "takes no interest in politics." Such minds devour everything with a keen appetite— fiction, science, gossip, politics, technical processes, sport, everything. Shakespear is full of little lectures of the concrete English kind, from Cassio on temperance to Hamlet on suicide. Goethe, in his German way, is always discussing metaphysical points. To master Wagner's music dramas is to learn a philosophy. It was so with all the great men until the present century. They swallowed all the discussions, all the social questions, all the topics, all the fads, all the enthusiasms, all the fashions of their day in their non-age; but their theme finally was not this social question or that social question, this reform or that reform, but humanity as a whole. To this day your great dramatic poet is never a socialist, nor an individualist, nor a positivist, nor a materialist, nor any other sort of "ist," though he comprehends all the "isms," and is generally quoted and claimed by all the sections as an adherent. Social questions are too sectional, too topical, too temporal to move a man to the mighty effort which is needed to produce great poetry. Prison reform may nerve Charles Reade to produce an effective and businesslike prose melodrama; but it could never produce *Hamlet, Faust,* or *Peer Gynt.*

It must, however, be borne in mind that the huge size of modern populations and the development of the press make every social question more momentous than it was formerly. Only a very small percentage of the population commits murder; but the population is so large that the frequency of executions is appalling. Cases which might have come under Goethe's notice in Weimar perhaps once in ten years come daily under the notice of modern newspapers, and are described by them as sensa-

tionally as possible. We are therefore witnessing a steady intensification in the hold of social questions on the larger poetic
imagination. *Les Misérables,* with its rivulet of story running
through a continent of essays on all sorts of questions, from religion to main drainage, is a literary product peculiar to the nineteenth century: it shows how matters which were trifles to
Æschylus become stupendously impressive when they are multiplied by a million in a modern civilized state. Zola's novels are
the product of an imagination driven crazy by a colossal police
intelligence, by modern hospitals and surgery, by modern war
correspondence, and even by the railway system—for in one of
his books the hero is Jack the Ripper and his sweetheart a loco-
motive engine. What would Aristophanes have said to a city
with fifteen thousand lunatics in it? Might he not possibly have
devoted a comedy to the object of procuring some amelioration
in their treatment? At all events, we find Ibsen, after producing,
in *Brand, Peer Gynt,* and *Emperor and Galilean,* dramatic poems
on the grandest scale, deliberately turning to comparatively
prosaic topical plays on the most obviously transitory social
questions, finding in their immense magnitude under modern
conditions the stimulus which, a hundred years ago, or four
thousand, he would only have received from the eternal strife
of man with his own spirit. *A Doll's House* will be as flat
as ditchwater when *A Midsummer Night's Dream* will still
be as fresh as paint; but it will have done more work in the
world; and that is enough for the highest genius, which is always
intensely utilitarian.

Let us now hark back for a moment to the remark I made on
Mr. Grundy's *Sowing the Wind:*[2] namely, that its urgency and
consequently its dramatic interest are destroyed by the fact that
the social question it presents is really a solved one. Its production after *Les Surprises de Divorce* (which Mr. Grundy himself
adapted for England) was an anachronism. When we succeed in
adjusting our social structure in such a way as to enable us to
solve social questions as fast as they become really pressing, they
will no longer force their way into the theatre. Had Ibsen, for instance, had any reason to believe that the abuses to which he

---

[2] Evidently a slip for *Slaves of the Ring,* mentioned above. This play was the
subject of Shaw's first contribution to *The Saturday Review* as dramatic critic
(January 5, 1895). He had printed on March 23, 1895 a comment on a revival
of *Sowing the Wind,* which he found better than Grundy's usual product.

called attention in his prose plays would have been adequately attended to without his interference, he would no doubt have gladly left them alone. The same exigency drove William Morris in England from his tapestries, his epics, and his masterpieces of printing, to try and bring his fellow-citizens to their senses by the summary process of shouting at them in the streets and in Trafalgar Square. John Ruskin's writing began with *Modern Painters;* Carlyle began with literary studies of German culture and the like: both were driven to become revolutionary pamphleteers. If people are rotting and starving in all directions, and nobody else has the heart or brains to make a disturbance about it, the great writers must. In short, what is forcing our poets to follow Shelley in becoming political and social agitators, and to turn the theatre into a platform for propaganda and an arena for discussion, is that whilst social questions are being thrown up for solution almost daily by the fierce rapidity with which industrial processes change and supersede one another through the rivalry of the competitors who take no account of ulterior social consequences, and by the change in public feeling produced by popular "education," cheap literature, facilitated travelling, and so forth, the political machinery by which alone our institutions can be kept abreast of these changes is so old-fashioned, and so hindered in its action by the ignorance, the apathy, the stupidity, and the class feuds of the electorate, that social questions never get solved until the pressure becomes so desperate that even governments recognize the necessity for moving. And to bring the pressure to this point, the poets must lend a hand to the few who are willing to do public work in the stages at which nothing but abuse is to be gained by it.

Clearly, however, when the unhappy mobs which we now call nations and populations settle down into ordered commonwealths, ordinary bread-and-butter questions will be solved without troubling the poets and philosophers. The Shelleys, the Morrises, the Ruskins and Carlyles of that day will not need to spend their energies in trying to teach elementary political economy to the other members of the commonwealth; nor will the Ibsens be devising object lessons in spoiled womanhood, sickly consciences, and corrupt town councils, instead of writing great and enduring dramatic poems.

I need not elaborate the matter further. The conclusions to be drawn are:

1. Every social question, arising as it must from a conflict between human feeling and circumstances, affords material for drama.

2. The general preference of dramatists for subjects in which the conflict is between man and his apparently inevitable and eternal rather than his political and temporal circumstances, is due in the vast majority of cases to the dramatist's political ignorance (not to mention that of his audience), and in a few to the comprehensiveness of his philosophy.

3. The hugeness and complexity of modern civilizations and the development of our consciousness of them by means of the press, have the double effect of discrediting comprehensive philosophies by revealing more facts than the ablest man can generalize, and at the same time intensifying the urgency of social reforms sufficiently to set even the poetic faculty in action on their behalf.

4. The resultant tendency to drive social questions on to the stage, and into fiction and poetry, will eventually be counteracted by improvements in social organization, which will enable all prosaic social questions to be dealt with satisfactorily long before they become grave enough to absorb the energies which claim the devotion of the dramatist, the storyteller, and the poet.

Bertolt Brecht (1898–1956) is as much a social dramatist as Bernard Shaw, yet, at the same time, as far removed in style and technique from Shaw as Shaw is from Ben Jonson or Molière. Brecht instructs by parable and by placard, by theater song and any other device that can be infused with his left-wing political and social ironies. Those ironies sometimes exist at the expense of his Communist associates, whether by intention or not, leaving Brecht a figure of captivating elusiveness in the modern theater. He had succeeded too well, perhaps, in his efforts to alienate his audiences, to keep them from vicarious involvement with the events on his stage, even when he and they shared the same political convictions. But no one can seriously debate the mastery with which Brecht brought learning and pleasure together in his self-styled "epic theater." Even in performances less meticulous than those he himself mounted with his Berliner Ensemble, such plays as his The Threepenny Opera, Arturo Ui, Galileo, The Good Woman of Setzuan, Mother Courage, *and* The Caucasian Chalk Circle *entertain at least as much as they instruct. The principles outlined here thus seem applicable to the presentation of any serious point of view in the theater.*

THEATRE FOR LEARNING OR

THEATRE FOR PLEASURE

Bertolt Brecht

When anyone spoke of modern theater a few years ago, he mentioned the Moscow, the New York or the Berlin theatre. He may also have spoken of a particular production of Jouvet's in Paris, of Cochran's in London, or the Habima performance of "The Dybbuk,"[1] which, in fact, belonged to Russian

---

[1] Louis Jouvet (1887–1951), French actor and producer, particularly well known for his production of the plays of Jean Giraudoux. Charles Cochran (1873–1951), most famous of London impresarios of his era. The Habima was the famous Moscow theatrical company formed by Stanislavsky's assistant, Eugene Vakhtangov in 1917 for the performance of plays in Hebrew; the name means "stage."

theater, since it was directed by Vakhtangov; but by and large, there were only three capitals as far as modern theatre was concerned.

The Russian, the American and the German theatres were very different from one another, but they were alike in being modern, i.e., in introducing technical and artistic innovations. In a certain sense they even developed stylistic similarities, probably because technique is international (not only the technique directly required for the stage, but also that which exerts an influence on it, the film, for example) and because the cities in question were great progressive cities in great industrial countries. Most recently, the Berlin theatre seemed to have taken the lead among the most advanced capitalist countries. What was common to modern theatre found there its strongest and, for the moment, most mature expression.

The last phase of the Berlin theatre, which as I said only revealed in its purest form the direction in which modern theatre was developing, was the so-called *epic theatre*. What was known as the "Zeitstueck" (a play dealing with current problems— Trans.) or Piscator theater or the didactic play all belonged to epic theatre.

EPIC THEATRE

The expression "epic theatre" seemed self-contradictory to many people, since according to the teachings of Aristotle the epic and the dramatic forms of presenting a story were considered basically different from one another. The difference between the two forms was by no means merely seen in the fact that one was performed by living people while the other made use of a book—epic works like those of Homer and the *minnesingers* of the Middle Ages were likewise theatrical performances, and dramas like Goethe's "Faust" or Byron's "Manfred" admittedly achieved their greatest effect as books. Aristotle's teachings themselves distinguished the dramatic from the epic form as a difference in construction, whose laws were dealt with under two different branches of aesthetics. This construction depended on the different way in which the works were presented to the public, either on the stage or through a book, but nevertheless,

Mother Courage, *Berliner Ensemble, East Berlin.*
Photograph by René Burri. Magnum.

apart from that, "the dramatic" could also be found in epic works and "the epic" in dramatic works. The bourgeois novel in the last century considerably developed "the dramatic," which meant the strong centralization of plot and an organic interdependence of the separate parts. "The dramatic" is characterized by a certain passion in the tone of the exposition and a working out of the collision of forces. The epic writer, Döblin,[2] gave an excellent description when he said that the epic, in contrast to the dramatic, could practically be cut up with a scissors into single pieces, each of which could stand alone.

I do not wish to discuss here in what way the contrasts between epic and dramatic, long regarded as irreconcilable, lost their rigidity, but simply to point out that (other causes aside) technical achievements enabled the stage to include narrative elements in dramatic presentations. The potentialities of projection, the film, the greater facility in changing sets through machinery, completed the equipment of the stage and did so at a moment when the most important human events could no longer be so simply portrayed as through personification of the moving forces or through subordinating the characters to invisible, metaphysical powers. To make the events understandable, it had become necessary to play up the "bearing" of the *environment* upon the people living in it.

Of course this environment had been shown in plays before, not, however, as an independent element but only from the viewpoint of the main figure of the drama. It rose out of the hero's reaction to it. It was seen as a storm may be "seen" if you observe on the sea a ship spreading its sails and the sails bellying. But in the epic theatre it was now to appear as an independent element.

The stage began to narrate. The narrator no longer vanished with the fourth wall. Not only did the background make its own comment on stage happenings through large screens which evoked other events occurring at the same time in other places, documenting or contradicting statements by characters through quotations projected onto a screen, lending tangible, concrete statistics to abstract discussions, providing facts and figures for happenings which were plastic but unclear in their meaning; the

---

[2] Alfred Döblin (1878–1957), German novelist and essayist. His best-known work was the novel *Berlin-Alexanderplatz*.

actors no longer threw themselves completely into their roles but maintained a certain distance from the character performed by them, even distinctly inviting criticism.

Nothing permitted the audience any more to lose itself through simple empathy, uncritically (and practically without any consequences) in the experiences of the characters on the stage. The presentation exposed the subject matter and the happenings to a process of de-familiarization.[3] De-familiarization was required to make things understood. When things are "self-evident," understanding is simply dispensed with. The "natural" had to be given an element of the *conspicuous*. Only in this way could the laws of cause and effect become plain. Characters had to behave as they *did* behave, and at the same time be capable of behaving otherwise.

These were great changes.

TWO OUTLINES

The following little outlines may indicate in what respect the function of the epic is distinguished from that of the dramatic theatre.

1.

Dramatic form	*Epic form*
The stage "incarnates" an event.	It relates it.
Involves the audience in an action, uses up its activity.	Makes the audience an observer, but arouses its activity.
Helps it to feel.	Compels it to make decisions.
Communicates experiences.	Communicates insights.
The audience is projected into an event.	Is confronted with it.
Suggestion is used.	Arguments are used.
Sensations are preserved.	Impelled to the level of perceptions.

[3] In German, "Entfremdung," sometimes translated as "alienation," and sometimes called "Verfremdung" by Brecht. The latter is an invented word like "defamiliarization."—*Translator's note.*

Dramatic form	*Epic form*
The character is a known quantity.	The character is subjected to investigation.
Man unchangeable.	Man who can change and make changes.
His drives.	His motives.
Events move in a straight line.	In "irregular" curves.
Natura non facit saltus.	Facit saltus.
The world as it is.	The world as it is becoming.

2.

The audience in the dramatic theater says:
Yes, I have felt that too.—That's how I am.—That is only natural.—That will always be so.—This person's suffering shocks me because he has no way out. This is great art: everything in it is self-evident.—I weep with the weeping, I laugh with the laughing.

The audience in the epic theater says:
I wouldn't have thought that.—People shouldn't do things like that.—That's extremely odd, almost unbelievable.—This has to stop.—This person's suffering shocks me, because there might be a way out for him.—This is great art: nothing in it is self-evident. —I laugh over the weeping, I weep over the laughing.

DIDACTIC THEATER

The stage began to instruct.

Oil, inflation, war, social struggles, the family, religion, wheat, the meat-packing industry became subjects for theatrical portrayal. Choruses informed the audience about facts it did not know. In montage form, films showed events all over the world. Projections provided statistical data. As the "background" came to the fore, the actions of the characters became exposed to criticism. Wrong and right actions were exhibited. People were shown who knew what they were doing, and other people were shown who did not know. The theater entered the province of the philosophers—at any rate, the sort of philosophers who wanted not only to explain the world but also to change it. Hence the theater philosophized; hence it instructed. And what became of entertainment? Were the audiences put back in school, treated as illiterates? Were they to take examinations and be given marks?

It is the general opinion that a very decided difference exists between learning and being entertained. The former may be useful, but only the latter is pleasant. Thus we have to defend the epic theater against a suspicion that it must be an extremely unpleasant, a joyless, indeed a wearing business.

Well, we can only say that the contrast between learning and being entertained does not necessarily exist in nature, it has not always existed and it need not always exist.

Undoubtedly, the kind of learning we did in school, in training for a profession, etc., is a laborious business. But consider under what circumstances and for what purpose it is done. It is, in fact, a purchase. Knowledge is simply a commodity. It is acquired for the purpose of being re-sold. All those who have grown too old for school have to pursue knowledge on the Q.T., so to speak, because anybody who admits he still has to study depreciates himself as one who knows too little. Apart from that, the utility of learning is very much limited by factors over which the student has no control. There is unemployment, against which no knowledge protects. There is the division of labor, which makes comprehensive knowledge unnecessary and impossible. Often, those who study do it only when they see no other possibility of getting ahead. There is not much knowledge that procures power, but much knowledge is only procured through power.

Learning means something very different to people in different strata of society. There are people who cannot conceive of any improvement in conditions; conditions seem good enough to them. Whatever may happen to petroleum, they make a profit out of it. And they feel, after all, that they are getting rather old. They can scarcely expect many more years of life. So why continue to learn? They have already spoken their "Ugh!"[4] But there are also people who have not yet "had their turn," who are discontented with the way things are, who have an immense practical interest in learning, who want orientation badly, who know they are lost without learning—these are the best and most ambitious learners. Such differences also exist among nations and peoples. Thus the lust for learning is dependent on various

4 Reference to popular German literature about American Indians, by the author Karl May, in which, after a chieftain had given his opinion at a pow-wow he would conclude, "I have spoken. Ugh!"—*Translator's note.*

things; in short, there *is* thrilling learning, joyous and militant learning.

If learning could not be delightful, then the theater, by its very nature, would not be in a position to instruct.

Theater remains theater, even when it is didactic theater, and if it is good theater it will entertain.

THEATER AND SCIENCE

"But what has science to do with art? We know very well that science can be diverting, but not everything that diverts belongs in the theater."

I have often been told when I pointed out the inestimable services that modern science, properly utilized, could render to art, especially to the theater, that art and science were two admirable but completely different fields of human activity. This is a dreadful platitude, of course, and the best thing to do is admit at once that it is quite right, like most platitudes. Art and science operate in very different ways—agreed. Still, I must admit—bad as this may sound—that I cannot manage as an artist without making use of certain sciences. This may make many people seriously doubt my artistic ability. They are accustomed to regarding poets as unique, almost unnatural beings who unerringly, practically like gods, perceive things that others can only perceive through the greatest efforts and hard work. Naturally, it is unpleasant to have to admit not being one of those so endowed. But it must be admitted. It must also be denied that this application to science has anything to do with some pardonable avocation indulged in the evening after work is done. Everyone knows that Goethe also went in for natural science, Schiller for history—presumably this is the charitable assumption —as a sort of hobby. I would not simply accuse these two of having needed the science for their poetic labors, nor would I use them to excuse myself, but I must say I need the sciences. And I must even admit that I regard suspiciously all sorts of people who I know do not keep abreast of science, who, in other words, sing as the birds sing, or as they imagine the birds sing. This does not mean that I would reject a nice poem about the taste of a flounder or the pleasure of a boating party just because the author had not studied gastronomy or navigation. But I think that unless every resource is employed towards understanding the great, complicated events in the world of man, they cannot be seen adequately for what they are.

Let us assume that we want to portray great passions or events which influence the fates of peoples. Such a passion today might be the drive for power. Supposing that a poet "felt" this drive and wanted to show someone striving for power—how could he absorb into his own experience the extremely complicated mechanism within which the struggle for power today takes place? If his hero is a political man, what are the workings of politics, if he is a business man, what are the workings of business? And then there are poets who are much less passionately interested in any individual's drive for power than in business affairs and politics as such! How are they to acquire the necessary knowledge? They will scarcely find out enough by going around and keeping their eyes open, although that is at least better than rolling their eyes in a fine frenzy. The establishment of a newspaper like the *Voelkische Beobachter* or a business like Standard Oil is a rather complicated matter, and these things are not simply absorbed through the pores. Psychology is an important field for the dramatist. It is supposed that while an ordinary person may not be in a position to discover, without special instruction, what makes a man commit murder, certainly a writer ought to have the "inner resources" to be able to give a picture of a murderer's mental state. The assumption is that you only need look into yourself in such a case; after all, there is such a thing as imagination. . . . For a number of reasons I can no longer abandon myself to this amiable hope of managing so comfortably. I cannot find in myself alone all the motives which, as we learn from newspapers and scientific reports, are discovered in human beings. No more than any judge passing sentence am I able to imagine adequately, unaided, the mental state of a murderer. Modern psychology, from psychoanalysis to behaviorism, provides me with insights which help me to form a quite different judgment of the case, especially when I take into consideration the findings of sociology, and do not ignore economics or history. You may say: this is getting complicated. I must answer, it *is* complicated. Perhaps I can talk you into agreeing with me that a lot of literature is extremely primitive; yet you will ask in grave concern: Wouldn't such an evening in the theater be a pretty alarming business? The answer to that is: No.

Whatever knowledge may be contained in a poetic work, it must be completely converted into poetry. In its transmuted form, it gives the same type of satisfaction as any poetic work. And although it does not provide that satisfaction found in science as such, a certain inclination to penetrate more deeply into the nature of things, a desire to make the world controllable, are necessary to ensure enjoyment of poetic works generated by this era of great discoveries and inventions.

IS THE EPIC THEATER A SORT OF "MORAL INSTITUTION"?

According to Friedrich Schiller the theater should be a moral institution. When Schiller posed this demand it scarcely occurred to him that by moralizing from the stage he might drive the audience out of the theater. In his day the audience had no objection to moralizing. Only later on did Friedrich Nietzsche abuse him as the moral trumpeter of Säckingen.[5] To Nietzsche a concern with morality seemed a dismal affair; to Schiller it seemed completely gratifying. He knew of nothing more entertaining and satisfying than to propagate ideals. The bourgeoisie was just establishing the concept of the nation. To furnish your house, show off your new hat, present your bills for payment is highly gratifying. But to speak of the decay of your house, to have to sell your old hat and pay the bills yourself is a truly dismal affair, and that was how Friedrich Nietzsche saw it a century later. It was no use talking to him about morality or, in consequence, about the other Friedrich. Many people also attacked the epic theater, claiming it was too moralistic. Yet moral utterances were secondary in the epic theater. Its intention was less to moralize than to study. And it did study, but then came the rub: the moral of the story. Naturally, we cannot claim that we began making studies just because studying was so much fun and not for any concrete reason, or that the results of our studies then took us completely by surprise. Undoubtedly there were painful discrepancies in the world around us, conditions that were hard to bear, conditions of a kind not only hard to bear for

---

[5] Nietzsche's quip referred to a banal verse tale by Viktor Scheffel, *Der Trompeter von Säckingen,* a standard favorite in Germany's "plush sofa kultur"—a parallel of Victorianism—in the second half of the nineteenth century.—*Translator's note.*

moral reasons. Hunger, cold and hardship are not only burden-some for moral reasons. And the purpose of our investigation was not merely to arouse moral misgivings about certain condi-tions (although such misgivings might easily be felt, if not by every member of the audience; such misgivings, for example, were seldom felt by those who profited by the conditions in question). The purpose of our investigation was to make visible the means by which those onerous conditions could be done away with. We were not speaking on behalf of morality but on behalf of the wronged. These are really two different things, for moral allusions are often used in telling the wronged that they must put up with their situation. For such moralists, people exist for morality, not morality for people.

Nevertheless it can be deduced from these remarks to what extent and in what sense the epic theater is a moral institution.

CAN EPIC THEATER
BE PERFORMED ANYWHERE?

From the standpoint of style, the epic theater is nothing espe-cially new. In its character of show, of demonstration, and its emphasis on the artistic, it is related to the ancient Asian theater. The medieval mystery play, and also the classical Spanish and Jesuit theaters, showed an instructive tendency.

Those theater forms corresponded to certain tendencies of their time and disappeared with them. The modern epic theater is also linked with definite tendencies. It can by no means be per-formed anywhere. Few of the great nations today are inclined to discuss their problems in the theater. London, Paris, Tokyo and Rome maintain their theaters for quite different purposes. Only in a few places, and not for long, have circumstances been favorable to an epic, instructive theater. In Berlin, fascism put a violent end to the development of such a theater.[6]

Besides a certain technical standard, it presupposes a powerful social movement which has an interest in the free discussion of

[6] After the defeat of the Nazis in 1945, the German administrators of the then Soviet-occupied zone—now the German Democratic Republic—invited Brecht to establish his own theater in East Berlin. This theater, the "Berliner Ensemble," is recognized today all over the world as a classical type of epic theater.—*Translator's note.*

vital problems, the better to solve them, and can defend this interest against all opposing tendencies.

The epic theater is the broadest and most far-reaching experiment in great modern theater, and it has to overcome all the enormous difficulties that all vital forces in the area of politics, philosophy, science and art have to overcome.

Translated from the German by Edith Anderson.

THE ETERNAL LAW OF THE DRAMATIST

Jean Giraudoux

If there is a social consciousness in either the plays or the dramatic theory of Jean Giraudoux (1882–1944), it springs from a world of vision, one constantly and perilously at odds with the world of drab reality. Wherever possible, Giraudoux's fanciful figures elect illusion and dream in their combat with the tyrannies that bedevil their lives— the tyrannies of war and super-finance, of nationalist and religious and sexual simplifications, of huge things and of little things. His Judith, La Guerre de Troie n'aura pas lieu (The Trojan War Will Not Take Place, *translated by Christopher Fry as* Tiger at the Gates), Ondine, Sodom and Gomorrah, *and* The Madwoman of Chaillot *are perhaps the most considerable body of plays contributed to the French theater in the first half of this century. Tragedy, irony, fantasy, paradox—all are in Giraudoux, all are part of the dramatic credo so swiftly and so engagingly sketched here. The words in which this most elegant of prophets defines his prophetic theater, the concluding words of this piece, are worthy of pondering and, it may be, just the faintest* amen—*or, as one of Giraudoux's characters would murmur,* ainsi soit-il, *"so be it."*

Two rules govern, if I may speak in this way, the eternal law of the dramatist.

The first consecrates the sorry and somewhat ridiculous position of the author in relation to those of his characters that he has created and given to the theatre. To the extent that he finds a character to be docile, familiar, belonging to him, to that extent the character becomes foreign and indifferent to the author once it is given to the public. The first actor to play the part constitutes the first in a series of reincarnations in which the character becomes more and more distant from its author and steals away from him forever. This is also true of the play as a whole. After the first performance it belongs to the actors, and the author who haunts the wings become a sort of ghost, detested by the stagehands if he listens or is indiscreet; after the hundredth performance, especially if the play is a good one, it belongs to the public. The truth is that the playwright really owns only his bad plays. The independence of those of his characters who have succeeded is complete; the life they lead on tour or in America is a constant denial of their filial obligations, and, while the heroes of your novels follow you everywhere calling you Father or Daddy, dramatic characters among those whom you meet by chance, as has happened to me in Carcassonne or in Los Angeles, have become total strangers. To a large extent it is to punish them for this independence that Goethe, Claudel, and many others have made new versions of plays with their favorite heroines. In vain. The new Margaret, the new Helen, the new Violaine were no less prompt to abandon them. I once went to a performance of *The Tidings Brought to Mary* with Claudel and, on that occasion at least, this situation worked in my favor: the play, I observed, was infinitely more mine than it was his.

How many authors are obliged to search in an actress or actor for the memory of the reflection of a daughter or son who has gone off—much as parents, in a more everyday setting, must do in a son-in-law or daughter-in-law. . . . On the terrace of Weber, in the generals' vestibule, on the lawn of the country house of a famous actress, how many of these couples have we met: Feydeau and Cassive, Jules Renard and Suzanne Deprès, Réjane and Maurice Donnay [famous pairings of the late nineteenth- and early twentieth-century French writers and actresses], the woman just a little absent-minded, the man attentive and absorbed in memories, loquacious and questioning, talking about the woman who was not there.

The second law, a corollary and the reverse of the first, consecrates the wonderful position of the dramatic author in relation to his epoch and its events, and indicates his role. And here, if I wish to be truthful, I surely must relieve my colleagues and myself of any false modesty. This narrator, who in the play is but a voice, without personality, without responsibility, but who is also an historian and an avenger, exists in the age as flesh and bone; he is the dramatic author himself. For every playwright worthy of the name, one should be able to say, when his work is performed: "Add the archangel to your play!" It is vain to believe that a year or a century can find the resonance and the elevation which are necessary, in the long run, to this pathetic debate and this sorry effort which is each moment of our passage on earth, if there were not a spokesman for the tragedy or the drama to fix its height and to plumb its foundation and vault. Tragedy and drama are the confession this army of salvation and damnation which is humanity must also make in public, without reticence and in its highest pitch, for the echo of its voice is more distinct and more real than the voice itself. We should not delude ourselves on this point. The relationship between the theatre and religious solemnity is evident, and it is not by chance that in front of our cathedrals there used to be dramatic performances at every occasion. The theatre is at its best in the church courtyard. It is there that the public goes to the theater on holiday nights, to the illuminated confession of its dwarfed and gigantic destinies. Calderón is humanity confessing its desire for eternity, Corneille its dignity, Racine its weakness, Shakespeare its passion for life, Claudel its condition of sin and salvation, Goethe its humanity, Kleist its lightning. Epochs are in accord with themselves only if the crowd comes into these radiant confessionals which are the theatres or the arenas, and as much as possible, in its most brilliant confessional dress, in order to increase the solemnity of the event, to listen to its own confessions of cowardice and sacrifice, of hate and passion. And what if the crowd too should exclaim: "Add the prophet to the play!" For there is no theatre which is not prophecy. Not this false divination which gives names and dates, but true prophecy, that which reveals to men these surprising truths: that the living must live, that the living must die, that autumn must follow summer, spring follow winter, that there are four elements, that there is happiness, that there are innumerable miseries, that life is a reality, that it is a dream, that man lives in peace, that man lives on blood; in short, those things they will never know. Such is the theatre, the public restoration of these incredible prodigies whose visions will disturb and overwhelm the night of the onlookers, but whose dawn, no doubt—my faith rejoices in it— to make the author's mission an everyday reality, will have already diluted in them the lesson and the memory. This is dramatic representation, the spectator's sudden consciousness of the permanent condition of this living and indifferent humanity: passion and death.

For some years in the 1950s and 1960s, one standard piece in the Sunday supplements of British and American newspapers was that on the "Theater of the Absurd." This piece was received by readers who were almost invariably bewildered, beguiled, infuriated, or delighted, if one could gather correctly from the mail that followed. If the piece was written, as it often enough was, by Martin Esslin (1918–), the reader was also informed— at length and with incontrovertible authority. Esslin is the master biographer and geographer of the Theater of the Absurd, the author of a book on it and of another on Brecht, one of its major progenitors. He has produced its plays for BBC radio and television. He has made himself familiar with every hill and valley, every contour of the

THE THEATRE OF THE

world of the Absurd. And he has linked that world with others in the theater, demonstrating as he does so the considerable range and depth of this particular theater. The Absurd is clearly not, he shows, an arriviste, a crude upstart in the modern world. It is, in fact, the very mirror of our world. If we dismiss it, we may be dismissing ourselves.

ABSURD

Martin Esslin

The plays of Samuel Beckett, Arthur Adamov, and Eugène Ionesco have been performed with astonishing success in France, Germany, Scandinavia, and the English-speaking countries. This reception is all the more puzzling when one considers that the audiences concerned were amused by and applauded these plays fully aware that they could not understand what they meant or what their authors were driving at.

At first sight these plays do, indeed, confront their public with a bewildering experience, a veritable barrage of wildly irrational, often nonsensical goings-on that seem to go counter to all accepted standards of stage convention. In these

plays, some of which are labeled "antiplays," neither the time
nor the place of the action are ever clearly stated. (At the beginning of Ionesco's *The Bald Soprano* the clock strikes seventeen.) The characters hardly have any individuality and often
even lack a name; moreover, halfway through the action they
tend to change their nature completely. Pozzo and Lucky in
Beckett's *Waiting for Godot*, for example, appear as master and
slave at one moment only to return after a while with their respective positions mysteriously reversed. The laws of probability
as well as those of physics are suspended when we meet young
ladies with two or even three noses (Ionesco's *Jack or the Submission*), or a corpse that has been hidden in the next room that
suddenly begins to grow to monstrous size until a giant foot
crashes through the door onto the stage (Ionesco's *Amédée*). As
a result, it is often unclear whether the action is meant to represent a dream world of nightmares or real happenings. Within
the same scene the action may switch from the nightmarish
poetry of high emotions to pure knock-about farce or cabaret,
and above all, the dialogue tends to get out of hand so that at
times the words seem to go counter to the actions of the characters on the stage, to degenerate into lists of words and phrases
from a dictionary or traveler's conversation book, or to get
bogged down in endless repetitions like a phonograph record
stuck in one groove. Only in this kind of demented world can
strangers meet and discover, after a long polite conversation and
close cross-questioning, that, to their immense surprise, they
must be man and wife as they are living on the same street, in the
same house, apartment, room, and bed (Ionesco's *The Bald Soprano*). Only here can the whole life of a group of characters
revolve around the passionate discussion of the aesthetics and
economics of pinball machines (Adamov's *Ping-Pong*). Above
all, everything that happens seems to be beyond rational motivation, happening at random or through the demented caprice of
an unaccountable idiot fate. Yet, these wildly extravagant tragic
farces and farcial tragedies, although they have suffered their
share of protests and scandals, do arouse interest and are received
with laughter and thoughtful respect. What is the explanation
for this curious phenomenon?

The most obvious, but perhaps too facile answer that suggests
itself is that these plays are prime examples of "pure theatre."
They are living proof that the magic of the stage can persist even

outside, and divorced from, any framework of conceptual rationality. They prove that exits and entrances, light and shadow, contrasts in costume, voice, gait and behavior, pratfalls and embraces, all the manifold mechanical interactions of human puppets in groupings that suggest tension, conflict, or the relaxation of tensions, can arouse laughter or gloom and conjure up an atmosphere of poetry even if devoid of logical motivation and unrelated to recognizable human characters, emotions, and objectives.

But this is only a partial explanation. While the element of "pure theatre" and abstract stagecraft is certainly at work in the plays concerned, they also have a much more substantial content and meaning. Not only *do* all these plays make sense, though perhaps not obvious or conventional sense, they also give expression to some of the basic issues and problems of our age, in a uniquely efficient and meaningful manner, so that they meet some of the deepest needs and unexpressed yearnings of their audience.

The three dramatists that have been grouped together here would probably most energetically deny that they form anything like a school or movement. Each of them, in fact, has his own roots and sources, his own very personal approach to both form and subject matter. Yet they also clearly have a good deal in common. This common denominator that characterizes their works might well be described as the element of *the absurd*. "Est absurde ce qui n'a pas de but . . ." ("Absurd is that which has no purpose, or goal, or objective"), the definition given by Ionesco in a note on Kafka,[1] certainly applies to the plays of Beckett and Ionesco as well as those of Arthur Adamov up to his latest play, *Paolo Paoli*, when he returned to a more traditional form of social drama.

Each of these writers, however, has his own special type of absurdity: in Beckett it is melancholic, colored by a feeling of futility born from the disillusionment of old age and chronic hopelessness; Adamov's is more active, aggressive, earthy, and tinged with social and political overtones; while Ionesco's absurdity has its own fantastic knock-about flavor of tragical clowning. But they all share the same deep sense of human isolation and of the irremediable character of the human condition.

As Arthur Adamov put it in describing how he came to write his first play *La Parodie* (1947):

[1] Ionesco, "Dans les Armes de la Ville," *Cahiers de la Compagnie Madeleine Renaud-Jean-Louis Barrault*, No. 20 (October, 1957).

I began to discover stage scenes in the most commonplace everyday events. [One day I saw] a blind man begging; two girls went by without seeing him, singing: "I closed my eyes; it was marvelous!" This gave me the idea of showing on stage, as crudely and as visibly as possible, the loneliness of man, the absence of communication among human beings.[2]

Looking back at his earliest effort (which he now regards as unsuccessful) Adamov defines his basic idea in it, and a number of subsequent plays, as the idea "that the destinies of all human beings are of equal futility, that the refusal to live (of the character called N.) and the joyful acceptance of life (by the employee) both lead, by the same path, to inevitable failure, total destruction."[3] It is the same futility and pointlessness of human effort, the same impossibility of human communication which Ionesco expresses in ever new and ingenious variations. The two old people making conversation with the empty air and living in the expectation of an orator who is to pronounce truths about life, but turns out to be deaf and dumb (*The Chairs*), are as sardonically cruel a symbol of this fundamentally tragic view of human existence as Jack (*Jack or the Submission*), who stubbornly resists the concerted urgings of his entire family to subscribe to the most sacred principle of his clan—which, when his resistance finally yields to their entreaties, turns out to be the profound truth: "I love potatoes with bacon" ("J'adore les pommes de terre au lard").

The Theatre of the Absurd shows the world as an incomprehensible place. The spectators see the happenings on the stage entirely from the outside, without ever understanding the full meaning of these strange patterns of events, as newly arrived visitors might watch life in a country of which they have not yet mastered the language.[4] The confrontation of the audience with characters and happenings which they are not quite able to comprehend makes it impossible for them to share the aspirations and emotions depicted in the play. Brecht's famous "Verfrem-

---

[2] Adamov, "Note Préliminaire," *Théâtre II*, Paris, 1955.
[3] *Ibid.*
[4] It may be significant that the three writers concerned, although they now all live in France and write in French have all come to live there from outside and must have experienced a period of adjustment to the country and its language. Samuel Beckett (b. 1906) came from Ireland; Arthur Adamov (b. 1908) from Russia, and Eugène Ionesco (b. 1912) from Rumania.

dungseffekt" (alienation effect), the inhibition of any identification between spectator and actor, which Brecht could never successfully achieve in his own highly rational theatre, really comes
into its own in the Theatre of the Absurd. It is impossible to
identify oneself with characters one does not understand or
whose motives remain a closed book, and so the distance between the public and the happenings on the stage can be maintained. Emotional identification with the characters is replaced
by a puzzled, critical attention. For while the happenings on the
stage are absurd, they yet remain recognizable as somehow related to real life with *its* absurdity, so that eventually the spectators are brought face to face with the irrational side of their
existence. Thus, the absurd and fantastic goings-on of the Theatre of the Absurd will, in the end, be found to reveal the irrationality of the human condition and the illusion of what we
thought was its apparent logical structure.

If the dialogue in these plays consists of meaningless clichés and
the mechanical, circular repetition of stereotyped phrases—how
many meaningless clichés and stereotyped phrases do we use in
our day-to-day conversation? If the characters change their personality halfway through the action, how consistent and truly
integrated are the people we meet in our real life? And if people
in these plays appear as mere marionettes, helpless puppets without any will of their own, passively at the mercy of blind fate
and meaningless circumstance, do we, in fact, in our over-
organized world, still possess any genuine initiative or power to
decide our own destiny? The spectators of the Theatre of the
Absurd are thus confronted with a grotesquely heightened picture of their own world: a world without faith, meaning, and
genuine freedom of will. In this sense, the Theatre of the Absurd is the true theatre of our time.

The theatre of most previous epochs reflected an accepted
moral order, a world whose aims and objectives were clearly
present to the minds of all its public, whether it was the audience
of the medieval mystery plays with their solidly accepted faith
in the Christian world order or the audience of the drama of
Ibsen, Shaw, or Hauptmann with their unquestioned belief in
evolution and progress. To such audiences, right and wrong were
never in doubt, nor did they question the then accepted goals of
human endeavor. Our own time, at least in the Western world,
wholly lacks such a generally accepted and completely integrated

world picture. The decline of religious faith, the destruction of the belief in automatic social and biological progress, the discovery of vast areas of irrational and unconscious forces within the human psyche, the loss of a sense of control over rational human development in an age of totalitarianism and weapons of mass destruction, have all contributed to the erosion of the basis for a dramatic convention in which the action proceeds within a fixed and self-evident framework of generally accepted values. Faced with the vacuum left by the destruction of a universally accepted and unified set of beliefs, most serious playwrights have felt the need to fit their work into the frame of values and objectives expressed in one of the contemporary ideologies: Marxism, psychoanalysis, aestheticism, or nature worship. But these, in the eyes of a writer like Adamov, are nothing but superficial rationalizations which try to hide the depth of man's predicament, his loneliness and his anxiety. Or, as Ionesco puts it:

As far as I am concerned, I believe sincerely in the poverty of the poor, I deplore it; it is real; it can become a subject for the theatre; I also believe in the anxieties and serious troubles the rich may suffer from; but it is neither in the misery of the former nor in the melancholia of the latter, that I, for one, find my dramatic subject matter. Theatre is for me the outward projection onto the stage of an inner world; it is in my dreams, in my anxieties, in my obscure desires, in my internal contradictions that I, for one, reserve for myself the right of finding my dramatic subject matter. As I am not alone in the world, as each of us, in the depth of his being, is at the same time part and parcel of all others, my dreams, my desires, my anxieties, my obsessions do not belong to me alone. They form part of an ancestral heritage, a very ancient storehouse which is a portion of the common property of all mankind. It is this, which, transcending their outward diversity, reunites all human beings and constitutes our profound common patrimony, the universal language. . . .[5]

In other words, the commonly acceptable framework of beliefs and values of former epochs which has now been shattered is to be replaced by the community of dreams and desires of a collective unconscious. And, to quote Ionesco again:

. . . the new dramatist is one . . . who tries to link up with what is most ancient: new language and subject matter in a dramatic struc-

[5] Ionesco, "L'Impromptu de l'Alma," *Théâtre II,* Paris, 1958.

ture which aims at being clearer, more stripped of non-essentials and more purely theatrical; the rejection of traditionalism to rediscover tradition; a synthesis of knowledge and invention, of the real and imaginary, of the particular and the universal, or as they say now, of the individual and the collective. . . . By expressing my deepest obsessions, I express my deepest humanity. I become one with all others, spontaneously, over and above all the barriers of caste and different psychologies. I express my solitude and become one with all other solitudes. . . .[6]

What is the tradition with which the Theatre of the Absurd—at first sight the most revolutionary and radically new movement—is trying to link itself? It is in fact a very ancient and a very rich tradition, nourished from many and varied sources: the verbal exuberance and extravagant inventions of Rabelais, the age-old clowning of the Roman mimes and the Italian *Commedia dell'Arte*, the knock-about humor of circus clowns like Grock; the wild, archetypal symbolism of English nonsense verse, the baroque horror of Jacobean dramatists like Webster or Tourneur, the harsh, incisive and often brutal tones of the German drama of Grabbe, Büchner, Kleist, and Wedekind with its delirious language and grotesque inventiveness; and the Nordic paranoia of the dreams and persecution fantasies of Strindberg.

All these streams, however, first came together and crystallized in the more direct ancestors of the present Theatre of the Absurd. Of these, undoubtedly the first and foremost is Alfred Jarry (1873–1907), the creator of *Ubu Roi*, the first play which clearly belongs in the category of the Theatre of the Absurd. *Ubu Roi*, first performed in Paris on December 10, 1896, is a Rabelaisian nonsense drama about the fantastic adventures of a fat, cowardly, and brutal figure, *le père* Ubu, who makes himself King of Poland, fights a series of Falstaffian battles, and is finally routed. As if to challenge all accepted codes of propriety and thus to open a new era of irreverence, the play opens with the defiant expletive, *"Merdre!"* which immediately provoked a scandal. This, of course, was what Jarry had intended. *Ubu*, in its rollicking Rabelaisian parody of a Shakespearean history play, was to confront the Parisian bourgeois with a monstrous portrait of his own greed, selfishness, and philistinism: "As the curtain went up I wanted to confront the public with a theatre in

[6] Ionesco, "The Avant-Garde Theatre," *World Theatre*, VIII, No. 3 (Autumn, 1959).

which, as in the big magic mirror . . . of the fairy tales . . . the vicious man sees his reflection with bulls' horns and the body of a dragon, the projections of his viciousness. . . ."[7] But Ubu is more than a mere monstrous exaggeration of the selfishness and crude sensuality of the French bourgeois. He is at the same time the personification of the grossness of human nature, an enormous belly walking on two legs. That is why Jarry put him on the stage as a monstrous pot-bellied figure in a highly stylized costume and mask—a mythical, archetypal externalization of human instincts of the lowest kind. Thus, Ubu, the false king of Poland, pretended doctor of the pseudoscience of Pataphysics, clearly anticipates one of the main characteristics of the Theatre of the Absurd, its tendency to externalize and project outwards what is happening in the deeper recesses of the mind. Examples of this tendency are: the disembodied voices of "monitors" shouting commands at the hero of Adamov's *La Grande et la Petite Manoeuvre* which concretizes his neurotic compulsions; the mutilated trunks of the parents in Beckett's *Endgame* emerging from ashcans—the ashcans of the main character's subconscious to which he has banished his past and his conscience; or the proliferations of fungi that invade the married couple's apartment in Ionesco's *Amédée* and express the rottenness and decay of their relationship. All these psychological factors are not only projected outwards, they are also, as in Jarry's *Ubu Roi*, grotesquely magnified and exaggerated. This scornful rejection of all subtleties is a reaction against the supposed *finesse* of the psychology of the naturalistic theatre in which everything was to be inferred between the lines. The Theatre of the Absurd, from Jarry onwards, stands for explicitness as against implicit psychology, and in this resembles the highly explicit theatre of the Expressionists or the political theatre of Piscator or Brecht.

To be larger and more real than life was also the aim of Guillaume Apollinaire (1880–1918), the great poet who was one of the seminal forces in the rise of Cubism and who had close personal artistic links with Jarry. If Apollinaire labeled his play *Les Mamelles de Tirésias* a "*drama surrealiste,*" he did not intend that term, of which he was one of the earliest users, in the sense in which it later became famous. He wanted it to describe a play

---

[7] Jarry, "Questions de Théâtre," in *Ubu Roi, Ubu Enchaîné,* and other Ubuesque writings. Ed. Rene Massat, Lausanne, 1948.

in which everything was *larger than life,* for he believed in an
art which was to be "modern, simple, rapid, with the shortcuts
and enlargements that are needed to shock the spectator."[8] . . .

But Antonin Artaud (1896–1948), another major influence in
the development of the Theatre of the Absurd, did at one time
belong to the Surrealist group, although his main activity in the
theatre took place after he had broken with Breton. Artaud was
one of the most unhappy men of genius of his age, an artist consumed by the most intense passions; poet, actor, director, designer, immensely fertile and original in his inventions and ideas,
yet always living on the borders of sanity and never able to realize his ambitions, plans, and projects.

Artaud, who had been an actor in Charles Dullin's company at
the Atelier, began his venture into the realm of experimental
theatre in a series of productions characteristically sailing under
the label *Théâtre Alfred Jarry* (1927–29). But his theories of a
new and revolutionary theatre only crystallized after he had
been deeply stirred by a performance of Balinese dancers at the
Colonial Exhibition of 1931. He formulated his ideas in a series
of impassioned manifestos later collected in the volume *The
Theatre and Its Double* (1938), which continues to exercise an
important influence on the contemporary French theatre. Artaud
named the theatre of his dreams *Théâtre de la Cruauté,* a theatre
of cruelty, which, he said, "means a theatre difficult and cruel
above all for myself." "Everything that is really active is cruelty.
It is around this idea of action carried to the extreme that the
theatre must renew itself." Here too the idea of action larger
and more real than life is the dominant theme. "Every performance will contain a physical and objective element that will be
felt by all. Cries, Wails, Apparitions, Surprises, *Coups de Théâtre*
of all kinds, the magical beauty of costumes inspired by the model
of certain rituals. . . ." The language of the drama must also
undergo a change: "It is not a matter of suppressing articulate
speech but of giving to the words something like the importance
they have in dreams." In Artaud's new theatre "not only the
obverse side of man will appear but also the reverse side of the
coin: the reality of imagination and of dreams will here be seen
on an equal footing with everyday life."

Artaud's only attempt at putting these theories to the test on

---

[8] Apollinaire, *Les Mamelles de Tirésias,* Preface.

the stage took place on May 6, 1935 at the Folies-Wagram. Artaud had made his own adaptation ("after Shelley and Stendhal") of the story of the Cenci, that sombre Renaissance story of incest and patricide. It was in many ways a beautiful and memorable performance, but full of imperfections and a financial disaster which marked the beginning of Artaud's eventual descent into despair, insanity, and abject poverty. Jean-Louis Barrault had some small part in this venture and Roger Blin, the actor and director who later played an important part in bringing Adamov, Beckett, and Ionesco to the stage, appeared in the small role of one of the hired assassins.

Jean-Louis Barrault, one of the most creative figures in the theatre of our time, was, in turn, responsible for another venture which played an important part in the development of the Theatre of the Absurd. He staged André Gide's adaptation of Franz Kafka's novel, *The Trial*, in 1947 and played the part of the hero K. himself. Undoubtedly this performance which brought the dreamworld of Kafka to a triumphant unfolding on the stage and demonstrated the effectiveness of this particular brand of fantasy in practical theatrical terms exercised a profound influence on the practitioners of the new movement. For here, too, they saw the externalization of mental processes, the acting out of nightmarish dreams by schematized figures in a world of torment and absurdity.

The dream element in the Theatre of the Absurd can also be traced, in the case of Adamov, to Strindberg, acknowledged by him as his inspiration at the time when he began to think of writing for the theatre. This is the Strindberg of *The Ghost Sonata, The Dream Play* and of *To Damascus*. (Adamov is the author of an excellent brief monograph on Strindberg.)

But if Jarry, Artaud, Kafka, and Strindberg can be regarded as the decisive influences in the development of the Theatre of the Absurd, there is another giant of European literature that must not be omitted from the list—James Joyce, for whom Beckett at one time is supposed to have acted as helper and secretary. Not only is the Nighttown episode of *Ulysses* one of the earliest examples of the Theatre of the Absurd—with its exuberant mingling of the real and the nightmarish, its wild fantasies and externalizations of subconscious yearnings and fears—but Joyce's experimentation with language, his attempts to smash the limitations of conventional vocabulary and syntax has probably exercised an even more powerful impact on all the writers concerned.

It is in its attitude to language that the Theatre of the Absurd is most revolutionary. It deliberately attempts to renew the language of drama and to expose the barrenness of conventional stage dialogue. Ionesco once described how he came to write his first play. (Cf. his "The Tragedy of Language," *Tulane Drama Review*, Spring, 1960.) He had decided to take English lessons and began to study at the Berlitz school. When he read and repeated the sentences in his phrase book, those petrified corpses of once living speech, he was suddenly overcome by their tragic quality. From them he composed his first play, *The Bald Soprano*. The absurdity of its dialogue and its fantastic quality springs directly from its basic ordinariness. It exposes the emptiness of stereotyped language; "What is sometimes labeled the absurd," Ionesco says, "is only the denunciation of the ridiculous nature of a language which is empty of substance, made up of clichés and slogans. . . ."[9] Such a language has atrophied; it has ceased to be the expression of anything alive or vital and has been degraded into a mere conventional token of human intercourse, a mask for genuine meaning and emotion. That is why so often in the Theatre of the Absurd the dialogue becomes divorced from the real happenings in the play and is even put into direct contradiction with the action. The Professor and the Pupil in Ionesco's *The Lesson* "seem" to be going through a repetition of conventional school book phrases, but behind this smoke screen of language the *real* action of the play pursues an entirely different course with the Professor, vampire-like, draining the vitality from the young girl up to the final moment when he plunges his knife into her body. In Beckett's *Waiting for Godot* Lucky's much vaunted philosophical wisdom is revealed to be a flood of completely meaningless gibberish that vaguely resembles the language of philosophical argument. And in Adamov's remarkable play, *Ping-Pong*, a good deal of the dramatic power lies in the contrapuntal contrast between the triviality of the theme—the improvement of pinball machines—and the almost religious fervor with which it is discussed. Here, in order to bring out the full meaning of the play, the actors have to act *against* the dialogue rather than with it, the fervor of the delivery

---

[9] Ionesco, "The Avant-Garde Theatre."

must stand in a dialectical contrast to the pointlessness of the meaning of the lines. In the same way, the author implies that most of the fervent and passionate discussion of real life (of political controversy, to give but one example) also turns around empty and meaningless clichés. Or, as Ionesco says in an essay on Antonin Artaud:

As our knowledge becomes increasingly divorced from real life, our culture no longer contains ourselves (or only contains an insignificant part of ourselves) and forms a "social" context in which we are not integrated. The problem thus becomes that of again reconciling our culture with our life by making our culture a living culture once more. But to achieve this end we shall first have to kill the "respect for that which is written" . . . it becomes necessary to break up our language so that it may become possible to put it together again and to re-establish contact with the absolute, or as I should prefer to call it, with multiple reality.[10]

This quest for the multiple reality of the world which is real *because* it exists on many planes simultaneously and is more than a mere unidirectional abstraction is not only in itself a search for a re-established *poetical* reality (poetry in its essence expressing reality in its ambiguity and multidimensional depth); it is also in close accord with important movements of our age in what appear to be entirely different fields: psychology and philosophy. The dissolution, devaluation, and relativization of language is, after all, also the theme of much of present-day depth psychology, which has shown what in former times was regarded as a rational expression of logically arrived at conclusions to be the mere rationalization of subconscious emotional impulses. Not everything we say means what we intend it to mean. And likewise, in present-day Logical Positivism a large proportion of all statements is regarded as devoid of conceptual meaning and merely emotive. A philosopher like Ludwig Wittgenstein, in his later phases, even tried to break through what he regarded as the opacity, the misleading nature of language and grammar; for if all our thinking is in terms of language, and language obeys what after all are the arbitrary conventions of grammar, we must strive to penetrate to the real content of thought that is masked by grammatical rules and conventions. Here, too, then, is a matter of

[10] Ionesco, "Ni un Dieu, ni un Demon," *Cahiers de la Compagnie Madeleine Renaud-Jean-Louis Barrault*, No. 22–23 (May, 1958).

getting behind the surface of linguistic clichés and of finding
reality through the break-up of language.

In the Theatre of the Absurd, therefore, the real content of
the play lies in the action. Language may be discarded altogether,
as in Beckett's *Act Without Words* or in Ionesco's *The New
Tenant*, in which the whole sense of the play is contained in the
incessant arrival of more and more furniture so that the occupant
of the room is, in the end, literally drowned in it. Here the movement of objects alone carries the dramatic action, the language
has become purely incidental, less important than the contribution of the property department. In this, the Theatre of the
Absurd also reveals its anti-literary character, its endeavor to
link up with the pre-literary strata of stage history: the circus,
the performances of itinerant jugglers and mountebanks, the
music hall, fairground barkers, acrobats, and also the robust
world of the silent film. Ionesco, in particular, clearly owes a
great deal to Chaplin, Buster Keaton, the Keystone Cops, Laurel
and Hardy, and the Marx Brothers. And it is surely significant
that so much of successful popular entertainment in our age
shows affinities with the subject matter and preoccupation of the
avant-garde Theatre of the Absurd. A sophisticated, but nevertheless highly popular, film comedian like Jacques Tati uses
dialogue merely as a barely comprehensible babble of noises, and
also dwells on the loneliness of man in our age, the horror of
overmechanization and overorganization gone mad. Danny Kaye
excels in streams of gibberish closely akin to Lucky's oration in
Waiting for Godot. The brilliant and greatly liked team of
British radio (and occasionally television) comedians, the Goons,
have a sense of the absurd that resembles Kafka's or Ionesco's and
a team of grotesque singers like "Les Frères Jacques" seems more
closely in line with the Theatre of the Absurd than with the
conventional cabaret.

Yet the defiant rejection of language as the main vehicle of the
dramatic action, the onslaught on conventional logic and unilinear
conceptual thinking in the Theatre of the Absurd is by no means
equivalent to a total rejection of all meaning. On the contrary, it
constitutes an earnest endeavor to penetrate to deeper layers of
meaning and to give a truer, because more complex, picture of
reality in avoiding the simplification which results from leaving
out all the undertones, overtones, and inherent absurdities and
contradictions of any human situation. In the conventional drama
every word means what it says, the situations are clearcut, and at

the end all conflicts are tidily resolved. But reality, as Ionesco points out in the passage we have quoted, is never like that; it is multiple, complex, many-dimensional and exists on a number of different levels at one and the same time. Language is far too straight-forward an instrument to express all this by itself. Reality can only be conveyed by being *acted out* in all its complexity. Hence, it is the theatre, which is multidimensional and more than merely language or literature, which is the only instrument to express the bewildering complexity of the human condition. The human condition being what it is, with man small, helpless, in-secure, and unable ever to fathom the world in all its hopelessness, death, and absurdity, the theatre has to confront him with the bitter truth that most human endeavor is irrational and senseless, that communication between human beings is well-nigh impos-sible, and that the world will forever remain an impenetrable mystery. At the same time, the recognition of all these bitter truths will have a liberating effect: if we realize the basic ab-surdity of most of our objectives we are freed from being ob-sessed with them and this release expresses itself in laughter.

Moreover, while the world is being shown as complex, harsh, and absurd and as difficult to interpret as reality itself, the audi-ence is yet spurred on to attempt their own interpretation, to wonder what it is all about. In that sense they are being invited to school their critical faculties, to train themselves in adjusting to reality. As the world is being represented as highly complex and devoid of a clear-cut purpose or design, there will always be an infinite number of possible interpretations. . . . Thus, it may be that the pinball machines in Adamov's *Ping-Pong* and the ideol-ogy which is developed around them stand for the futility of political or religious ideologies that are pursued with equal fervor and equal futility in the final results. Others have in-terpreted the play as a parable on the greed and sordidness of the profit motive. Others again may give it quite different meanings. The mysterious transformation of human beings into rhinos in Ionesco's latest play, *Rhinoceros*, was felt by the audience of its world premier at Duesseldorf (November 6, 1959) to depict the transformation of human beings into Nazis. It is known that Ionesco himself intended the play to express his feelings at the time when more and more of his friends in Rumania joined the Fascist Iron Guard and, in effect, left the ranks of thin-skinned humans to turn themselves into moral pachyderms. But to spec-tators less intimately aware of the moral climate of such a situation than the German audience, other interpretations might impose themselves: if the hero, Bérenger, is at the end left alone as the only human being in his native town, now entirely inhabited by rhinos, they might regard this as a poetic symbol of the gradual isolation of man growing old and imprisoned in the strait jacket of his own habits and memories. Does Godot, so fervently and vainly awaited by Vladimir and Estragon, stand for God? Or does he merely represent the ever elusive tomorrow, man's hope that one day something will happen that will render his existence meaningful? The force and poetic power of the play lie precisely in the impossibility of ever reaching a conclusive answer to this question.

Here we touch the essential point of difference between the conventional theatre and the Theatre of the Absurd. The former, based as it is on a known framework of accepted values and a rational view of life, always starts out by indicating a fixed objective towards which the action will be moving or by posing a definite problem to which it will supply an answer. Will Hamlet revenge the murder of his father? Will Iago succeed in destroying Othello? Will Nora leave her husband? In the conventional theatre the action always proceeds toward a definable end. The spectators do not know whether that end will be reached and how it will be reached. Hence, they are in suspense, eager to find out *what* will happen. In the Theatre of the Absurd, on the other hand, the action does not proceed in the manner of a logical syllogism. It does not go from A to B but travels from an unknown premise X toward an unknowable conclusion Y. The spectators, not knowing what their author is driving at, cannot be in suspense as to how or whether an expected objective is going to be reached. They are not, therefore, so much in suspense as to *what* is going to happen *next* (although the most unexpected and unpredictable things do happen) as they are in suspense about what the next event to take place will add to their understanding of *what is happening*. The action supplies an increasing number of contradictory and bewildering clues on a number of different levels, but the final question is never wholly answered. Thus, instead of being in suspense as to what will happen next, the spectators are, in the Theatre of the Absurd, put into suspense as to *what* the play *may mean*. This suspense continues even after the curtain has come down. Here again the Theatre of the Absurd fulfills Brecht's postulate of a critical, detached audience,

A Scene from The Balcony *by Jean Genet, a Circle in the Square Production, New York, 1961. Photograph by Martha Swope.*

who will have to sharpen their wits on the play and be stimulated
by it to think for themselves, far more effectively than Brecht's
own theatre. Not only are the members of the audience unable to
identify with the characters, they are compelled to puzzle out the
meaning of what they have seen. Each of them will probably find
his own, personal meaning, which will differ from the solution
found by most others. But he will have been forced to make a
mental effort and to evaluate an experience he has undergone. In
this sense, the Theatre of the Absurd is the most demanding, the
most intellectual theatre. It may be riotously funny, wildly exaggerated and oversimplified, vulgar and garish, but it will always
confront the spectator with a genuine intellectual problem, a
philosophical paradox, which he will have to try to solve even if
he knows that it is most probably insoluble.

   In this respect, the Theatre of the Absurd links up with an
older tradition which has almost completely disappeared from
Western culture: the tradition of allegory and the symbolical
representation of abstract concepts personified by characters
whose costumes and accoutrements subtly suggested whether
they represented Time, Chastity, Winter, Fortune, the World,
etc. . . . Although the living riddles the characters represented in
these entertainments were by no means difficult to solve, as
everyone knew that a character with a scythe and an hourglass
represented Time, and although the characters soon revealed
their identity and explained their attributes, there was an element
of intellectual challenge which stimulated the audience in the
moments between the appearance of the riddle and its solution
and which provided them with the pleasure of having solved a
puzzle. And what is more, in the elaborate allegorical dramas
like Calderón's *El Gran Teatro del Mundo* the subtle interplay
of allegorical characters itself presented the audience with a great
deal to think out for themselves. They had, as it were, to translate the abstractly presented action into terms of their everyday
experience; they could ponder on the deeper meaning of such
facts as death having taken the characters representing Riches or
Poverty in a Dance of Death equally quickly and equally harshly,
or that Mammon had deserted his master Everyman in the hour
of death. The dramatic riddles of our time present no such clear-
cut solutions. All they can show is that while the solutions have
evaporated the riddle of our existence remains—complex, unfathomable, and paradoxical.

The subject of this piece is really the "collage-event," a multimedia performance that brings material together from any number of arts. If the resultant gathering of the arts has an association with any one art more than another, it is the theatre, whether or not the stage is directly involved or dramatic elements are conspicuous in the work. Significantly, the title of the piece is a quotation from an American composer, John Cage, while the author is a British painter, poet, art critic, and gallery director. "Art is the objectification of the real," Coutts-Smith says in the opening pages of The Dream of Icarus, *his study of art and society in the twentieth century, from which these pages are taken. For him that objectification became, in modern times, a process in which "the radical political left and the radical 'art' underground" could be seen in exact parallel: "Both stem from the same roots and causes, both are groping towards the same ends and both are interrelated in the same utopian tradition." Boundary lines break down. The arts move to meet each other in happenings that may presage great changes in the structure of society and in human consciousness. "Theatre takes place all the time, . . ."*

THEATRE TAKES PLACE ALL THE TIME, WHEREVER ONE IS

Kenneth
Coutts-Smith

In recent years the defining lines between the boundaries of various art forms have become more and more blurred. To a certain extent painting and sculpture have become enmeshed with each other, and with a great deal of work it is no longer possible to classify individual art objects; *environment* and *participation* are frequent critical catchwords. Poetry also has become abstracted, relying often on visual patterns across the page while the boundaries between verbal and musical imagery are no longer as sharp as they used to be. Earlier poetry was of course always "musical" in that it responded to the cadences and rhythms of the human voice; the sound patterns of "concrete" poetry, however, owe their origins more to synthetic or accidentally discovered noise, the overheard sounds of city life, of traffic for example. *Avant-garde* music has learnt the collage techniques of the plastic arts, and the tape recorder has enabled it, as it were, to spill over into other disciplines. A similar pattern is very obvious in the theatre; from Brecht and Artaud onwards the drama is conditioning a new relationship between the stage and the audience.

This drift towards multi-media is most evident in the area known as Happenings, which as defined by Al Hansen, one of the originators of the idiom, are "theatre pieces in the manner of collage, and that each action or situation or event that occurs within their framework is related in the same way as is each part of an Abstract Expressionist painting." Here the collage moves out of a purely static position conditioned by the assembling of objects; it now has the added dimension of time and event. Happenings as we now know them developed during the middle to the late '50s in America. There were, of course, earlier precedents; the provocative goings-on at the Cabaret Voltaire in Zurich from 1916 to 1919, where Hugo Ball, Tristan Tzara, Richard Huelsenbeck, Marcel Janco, Hans Arp and others anticipated much of what was to happen in the 1950s.

The orientation was different, however. Zurich Dada, and its parallel manifestations in New York, Barcelona, Cologne, Hanover, and Berlin was, in general, like that of Alfred Jarry before them, an anarchic protest against bourgeois society exacerbated by a disillusionment and pessimism engendered by the war. Though the Futurists anticipated them in certain areas, particularly in typographical innovations and strident manifestoes, they were the first "urban guerrillas," the prototypes of the Portobello Road anarchists who maintain a sort of social terrorism by aerosoling in large lettering on walls and hoardings such slogans as the one recently noticed in North Kensington, "Crime is the Highest form of Sensuality." This original Dada role of somewhat nihilistic provocation was deviated from by only a few individuals such as Duchamp and Picabia who searched for a philosophical basis and justification, and John Heartfield and his Berlin colleagues who transformed Dada into a political and polemic weapon in the climate of actual revolution in 1918 Germany.

Dada was on the whole orientated to literature; it was at the first major Dada evening that Hugo Ball is supposed to have "invented" abstract phonetic poetry, a recitative consisting only of rhythmically uttered vowel and consonant sounds. Later Huelsenbeck, Tzara and Janco were to perform *poéms simultanés*, which in Ball's words are "a contrapuntal recitative in which three or more voices speak, sing, whistle, etc., simultaneously, in such a way that the resulting combinations account for the total effect of the work, elegaic, funny, or bizarre. The simultaneous poem is a powerful illustration of the fact that an organic work of art has a will of its own, and also illustrates the decisive role played by accompaniment. Noises (a drawn-out rrrr sustained for minutes on end, sudden crashes, sirens wailing) are existentially more powerful than the human voice."

As far as the visual arts were concerned the Dadaists were mainly concerned with promoting (at first, that is, in their comparatively provincial Swiss backwater) the already existing *avant-garde* of Paris and Munich; the early exhibitions they mounted consisted of works by the *Der Sturm* Group, and of one-man shows by Klee and Kandinsky. Though not in terms of the visual arts, the latter was a considerable influence through his ideas of *Gesamtkunstwerke*, the "total" work of art, embodying what up until then had been disparate disciplines. In Kandinsky's case, of course, the preoccupation was in the confrontation of music with painting. The actual use of the plastic arts was restricted in the Zurich events to the costumes and masks designed by Janco and to the adoption of Futurist typography. Hans Arp was the exception, developing the ideas of "chance" already implicit in their theatrical events, and it was at this time that he made his first collages by tearing paper into random forms, letting them flutter to the ground and gumming them into the position into which they had fallen. Some of these were later developed into his characteristic wooden constructions. He also experimented with a sort of early assemblage, "nailing pieces of wood . . . onto oblong box-like lids. He found some wooden rods, coloured variously by age and dirt, and set them side by side to produce their own kind of harmony."

Duchamp also, of course, was concerned with chance; his famous *Stoppages Etalon*, his own private units of measurement, were made in 1916. Questioning that one should accept the metric standard as unchangingly and absolutely valid, regarding that bar of platinum kept under conditions of controlled temperature in the basement of the Bureau of Weights and Measurements in Paris as being somewhat "arbitary," he produced with a careful and ironic seriousness "a new form to the unit of length." Taking a thread one metre in length, and dropping in onto a canvas from a height of one metre, he fixed it to the surface with varnish. This was repeated three times, and from these chance forms wooden "rulers" were made, indicating with all the precision of surveyor's instruments the shapes discovered in this way.

Chance, perhaps, interested Duchamp in a rather unique way, as Calvin Tomkins has pointed out. He writes that Duchamp believed "that chance is an expression of the subconscious personality. 'Your chance is not the same as my chance,' he has explained, 'just as your throw of the dice will rarely be the same as mine.' When Duchamp and his sisters Yvonne and Magdeleine amused themselves in 1913 by drawing the notes of the musical scale at random from a hat and then setting them down in the order drawn, the resulting composition, which they called *Musical Erratum*, was in Duchamp's mind a lighthearted expression of their own personal chance rather than a purely random creation."

This comment of Tomkins' is particularly interesting in that "aleatory" music, to use the phrase coined by Boulez, has had the most profound influence on the visual arts, for there has been a feed-back situation between painting and the music of the *avant-garde*. It is at this poi .t that the importance of John Cage must be stressed. Predecessors such as Varèse and Satie, of course, have been associated with modern art. Varèse, for instance, developed from the interest in percussion music of the '20s, remembering that the Futurist Luigi Russolo called for an "art of noise"; his *Ionization* of 1931 is an important work in this context. Satie, through his ironic inventions and deliberate subversion of accepted musical canon, is clearly related to Dada. Cage, much influenced by these two, and trained by Schönberg, was the first, however, to consistently explore elements of chance, and created the idiom now widely followed by such composers as Stockhausen, La Monte Young and Chiari.

It was in the early '50s, when writing music for the followers of Martha Graham, dancers like Merce Cunningham with whom he built up a life-long collaboration, and who was the first to take the composer seriously, that he stumbled upon the *I Ching*, the Chinese prophetic "book of changes," where guidance is elicited from the chance configuration of thrown twigs or, traditionally, yarrow-stalks. Here the aleatory element joins with a concern about Oriental philosophy which was soon to become a dominant element in the *avant-garde* scene. For instance, one of Cage's best known techniques of composition was to use transparent sheets on which were inked "lines, dots or biomorphic shapes; the lines and dots were understood to refer to the various aspects of sound that would be used, and when the performer superimposed one sheet over another, the intersection of the lines and dots on one of the biomorphic shapes on another would give him the information he needed to 'compose' the piece. Since Cage had no idea how the performer would superimpose one sheet over another, he could not foresee what would take place. Implicit in this whole process, he has explained, is the Buddhist belief that all things in the world are related and thus *relevant* to each other, so that no matter who used the transparencies or how he used them, each performance would be simply another aspect of the same (indeterminate) work."

A certain philosophic approach conditioned by Chinese magic and Zen Buddhism is also apparent in his use of "silent" music, particularly in the much-discussed piece entitled 4' 33", a silent work for the piano where the performer sits for this length of time perfectly still at his instrument, except for solemnly closing the lid of the keyboard three times to mark the divisions between sections of the work. Here the "music" consists entirely of random sounds filtering into the concert hall together with those contributed by the audience in the form of coughs, shuffles and other noises. Cage had once visited a totally sound-proof room in the physics laboratory of Harvard University, and was surprised not to find the dead and absolute silence that he had expected. Instead he heard two distinct and continuous sounds which he was told were noises made by his blood circulating and by the operation of his nervous system. He began to see music as something that was continually present, permanently in a flux with other aspects of perceptual experience, indeed he came to regard it only as part of a total experience, and that its expression in art must become something rather in the nature of theatre. "Theatre," he once said, "takes place all the time wherever one is, and art simply facilitates persuading one that this is the case."

In this he was close to the ideas of Robert Rauschenberg, who in his early "field" paintings of 1952, saw the canvas as a sort of mirror which recorded aspects of the environment, a work in the process of permanent creation by events taking place outside of the picture. "I always thought," he said, "of the white paintings as being not passive, but very—well, hypersensitive. So that one could look at them and almost see how many people were in the room by the shadows cast, or what time of day it was."

The meeting between Cage and Rauschenberg at Black Mountain College, and their joint collaboration with Merce Cunningham, was to be very fruitful. Similar ideas to that of the composer were expressed by the painter when he made his much quoted statement, "Painting relates to both art and life. Neither can be made. I try to act in the gap between the two." Rauschenberg also wanted to step back into some sort of anonymity in the face of the picture itself, to take an opposite standpoint to that of the emotional self-expression of the Abstract Expressionists. He speaks of *collaboration* with his materials, "I don't want a painting to be an expression of my personality . . . I'd really like to think that the artist could be just another kind of material in the picture . . . I don't want a picture to look like something it isn't. I want it to look like something it is. And I think a picture is more like the real world when it is made out of the real world."

This insistence on "realism," like Cage's incorporation of actual pre-existing sounds, is perhaps not sufficiently emphasized in the average consideration of the art today. It is here that a distinction can be made between two separate trends. The direction we are considering at this moment, though technically enormously different, can be regarded as a descendant of much "realist" art of the past. It is distinct from the parallel direction which is subjective and "idealist" in nature. Frequently works from one category are confused with works from the other as the result of similar technical aspect or superficial qualities. A lot of pop art, for instance, is clearly "idealist," while some hard-edge is "realist"; the question revolves around intentions, and is basically the dichotomy between existence and essence.

The collaboration between Cage, Rauschenberg and Merce Cunningham led to a series of "theatre" pieces dependent on random events during 1953 and 1954. The term Happening had not then been coined; this was to wait another four years when circumstances brought a particularly talented group of young artists together in one of Cage's classes at the New School for Social Research in New York. Al Hansen, Dick Higgins, Allen Kaprow and George Brecht were all enrolled, and they also brought in friends such as George Segal, Jim Dine and Larry Poons. These young artists developed the idea of the collage event in various directions, exploring audience participation and "total" theatre.

Merce Cunningham (1922–   ) is an uncommonly articulate dancer and choreographer. He thinks on his feet; that is clear to anyone who has ever seen him dance, with his own troupe or earlier as soloist with Martha Graham's company. Whatever he thinks comes out in strong movements of the body and even his words seem to spring from some all but visible gesture or posture of the dancer. In the general development of modern American dance toward the abstract, Cunningham has been perhaps the most forceful of choreographers, with the clearest notion of what he has been doing and why, as this brief statement shows so well. He has the gift of terseness and relevance, avoiding glib and final definitions. All of life is compact in the dance for Cunningham; neither an article such as this one nor any of his dance compositions can offer a finished definition or an ultimate statement. The central point of his art remains, in the words of this piece, that "dance is free to act as it chooses. . . ."

SPACE, TIME, AND DANCE

Merce Cunningham

The dance is an art in space and time.
The object of the dancer is to obliterate that.

The classical ballet, by maintaining the image of the Renaissance perspective in stage thought, kept a linear form of space. The modern American dance, stemming from German expressionism and the personal feelings of the various American pioneers, made space into a series of lumps, or often just static hills on the stage with actually no relation to the larger space of the stage area, but simply forms that by their connection in time made a shape. Some of the space-thought coming from the German dance opened the space out, and left a momentary feeling of connection with it, but too often the space was not visible enough because the physical action was all of a lightness, like sky without earth, or heaven without hell.

The fortunate thing in dancing is that space and time cannot be disconnected, and everyone can see and understand that. A body still is taking up just as much space and time as a body moving. The result is that neither the one nor the other—moving or being still—is more or less important, except it's nice to see a dancer moving. But the moving becomes more clear if the space and time around the moving are one of its opposites—stillness. Aside from the personal skill and clarity of the individual dancer, there are certain things that make clear to a spectator what the dancer is doing. In the ballet the various steps that lead to the larger movements or poses have, by usage and by their momentum, become common ground upon which the spectator can lead his eyes and his feelings into the resulting action. This also helps define the rhythm, in fact more often than not does define it. In the modern dance, the tendency or the wish has been to get rid of these "unnecessary and balletic" movements, at the same time wanting the same result in the size and vigor of the movement as the balletic action, and this has often left the dancer and the spectator slightly short.

To quibble with that on the other side: one of the best discoveries the modern dance has made use of is the gravity of the body in weight, that is, as opposite from denying (and thus affirming) gravity by ascent into the air, the weight of the body in going with gravity, down. The word "heavy" connotes something incorrect, since what is meant is not the heaviness of a bag of cement falling, although we've all been spectators of that too, but the heaviness of a living body falling with full intent of eventual rise. This is not a fetish or a use of heaviness as an accent against a predominantly light quality, but a thing in itself. By its nature this kind of moving would make the space seem a series of unconnected spots, along with the lack of clear-connecting movements in the modern dance.

A prevalent feeling among many painters that lets them make a space in which anything can happen is a feeling dancers may have too. Imitating the way nature makes a space and puts lots of things in it, heavy and light, little and big, all unrelated, yet each affecting all the others.

About the formal methods of choreography—some due to the conviction that a communication of one order or another is necessary; others to the feeling that mind follows heart, that is, form follows content; some due to the feeling that the musical form is the most logical to follow—the most curious to me is the general feeling in the modern dance that nineteenth-century forms stemming from earlier pre-classical forms are the only formal actions advisable, or even possible to take. This seems a flat contradiction of the modern dance—agreeing with the thought of discovering new or allegedly new movement for contemporary reasons, the using of psychology as a tremendous elastic basis for content, and wishing to be expressive of the "times" (although how can one be expressive of anything else?)— but not feeling the need for a different basis upon which to put this expression, in fact being mainly content to indicate that either the old forms are good enough, or further that the old forms are the only possible forms. These consist mainly of theme and variation, and associated devices—repetition, inversion, development and manipulation. There is also a tendency to imply a crisis to which one goes and then in some way retreats from. Now I can't see that crisis any longer means a climax, unless we are willing to grant that every breath of wind has a climax (which I am), but then that obliterates climax, being a surfeit of such. And since our lives, both by nature and by the newspapers, are so full of crisis that one is no longer aware of it, then it is clear that life goes on regardless, and further that each thing can be and is separate from each and every other, viz: the continuity of the newspaper headlines. Climax is for those who are swept by New Year's Eve.

More freeing into *space* than the theme and manipulation 'holdup' would be a formal structure based on *time*. Now time can be an awful lot of bother with the ordinary pinch-penny counting that has to go with it, but if one can think of the structure as a space of time in which anything can happen in any sequence of movement event, and any length of stillness can take place, then the counting is an aid towards freedom, rather than a discipline towards mechanization. A use of time-structure also frees the music into space, making the connection between the dance and the music one of individual autonomy connected at structural points. The result is that the dance is free to act as it chooses, as is the music. The music doesn't have to work itself to death to underline the dance, or the dance create havoc in trying to be as flashy as the music.

Merce Cunningham.
Photograph courtesy of Merce Cunningham.

For me, it seems enough that dancing is a spiritual exercise in physical form, and that what is seen, is what it is. And I do not believe it is possible to be "too simple." What the dancer does is the most realistic of all possible things, and to pretend that a man standing on a hill could be doing everything except just standing is simply divorce—divorce from life, from the sun coming up and going down, from clouds in front of the sun, from the rain that comes from the clouds and sends you into the drugstore for a cup of coffee, from each thing that succeeds each thing. Dancing is a visible action of life.

In any discussion of the art of Mary Wigman (1886–   ), words like "primordial" inevitably appear. This extraordinary dancer seemed to have gone right back to the beginning of things when she began to display her ecstatic creations in Germany just after the First World War. She has said herself that "Art grows out of the basic cause of existence." She looked for essences, caught with a spontaneity that no one should mistake for anything else. The body was her means and her end. In its movements were compounded the totality of being, made visible, with no emotion restrained, no feeling repressed. In speaking of her, one is not ashamed to use the grandest terms, to talk of Death and Life. Wigman, probably more than anyone, forced the modern dance toward a free expression, but free expression that remained a controlled art form, and was never mere yielding to impulse. In describing

COMPOSITION IN PURE MOVEMENT

Mary Wigman

the creation of her dances, she presents the reader with a very palpable impression of the force that she still exerts in the dance.

Charged as I frequently am with "freeing" the dance from music, the question often arises, what can be the source and basic structure of my own dancing. I cannot define its principles more clearly than to say that the fundamental idea of any creation arises in me or, rather, out of me as a completely independent dance theme. This theme, however primitive or obscure at first, already contains its own development and alone dictates its singular and logical sequence. What I feel as the germinal source of any dance may be compared perhaps to the melodic or rhythmic "subject" as it is first conceived by a composer, or to the compelling image that haunts a poet. But beyond that I can draw no parallels. In working out a dance I do not follow the models of any other art, nor have I evolved a general routine for my own. Each dance is unique and free, a separate organism whose form is self-determined.

Neither is my dancing abstract, in intention at any rate, for its origin is not in the mind. If there is an abstract effect it is incidental. On the other hand my purpose is not to "interpret" the emotions. Grief, joy, fear, are terms too fixed and static to describe the sources of my work. My dances flow rather from certain states of being, different stages of vitality which release in me a varying play of the emotions, and in themselves dictate the distinguishing atmospheres of the dances.

I can at this moment clearly recall the origin of my *Festlicher Rhythmus* ["Festive Rhythm"]. Coming back from the holidays, rested, restored by sun and fresh air, I was eager to begin dancing again. When I stepped into the studio and saw my co-workers there waiting for me, I beat my hands together and out of this spontaneous expression of happiness, of joy, the dance developed.

My first tentative attempts to compose were made when I was studying the Dalcroze system [a technique for translating musical rhythms into bodily movement conceived by the modern Swiss composer Émile Jaque-Dalcroze; known as "eurythmics"]. Though I have always had a strong feeling for music it seemed from the very start most natural for me to express my own nature by means of pure movement. Perhaps it was just because there was so much musical work to be done at that time, that all these little dances and dance studies took form without music. A German painter observing my modest experiments advised me to go to Munich and work with [German theorist and teacher Rudolf] Von Laban who was also interested in such dancing. On Laban's system of gymnastics I founded my body technique; and during this period of apprenticeship I continued the gradual evolution of my own work.

After years of trial I have come to realize in a very final way, that for me the creation of a dance to music already written cannot be complete and satisfactory. I have danced with several of the great European orchestras, and to music (always generically dance music) old and new. I have even attempted to work out Hindemith's *Daemon*, and some compositions of Bartók, Kodaly, and other contemporaries. But while music easily evokes in me a dance reaction, it is in the development of the dance that a great divergence so often occurs. For usually a dance idea, a "theme," however inspired, by a state of feeling, or indirectly by music, sets up independent reactions. The theme calls for its own development. It is in working this out that I find my dance parting company with the music. The parallel development of the dance with the already completely worked out musical idea is what I find in most instances to be functionally wrong. Each dance demands organic autonomy.

So I have come gradually to feel my way toward a new reintegration of music with the dance. I do not create a dance and then order music written for it. As soon as I conceive a theme, and before it is completely defined, I call in my musical assistants. Catching my idea, and observing me for atmosphere, they begin to improvise with me. Every step of the development is built up co-operatively. Experiments are made with various instruments, accents, climaxes, until we feel the work has indissoluble unity.

My *Pastorale* was developed in the following way: I came into my studio one day and sank down with a feeling of complete relaxation. Out of a sense of deepest peace and quietude I began slowly to move my arms and body. Calling to my assistants I said, "I do not know if anything will come of this feeling, but I should like a reed instrument that would play over and over again a simple little tune, not at all important, always the same one." Then with the monotonous sound of the little tune, with its gentle lyric suggestion, the whole dance took form. Afterwards we found that it was built on six-eighths time, neither myself nor the musician being conscious of the rhythm until we came to the end.

The monumental *Totenmal* ["Funeral Games"] which we presented in Munich last year was accompanied by a whole orchestra of percussion instruments. During the period of preparation these instruments were handled by dancers. The improvisation of dancing and music was so dovetailed that in the long hours of practice the girls dancing constantly changed places with those making the music. The final result was one of the greatest possible harmony. In group creations, as in my individual work, movement and sound are always evolved together.

Working with a group my effort is to seek out a common feeling. I present the main idea, each one improvises. No matter how wide the range of individuality, I must find some common denominator from these different emanations of personality. Thus, on the rock of basic feeling, I slowly build each structure.

Of course all that I have said here should be accepted as a very personal credo. I do not propose to erect a general system for I am a firm believer in individual freedom. Creative work will always assume new and varying forms. Any profound expression of self for which its creator assumes responsibility in the most complete sense must give authentic impetus to a new or an old idea in art.

TELEVISION AND MOTION PICTURES

Few essays—or books, for that matter—written about the film say as much about the nature of the medium and its stylistic possibilities as this piece by the German-American art historian Erwin Panofsky (1892–1968). Originally developed from an address in support of the creation of the Museum of Modern Art Film Library, it was first published in 1934. Its understanding of the problems and achievements of film is timeless, however; the essay needs no bringing up to date to make current what it says about the recording of movement, the dynamization of space and the spatialization of time, the place of speech in the film, the communicability of film and its translation into and out of commercial and noncommercial values. Panofsky's great experience and understanding as an historian of the visual arts allow him to make large-scale comparisons between the development of the film, and, for example, the mosaic and line engraving, and to make them convincingly. He sees the films of the first years of this century as establishing "the subject-matter and methods of the moving picture as we know it." The central problem remains the one with which film has always been confronted: "to manipulate and shoot unstylized reality in such a way that the result has style. This is a proposition no less difficult than any proposition in the older arts."

STYLE AND MEDIUM IN THE MOTION PICTURES

Erwin Panofsky

Film art is the only art the development of which men now living have witnessed from the very beginnings; and this development is all the more interesting as it took place under conditions contrary to precedent. It was not an artistic urge that gave rise to the discovery and gradual perfection of a new technique; it was a technical invention that gave rise to the discovery and gradual perfection of a new art.

From this we understand two fundamental facts. First, that the primordial basis of the enjoyment of moving pictures was not an objective interest in a specific subject matter, much less an aesthetic interest in the formal presentation of subject matter, but the sheer delight in the fact that things seemed to move, no matter what things they were. Second, that films—first exhibited in "kinetoscopes," viz., cinematographic peep shows, but projectable to a screen since as early as 1894—are, originally, a product of genuine folk art (whereas, as a rule, folk art derives from what is known as "higher art"). At the very beginning of things we find the simple recording of movements: galloping horses, railroad trains, fire engines, sporting events, street scenes. And when it had come to the making of narrative films these were produced by photographers who were anything but "producers" or "directors," performed by people who were anything but actors, and enjoyed by people who would have been much offended had anyone called them "art lovers."

The casts of these archaic films were usually collected in a "café" where unemployed supers or ordinary citizens possessed of a suitable exterior were wont to assemble at a given hour. An enterprising photographer would walk in, hire four or five convenient characters and make the picture while carefully instructing them what to do: "Now, you pretend to hit this lady over the head"; and (to the lady): "And you pretend to fall down in a heap." Productions like these were shown, together with those purely factual recordings of "movement for movement's sake," in a few small and dingy cinemas mostly frequented by the "lower classes" and a sprinkling of youngsters in quest of adventure (about 1905, I happen to remember, there was only one obscure and faintly disreputable *kino* in the whole city of Berlin, bearing, for some unfathomable reason, the English name of "The Meeting Room"). Small wonder that the "better classes," when they slowly began to venture into these early picture theaters, did so, not by way of seeking normal and possibly serious entertainment, but with that characteristic sensation of self-conscious condescension with which we may plunge, in gay company, into the folkloristic depths of Coney Island or a European kermis; even a few years ago it was the regulation attitude of the socially or intellectually prominent that one could confess to enjoying such austerely educational films as *The Sex Life of the Starfish* or films with "beautiful scenery," but never to a serious liking for narratives.

Today there is no denying that narrative films are not only "art"—not often good art, to be sure, but this applies to other media as well—but also, besides architecture, cartooning and "commercial design," the only visual art entirely alive. The "movies" have re-established that dynamic contact between art production and art consumption which, for reasons too complex to be considered here, is sorely attenuated, if not entirely inter-rupted, in many other fields of artistic endeavor. Whether we like it or not, it is the movies that mold, more than any other single force, the opinions, the taste, the language, the dress, the behavior, and even the physical appearance of a public com-prising more than 60 per cent of the population of the earth. If all the serious lyrical poets, composers, painters and sculptors were forced by law to stop their activities, a rather small fraction of the general public would become aware of the fact and a still smaller fraction would seriously regret it. If the same thing were to happen with the movies the social consequences would be catastrophic.

In the beginning, then, there were the straight recordings of movement no matter what moved, viz., the prehistoric ancestors of our "documentaries"; and, soon after, the early narratives, viz., the prehistoric ancestors of our "feature films." The craving for a narrative element could be satisfied only by borrowing from older arts, and one should expect that the natural thing would have been to borrow from the theater, a theater play being ap-parently the *genus proximum* to a narrative film in that it consists of a narrative enacted by persons that move. But in reality the imitation of stage performances was a comparatively late and thoroughly frustrated development. What happened at the start was a very different thing. Instead of imitating a theatrical per-formance already endowed with a certain amount of motion, the earliest films added movement to works of art originally station-ary, so that the dazzling technical invention might achieve a triumph of its own without intruding upon the sphere of higher culture. The living language, which is always right, has endorsed this sensible choice when it still speaks of a "moving picture" or, simply, a "picture," instead of accepting the pretentious and fundamentally erroneous "screen play."

The stationary works enlivened in the earliest movies were indeed pictures: bad nineteenth-century paintings and postcards (or waxworks à la Madame Tussaud's), supplemented by the comic strips—a most important root of cinematic art—and the subject matter of popular songs, pulp magazines and dime novels; and the films descending from this ancestry appealed directly and very intensely to a folk art mentality. They gratified—often simultaneously—first, a primitive sense of justice and decorum when virtue and industry were rewarded while vice and laziness were punished; second, plain sentimentality when "the thin trickle of a fictive love interest" took its course "through somewhat serpentine channels," or when Father, dear Father returned from the saloon to find his child dying of diphtheria; third, a primordial instinct for bloodshed and cruelty when Andreas Hofer faced the firing squad, or when (in a film of 1893–94) the head of Mary Queen of Scots actually came off; fourth, a taste for mild pornography (I remember with great pleasure a French film of *ca.* 1900 wherein a seemingly but not really well-rounded lady as well as a seemingly but not really slender one were shown changing to bathing suits—an honest, straightforward *porcheria* much less objectionable than the now extinct Betty Boop films and, I am sorry to say, some of the more recent Walt Disney productions); and, finally, that crude sense of humor, graphically described as "slapstick," which feeds upon the sadistic and the pornographic instinct, either singly or in combination.

Not until as late as *ca.* 1905 was a film adaptation of *Faust* ventured upon (cast still "unknown," characteristically enough), and not until 1911 did Sarah Bernhardt lend her prestige to an unbelievably funny film tragedy, *Queen Elizabeth of England*. These films represent the first conscious attempt at transplanting the movies from the folk art level to that of "real art"; but they also bear witness to the fact that this commendable goal could not be reached in so simple a manner. It was soon realized that the imitation of a theater performance with a set stage, fixed entries and exists, and distinctly literary ambitions is the one thing the film must avoid.

The legitimate paths of evolution were opened, not by running away from the folk art character of the primitive film but by developing it within the limits of its own possibilities. Those primordial archetypes of film productions on the folk art level—success or retribution, sentiment, sensation, pornography, and crude humor—could blossom forth into genuine history, tragedy and romance, crime and adventure, and comedy, as soon as it was realized that they could be transfigured—not by an artifical injection of literary values but by the exploitation of the unique and specific possibilities of the new medium. Significantly, the beginnings of this legitimate development antedate the attempts at endowing the film with higher values of a foreign order (the crucial period being the years from 1902 to *ca.* 1905), and the decisive steps were taken by people who were laymen or outsiders from the viewpoint of the serious stage.

These unique and specific possibilities can be defined as *dynamization of space* and, accordingly, *spatialization of time*. This statement is self-evident to the point of triviality but it belongs to that kind of truths which, just because of their triviality, are easily forgotten or neglected.

In a theater, space is static, that is, the space represented on the stage, as well as the spatial relation of the beholder to the spectacle, is unalterably fixed. The spectator cannot leave his seat, and the setting of the stage cannot change, during one act (except for such incidentals as rising moons or gathering clouds and such illegitimate reborrowings from the film as turning wings or gliding backdrops). But, in return for this restriction, the theater has the advantage that time, the medium of emotion and thought conveyable by speech, is free and independent of anything that may happen in visible space. Hamlet may deliver his famous monologue lying on a couch in the middle distance, doing nothing and only dimly discernible to the spectator and listener, and yet by his mere words enthrall him with a feeling of intensest emotional action.

With the movies the situation is reversed. Here, too, the spectator occupies a fixed seat, but only physically, not as the subject of an aesthetic experience. Aesthetically, he is in permanent motion as his eye identifies itself with the lens of the camera, which permanently shifts in distance and direction. And as movable as the spectator is, as moveable is, for the same reason, the space presented to him. Not only bodies move in space, but space itself does, approaching, receding, turning, dissolving and recrystallizing

as it appears through the controlled locomotion and focusing of
the camera and through the cutting and editing of the various
shots—not to mention such special effects as visions, transforma-
tions, disappearances, slow-motion and fast-motion shots, reversals
and trick films. This opens up a world of possibilities of which the
stage can never dream. Quite apart from such photographic
tricks as the participation of disembodied spirits in the action of
the *Topper* series, or the more effective wonders wrought by
Roland Young in *The Man Who Could Work Miracles*, there is,
on the purely factual level, an untold wealth of themes as inaccessible to the "legitimate" stage as a fog or a snowstorm is to the
sculptor; all sorts of violent elemental phenomena and, conversely,
events too microscopic to be visible under normal conditions
(such as the life-saving injection with the serum flown in at the
very last moment, or the fatal bite of the yellow-fever mosquito);
full-scale battle scenes; all kinds of operations, not only in the
surgical sense but also in the sense of any actual construction,
destruction or experimentation, as in *Louis Pasteur* or *Madame
Curie*; a really grand party, moving through many rooms of a
mansion or a palace. Features like these, even the mere shifting of
the scene from one place to another by means of a car perilously
negotiating heavy traffic or a motorboat steered through a nocturnal harbor, will not only always retain their primitive cinematic
appeal but also remain enormously effective as a means of stirring
the emotions and creating suspense. In addition, the movies have
the power, entirely denied to the theater, to convey psychological
experiences by directly projecting their content to the screen,
substituting, as it were, the eye of the beholder for the consciousness of the character (as when the imaginings and hallucinations
of the drunkard in the otherwise overrated *Lost Weekend* appear
as stark realities instead of being described by mere words). But
any attempt to convey thought and feelings exclusively, or even
primarily, by speech leaves us with a feeling of embarrassment,
boredom, or both.

What I mean by thoughts and feelings "conveyed exclusively,
or even primarily, by speech" is simply this: Contrary to naïve
expectation, the invention of the sound track in 1928 has been
unable to change the basic fact that a moving picture, even when
it has learned to talk, remains a picture that moves and does not
convert itself into a piece of writing that is enacted. Its substance
remains a series of visual sequences held together by an uninter-

rupted flow of movement in space (except, of course, for such checks and pauses as have the same compositional value as a rest in music), and not a sustained study in human character and destiny transmitted by effective, let alone "beautiful," diction. I cannot remember a more misleading statement about the movies than Mr. Eric Russell Bentley's in the spring number of the *Kenyon Review*, 1945: "The potentialities of the talking screen differ from those of the silent screen in adding the dimension of dialogue—which could be poetry." I would suggest: "The potentialities of the talking screen differ from those of the silent screen in integrating visible movement with dialogue which, therefore, had better not be poetry."

All of us, if we are old enough to remember the period prior to 1928, recall the old-time pianist who, with his eyes glued on the screen, would accompany the events with music adapted to their mood and rhythm; and we also recall the weird and spectral feeling overtaking us when this pianist left his post for a few minutes and the film was allowed to run by itself, the darkness haunted by the monotonous rattle of the machinery. Even the silent film, then, was never mute. The visible spectacle always required, and received, an audible accompaniment which, from the very beginning, distinguished the film from simple pantomine and rather classed it—*mutatis mutandis*—with the ballet. The advent of the talkie meant not so much an "addition" as a transformation: the transformation of musical sound into articulate speech and, therefore, of quasi pantomime into an entirely new species of spectacle which differs from the ballet, and agrees with the stage play, in that its acoustic component consists of intelligible words, but differs from the stage play and agrees with the ballet in that this acoustic component is not detachable from the visual. In a film, that which we hear remains, for good or worse, inextricably fused with that which we see; the sound, articulate or not, cannot express any more than is expressed, at the same time, by visible movement; and in a good film it does not even attempt to do so. To put it briefly, the play—or, as it is very properly called, the "script"—of a moving picture is subject to what might be termed the *principle of coexpressibility*.

Empirical proof of this principle is furnished by the fact that, wherever the dialogical or monological element gains temporary prominence, there appears, with the inevitability of a natural law, the "close-up." What does the close-up achieve? In showing us, in magnification, either the face of the speaker or the face of the listeners or both in alternation, the camera transforms the human physiognomy into a huge field of action where—given the qualification of the performers—every subtle movement of the features, almost imperceptible from a natural distance, becomes an expressive event in visible space and thereby completely integrates itself with the expressive content of the spoken word; whereas, on the stage, the spoken word makes a stronger rather than a weaker impression if we are not permitted to count the hairs in Romeo's mustache.

This does not mean that the scenario is a negligible factor in the making of a moving picture. It only means that its artistic intention differs in kind from that of a stage play, and much more from that of a novel or a piece of poetry. As the success of a Gothic jamb figure depends not only upon its quality as a piece of sculpture but also, or even more so, upon its integrability with the architecture of the portal, so does the success of a movie script—not unlike that of an opera libretto—depend, not only upon its quality as a piece of literature but also, or even more so, upon its integrability with the events on the screen.

As a result—another empirical proof of the coexpressibility principle—good movie scripts are unlikely to make good reading and have seldom been published in book form; whereas, conversely, good stage plays have to be severely altered, cut, and, on the other hand, enriched by interpolations to make good movie scripts. In Shaw's *Pygmalion*, for instance, the actual process of Eliza's phonetic education and, still more important, her final triumph at the grand party, are wisely omitted; we see—or, rather, hear—some samples of her gradual linguistic improvement and finally encounter her, upon her return from the reception, victorious and splendidly arrayed but deeply hurt for want of recognition and sympathy. In the film adaptation, precisely these two scenes are not only supplied but also strongly emphasized; we witness the fascinating activities in the laboratory with its array of spinning disks and mirrors, organ pipes and dancing flames, and we participate in the ambassadorial party, with many moments of impending catastrophe and a little counterintrigue thrown in for suspense. Unquestionably these two scenes, entirely absent from the play, and indeed unachievable upon the stage, were the highlights of the film; whereas the Shavian dialogue, however severely cut, turned out to fall a little flat in certain

moments. And wherever, as in so many other films, a poetic emotion, a musical outburst, or a literary conceit (even, I am grieved
to say, some of the wisecracks of Groucho Marx) entirely lose
contact with visible movement, they strike the sensitive spectator
as, literally, out of place. It is certainly terrible when a soft-boiled
he-man, after the suicide of his mistress, casts a twelve-foot glance
upon her photograph and says something less-than-coexpressible
to the effect that he will never forget her. But when he recites,
instead, a piece of poetry as sublimely more-than-coexpressible
as Romeo's monologue at the bier of Juliet, it is still worse.
Reinhardt's *Midsummer Night's Dream* is probably the most unfortunate major film ever produced; and Olivier's *Henry V* owes
its comparative success, apart from the all but providential adapta-
bility of this particular play, to so many *tours de force* that it
will, God willing, remain an exception rather than set a pattern. It
combines "judicious pruning" with the interpolation of pageantry,
nonverbal comedy and melodrama; it uses a device perhaps best
designated as "oblique close-up" (Mr. Olivier's beautiful face
inwardly listening to but not pronouncing the great soliloquy);
and, most notably, it shifts between three levels of archaeological
reality: a reconstruction of Elizabethan London, a reconstruction
of the events of 1415 as laid down in Shakespeare's play, and the
reconstruction of a performance of this play on Shakespeare's
own stage. All this is perfectly legitimate; but, even so, the highest praise of the film will always come from those who, like the
critic of the *New Yorker*, are not quite in sympathy with either
the movies *au naturel* or Shakespeare *au naturel*.

As the writings of Conan Doyle potentially contain all modern
mystery stories (except for the tough specimens of the Dashiell
Hammett school), so do the films produced between 1900 and
1910 preestablish the subject matter and methods of the moving
picture as we know it. This period produced the incunabula of
the Western and the crime film (Edwin S. Porter's amazing *Great
Train Robbery* of 1903) from which developed the modern
gangster, adventure, and mystery pictures (the latter, if well done,
is still one of the most honest and genuine forms of film entertainment, space being doubly charged with time as the beholder asks
himself not only "What is going to happen?" but also "What has
happened before?"). The same period saw the emergence of the
fantastically imaginative film (*Méliès*) which was to lead to the

expressionist and surrealist experiments (*The Cabinet of Dr. Caligari, Sang d'un Poète*, etc.), on the one hand, and to the more superficial and spectacular fairy tales à la Arabian Nights, on the other. Comedy, later to triumph in Charlie Chaplin, the still insufficiently appreciated Buster Keaton, the Marx Brothers and the pre-Hollywood creations of René Clair, reached a respectable level in Max Linder and others. In historical and melodramatic films the foundations were laid for movie iconography and movie symbolism, and in the early work of D. W. Griffith we find, not only remarkable attempts at psychological analysis (*Edgar Allan Poe*) and social criticism (*A Corner in Wheat*) but also such basic technical innovations as the long shot, the flashback and the close-up. And modest trick films and cartoons paved the way to Felix the Cat, Popeye the Sailor, and Felix's prodigious offspring, Mickey Mouse.

Within their self-imposed limitations the earlier Disney films, and certain sequences in the later ones, represent, as it were, a chemically pure distillation of cinematic possibilities. They retain the most important folkloristic elements—sadism, pornography, the humor engendered by both, and moral justice—almost without dilution and often fuse these elements into a variation on the primitive and inexhautible David-and-Goliath motif, the triumph of the seemingly weak over the seemingly strong; and their fantastic independence of the natural laws gives them the power to integrate space with time to such perfection that the spatial and temporal experiences of sight and hearing come to be almost inter-convertible. A series of soap bubbles, successively punctured, emits a series of sounds exactly corresponding in pitch and volume to the size of the bubbles; the three uvulae of Willie the Whale—small, large and medium—vibrate in consonance with tenor, bass and baritone notes; and the very concept of stationary existence is completely abolished. No object in creation, whether it be a house, a piano, a tree or an alarm clock, lacks the faculties of organic, in fact anthropomorphic, movement, facial expression and phonetic articulation. Incidentally, even in normal, "realistic" films the inanimate object, provided that it is dynamizable, can play the role of a leading character as do the ancient railroad engines in Buster Keaton's *General* and *Niagara Falls*. How the earlier Russian films exploited the possibility of heroizing all sorts of machinery lives in everybody's memory; and it is perhaps more than an accident that the two films which will go down in history as the great comical and the great serious masterpiece of the silent period bear the names and immortalize the personalities of two big ships: Keaton's *Navigator* (1924) and Eisenstein's *Potemkin* (1925).

The evolution from the jerky beginnings to this grand climax offers the fascinating spectacle of a new artistic medium gradually becoming conscious of its legitimate, that is, exclusive, possibilities and limitations—a spectacle not unlike the development of the mosaic, which started out with transposing illusionistic genre pictures into a more durable material and culminated in the hieratic supernaturalism of Ravenna; or the development of line engraving, which started out as a cheap and handy substitute for book illumination and culminated in the purely "graphic" style of Dürer.

Just so the silent movies developed a definite style of their own, adapted to the specific conditions of the medium. A hitherto unknown language was forced upon a public not yet capable of reading it, and the more proficient the public became the more refinement could develop in the language. For a Saxon peasant of around 800 it was not easy to understand the meaning of a picture showing a man as he pours water over the head of another man, and even later many people found it difficult to grasp the significance of two ladies standing behind the throne of an emperor. For the public of around 1910 it was no less difficult to understand the meaning of the speechless action in a moving picture, and the producers employed means of clarification similar to those we find in medieval art. One of these were printed titles or letters, striking equivalents of the medieval *tituli* and scrolls (at a still earlier date there even used to be explainers who would say, *viva voce*, "Now he thinks his wife is dead but she isn't" or "I don't wish to offend the ladies in the audience but I doubt that any of them would have done that much for her child"). Another, less obtrusive method of explanation was the introduction of a fixed iconography which from the outset informed the spectator about the basic facts and characters, much as the two ladies behind the emperor, when carrying a sword and a cross respectively, were uniquely determined as Fortitude and Faith. There arose, identifiable by standardized appearance, behavior and attributes, the well-remembered types of the Vamp and the Straight Girl (perhaps the most convincing modern equivalents of the medieval personifications of the Vices and Virtues), the Family Man, and the Villain, the latter marked by a black mustache and walking stick. Nocturnal scenes were printed on blue or green film. A checkered tablecloth meant, once for all, a "poor but honest" milieu; a happy marriage, soon to be endangered by the shadows from the past, was symbolized by the young wife's pouring the breakfast coffee for her husband; the first kiss was invariably announced by the lady's gently playing with her partner's necktie and was invariably accompanied by her kicking out with her left foot. The conduct of the characters was predetermined accordingly. The poor but honest laborer who, after leaving his little house with the checkered tablecloth, came upon an abandoned baby could not but take it to his home and bring it up as best he could; the Family Man could not but yield, however temporarily, to the temptations of the Vamp. As a result these early melodramas had a highly gratifying and soothing quality in that events took shape, without the complications of individual psychology, according to a pure Aristotelian logic so badly missed in real life.

Devices like these became gradually less necessary as the public grew accustomed to interpret the action by itself and were virtually abolished by the invention of the talking film. But even now there survive—quite legitimately, I think—the remants of a "fixed attitude and attribute" principle and, more basic, a primitive or folkloristic concept of plot construction. Even today we take it for granted that the diphtheria of a baby tends to occur when the parents are out and, having occurred, solves all their matrimonial problems. Even today we demand of a decent mystery film that the butler, though he may be anything from an agent of the British Secret Service to the real father of the daughter of the house, must not turn out to be the murderer. Even today we love to see Pasteur, Zola or Ehrlich win out against stupidity and wickedness, with their respective wives trusting and trusting all the time. Even today we much prefer a happy finale to a gloomy one and insist, at the very least, on the observance of the Aristotelian rule that the story have a beginning, a middle and an ending—a rule the abrogation of which has done so much to estrange the general public from the more elevated spheres of modern writing. Primitive symbolism, too, survives in such amusing details as the last sequence of *Casablanca* where the delightfully crooked and right-minded *préfet de police* casts an empty bottle of Vichy water into the wastepaper basket; and in such telling symbols of the supernatural as Sir Cedric Hardwicke's Death in the guise of a "gentleman in a dustcoat trying" (*On Borrowed Time*) or Claude Rains's Hermes Psychopompos in the striped trousers of an airline manager (*Here Comes Mister Jordan*).

The most conspicuous advances were made in directing, lighting, camera work, cutting and acting proper. But while in most of these fields the evolution proceeded continuously—though, of course, not without detours, breakdowns and archaic relapses— the development of acting suffered a sudden interruption by the invention of the talking film; so that the style of acting in the silents can already be evaluated in retrospect, as a lost art not unlike the painting technique of Jan van Eyck or, to take up our previous simile, the burin technique of Dürer. It was soon realized that acting in a silent film neither meant a pantomimic exaggeration of stage acting (as was generally and erroneously assumed by professional stage actors who more and more frequently condescended to perform in the movies), nor could dispense with stylization altogether; a man photographed while walking down a gangway in ordinary, everyday-life fashion looked like anything but a man walking down a gangway when the result appeared on the screen. If the picture was to look both natural and meaningful the acting had to be done in a manner equally different from the style of the stage and the reality of ordinary life; speech had to be made dispensable by establishing an organic relation between the acting and the technical procedure of cinephotography—much as in Dürer's prints color had been made dispensable by establishing an organic relation between the design and the technical procedure of line engraving.

This was precisely what the great actors of the silent period accomplished, and it is a significant fact that the best of them did not come from the stage, whose crystallized tradition prevented Duse's only film, *Cenere*, from being more than a priceless record of Duse. They came instead from the circus or the variety, as was the case of Chaplin, Keaton and Will Rogers; from nothing in particular, as was the case of Theda Bara, of her greater European parallel, the Danish actress Asta Nielsen, and of Garbo; or from everything under the sun, as was the case of Douglas Fairbanks. The style of these "old masters" was indeed comparable to the style of line engraving in that it was, and had to be, exaggerated in comparison with stage acting (just as the sharply incised and vigorously curved *tailles* of the burin are exaggerated in comparison with pencil strokes or brushwork), but richer, subtler and infinitely more precise. The advent of the talkies, reducing if not abolishing this difference between screen acting and stage acting, thus confronted the actors and actresses of the silent screen with a serious problem. Buster Keaton yielded to temptation and fell. Chaplin first tried to stand his ground and to remain an exquisite archaist but finally gave in, with only moderate success (*The Great Dictator*). Only the glorious Harpo has thus far successfully refused to utter a single articulate sound; and only Greta Garbo succeeded, in a measure, in transforming her style in principle. But even in her case one cannot help feeling that her first talking picture, *Anna Christie*, where she could ensconce herself, most of the time, in mute or monosyllabic sullenness, was better than her later performances; and in the second, talking version of *Anna Karenina*, the weakest moment is certainly when she delivers a big Ibsenian speech to her husband, and the strongest when she silently moves along the platform of the railroad station while her despair takes shape in the consonance of her movement (and expression) with the movement of the nocturnal space around her, filled with the real noises of the trains and the imaginary sound of the "little men with the iron hammers" that drives her, relentlessly and almost without her realizing it, under the wheels.

Small wonder that there is sometimes felt a kind of nostalgia for the silent period and that devices have been worked out to combine the virtues of sound and speech with those of silent acting, such as the "oblique close-up" already mentioned in connection with *Henry V*; the dance behind glass doors in *Sous les Toits de Paris*; or, in the *Histoire d'un Tricheur*, Sacha Guitry's recital of the events of his youth while the events themselves are "silently" enacted on the screen. However, this nostalgic feeling is no argument against the talkies as such. Their evolution has shown that, in art, every gain entails a certain loss on the other side of the ledger; but that the gain remains a gain, provided that the basic nature of the medium is realized and respected. One can imagine that, when the cavemen of Altamira began to paint their buffaloes in natural colors instead of merely incising the contours, the more conservative cavemen foretold the end of paleolithic art. But paleolithic art went on, and so will the movies. New technical inventions always tend to dwarf the values already attained, especially in a medium that owes its very existence to technical experimentation. The earliest talkies were infinitely inferior to the then mature silents, and most of the present technicolor films are still inferior to the now mature talkies in black and white. But even if Aldous Huxley's nightmare should come true and the experiences of taste, smell and touch should be added to those of sight and hearing, even then we may say with the Apostle, as we have said when first confronted with the sound track and the technicolor film, "We are troubled on every side, yet not distressed; we are perplexed, but not in despair."

From the law of time-charged space and space-bound time, there follows the fact that the screenplay, in contrast to the theater play, *has no aesthetic existence independent of its performance, and that its characters have no aesthetic existence outside the actors.*

The playwright writes in the fond hope that his work will be an imperishable jewel in the treasure house of civilization and will be presented in hundreds of performances that are but transient variations on a "work" that is constant. The script-writer, on the other hand, writes for one producer, one director and one cast. Their work achieves the same degree of permanence as does his; and should the same or a similar scenario ever be filmed by a different director and a different cast there will result an altogether different "play."

Othello or Nora are definite, substantial figures created by the playwright. They can be played well or badly, and they can be "interpreted" in one way or another; but they most definitely exist, no matter who plays them or even whether they are played at all. The character in a film, however, lives and dies with the actor. It is not the entity "Othello" interpreted by Robeson or the entity "Nora" interpreted by Duse; it is the entity "Greta Garbo" incarnate in a figure called Anna Christie or the entity "Robert Montgomery" incarnate in a murderer who, for all we know or care to know, may forever remain anonymous but will never cease to haunt our memories. Even when the names of the characters happen to be Henry VIII or Anna Karenina, the king who ruled England from 1509 to 1547 and the woman created by Tolstoy, they do not exist outside the being of Garbo and Laughton. They are but empty and incorporeal outlines like the shadows in

Homer's Hades, assuming the character of reality only when filled with the lifeblood of an actor. Conversely, if a movie role is badly played there remains literally nothing of it, no matter how interesting the character's psychology or how elaborate the words.

What applies to the actor applies, *mutatis mutandis*, to most of the other artists, or artisans, who contribute to the making of a film: the director, the sound man, the enormously important cameraman, even the make-up man. A stage production is rehearsed until everything is ready, and then it is repeatedly performed in three consecutive hours. At each performance everybody has to be on hand and does his work; and afterward he goes home and to bed. The work of the stage actor may thus be likened to that of a musician, and that of the stage director to that of a conductor. Like these, they have a certain repertoire which they have studied and present in a number of complete but transitory performances, be it *Hamlet* today and *Ghosts* tomorrow, or *Life with Father per saecula saeculorum*. The activities of the film actor and the film director, however, are comparable, respectively, to those of the plastic artist and the architect, rather than to those of the musician and the conductor. Stage work is continuous but transitory; film work is discontinuous but permanent. Individual sequences are done piecemeal and out of order according to the most efficient use of sets and personnel. Each bit is done over and over again until it stands; and when the whole has been cut and composed everyone is through with it forever. Needless to say that this very procedure cannot but emphasize the curious consubstantiality that exists between the person of the movie actor and his role. Coming into existence piece by piece, regardless of the natural sequence of events, the "character" can grow into a unified whole only if the actor manages to be, not merely to play, Henry VIII or Anna Karenina throughout the entire wearisome period of shooting. I have it on the best of authorities that Laughton was really difficult to live with in the particular six or eight weeks during which he was doing—or rather being—Captain Bligh.

It might be said that a film, called into being by a co-operative effort in which all contributions have the same degree of permanence, is the nearest modern equivalent of a medieval cathedral; the role of the producer corresponding, more or less, to that of the bishop or archbishop; that of the director to that of the architect in chief; that of the scenario writers to that of the scholastic advisers establishing the iconographical program; and that of the actors, camermen, cutters, sound men, make-up men and the divers technicians to that of those whose work provided the physical entity of the finished product, from the sculptors, glass painters, bronze casters, carpenters and skilled masons down to the quarry men and woodsmen. And if you speak to any one of these collaborators he will tell you, with perfect *bona fides*, that his is really the most important job—which is quite true to the extent that it is indispensable.

This comparison may seem sacrilegious, not only because there are, proportionally, fewer good films than there are good cathedrals but also because the movies are commercial. However, if commercial art be defined as all art not primarily produced in order to gratify the creative urge of its maker but primarily intended to meet the requirements of a patron or a buying public, it must be said that noncommercial art is the exception rather than the rule, and a fairly recent and not always felicitous exception at that. While it is true that commercial art is always in danger of ending up as a prostitute, it is equally true that noncommercial art is always in danger of ending up as an old maid. Noncommercial art has given us Seurat's "Grande Jatte" and Shakespeare's sonnets, but also much that is esoteric to the point of incommunicability. Conversely, commercial art has given us much that is vulgar or snobbish (two aspects of the same thing) to the point of loathsomeness, but also Dürer's prints and Shakespeare's plays. For, we must not forget that Dürer's prints were partly made on commission and partly intended to be sold in the open market; and that Shakespeare's plays—in contrast to the earlier masques and intermezzi which were produced at court by aristocratic amateurs and could afford to be so incomprehensible that even those who described them in printed monographs occasionally failed to grasp their intended significance—were meant to appeal, and did appeal, not only to the select few but also to everyone who was prepared to pay a shilling for admission.

It is this requirement of communicability that makes commercial art more vital than noncommercial, and therefore potentially much more effective for better or for worse. The commercial producer can both educate and pervert the general public, and can allow the general public—or rather his idea of the general public—both to educate and to pervert himself. As is demonstrated by a number of excellent films that proved to be great box

office successes, the public does not refuse to accept good
products if it gets them. That it does not get them very often is
caused not so much by commercialism as such as by too little
discernment and, paradoxical though it may seem, too much
timidity in its application. Hollywood believes that it must produce "what the public wants" while the public would take whatever Hollywood produces. If Hollywood were to decide for
itself what it wants it would get away with it—even if it should
decide to "depart from evil and do good." For, to revert to
whence we started, in modern life the movies are what most other
forms of art have ceased to be, not an adornment but a necessity.

That this should be so is understandable, not only from a sociological but also from an art-historical point of view. The processes
of all the earlier representational arts conform, in a higher or
lesser degree, to an idealistic conception of the world. These arts
operate from top to bottom, so to speak, and not from bottom to
top; they start with an idea to be projected into shapeless matter
and not with the objects that constitute the physical world. The
painter works on a blank wall or canvas which he organizes into
a likeness of things and persons according to his idea (however
much this idea may have been nourished by reality); he does not
work with the things and persons themselves even if he works
"from the model." The same is true of the sculptor with his
shapeless mass of clay or his untooled block of stone or wood; of
the writer with his sheet of paper or his dictaphone; and even of
the stage designer with his empty and sorely limited section of
space. It is the movies, and only the movies, that do justice to that
materialistic interpretation of the universe which, whether we
like it or not, pervades contemporary civilization. Excepting the
very special case of the animated cartoon, the movies organize
material things and persons, not a neutral medium, into a composition that receives its style, and may even become fantastic or
pretervoluntarily symbolic,[1] not so much by an interpretation in
the artist's mind as by the actual manipulation of physical objects
and recording machinery. The medium of the movies is physical
reality as such: the physical reality of eighteenth-century Ver-

[1] I cannot help feeling that the final sequence of the new Marx Brothers film *Night in Cassa-
blanca*—where Harpo unaccountably usurps the pilot's seat of a big airplane, causes incalculable
havoc by flicking one tiny little control after another, and waxes the more insane with joy the
greater the disproportion between the smallness of his effort and the magnitude of the disaster—
is a magnificent and terrifying symbol of man's behavior in the atomic age. No doubt the Marx
Brothers would vigorously reject this interpretation; but so would Dürer have done had anyone
told him that his "Apocalypse" foreshadowed the cataclysm of the Reformation.

sailles—no matter whether it be the original or a Hollywood facsimile indistinguishable therefrom for all aesthetic intents and purposes—or of a suburban home in Westchester; the physical reality of the Rue de Lappe in Paris or of the Gobi Desert, of Paul Ehrlich's apartment in Frankfurt or of the streets of New York in the rain; the physical reality of engines and animals, of Edward G. Robinson and Jimmy Cagney. All these objects and persons must be organized into a work of art. They can be arranged in all sorts of ways ("arrangement" comprising, of course, such things as make-up, lighting and camera work); but there is no running away from them. From this point of view it becomes evident that an attempt at subjecting the world to artistic prestylization, as in the expressionist settings of *The Cabinet of Dr. Caligari* (1919), could be no more than an exciting experiment that could exert but little influence upon the general course of events. To prestylize reality prior to tackling it amounts to dodging the problem. The problem is to manipulate and shoot unstylized reality in such a way that the result has style. This is a proposition no less legitimate and no less difficult than any proposition in the older arts.

Only in very recent decades has the criticism of film become an accepted part of the artistic and intellectual life in America. Thus the work of Andrew Sarris (1928–   ) is pioneering in nature, especially the articles of film criticism which began to appear in 1960 in the Village Voice *(New York City); in addition, Sarris is the New York editor of* Cahiers du Cinéma. *A teacher of screenwriting and cinema, he is also an editor and member of the National Society of Film Critics, and the Society of Cinematologists. In his critical work Sarris argues convincingly for the support of experimental and independent films and suggests these films contribute to the improvement of all film production. For further reading, see "The Independent Cinema," reprinted in an interesting anthology,* New American Cinema *(1967).*

THE FALL AND RISE OF THE FILM DIRECTOR

Andrew Sarris

Greta Garbo's creakiest vehicle of the Thirties was an opus entitled *Susan Lenox—Her Fall and Rise*. Film historians and archivists have repeatedly restored the classical cadence of "Rise and Fall" to the title in defiance of the plot line and the aggressively American optimism it presents. Film directors are comparable to sudsy Susan Lenox in that their tarnished professional image has regained its gloss after a long period of neglect and downright disrepute. In fact, the renewed awareness of the film director as a conscious artist is one of the more interesting cultural phenomena of the past decade. This renewal can be described as a rise only in the most relative terms. The director has risen no more than the sun rises. As the latter is a figure of speech describing the diurnal rotation of the earth from the point of view of the fallible human eye, the pre-eminence of the director has been a matter of public and critical fancy.

Like the sun, the director has always been out there on the set, and his turn to be worshiped has come full circle from the earliest days of his solitary pre-eminence behind primitive tripod cameras pointed at a world still visually virginal. This intimation of lost innocence is invoked in Billy Wilder's *Sunset Boulevard* when Erich von Stroheim commands the newsreel cameras to turn on Gloria Swanson as she descends the staircase to utter madness. There is more than the numbing nostalgia for a burnt-out star in this sequence; there is also the evocation of an era when movie-making was more individual, less industrial. It is immaterial whether there ever was an era of directional enlightenment. Many film historians have testified to the existence of a Golden Age in order to create a frame of reference. The gold may have turned to brass before 1925 or 1920 or 1915, but somewhere along the line, the legend persists, the film director lost all his freedom and integrity to some monstrous entity known as the motion picture industry—code name: Hollywood.

Confirmation of this legend of directorial decline and decadence has been provided by veteran Hollywood director George Stevens: "When the movie industry was young, the film-maker was its core and the man who handled the business details his partner . . . When [the director] finally looked around, he found his partner's name on the door. Thus the film-maker became the employee, and the man who had the time to attend to the business details became the head of the studio."

Studio head Samuel Goldwyn put the matter somewhat more brutally when a reporter had the temerity to begin a sentence with the statement: "When William Wyler made *Wuthering Heights* . . ." The reporter never passed beyond the premise. "*I* made *Wuthering Heights*," Goldwyn snapped. "Wyler only directed it."

"Only directed" is more precisely defined in the appendix of *The Film Till Now* by Paul Rotha and Richard Griffith: "Director—(a) In feature films the Director is usually the technician who directs the shooting of the film, that is, he tells the players what to do and the cameraman what to shoot, and usually supervises the editing. Most feature films are directed from scripts written by the script department or by an independent script-writer. The editing is carried out by a department under a super-

vising editor working in consultation with the director and producer. Sometimes a director will write his own shooting-script
and do his own editing; thus the film will tend much more to
carry his individual mark.

"(b) In documentary films the Director usually writes his own
script after first-hand investigation of the subject, although sometimes he may employ a dialogue writer. He not only directs the
action of the film, but controls it through all stages of editing,
music, dubbing, etc. Wartime developments have tended to departmentalize documentary production as in story films."

The most interesting aspect of this duplex definition, devised
during the Forties, is its ingrained bias in favor of the documentary director. Directors of "feature" or "story" films were
presumably less artists than artisans not only because they were
more closely supervised, but also because "feature" films were
considered more frivolous than documentary films. Thus, most
movie directors were doubly denigrated in the scholarly texts of
the period. On the one hand, most directors were charged with
having too little control over their movies, and on the other, their
movies were not considered worth doing in the first place.

Not that scholarly texts had any appreciable influence on the
motion picture industry. Like so many other products of capitalism, movies were designed for immediate consumption and rapid
expendability. Once a movie became "old," it was returned to the
vaults, never to be shown publicly again. Thus, even if there had
been any interest in directorial careers, the necessary research
materials were split in two by the advent of sound in the late
Twenties.

People who grew up in the Thirties were completely unaware
of the cinema of the Twenties except for infrequent custard pie
two-reelers or an occasional revival of the foreign repertory—
from *Caligari* to *Potemkin*. By about 1934, censorship had placed
many movies of the early Thirties out of bounds, a condition that
existed until the Forties and Fifties when television gold made it
lucrative for studios to open their vaults. We are still a long way
from the day when scholars can obtain the films they need from
film libraries, but the proliferation of old films has had its effect
on contemporary criticism. A greater awareness of the past, a
sense of stylistic continuity in the works of individual directors,
a cyclical pattern of period mannerisms—these are some of the
dividends of the improved distribution of movies in the Sixties.

The most hardheaded businessman in the movie industry must now be at least marginally concerned with the burgeoning scholarship in the medium. By the same token, the most serious-minded scholar cannot avoid taking movies more seriously than heretofore, particularly when it is now possible to trace links between the Marx Brothers and Ionesco, between Buster Keaton and Samuel Beckett.

Unfortunately, most scholarly works on the cinema are still written from a predominantly sociological viewpoint, and most directors are still subordinated to both the studio and the star system that allegedly enslave them. Indeed most directors have always been considered less as creators than as decorators of other people's scenarios. That most directors do not write their own scripts is enough to discredit these directors in the eyes of the literary establishment. Such discredit is often unjustified even on literary grounds simply because many directors decline to take credit for collaboration on the writing of their films.

Furthermore, screenwriting involves more than mere dialogue and plot. The choice between a close-up and a long-shot, for example, may quite often transcend the plot. If the story of Little Red Riding Hood is told with the Wolf in close-up and Little Red Riding Hood in long-shot, the director is concerned primarily with the emotional problems of a wolf with a compulsion to eat little girls. If Little Red Riding Hood is in close-up and the Wolf in long-shot, the emphasis is shifted to the emotional problems of vestigial virginity in a wicked world. Thus, two different stories are being told with the same basic anecdotal material. What is at stake in the two versions of Little Red Riding Hood are two contrasting directorial attitudes toward life. One director identifies more with the Wolf—the male, the compulsive, the corrupted, even evil itself. The second director identifies with the little girl—the innocence, the illusion, the ideal and hope of the race. Needless to say, few critics bother to make any distinction, proving perhaps that direction as creation is still only dimly understood.

As a consequence, contemporary film criticism has tended to diverge into two conflicting camps, the poor film director caught in the middle. First and foremost, we have the literary establishment, which relegates visual style to subordinate paragraphs in reviews. Then we have the visualists, who disdain plots and dialogues as literary impurities. Since most directors worthy of note work in the impure realm of the dramatic sound film, it is difficult to isolate their personal contributions to the cinema. The literary critics prefer to synopsize the plot, discuss the theme, if any, evaluate the performances, comment on the photography, editing, etc., and credit the director only for "pacing," usually in the three speeds—fast, deliberate, and most often of all, too slow. Conversely, the visual critics concentrate on landscapes and abstractions as "pure" cinema, and castigate dramatic scenes as "talky," "stagey," "literary," etc. That is why the coming of sound was such a traumatic experience for serious film aestheticians of the late Twenties and early Thirties, and why much of what we call film history is actually the thinly disguised nostalgia of elderly film historians for the mute movies of their youth.

Through the haze of selective recollection, the silent film had apparently flown to an extraordinary elevation in the Twenties only to crash through the sound barrier with a screech and a squeak. It became fashionable to mourn the tragedy of talkies until well into the Forties, and after to talk about the cinema in terms of artistic decline until well into the Fifties.

The biographical pattern of almost every director went something like this: He started off very promisingly, but was soon corrupted by Hollywood (if he were foreign), or by big budgets (if he were American). His work became more and more "commercial," less and less "significant." Because distribution was so erratic, it was always reasonably safe to say that yesterday's movies were superior to today's.

On the whole, however, directors were penalized more by critical indifference than by critical captiousness. Few people cared to read about directors; a volume of interviews of directors would have been inconceivable even as late as ten years ago. If the role of the director is now taken more seriously, it is because the cinema itself is taken more seriously. The director never really had any serious rival in the creative process. No one, least of all the serious scholar, was ever taken in by the pufferies of the producers. Selznick, Zanuck, Hughes, Goldwyn, and Thalberg did exercise great control over their productions, but few of their contributions were regarded as genuinely creative. Mostly, they maintained a certain level of technical quality in their productions, but production control without creative responsibility falls generally under the heading of interference.

The writer was even less serious a challenge to the director. Although the director was shackled to some extent by the studio system through the Thirties and Forties, the writer was virtually deprived of his identity. As far as studios were concerned, there was never a question of too many scribes spoiling the script. Quite to the contrary, most producers believed strongly in the safety of numbers, and the multiple writing credits on the screen made it difficult for screenwriters to be taken seriously as screen authors.

By contrast, directors almost invariably received sole credit for their efforts, however craven and controlled these efforts may have been considered. In addition, the director's credit always appeared last on the screen—or almost always—one contractual exception being the aforementioned Samuel Goldwyn, a producer with a passion for having his name follow the director's. Nevertheless, the director's position, even in Hollywood, has always been strategically superior to the writer's. In the early Forties, the Screenwriter's Guild felt obliged to agitate for greater critical recognition, and the conflict became so exaggerated that, at one point, Stephen Longstreet attacked Vincente Minnelli for distracting audiences from dialogue with fancy camera angles in the 1945 Judy Garland-Robert Walker romance, *The Clock*. Needless to say, no screenwriter today would dare make a comparable objection.

Even today, however, the film director faces massive obstacles to critical recognition. Writers, actors, producers, and technicians challenge him at every turn. Also, the analogous and yet anomalous relationship with stage directors tends to confuse the issue. It is fashionable to say that the screen is a director's medium and the stage a writer's medium, but it is difficult to demonstrate that a Broadway-to-Hollywood-and-back director like Elia Kazan is any less in command in one medium than in another. To some extent, of course, the role of the director, stage or screen, depends on the person playing it. Many, if not most, film directors are little more than glorified stage managers charged with maintaining a schedule for the execution of the preordained plans of the studio, the stars, the producer, the writer or writers, the technicians, the distributors, and even the vulgar public. At his least or his worst, the director is reduced to the level of a technician without the technician's pride in his craft. Such directors are like absolute despots compelled to act as constitutional monarchs, but lacking the style to conceal or circumvent their subservience.

At the other extreme, we have a new breed of film-makers who do not even call themselves "directors." These are the so-called independents, the "poets," the perpetual avant-garde of the cinema. They scorn or pretend to scorn the elaborate technical and industrial processes of movie production for the sake of a more individualized creation. They are descended, if only atavistically, from the first film-makers, the curious cameramen who were playing with a new toy. Ironically, the avant-garde has generally resisted the stylistic and technological innovations initiated by so-called commercial movie-makers. Sound, color, music, variable screens were all devoloped by the film industry while the avant-garde was publishing manifestoes against them. The avant-garde has thus led the way not in form, but in content—anarchic, subversive, sacrilegious, scatological, and pornographic.

Through the years and decades, however, avant-garde attitudes in America have relied on the foreign "art film" for intellectual authority. The Germans and the Russians were particularly fashionable in the Twenties, before Hitler and Stalin stultified experimentation. Movies like *The Last Laugh* and *Variety* dramatized the expressive potentialities of the moving camera along with downbeat subjects considered too grim for Hollywood, but it was Sergei Eisenstein's *Potemkin* that galvanized a whole generation of intellectuals and aesthetes into wild enthusiasm over the creative possibilities of montage, a term that reverberated through the Twenties and Thirties the way *mise en scène* has reverberated through the Fifties and Sixties. Normally, montage is merely a fancy word for editing or cutting, but Eisenstein gave montage a mystique by linking it to the philosophical processes of dialectical materialism. As Eisenstein conceived of film-making, images equaled ideas, and the collision of two dynamically opposed images created a new idea. Eisenstein's montage theory was ideal for describing the collisions of the Russian Revolution, but there did not seem to be many other plots for which incessant montage was appropriate. The great majority of movies developed a dramatic style of expression to enhance audience identification with star personalities. Since in the world cinema the mystique of montage was thereafter honored more in the breach than in the observance, film histories turned sour with acid critiques of alleged betrayals of the medium. As the gap widened between what was popular and what was intellectually fashionable, Eisensteinian aesthetics were supplemented by Marxist politics. Movies were not merely vulgar; they were instruments of capitalism in the never-ending class struggle. Film directors were thus presented with two choices: fight the establishment, or "sell out."

It remained for the illustrious French film critic André Bazin to eliminate much of the confusion arising from Eisenstein's half-digested montage theories. Bazin pinpointed psychological and physical situations in which montage disrupted the unity of man with his environment. Indeed it was French criticism in the late Forties and early Fifties that introduced the mystique of *mise en scène* to counterbalance that of montage. The more extreme of Einsenstein disciples had reached a stage of absurdity in which what was actually on the screen was secondary to the "rhythm" of the film. The montage maniacs had thus enthroned punctuation at the expense of language. At times, it seemed that the camera was merely an excuse to get into the cutting room.

Ironically, the producers shared the highbrow enthusiasm over montage. "We'll save it in the cutting room" became one of the hackneyed slogans of bad producers. *Mise en scène*, with its connotation of design and decor, reintroduced pictorial values to a medium that had become obsessed with the musical rhythms of images flashing by to be slashed on the moviola.

Because French critics were less awed by montage, they tended to be more appreciative of Hollywood than their cultivated counterparts in America and England. Most Hollywood directors of the Thirties were disqualified from serious consideration because they did not supervise the final editing (montage) of their films, for editing was then considered, by the aestheticians, the supreme function of cinematic creation. With the collapse of the montage mystique, however, many directors of the Thirties have been rediscovered as undeniably personal artists. Not only do the best directors cut "in the mind" rather than in the cutting room, but montage is only one aspect of a directorial personality.

Nonetheless, the Hollywood director is still taken less seriously than his foreign counterpart, and, in interviews, he generally regards himself with the same lack of seriousness. Part of his problem is the Hollywood ethos of the "team"; part is the tendency of Hollywood movies to conceal the inner workings for the sake of popular illusionism. Audiences are not supposed to be conscious that a movie is directed; the movie just happens by some mysterious conjunction of the players with their plot. Quite often, Hollywood directors have labored in obscurity to evolve an extraordinary economy of expression that escapes so-called highbrow critics in search of the obvious stylistic flourish. Consequently, there has been a tendency to overrate the European directors because of their relative articulateness about their artistic *angst*, and now a reaction has set in against some of the disproportionate pomposity that has ensued. Some of the recent cults for Ingmar Bergman, Federico Fellini, and Michelangelo Antonioni create the impression that the cinema was born sometime between 1950 and 1960. Not that European directors are entirely to blame for occasionally appearing pretentious. They are merely playing the role that is expected of them, just as Hollywood directors are conditioned to pretend that they are all hardheaded businessmen. But here, too, the gap is narrowing as Hollywood directors venture to be more explicit about their artistic intentions and European directors dare to be more candid about commercial and professional problems.

As film scholarship becomes more sophisticated, the facile distinctions between so-called "art" films and so-called "commercial" films become less meaningful. Out of the sifting and winnowing emerges a new division of good "art" and "commercial" films on one side and bad "art" and "commercial" films on the other. Not only do art and commerce intersect; they are intertwined with the muddled processes of film-making. Even art films have to make money, and even commercial films have to make some statement. To put it another way, more and more critics are demanding that there should be more fun in art, and more art in fun. The post-Marxist pop and camp movements have perhaps overreacted to the socially conscious solemnity of the past, but the increasing skepticism about mere good intentions is a healthy sign of higher standards. Unfortunately, the pendulum has swung from the extreme of sobriety to the extreme of silliness. In the process, however, it has become possible to speak of Alfred Hitchcock and Michelangelo Antonioni in the same breath and with the same critical terminology. Amid the conflicting critical camps, both Rays, Nicholas and Satyajit, have gained a respectful hearing. Suddenly every director is entitled to equal time on the international critical scene in which critics are compelled to abandon many of their cherished prejudices and snobberies. In a more open-minded atmosphere of critical recognition, it is only natural that film directors should abandon some of their defensive attitudes toward their roles. However, as instructive as the new frankness of film directors may be, interviews with directors cannot usurp the role of critical analysis.

André Bazin has summed up the situation admirably: "There are, occasionally, good directors, like René Clement or Lattuada, who profess a precise aesthetic consciousness and accept a discussion on this level, but most of their colleagues react to aesthetic analysis with an attitude ranging from astonishment to irritation. Moreover, the astonishment is perfectly sincere and comprehensible. As for the irritation, this often springs from an instinctive resistance to the dismantling of a mechanism whose purpose is to create an illusion, and only mediocrities gain, in effect, from malfunctioning mechanisms. The director's irritation springs also from his resentment at being placed in a position that is foreign to him. Thus, I have seen a director as intelligent (and conscious) as Jean Grémillon play the village idiot and sabotage our discussion of *Lumière d'été* evidently because he did not agree with me. And how can I say he is wrong? Is not this impasse reminiscent of Paul Valéry leaving the lecture hall where Gustave Cohen has presented his famous commentary on *Cimitière Marin* with a word of ironic admiration for the professor's imagination? Must we conclude therefore that Paul Valéry is only an intuitive artist betrayed by a pedant's textual analysis and that *Cimitière Marin* is merely automatic writing?

"As a matter of fact," Bazin declares, "this apparent contradiction between the critic and the author should not trouble us. It is in the natural order of things, both subjectively and objectively. Subjectively because artistic creation—even with the most intellectual temperaments—is essentially intuitive and practical: it is a matter of effects to attain and materials to conquer. Objectively, because a work of art escapes its creator and bypasses his conscious intentions, in direct proportion to its quality. The foundation of this objectivity also resides in the psychology of the creation to the inappreciable extent to which the artist does not really create but sets himself to crystallize, to order the sociological forces and the technical conditions into which he is thrust. This is particularly true of the American cinema in which you often find quasi-anonymous successes whose merit reflects, not on the director, but on the production system. But an objective criticism, methodically ignoring 'intentions,' is as applicable to the most personal work imaginable, like a poem or a painting, for example.

"This does not mean that knowing authors (*auteurs*) personally, or what they say about themselves and their work, may not clarify the critic's conception, and this is proven by taped interviews we have published in *Cahiers du Cinema* through the Fifties.

These confidences, on the contrary, are infinitely precious, but they are not on the same plane as the criticism I am discussing; or, if you will, they constitute a pre-critical, unrefined documentation, and the critic still retains the liberty of interpretation."

Bazin's actual acceptance of the director as author or *"auteur"* is typical of the French critical orientation toward the director as the sole creative artist of consequence in the cinema. Although the personal and poetic artistry of Ingmar Bergman and Federico Fellini in their films of the early Fifties helped encourage a resurgence of serious interest in the cinema, it was not until the *nouvelle vague* emerged that the role of the director became fully romanticized for young people around the world. Bergman and Fellini were, after all, mature artists and remote figures to most of their admirers. Truffaut and Godard were young men in their twenties without practical experience. They were critics and enthusiasts, and they obviously loved movies with none of the dead chill of professionals. They also admired many of their predecessors, artists as disparate as Jean Renoir and Alfred Hitchcock. Above all, they had resurrected many directors from the limbo of low regard and had popularized the *Politique des Auteurs*, a mystique for reviewing directorial careers rather than individual films.

Overnight the director was king. Truffaut expressed the lyricism of being a director simply by freezing Jeanne Moreau on the screen, thus immortalizing her in a medium where montage implies mortality. Rouben Mamoulian did almost the same thing with Garbo in *Queen Christina* in 1933, but he could never go the whole way to freeze her, not because he didn't know how, but because the world of the Thirties was not interested in how Mamoulian felt about Garbo. Mamoulian had been hired simply to present Garbo to her public. By contrast, Truffaut felt empowered to tell the whole world how he felt about Moreau. Jean-Luc Godard has been even more audacious in breaking every possible rule imposed upon a director by producers and aestheticians. If Godard has been abused for his impudence, Federico Fellini (*8½*), Richard Lester (*A Hard Day's Night*), and Tony Richardson (*Tom Jones*) have struck a post-*Breathless* bonanza by exploiting Godard's gimmicks to the hilt. The meaning of all the freezes, jump cuts, and zany camera speeds of the Sixties is simply that directors have found the courage at long last to call attention to their techniques and personalities. . . .

*Luis Buñuel (1900–   ) is the Goya of the film,
a brilliant and cutting social commentator and at
the same time a psychologist of extraordinary
perception who has recorded better than almost
anyone else in film the madnesses of modern life,
whether caused by economic or social imbalance
or by some interior disturbance in his characters.
The five propositons presented here were written in
1960 and thus antedate such films as* Viridiana,
Belle de Jour, *and* Tristana. *However, they represent
quite fairly these late masterpieces and the rest of
Buñuel, from the early surrealist works,* Un Chien
Andalou *and* L'Age d'Or, *through the social
testaments,* Spanish Earth *and* Los Olvidados, *to the
extraordinary mixtures of anticlericalism,
religiosity, social documentation, and
psychological analysis of recent years.*

A
STATEMENT

*Luis
Buñuel*

*"The screen," he says here,
"is a dangerous and won-
derful instrument,
if a free spirit uses it." Luis Buñuel's own films
demonstrate the accuracy of the statement
and its surrounding arguments.*

1. In none of the traditional arts is there such a
wide gap between possibilities and facts as in the
cinema. Motion pictures act directly upon the
spectator; they offer him concrete persons and
things; they isolate him, through silence and darkness, from the usual psychological atmosphere.
Because of all this, the cinema is capable of stirring the spectator as perhaps no other art. But
as no other art, it is also capable of stupefying
him. Unfortunately, the great majority of today's
films seem to have exactly that purpose; they
glory in an intellectual and moral vacuum. In this
vacuum, movies seem to prosper.

2. Mystery is a basic element of all works of
art. It is generally lacking on the screen. Writers,
directors and producers take good care in avoiding anything that may upset us. They keep the

marvelous window on the liberating world of poetry shut. They prefer stories which seem to continue our ordinary lives, which repeat for the umpteenth time the same drama, which help us forget the hard hours of our daily work. And all this, of course, carefully watched over by traditional morals, government and international censorship, religion, good taste, white humour and other flat dicteria of reality.

3. The screen is a dangerous and wonderful instrument, if a free spirit uses it. It is the superior way of expressing the world of dreams, emotions and instinct. The cinema seems to have been invented for the expression of the subconscious, so profoundly is it rooted in poetry. Nevertheless, it almost never pursues these ends.

4. We rarely see good cinema in the mammoth productions, or in the works that have received the praise of critics and audience. The particular story, the private drama of an individual, cannot interest—I believe—anyone worthy of living in our time. If a man in the audience shares the joys and sorrows of a character on the screen, it should be because that character reflects the joys and sorrows of all society and so the personal feelings of that man in the audience. Unemployment, insecurity, the fear of war, social injustice, etc., affect all men of our time, and thus, they also affect the individual spectator. But when the screen tells me that Mr. X is not happy at home and finds amusement with a girl-friend whom he finally abandons to reunite himself with his faithful wife, I find it all very moral and edifying, but it leaves me completely indifferent.

5. Octavio Paz has said: "But that a man in chains should shut his eyes, the world would explode." And I could say: But that the white eye-lid of the screen reflect its proper light, the Universe would go up in flames. But for the moment we can sleep in peace: the light of the cinema is conveniently dosified and shackled.

It is clear from his films that Ingmar Bergman (1918–) pursues ideas with a relentlessness and determination unmatched among film directors. His pursuit is manifest in the films themselves, not in the construction of scripts or the literary interpretation of the novels or plays that may inspire them. Nonetheless, there is no mistaking the great influence upon Bergman of Strindberg, several of whose plays the director produced when he was head of the Swedish National Theatre in Stockholm. Nor can one miss the large literary traditions, medieval and modern, Swedish, European, American, that feed the hungry speculations of such Bergman films as The Seventh Seal, The Virgin Spring, Wild Strawberries, Winter Light, The Silence, Persona, *and* The Passion of Anna. *There is something paradoxical, then, about the assertions in this statement, something not quite complete. The assertions are necessary; they add much to our understanding of Bergman without destroying the air of mystification that pervades all Bergman films.*

FILM HAS NOTHING TO DO WITH LITERATURE

Ingmar Bergman

A film for me begins with something very vague—a chance remark or a bit of conversation, a hazy but agreeable event unrelated to any particular situation. It can be a few bars of music, a shaft of light across the street. Sometimes in my work at the theatre I have envisioned actors made up for yet unplayed roles.

These are split-second impressions that disappear as quickly as they come, yet leave behind a mood—like pleasant dreams. It is a mental state, not an actual story, but one abounding in fertile associations and images. Most of all, it is a brightly colored thread sticking out of the dark sack of the unconscious. If I begin to wind up this thread, and do it carefully, a complete film will emerge.

This primitive nucleus strives to achieve definite form, moving in a way that may be lazy and half asleep at first. Its stirring is accompanied by vibrations and rhythms which are very special and unique to each film. The picture sequences then assume a pattern in accordance with these rhythms, obeying laws born out of and conditioned by my original stimulus.

If that embryonic substance seems to have enough strength to be made into a film, I decide to materialize it. Then comes something very complicated and difficult: the transformation of rhythms, moods, atmosphere, tensions, sequences, tones and scents into words and sentences, into an understandable screenplay.

This is an almost impossible task.

The only thing that can be satisfactorily transferred from that original complex of rhythms and moods is the dialogue, and even dialogue is a sensitive substance which may offer resistance. Written dialogue is like a musical score, almost incomprehensible to the average person. Its interpretation demands a technical knack plus a certain kind of imagination and feeling—qualities which are so often lacking, even among actors. One can write dialogue, but how it should be delivered, its rhythm and tempo, what is to take place between lines—all this must be omitted for practical reasons. Such a detailed script would be unreadable. I try to squeeze instructions as to location, characterization and atmosphere into my screenplays in understandable terms, but the success of this depends on my writing ability and the perceptiveness of the reader, which are not always predictable.

Now we come to essentials, by which I mean montage, rhythm and the relation of one picture to another—the vital third dimension without which the film is merely a dead product from a factory. Here I cannot clearly give a key, as in a musical score, nor a specific idea of the tempo which determines the relationship of the elements involved. It is quite impossible for me to indicate the way in which the film "breathes" and pulsates.

I have often wished for a kind of notation which would enable me to put on paper all the shades and tones of my vision, to record distinctly the inner structure of a film. For when I stand in the artistically devastating atmosphere of the studio, my hands and head full of all the trivial and irritating details that go with motion-picture production, it often takes a tremendous effort to remember how I originally saw and thought out this or that sequence, or what was the relation between the scene of four weeks ago and that of today. If I could express myself clearly, in explicit symbols, then this problem would be almost eliminated and I could work with absolute confidence that whenever I liked I could prove the relationship between the part and the whole and put my finger on the rhythm, the continuity of the film.

Thus the script is a very imperfect *technical* basis for a film. And there is another important point in this connection which I should like to mention. Film has nothing to do with literature; the character and substance of the two art forms are usually in conflict. This probably has something to do with the receptive process of the mind. The written word is read and assimilated by a conscious act of the will in alliance with the intellect; little by little it affects the imagination and the emotions. The process is different with a motion picture. When we experience a film, we consciously prime ourselves for illusion. Putting aside will and intellect, we make way for it in our imagination. The sequence of pictures plays directly on our feelings.

Music works in the same fashion; I would say that there is no art form that has so much in common with film as music. Both affect our emotions directly, not via the intellect. And film is mainly rhythm; it is inhalation and exhalation in continuous sequence. Ever since childhood, music has been my great source of recreation and stimulation, and I often experience a film or play musically.

It is mainly because of this difference between film and literature that we should avoid making films out of books. The irrational dimension of a literary work, the germ of its existence, is often untranslatable into visual terms—and it, in turn, destroys the special, irrational dimension of the film. If, despite this, we wish to translate something literary into film terms, we must make an infinite number of complicated adjustments which often bear little or no fruit in proportion to the effort expended.

I myself have never had any ambition to be an author. I do not want to write novels, short stories, essays, biographies, or even plays for the theatre. I only want to make films—films about conditions, tensions, pictures, rhythms and characters which are in one way or another important to me. The motion picture, with its complicated process of birth, is my method of saying what I want to my fellow men. I am a film-maker, not an author.

People ask what are my intentions with my films—my aims. It is a difficult and dangerous question, and I usually give an evasive answer: I try to tell the truth about the human condition, the truth as I see it. This answer seems to satisfy everyone, but it is not quite correct. I prefer to describe what I *would like* my aim to be.

There is an old story of how the cathedral of Chartres was struck by lightning and burned to the ground. Then thousands of people came from all points of the compass, like a giant procession of ants, and together they began to rebuild the cathedral on its old site. They worked until the building was completed— master builders, artists, laborers, clowns, noblemen, priests, burghers. But they all remained anonymous, and no one knows to this day who built the cathedral of Chartres.

Regardless of my own beliefs and my own doubts, which are unimportant in this connection, it is my opinion that art lost its basic creative drive the moment it was separated from worship. It severed an umbilical cord and now lives its own sterile life, generating and degenerating itself. In former days the artist remained unknown and his work was to the glory of God. He lived and died without being more or less important than other artisans; "eternal values," "immortality" and "masterpiece" were terms not applicable in his case. The ability to create was a gift. In such a world flourished invulnerable assurance and natural humility.

Today the individual has become the highest form and the greatest bane of artistic creation. The smallest wound or pain of the ego is examined under a microscope as if it were of eternal importance. The artist considers his isolation, his subjectivity, his individualism almost holy. Thus we finally gather in one large pen, where we stand and bleat about our loneliness without listening to each other and without realizing that we are smothering each other to death. The individualists stare into each other's eyes and yet deny the existence of each other. We walk in circles, so limited by our own anxieties that we can no longer distinguish between true and false, between the gangster's whim and the purest ideal.

Thus if I am asked what I would like the general purpose of my films to be, I would reply that I want to be one of the artists in the cathedral on the great plain. I want to make a dragon's head, an angel, a devil—or perhaps a saint—out of stone. It does not matter which; it is the sense of satisfaction that counts. Regardless of whether I believe or not, whether I am a Christian or not, I would play my part in the collective building of the cathedral.

Ernest Callenbach (1930–   ) is the founder and editor of Film Quarterly. *In addition to writing film criticism which often appears in that journal, he has made several short films of his own. Thus, in both theory and practice, Callenbach confronts the film establishment, which in most countries, including America, can operate only by the use of large sums of money furnished by major financial institutions. Understandably, the "success" or "failure" of the film-establishment product is calculated largely in terms of "box office," the return on capital investment. In the following essay Callenbach explicates the major issues raised by the comparatively low-budget, presumably nonestablishment film: the nature of the camera and the concept of the camera itself; the lighting, the direction, acting styles, and the kind of appeal the newer "counter-culture" film has for the present-day audience.*

ACTING, BEING, AND THE DEATH OF THE MOVIE AESTHETIC

Ernest Callenbach

. . . In the last few years an awesome gulf has opened under the [film] industry: the actual drawing power of well-known performers has become totally erratic. Not only Elizabeth Taylor but *all* high-priced stars are now dubious commodities. In the plaintive words of old-time producer Joe Pasternak, "You're not buying box office anymore.". . . I think . . . it is only one among many consequences of a . . . fundamental change the cinema is going through—an artistic, technical, industrial, and social revolution in which the stars are merely the first and most spectacular casualties. . . . This [revolution] cannot be traced to any single cause, but it has one remarkable technical root: the portable 16-mm sound camera. Most models . . . are awkwardly shaped, knobby devices roughly the size of a football, with various protruding lenses, handles, and cables, and weigh around fifteen pounds. But this camera, with its companion cigarbox-size synchronous tape recorder, has dealt a decisive blow to the entire tradition of the theatrical film. . . .

The new portable equipment was first used mainly for television reportage, where speed and flexibility in shooting counted for more than studio perfection. But little by little its impact spread. More and more technicians learned to operate the new, simpler equipment, and more millions of feet of film were shown to more millions of viewers, both on TV and through documentary films.

Most of this footage remained mundane reportage: interviews, hasty newsreel material. But it was still film, and it has had drastic aesthetic consequences. In time some practitioners, growing more ambitious and sophisticated, adopted the battlecry of *cinéma-vérité*; others preferred the alternate name "direct cinema." Sometimes—more sinister still—the new practices went under no name at all. But they have profoundly altered our notion of what a film is and what the filmmaking act is.

Canadian filmmakers first seized on the new light equipment to make films about pop singers (*Lonely Boy*), tobacco farmers (*Back-Breaking Leaf*), street-railway switchmen, even the publisher of *Playboy* (*The Most*). Americans followed, filming race-car drivers (*On the Pole*), politicians (*Primary*), convicts (*The Chair*), high-school football players and coaches (*Football*), inmates of prisons for "the criminally insane" (*Titicut Follies*), film magnates (*Showman*). . . .

The conventional movies had offered various pleasures. People went to them partly because they expected to be excited by a "suspenseful" story, with a beginning, middle, and end, in which they could to some extent believe. Partly they went for spectacle (one of the proper elements of tragedy, said Aristotle): battles, explosions, dancing girls—colorful, impressive, large-scale experiences few viewers could hope to encounter in their workaday lives. . . . And spectacle, if handled in a documentary spirit, still has an appeal—as for instance in racing-car pictures. But the expectations of most moviegoers until very recently have essentially depended on actors' performances. . . . We all look forward to an actor playing a part that suits him exactly, in that intimate, direct, unstagy way. Such performances can seem good enough to be nonperformances. . . . [Yet] certainly there is an indefinable electricity about people who are "personalities"—which is to say, people who have discovered for themselves a powerful, intriguing role that they continue to play even when they are supposed to be enacting some other role. . . . We may not believe Brigitte Bardot or John Wayne are exactly serious artists, but if we are honest we admit that they are more important—to us and to society—than hosts of dedicated and highly trained actors.

But what do such performers do, when they are on camera? Direct cinema, which may show us people shifting from foot to foot or going about their ordinary business of selling Bibles or shoveling snow from streetcar tracks, gives us the perspective to see that a very special agreement lies behind fiction filming. The director is saying, through devices of photography and cutting as well as through the ways he has the actors behave, that we are entering into a kind of game. "We will put on a show for you— we will be artful and entertaining and reasonably convincing and a little naughty, so that you will love us in return and come back to see us again.". . .

The compact has many aesthetic clauses, which make themselves felt in every aspect of filmmaking. In traditional filming, for instance, there was an absolute taboo against looking at the camera—though in the early years vaudeville-trained comics like Chaplin had sometimes gotten away with it. The entire massive process of lighting and rehearsing a shot, marking positions, measuring focus, and so on was conducted with the camera's eye foremost in everyone's thoughts. But for that very reason the actors had to be forbidden to look at it, lest they play visibly to it. . . .

Another basic element of traditional film aesthetics lies in our feeling for the crucial creative act in filming. In "omniscient" studio cinema, the film as a whole was taken to represent the creative will of the director—or at any rate of the director-producer-writer-studio combine. It was made, and accepted by viewers, and criticized by critics, as a fully rounded, concocted, fabricated "work.". . .

With the advent of direct cinema, however, the crucial locus is seen to lie nearer to the cameraman—who is often, by a sort of inevitable default, the actual organizer of the shooting process itself and thus, in a sense, the director of it. It is impossible for anyone else to tell the direct cameraman what to do: when to start a shot, when to stop, how to frame a shot, and so on. He and the sound man must develop an instinctive, nonverbal way of working together; then they must just play by ear. (In *A Married Couple*, director Allan King properly gave cameraman Richard Leiterman a credit as associate director.) Where the basic act of the studio film was to invent, shape, and develop the story material, which the director and actors then froze onto film, the basic act of the direct cinema is to seize characters and actions as they exist in their own right.

This fundamental difference has immense repercussions through every aspect of film production. For instance, take the zoom lens. This lens was, as an invention, available before direct cinema; but it was cameramen filming sports and newsreel work who *needed* it in order to cover large events from a single camera position. Thereafter its applications became far more general. The zoom lens can achieve a fluid, continuous change of focal length (and hence of both framing and perspective) without actually having to move the camera—which can only be done smoothly by a complex system of tracks and dollies, and the crew of ten or fifteen people needed to lay down and operate that system. The aesthetic effect of the zoom shot is, to people used to studio techniques, almost always somewhat unpleasantly artificial. Its optical impression of enlargement rather than true approach to what is being photographed seems tricky and false. But this is felt only so long as one assumes that the camera's relation to the filmed material is being controlled by a director and hence carries some expressive meaning (as, in a dolly-forward shot, we get a "warmer" effect). If we begin to take it for granted that the cameraman must cope as best he can with a reality that is beyond his (or perhaps anybody's) control, then we accept the zoom as a natural weapon in his repertoire. Even the erratic focusing by trial-and-error which is inherent in much direct photography may be left in. . . . Even the cameraman's breathing and pulse can have visible consequences, like the steadiness of his shoulder or the smoothness of his stride.

But we must notice the perhaps dismaying converse aesthetic consequence: the great authority of point-of-view inherent in the tracking, craning studio camera has become largely irrelevant—or at least is on the verge of becoming insufferably pretentious. . . . Thus the remarkable subtleties of the fluid camera, developed over the years by Murnau, Renoir, Welles, and the rest, are going to go down the drain. . . . The wide screen, when it came, seemed the natural technical home for a cinema in which scenes were thus played in long takes, rather than broken up into the closer-up bits and pieces of Griffithian and "montage" cinema. But the wide screen no longer seems wide to us. Neorealism and its offspring are dead. The unity and integrity of the scene is no longer considered to be achievable through ordinary fictional means; and in the zippy works of Godard, Lester, and fashionably chic directors like Lelouche, Varda, and Widerberg, more abstract, ideational ways of putting films together are coming to predominate; their films come to resemble essays or monologues more than realistic stories.

Every element of film style will undergo similar sea changes. The cut from shot to shot, for instance, has always been, as V. I. Pudovkin properly said, the foundation of film art. But the meaning we attribute to it has changed before in film history, and it is changing again now. For in footage shot by direct means, we have a different feel for the film record itself, and particularly for the sound track. Direct material has a natural unity which the cutter messes with at his peril. In studio technique, the image was "built" to be cut. . . . The director, with his rushes watched over by the studio's chief editor, planned the shots so they would cut as called for; and the editor experimentally determined the best actual cuts which could be achieved with the resulting film strips. Hence the cut was a highly contrived artistic technique in which great meaning could be invested; some of the most remarkable moments in cinema have been achieved by cutting. This was true not only in very formal, almost abstract works, like Eisenstein's Odessa Steps massacre in *Potemkin*, where a "musical" visual form is achieved, but also of every film that made astute dramatic use of the suspense inherent in the image frame—for instance, when the sudden apparition of the convict is cut into the famous cemetery scene at the beginning of Lean's *Great Expectations*. . . .

Lighting, another massive and inert aspect of studio technique, has been utterly transformed from what it was before Raoul Coutard shot *Breathless* for Godard, using only light that came from natural sources—or seemed to. Before that, at least ever since the German filmmakers gave rein to their passion for chiaroscuro in the twenties and Cecil B. DeMille went in for "Rembrandt lighting," the art of the Hollywood lighting cameraman was an intricate manipulation of manifold light sources—a shaping, sculpting force that helped to dramatize the studio

image and could decorate it with tracery shadows, bars, and so
on. To handle the enormously heavy lights that provided the key
illumination, and the sometimes hundreds of smaller lights,
screens, reflectors, and shades that provided fill and balance and
special highlights, was the task of an industrial team of dozens
of men, including experienced electricians. The huge power-
requirements practically demanded studio facilities. Indeed, the
predilection of direct cinema for real locations, and its capacity
(because of faster lenses and emulsions) to shoot in existing real
light, have been more revolutionary than the miniaturization of
the camera itself. Today, though someone may have to position
a few small bounce lights that can run on house current, the
direct-filming team spends virtually no time on lighting. Above
all, it preserves the same lighting from shot to shot, so that the
attention of the team can be focused on what is going on.

But the most central artistic assumptions of the traditional
movies had to do with acting. Directors, who have mostly come
from some kind of stage or television background, instinctively
feel that the chief business of film is performance. . . . So vulner-
able is the film image to changes in manners and dress that a
performance which seems powerful and "realistic" today will
seem only delightfully campy ten years hence—while documentary footage, though it may appear quaint, never loses our credence. Still, as a practical matter, most films have had to be made
with actors. Until the sixties no one ventured to boast of using
non-actors. The turning point may have been the tremendously
powerful impression made by the non-actor father and son in
Bicycle Thief (1949) and by other non-actors in Italian neorealist
films. . . .

The biggest part of traditional acting has been the delivery of
lines, for even relatively "visual" films have been stuffed with
dialogue cunningly devised by scriptwriters to establish characters or indicate turns of plot. But under the impact of direct
films, we are now beginning to be much more sensitive to the
artificiality of pre-scripted lines, and directors are experimenting
with various degrees of improvisation. The script was once
treated as holy writ; now it is argued that part of the actor's job
is to prepare his own lines within a situation established by the
director—which gives the actor, in other words, much of the
freedom that a real person has in direct cinema. The obvious
danger in improvisation is that the actors will not in fact prove

very interesting; but there is no reason (except inexperience or laziness) for a director to put the burden of total improvisation upon his actors. What usually happens is that a director who works in the modern, flexible way plans his shots in a close relationship with his locations and cast. There is no prearranged plan into which he must fit his actors.

Such innovations, nervous-making as they may be, are not an indication of directorial laxity or megalomania. On the contrary, they are a painful and intelligent response to the great air-pockets created in film conventions by the direct cinema. For viewers and filmmakers with any considerable experience of direct films, the usual dramatic film, with its creaky machinery for expositions and climaxes, is beginning to seem intolerably false. Even (or perhaps especially) when it is "documentarized," like *The Battle of Algiers*, the fiction film has developed a fatal credibility gap. To the final question, Can you then photograph any kind of dramatic pretense without "exposing" it and making it ridiculous? there are purists who argue a vociferous No. If they had their way, there would be no more fictional cinema at all. Films would be devoted to seeing reality and seeing it unvarnished.

But if we look more carefully at the process of direct filming, we may discover subleties that undercut these apocalyptic conclusions. For in fact the direct-filming situation presupposes its own kind of compact, which is linked to stylistic possibilities rather in the same way as the fictional film's is. The existence of this compact is usually overlooked by the most ardent proponents of *cinéma-vérité*, who tend to talk as if they become invisible the moment they pick up their cameras. They do not, of course, pretend to be filming candid-camera style or like filmmakers operating from such a distance (with telephoto lenses) that people being photographed do not notice the camera. But they feel that by being unobtrusive and trying not to influence the outgoing development of events, they manage to obtain a neutral and unbiased account of what has happened. They forbear to do even the simplest kind of reenactment (which was practiced even by newsreel cameramen from the faked prizefights of the 1890's on), and they absolutely abstain from manipulating scenes.

But in actuality there is no such thing as complete authenticity in film. . . . In the cinema we cannot photograph someone, except from candid-camera ambush, without affecting his behavior. This is true whether we are photographing actors or non-actors. (It is in fact often *more* true with non-actors.) This is not to deny that people do get used to cameras when they have been followed around by a cameraman for a week or so. But we must be careful not to exaggerate this fact into a contention that people cease to be conscious of the camera. What does happen is that they achieve a kind of stable relationship with the camera, in which its presence is accepted rather as we might accept that of a close friend. Even so, there are obvious areas, both physical and psychological, where few people will allow the camera to follow—notably the bedroom and bathroom, and discussions of money, power, and private feelings.

What we are seeing in a direct-cinema film like *Salesman*, then, is the complex and subtle record of a real social process in which the camera figured as an important participant. As filming begins, the crew and "subjects" must quickly come to an understanding about this process or the filming is likely to break down. This understanding is often a quite limited one. In *Salesman* I would guess that none of the salesmen would have allowed the Maysles to photograph them in intimate moments with their wives, though such encounters in the lives of traveling men must be very significant. . . . They would demand the excision of childish outbursts of temper, serious errors of judgment, acts of stupidity or meanness (if they happened to recognize them as such, which often they do not)—in a word, precisely the stuff of which much drama is constructed. . . . In *Titicut Follies*, where many of the subjects were quite mad, the camera seems to have been only one more hallucinatory experience among the many provided for the inmates by institution life. Evidently, then, there are different levels of candor on which such films can operate. In . . . *Titicut Follies* . . . the films brought out a great deal of fascinating personal material. In *Salesman*, where the subjects are guarded, manipulative, uncandid, the film was able only to document a surface, though that surface has a certain gruelling fascination; in *A Married Couple*, despite a certain element of histrionics, we have the most realistic (and also comic) account of a marriage in trouble ever filmed.

Aside from such inherent factors in the filming itself, the filmmaker is also inevitably the architect of the overall filming situation. He must find, choose, negotiate with, and learn to work with his subjects. Except in a rare case like *Football*, where the coaches and players are caught up in an intensely absorbing situation, this involves delicate questions of attitude, objectives, time, and money. Routines must be worked out, explicitly or implicitly, to explain the presence of the filming team. And the relationship between the filmmakers and their subjects must be maintained, sometimes through difficult mixtures of feelings on both sides and sometimes through weeks of taxing real-life conditions.

Given the complexity of such situations, it is perhaps surprising that people are so easily able to fall into the role of acting themselves, even adopting the fiction-film convention of not looking at the camera. In this and other ways, what happens in such direct films as *Salesman* is an inter-penetration of influences from the old and new cinema. The most electrifying moments in direct cinema, like the one at the end of *Salesman* when Paul's comic-Irish imitation dies on his lips, have a way of seeming consummately fictional. . . . We may hazard that in *Salesman* the filming team soon discovered that Paul, perhaps the most sensitive and complex of the group, was also the most responsive and interesting in front of the camera; their interest in his discouragement doubtless led him, subtly, to emphasize and develop it; and when it came to the editing, his progressive disenchantment with the Bible racket seemed to provide a structure for a film which had no other organizing principle. Yet the film cannot really give us enough of Paul to make this development very convincing. (We are not surprised to learn that he later went into roofing-and-siding—an even worse racket.)

It must be kept in mind, in this connection, that every film, fictional or nonfictional, has some kind of dialectic which governs why things happen or are shown in the manner and order we see them. In the traditional movie this structure was provided by the plot—which, even if preposterous, could give the movie an ironclad logic. But mundane documentaries also, if they are any good, prove to have some subterranean conflict structure; and so do poetic nonnarrative films like those of Bruce Baillie or Stan Brakhage, for that matter. But direct cinema, with its reluctance to meddle with its subjects any more than absolutely necessary, is at the mercy of the subjects to provide a logic for the picture. The direct-film maker cannot invent lines or episodes which will help explain his characters' actions, as the fiction director can so easily do. . . . Thus, . . . a direct film about a draft-eligible youth would have an inherent logic. Either he will escape to Canada, or go to jail, or go into the army, or perhaps get

deferred. No matter what happened, a film following his activities, even apparently trivial ones, would have a distinct shape and
tension. Above all, it would have an ending. Everything the boy
did (or did not do) would relate in one way or another to the
main thematic line of the film. . . . But the Bible salesmen in *Salesman* are simply going on from day to day, as they have done for
years and will go on doing. The basic lines of force in their lives
are balanced, and after only a few minutes we settle down to
watch the film as information rather than drama. But curiosity is
not a strong enough motive to make very many people care about
a ninety-minute film. . . .

Even sexual curiosity has its limitations, as we can see by such
Andy Warhol films as *Blue Movie*, unless it can be given some
ongoing structural life. However tedious they may seem, Warhol's films are important experiments bearing on the problem of
acting versus being. Warhol takes nonperformers (calling them,
rather cruelly, "superstars") and asks them to perform; but by
giving them no instructions and by not framing them in specially
contrived "significant" settings, he reduces the filmmaker's part
virtually to turning the camera switch on and off. This is probably about as near as you can come to exerting no influence on
your subjects—especially since many of the subjects appear to be
stoned out of their minds while on camera. . . . The result is film
in which personal pretense of the everyday variety plays a substantial part, but in which the pretenses of acting have been eliminated. As in home movies, people play themselves, with faint
twinges of duress or indulgence in the air. The films are therefore in their primitive way films of performances as human
actions. . . .

What we are likely to see next are more films which, in one
way or another, chiefly rely on the new conventions but do not
entirely abandon the old—usually in the form of fictional films
using direct techniques and partaking of the direct tone and atmosphere. Thus John Cassavetes, whose *Shadows* (1960) was
important for breaking with studio story-structure and using the
portable 16-mm camera on a feature-length work, has pushed his
direct approach further with *Faces*. By using some actors and
some nonactors, but above all by using an improvisational, almost
psychodrama technique in shooting, Cassavetes has tried to eliminate the greatest drawback of acting; the tendency of behavior to
fall into familiar forms with no natural play of emotion. I, myself,
don't find the film as a whole terribly convincing: the business-

man husband seems to me altogether unbusinesslike, the whore rather too emptily spiritual, and the childlessness of the people allows them an unreal isolation from society. Yet many scenes in the movie work in a way no purely fictional director could have contrived (like the women's uneasy visit to the discothèque); and the portrayal of the up-tight wife has a painful veracity that could not have been achieved by any actress. The plot has been criticized as melodramatic, but I would criticize it rather for undue symmetry (husband goes to whore, wife sleeps with hustler); its sense of incident, the relative weights it gives to emotion and action, its problematic and anguishing ending, are like those of the direct cinema—too raggedy and ambiguous and weary for any neat fictional packaging.

Through such films, directors may reach some relatively stable mixed style—a synthesis arising out of the confrontation between the traditional aesthetic and the direct styles. . . . No artist can escape artfulness entirely. Sometimes, even in fictional films of a highly contrived kind, we have seen directors (Jean Renoir, for instance) marvelously effacing themselves and capturing the performers as people, whether in a trio like *Boudu* or a concerto like *Rules of the Game*. And sometimes, in an apparently neutral direct-cinema film, we will encounter performances so contrived that we would be appalled if we found them in an avowedly fictional film: can the Hugh Hefner we see in *The Most* be real? . . . The Hollywood industry is manned by people who can think only in the old dramatic-prefabrication terms. Though they cope well enough with the demands of the television serial, they are at a loss when confronted with films made through interaction with the real world and do not seem to be able to deal with filmmakers who operate that way. But fewer and fewer members of the movie audience share the old assumptions and predilections. Young people still tolerate films based on them, just as they will still ride in Detroit cars; but what they love are Porsches or old converted bread trucks—clean and cool or dirty and funky, they are what they are.

And thus it is that the movie industry, now a shrinking handmaiden to television and oil corporations, flutters along from quick bursts of optimism to fits of suicidal despair, depending on the ever more unpredictable reports from the box office. The closing of a great studio, however, is the kind of event at which a direct-cinema team would feel perfectly at home: it would make a nice film.

We are all aware of the dominant role played by inventions in modern history, but not at all clear as yet about the particular place of television, which may be the most important of all in its power to shape and direct human communication. A thoughtful attempt is made here to evaluate the resources of television and its failure to use them; at the same time, some cures are prescribed for the

TELEVISION:

peculiar rootlessness of the medium, which has resulted in its almost total inability to

THE

establish its identity or to evaluate itself. Henry Steele Commager (1902–   ) is an historian by

MEDIUM

profession, a notably learned and lucid commentator on American life, and obviously one who has spent many hours

IN

watching the great American public eye.

SEARCH
OF ITS
CHARACTER

Henry Steele Commager

Television has some claim to be considered the most important invention in the history of communication of knowledge since the two great inventions of the Middle Ages: the university in the 12th Century and printing in the 15th Century. The beneficent consequences of these earlier inventions made themselves felt almost at once and have made themselves felt, cumulatively, over the centuries. We have now had television for only a quarter of a century, a very short time as these things go. It is not yet clear whether television has added anything to the dimensions of knowledge; it is not even clear whether its quantitative contributions to information and to entertainment can be counted as qualitative contributions to understanding or to happiness.

We are speaking, of course, of television as we know it in America; we must ever be on guard against two pervasive but fallacious assumptions: first that the United States' pattern of private ownership and control is the normal one; and second, that television has already reached its final form, and that changes will be largely in the technical realm, e.g., color instead of black and white, or Telstar. And as we have not yet exhausted the potentialities of television, we should not try to render final judgment on it. This is an interim judgment, or perhaps merely an interim report.

Television is, after all, a new medium and it is not surprising that we have not yet come to terms with it or that we do not yet understand its character. We do not really know what role it should play, or how it should play whatever role is assigned to it. Those who sit in the seats of power—the members of the Federal Communications Commission and, more important, the overlords of the industry—are, almost all of them, suffering from an acute case of schizophrenia: They have not yet decided whether television is a public or a private enterprise. One might suppose that the answer was clear enough. The airways, after all, belong to the public; the original FCC Act of 1934 specifically required television to serve the public interest; everywhere else in the world, television is regarded as a public-service institution.

One might suppose, too, that the choice, if open, would be clear. There are, after all, enough private enterprises, enough ways to make money. All the opportunities, all the challenges, are in the arena of public enterprise; all the important contributions are to be made to the commonwealth, not the private wealth.

But television is controlled by men trained in the most competitive of private industries, and by great corporations with the most miscellaneous activities, controlled, for the most part, by men without vision or imagination in anything other than their major interests—manufacturing, marketing and finance. The humorist Finley Peter Dunne once observed that what looked like a stone wall to a layman was a triumphal arch to a corporation lawyer; we might reverse that and say that what looks like a royal road to public service to the layman looks like a stone wall to TV's overlords.

There are, to be sure, frequent gestures toward the public interest, and sometimes more than gestures. Every so often television shows what it can do when it really tries—when it devotes the talents and resources which it commands to the task. Thus television's presentation of the Kennedy assassination and funeral, of the Churchill funeral; thus documentaries like *The Valiant*

Years, or like those studies of civil-rights demonstrations in the South, or the effect of cigaret smoking; thus reports on Presidential campaigns and elections; thus presentations of symphonic music, or of conducting by a Pablo Casals or a Leonard Bernstein; thus, from time to time, a few entertainments like the lamented *That Was the Week That Was* and the equally lamented *Slattery's People;* thus news commentators like Eric Sevareid.

The inevitable observation here is, if television can do this well, why does it not habitually do this well? We do not, after all, single out a few issues of the *New York Times* or the *Manchester Guardian*, a few great performances by the Boston Symphony or Vienna Philharmonic, a few courses or research findings at Harvard or Columbia Universities, a few decisions of the Supreme Court, and use these to justify such institutions. Why should not television have the same standards of excellence that we take for granted in other institutions devoted to the public interests?

The trouble is that, after 25 years, television does not know where it belongs, or what is its character. Does it belong with the newspaper and magazine as a form of entertainment and of information? Or does it belong with the University and the Foundation as a form of education?

It is, of course, something of both, but who can doubt that the proportions are badly mixed? Who can doubt that in both areas a kind of Gresham's law operates, the bad features driving out the good? And, more important still, who can doubt that the principle of control which dictates the nature of the operation itself differs fundamentally and perniciously from that which obtains in the realms of journalism and of education alike?

The analogy to journalism is the closest and the most revealing. Newspapers and magazines are, for the most part, business enterprises devoted to making money, though even here distinguished newspapers like the *New York Times* and distinguished journals like *Foreign Affairs* consider themselves public enterprises. But newspapers and magazines, for all their dependence on advertisers, control everything connected with their content, editorial and otherwise. Advertisers buy space in newspapers, and that is all they buy; they do not buy editorial content or editorial policy nor—in proper papers—influence over these. But with television —and alone with television—it is not the owners but the advertisers (euphemistically called "sponsors") who determine policy and content. Thus, alone of major media of communication, television lacks independence. Spokesmen for television, to be sure, prate ceaselessly about independence, chiefly from Governmental regulation, but they have nothing to say about independence where it really counts.

TV's MOST PROMINENT FUNCTION

The most prominent, though not the most important, function of television is to entertain. That the networks perform this role in a manner acceptable to the great majority of viewers is clear enough. But relevant here is the observation of Lord Reith of the British Broadcasting Corporation:

"It will be admitted by all that to have exploited so great a scientific invention for the purpose and pursuit of entertainment alone, would have been a prostitution of its powers and an insult to the character and intelligence of the people."

Nor can the masters of television escape responsibility for the low level of much that passes for entertainment by insisting, as they invariably do, that they are merely giving the public what it wants. It is not clear whether it is the audience which has imposed its standards on television, or television which has imposed its standards—and its notions about how to make money —on the audience.

Nor is it clear that the good done by bringing some pleasure to the old, the infirm, the housebound, or the simple-minded, outweighs the harm done to a whole society by debasing the public taste or pandering to a taste already debased, and by discrediting or making obsolete the habits of self-entertainment which, after all, kept most people happy for a good many centuries.

The second major function of television is to inform and educate. Here the analogy is not to the newspaper, but to the University and the Foundation, or perhaps to schools generally. Television does the informing part of this task very well indeed —at least the major networks do. They seek out what appears to be newsworthy and report it with imagination and skill.

Never before in history have men generally been able to know so much about what happens everywhere, as now. They can sit in on deliberations of the United Nations, follow election campaigns at home and abroad, get the feel of life in Russia, in Mexico, in an English industrial town, participate in the drama of a civil-rights demonstration in Mississippi, share with a small audience the performances of a Bernstein, see the White House through the eyes of Mrs. Kennedy and Washington through the eyes of Mrs. Johnson.

It is in the realm of education that the failure of television is most conspicuous. If we compare television with the University, or with an institution almost as new as television itself, the Foundation, we see at once the nature of the failure. Even those departments of television devoted to information have greater resources than most universities or foundations, but what have they to show for these resources? There is "educational television," to be sure, but it is weak and miscellaneous, largely because it lacks the funds and the personnel to make educational television as palatable to the public as commercial television. Now and then television gives us a brief interlude of "culture"—the glory that was Greece, perhaps, or the saga of Columbus, but these are exceptions.

On the whole the contribution of this new and potentially great medium of television to education, or to the enlargement of intellectual horizons, is meager, and is more than counterbalanced by its contributions to noneducation and to the narrowing of intellectual horizons. Television performs none of the traditional services of the Academy except fortuitously—it neither transmits the knowledge of the past to the next generation, nor contributes to professional training, nor does it expand the boundaries of knowledge.

Perhaps nowhere is the contrast between television and the Academy more revealing than in the realm of professional practices and institutional character. Over the years the Academy has developed a body of institutions and practices designed to promote its purposes and safeguard its integrity: thus academic standards for both students and scholars, academic tenure, academic freedom, academic self-government; concentration on libraries and laboratories; rewards not to popularity but to contributions.

Television has developed nothing whatsoever of this. If it be asserted that the analogy is unsound because the Academy is wholly noncommercial and television is a business enterprise, the answer is that other institutions both business and professional, such as medicine, the Bench and the Bar, the Church, architecture, even journalism, have developed comparable practices and safeguards.

Indeed, of all major institutions devoted to communication or to knowledge, television is the most conventional and the most pusillanimous. And the reason for this is even more sobering than the consideration itself: Television lacks enterprise and courage chiefly because it has nothing to be enterprising or courageous about. It has not developed anything like academic freedom because it is not interested in freedom, except from Governmental restrictions.

There are, of course, in all the networks, men of enterprise, men of ideas, men of courage and of honor, but they operate largely in a vacuum, and these qualities, though they are not deprecated, are not prized. The University, the Foundations, the professions of medicine and law and religion and journalism, are engaged in something more than competition for sponsors: they are engaged in an honorable competition to advance knowledge, or justice, or truth.

OTHER GOALS NEEDED

That is something worth competing for. But we cannot expect television to develop professional standards, principles, loyalties or ideas until it dedicates itself to something more important than success in the Nielsens or increased earnings to shareholders.

How sobering it is that though TV has flourished, now, for a quarter-century, it has not yet developed its statesmen, as do such institutions as the University, Journalism, the Church, the Military, Labor Unions, and Philanthropy.

Most Americans regard criticism of television like criticism of the weather: It cannot be other than it is! But American television is not the norm of television; it is abnormal. We take private ownership for granted, but it is public ownership which is taken for granted elsewhere. We take for granted control of programs by "sponsors" but even in Canada and Britain, which permit private television, sponsors have no influence on the programs themselves: They buy time, and that is the end of the matter.

No less startling, the development of television in the United States appears to be contrary to the intentions of our own law, as it is to most of our legal and constitutional principles. Is it necessary to repeat anything so elementary as this? Television is not a private but a public enterprise. It is so recognized in the basic Communications Act of 1934 which required the FCC to "grant licenses to serve the public convenience, interest or necessity."

Such a broad mandate must be interpreted in the light of a century of public-utility regulation, and of a long line of Supreme Court decisions from Munn v. Illinois of 1877: "When one devotes his property to a use in which the public has an interest, he grants to the public an interest in that use and must submit to be controlled by the public for the common good. . . ."

Every other major utility has submitted to this control; television alone of public utilities still thinks itself exempt from public control, defies it or circumvents it. But those who sit in the seats of power should remember that the alternative to private ownership is public ownership; it is not an extreme alternative but one which almost every civilized country on the globe accepts as a matter of course.

If television continues to reveal to us how good a job it *can* do, and how bad a job it commonly does; if it continues to exploit the public air waves for purely private gain, to debase the public taste, it may yet force the people into the alternative of public ownership. What is called for is not so much revolution as reform.

Here are some of the reforms which might restore television to the public domain and insure its service to the commonwealth:

First, the television networks must resume control of the whole content of their programs, just as newspapers control their content. The most pernicious ingredient in the whole of television is advertiser control of the content of television programs.

Second, we should create within the Federal Communications Commission, or elsewhere, boards of regents comparable to the Board of Governors of the BBC or to the regents and trustees of universities and foundations, whose responsibility it would be to safeguard the public interest in television.

POWERS FCC ISN'T USING

Such boards should have authority to make findings and impose decisions with respect to such matters as content and advertising, and to refuse to license stations which fail to devote themselves to the public interest. The FCC, to be sure, has this authority even now, but has not exercised it since its establishment.

Third, the networks themselves should develop institutions which will safeguard their independence and integrity and provide them with the kind of leadership and loyal, disinterested service taken for granted in universities or in governments.

It might be desirable to add a fourth safeguard: The creation of a well-supported publicly owned and controlled television network which would function nationally as WNYC functions in New York, or perhaps as the Third Programme of the BBC functions, to provide standards of comparison for the existing networks and to carry on experiments which are now so rarely attempted.

THE
FILM
ARTS:
PHOTOGRAPHY

Spawned in the nineteenth century and, in turn, spawning hordes of enthusiasts who went, and still go about snapping everything in sight, photography as it is practiced by the masters undeniably ranks among the arts. Photography as an art can obviously be compared with painting in a number of ways. Picasso, for example, once explained the difference by comparing the painter to the magician or faith-healer who keeps a normal distance between himself and his subject's reality and the photographer to a surgeon who " 'operates' directly on the tissues of reality." Thus, the painter's image is total; the photographer's shows "a multiplicity of details coordinated according to a new law and resulting from an intensive penetration of reality." Some of the means by which that penetration is achieved are analyzed in the following article by a well-known photographer and critic. John Szarkowski (1925–) is Director of Photography at The Museum of Modern Art and head of the Edward Steichen Photography Center there.

THE PHOTOGRAPHER'S EYE

John Szarkowski

The invention of photography provided a radically new picture-making process—a process based not on synthesis but on selection. The difference was a basic one. Paintings were *made* —constructed from a storehouse of traditional schemes and skills and attitudes—but photographs, as the man on the street put it, were *taken*.

The difference raised a creative issue of a new order: how could this mechanical and mindless process be made to produce pictures meaningful in human terms—pictures with clarity and coherence and a point of view? It was soon demonstrated that an answer would not be found by those who loved too much the old forms, for in large part the photographer was bereft of the old artistic traditions. Speaking of photography Baudelaire said: "This industry, by invading the territories of art, has become art's most mortal enemy."[1] And in his own terms of reference Baudelaire was half right; certainly the new medium could not satisfy old standards. The photographer must find new ways to make his meaning clear.

These new ways might be found by men who could abandon their allegiance to traditional pictorial standards—or by the artistically ignorant who had no old allegiances to break. There have been many of the latter sort. Since its earliest days, photography has been practiced by thousands who shared no common tradition or training, who were disciplined and united by no academy or guild, who considered their medium variously as a science, an art, a trade, or an entertainment, and who were often unaware of each other's work. Those who invented photography were scientists and painters, but its professional practitioners were a very different lot. Hawthorne's daguerreotypist hero Holgrave in *The House of the Seven Gables* was perhaps not far from typical:

> Though now but twenty-two years old, he had already been a country schoolmaster; salesman in a country store; and the political editor of a country newspaper. He had subsequently travelled as a peddler of cologne water and other essences. He had studied and practiced dentistry. Still more recently he had been a public lecturer on mesmerism, for which science he had very remarkable endowments. His present phase as a daguerreotypist was of no more importance in his own view, nor likely to be more permanent, than any of the preceding ones.[2]

The enormous popularity of the new medium produced professionals by the thousands—converted silversmiths, tinkers, druggists, blacksmiths and printers. If photography was a new artistic problem, such men had the advantage of having nothing to unlearn. Among them they produced a flood of images. In 1853 the *New York Daily Tribune* estimated that three million daguerreotypes were being produced that year.[3] Some of these pictures were the product of knowledge and skill and sensibility

---

[1] Charles Baudelaire, "Salon de 1859," translated by Jonathan Mayne for *The Mirror of Art, Critical Studies by Charles Baudelaire*. London: Phaidon Press, 1955. (Quoted from *On Photography, A Source Book of Photo History in Facsimile*, edited by Beaumont Newhall. Watkins Glen, N.Y.: Century House, 1956, p. 106.)

[2] Nathaniel Hawthorne, *The House of the Seven Gables*. New York: Signet Classics edition, 1961, pp. 156–7.

[3] A. C. Willers, "Poet and Photography," in *Picturescope*, Vol. XI, No. 4. New York: Picture Division, Special Libraries Association, 1963, p. 46.

and invention; many were the product of accident, improvisation, misunderstanding, and empirical experiment. But whether produced by art or by luck, each picture was part of a massive assault on our traditional habits of seeing.

By the latter decades of the nineteenth century the professionals and the serious amateurs were joined by an even larger host of casual snapshooters. By the early eighties the dry plate, which could be purchased ready-to-use, had replaced the refractory and messy wet plate process, which demanded that the plate be prepared just before exposure and processed before its emulsion had dried. The dry plate spawned the hand camera and the snapshot. Photography had become easy. In 1893 an English writer complained that the new situation had "created an army of photographers who run rampant over the globe, photographing objects of all sorts, sizes and shapes, under almost every condition, without ever pausing to ask themselves, is this or that artistic? . . . They spy a view, it seems to please, the camera is focused, the shot taken! There is no pause, why should there be? For art may err but nature cannot miss, says the poet, and they listen to the dictum. To them, composition, light, shade, form and texture are so many catch phrases. . . ."[4]

These pictures, taken by the thousands by journeyman worker and Sunday hobbyist, were unlike any pictures before them. The variety of their imagery was prodigious. Each subtle variation in viewpoint or light, each passing moment, each change in the tonality of the print, created a new picture. The trained artist could draw a head or a hand from a dozen perspectives. The photographer discovered that the gestures of a hand were infinitely various, and that the wall of a building in the sun was never twice the same.

Most of this deluge of pictures seemed formless and accidental, but some achieved coherence, even in their strangeness. Some of the new images were memorable, and seemed significant beyond their limited intention. These remembered pictures enlarged one's sense of possibilities as he looked again at the real world. While they were remembered they survived, like organisms, to reproduce and evolve.

But it was not only the way that photography described things

---

[4] E. E. Cohen, "Bad Form in Photography," in *The International Annual of Anthony's Photographic Bulletin.* New York and London: E. and H. T. Anthony, 1893, p. 18.

that was new; it was also the things it chose to describe. Photographers shot ". . . objects of all sorts, sizes and shapes . . . without ever pausing to ask themselves, is that or that artistic?" Painting was difficult, expensive, and precious, and it recorded what was known to be important. Photography was easy, cheap and ubiquitous, and it recorded anything: shop windows and sod houses and family pets and steam engines and unimportant people. And once made objective and permanent, immortalized in a picture, these trivial things took on importance. By the end of the century, for the first time in history, even the poor man knew what his ancestors had looked like.

The photographer learned in two ways: first, from a worker's intimate understanding of his tools and materials (if his plate would not record the clouds, he could point his camera down and eliminate the sky); and second he learned from other photographs, which presented themselves in an unending stream. Whether his concern was commercial or artistic, his tradition was formed by all the photographs that had impressed themselves upon his consciousness. . . .

It should be possible to consider the history of the medium in terms of photographers' progressive awareness of characteristics and problems that have seemed inherent in the medium. Five such issues are considered below. These issues *do not* define discrete categories of work; on the contrary they should be regarded as interdependent aspects of a single problem— as section views through the body of photographic tradition. As such, it is hoped that they may contribute to the formulation of a vocabulary and a critical perspective more fully responsive to the unique phenomena of photography.

THE THING ITSELF

The first thing that the photographer learned was that photography dealt with the actual; he had not only to accept this fact, but to treasure it; unless he did, photography would defeat him. He learned that the world itself is an artist of incomparable inventiveness, and that to recognize its best works and moments, to anticipate them, to clarify them and make them permanent, requires intelligence both acute and supple.

But he learned also that the factuality of his pictures, no matter how convincing and unarguable, was a different thing than the reality itself. Much of the reality was filtered out in the static little black and white image, and some of it was exhibited with an unnatural clarity, an exaggerated importance. The subject and the picture were not the same thing, although they would afterwards seem so. It was the photographer's problem to see not simply the reality before him but the still invisible picture, and to make his choices in terms of the latter.

This was an artistic problem, not a scientific one, but the public believed that the photograph could not lie, and it was easier for the photographer if he believed it too, or pretended to. Thus he was likely to claim that what our eyes saw was an illusion, and what the camera saw was the truth. Hawthorne's Holgrave, speaking of a difficult portrait subject said:

"We give [heaven's broad and simple sunshine] credit only for depicting the merest surface, but it actually brings out the secret character with a truth that no painter would ever venture upon, even could he detect it. . . . The remarkable point is that the original wears, to the world's eye . . . an exceedingly pleasant countenance, indicative of benevolence, openness of heart, sunny good humor, and other praiseworthy qualities of that cast. The sun, as you see, tells quite another story, and will not be coaxed out of it, after half a 'dozen patient attempts on my part. Here we have a man, sly, subtle, hard, imperious, and withal, cold as ice."[5]

In a sense Holgrave was right in giving more credence to the camera image than to his own eyes, for the image would survive the subject, and become the remembered reality. William M. Ivins, Jr. said, "at any given moment the accepted report of an event is of greater importance than the event, for what we think about and act upon is the symbolic report and not the concrete event itself."[6] He also said: "The nineteenth century began by believing that what was reasonable was true and it would end up by believing that what it saw a photograph of was true."[7]

THE DETAIL

The photographer was tied to the facts of things, and it was his problem to force the facts to tell the truth. He could not, out-

5 Hawthorne, op. cit., p. 85.
6 William M. Ivins, Jr., *Prints and Visual Communication*. Cambridge, Mass.: Harvard University Press, 1953, p. 180.
7 Ibid., p. 94.

side the studio, pose the truth; he could only record it as he found it, and it was found in nature in a fragmented and unexplained form—not as a story, but as scattered and suggestive clues. The photographer could not assemble these clues into a coherent narrative, he could only isolate the fragment, document it, and by so doing claim for it some special significance, a meaning which went beyond simple description. The compelling clarity with which a photograph recorded the trivial suggested that the subject had never before been properly seen, that it was in fact perhaps *not* trivial, but filled with undiscovered meaning. If photographs could not be read as stories, they could be read as symbols.

The decline of narrative painting in the past century has been ascribed in large part to the rise of photography, which "relieved" the painter of the necessity of story telling. This is curious, since photography has never been successful at narrative. It has in fact seldom attempted it. The elaborate nineteenth century montages of Robinson and Rejlander, laboriously pieced together from several posed negatives, attempted to tell stories, but these works were recognized in their own time as pretentious failures. In the early days of the picture magazines the attempt was made to achieve narrative through photographic sequences, but the superficial coherence of these stories was generally achieved at the expense of photographic discovery. The heroic documentation of the American Civil War by the Brady group, and the incomparably larger photographic record of the Second World War, have this in common: neither explained, without extensive captioning, what was happening. The function of these pictures was not to make the story clear, it was to make it *real*. The great war photographer Robert Capa expressed both the narrative poverty and the symbolic power of photography when he said, "If your pictures aren't good, you're not close enough."

THE FRAME

Since the photographer's picture was not conceived but selected, his subject was never truly discrete, never wholly self-contained. The edges of his film demarcated what he thought most important, but the subject he had shot was something else; it had extended in four directions. If the photographer's frame surrounded two figures, isolating them from the crowd in which they stood, it created a relationship between those two figures that had not existed before.

The central act of photography, the act of choosing and eliminating, forces a concentration on the picture edge—the line that separates in from out—and on the shapes that are created by it.

During the first half-century of photography's lifetime, photographs were printed the same size as the exposed plate. Since enlarging was generally impractical, the photographer could not change his mind in the darkroom, and decide to use only a fragment of his picture, without reducing its size accordingly. If he had purchased an eight by ten inch plate (or worse, prepared it), had carried it as part of his back-bending load, and had processed it, he was not likely to settle for a picture half that size. A sense of simple economy was enough to make the photographer try to fill the picture to its edges.

The edges of the picture were seldom neat. Parts of figures or buildings or features of landscape were truncated, leaving a shape belonging not to the subject, but (if the picture was a good one) to the balance, the propriety, of the image. The photographer looked at the world as though it was a scroll painting, unrolled from hand to hand, exhibiting an infinite number of croppings— of compositions—as the frame moved onwards.

The sense of the picture's edge as a cropping device is one of the qualities of form that most interested the inventive painters of the latter nineteenth century. To what degree this awareness came from photography, and to what degree from oriental art, is still open to study. However, it is possible that the prevalence of the photographic image helped prepare the ground for an appreciation of the Japanese print, and also that the compositional attitudes of these prints owed much to habits of seeing which stemmed from the scroll tradition.

TIME

There is in fact no such thing as an instantaneous photograph. All photographs are time exposures, of shorter or longer duration, and each describes a discrete parcel of time. This time is always the present. Uniquely in the history of pictures, a photograph describes only that period of time in which it was made. Photography alludes to the past and the future only in so far as they exist in the present, the past through its surviving relics, the future through prophecy visible in the present.

In the days of slow films and slow lenses, photographs described a time segment of several seconds or more. If the subject moved, images resulted that had never been seen before: dogs with two heads and a sheaf of tails, faces without features, transparent men, spreading their diluted substance half across the plate. The fact that these pictures were considered (at best) as partial failures is less interesting than the fact that they were produced in quantity; they were familiar to all photographers, and to all customers who had posed with squirming babies for family portraits.

It is surprising that the prevalence of these radical images has not been of interest to art historians. The time-lapse painting of Duchamp and Balla, done before the First World War, has been compared to work done by photographers such as Edgerton and Mili, who worked consciously with similar ideas a quarter-century later, but the accidental time-lapse photographs of the nineteenth century have been ignored—presumably *because* they were accidental.

As photographic materials were made more sensitive, and lenses and shutters faster, photography turned to the exploration of rapidly moving subjects. Just as the eye is incapable of registering the single frames of a motion picture projected on the screen at the rate of twenty-four per second, so is it incapable of following the positions of a rapidly moving subject in life. The galloping horse is the classic example. As lovingly drawn countless thousands of times by Greeks and Egyptians and Persians and Chinese, and down through all the battle scenes and sporting prints of Christendom, the horse ran with four feet extended, like a fugitive from a carousel. Not till Muybridge successfully photographed a galloping horse in 1878 was the convention broken. It was this way also with the flight of birds, the play of muscles on an athlete's back, the drape of a pedestrian's clothing, and the fugitive expressions of a human face.

Immobilizing these thin slices of time has been a source of continuing fascination for the photographer. And while pursuing this experiment he discovered something else: he discovered that there was a pleasure and a beauty in this fragmenting of time that had little to do with what was happening. It had to do rather with seeing the momentary patterning of lines and shapes that had been previously concealed within the flux of movement. The famous French photographer Henri Cartier-Bresson defined his commitment to this new beauty with the phrase *"the decisive moment,"* but the phrase has been misunderstood; the thing that happens at the decisive moment is not a dramatic climax but a visual one. The result is not a story but a picture.

VANTAGE POINT

Much has been said about the clarity of photography, but little has been said about its obscurity. And yet it is photography that has taught us to see from the unexpected vantage point, and has shown us pictures that give the sense of the scene, while withholding its narrative meaning. Photographers from necessity choose from the options available to them, and often this means pictures from the other side of the proscenium, showing the actors' backs, pictures from the bird's view, or the worm's, or pictures in which the subject is distorted by extreme foreshortening, or by none, or by an unfamiliar pattern of light, or by a seeming ambiguity of action or gesture.

Ivins wrote with rare perception of the effect that such pictures had on nineteenth-century eyes:

At first the public had talked a great deal about what it called photographic distortion. . . . [But] it was not long before men began to think photographically, and thus to see for themselves things that it had previously taken the photograph to reveal to their astonished and protesting eyes. Just as nature had once imitated art, so now it began to imitate the picture made by the camera.[8]

After a century and a quarter, photography's ability to challenge and reject our schematized notions of reality is still fresh. In his monograph on Francis Bacon, Lawrence Alloway speaks of the effect of photography on that painter: "The evasive nature of his imagery, which is shocking but obscure, like accident or atrocity photographs, is arrived at by using photography's huge

[8] Ibid., p. 138.

repertory of visual images. . . . Uncaptioned news photographs, for instance, often appear as momentous and extraordinary. . . . Bacon used this property of photography to subvert the clarity of pose of figures in traditional painting."[9]

The influence of photography on modern painters (and on modern writers) has been great and inestimable. It is, strangely, easier to forget that photography has also influenced photographers. Not only great pictures by great photographers, but *photography*—the great undifferentiated, homogeneous whole of it—has been teacher, library, and laboratory for those who have consciously used the camera as artists. An artist is a man who seeks new structures in which to order and simplify his sense of the reality of life. For the artist photographer, much of his sense of reality (where his picture starts) and much of his sense of craft or structure (where his picture is completed) are anonymous and untraceable gifts from photography itself.

The history of photography has been less a journey than a growth. Its movement has not been linear and consecutive, but centrifugal. Photography, and our understanding of it, has spread from a center; it has, by infusion, penetrated our consciousness. Like an organism, photography was born whole. It is in our progressive discovery of it that its history lies.

[9] Lawrence Alloway, *Francis Bacon*. New York: Solomon R. Guggenheim Foundation, 1963, p. 22.

THE ONTOLOGY OF THE PHOTOGRAPHIC IMAGE

André Bazin

André Bazin (1918–1958) was an extraordinarily imaginative critic in both senses of the word "imaginative": he was inventive and he was fixated on the image. His writings about the motion-picture film and his work as a critic for Le Parisien Liberé *and as coeditor of* Les Cahiers du Cinéma *reveal everywhere an understanding of the photographic image that goes far beneath its surfaces and yet never fails to respect what is presented to the viewer's first glance. For film maker Jean Renoir, Bazin was the poet for "that king of our time, the cinema." He was also, as this essay demonstrates, the logician of the photographic image. He shows us its special place in our lives, its "objective character," the advantage it derives from the absence of man, its superiority—in certain areas, at least—to painting. Bazin takes his title seriously: being, he says, is enlarged by photography; photography "actually contributes something to the order of natural creation instead of providing a substitute for it." If we take him seriously, we are bound, literally, to see a new world.*

If the plastic arts were put under psychoanalysis, the practice of embalming the dead might turn out to be a fundamental factor in their creation. The process might reveal that at the origin of painting and sculpture there lies a mummy complex. The religion of ancient Egypt, aimed against death, saw survival as depending on the continued existence of the corporeal body. Thus, by providing a defense against the passage of time it satisfied a basic psychological need in man, for death is but the victory of time. To preserve, artificially, his bodily appearance is to snatch it from the flow of time, to stow it away neatly, so to speak, in the hold of life. It was natural, therefore, to keep up appearances in the face of the reality of death by preserving flesh and bone. The first Egyptian statue, then, was a mummy, tanned and petrified in sodium. But pyramids and labyrinthine corridors offered no certain guarantee against ultimate pillage.

Other forms of insurance were therefore sought. So, near the sarcophagus, alongside the corn that was to feed the dead, the Egyptians placed terra cotta statuettes, as substitute mummies which might replace the bodies if these were destroyed. It is this religious use, then, that lays bare the primordial function of statuary, namely, the preservation of life by a representation of life. Another manifestation of the same kind of thing is the arrow-pierced clay bear to be found in prehistoric caves, a magic identity-substitute for the living animal, that will ensure a successful hunt. The evolution, side by side, of art and civilization has relieved the plastic arts of their magic role. Louis XIV did not have himself embalmed. He was content to survive in his portrait by Le Brun. Civilization cannot, however, entirely cast out the bogy of time. It can only sublimate our concern with it to the level of rational thinking. No one believes any longer in the ontological identity of model and image, but all are agreed that the image helps us to remember the subject and to preserve him from a second spiritual death. Today the making of images no longer shares an anthropocentric, utilitarian purpose. It is no longer a question of survival after death, but of a larger concept, the creation of an ideal world in the likeness of the real, with its own temporal destiny. "How vain a thing is painting" if underneath our fond admiration for its works we do not discern man's primitive need to have the last word in the argument with death by means of the form that endures. If the history of the plastic arts is less a matter of their aesthetic than of their psychology then it will be seen to be essentially the story of resemblance, or, if you will, of realism.

Seen in this sociological perspective photography and cinema would provide a natural explanation for the great spiritual and technical crisis that overtook modern painting around the middle of the last century. André Malraux has described the cinema as the furthermost evolution to date of plastic realism, the beginnings of which were first manifest at the Renaissance and which found a limited expression in baroque painting.

It is true that painting, the world over, has struck a varied balance between the symbolic and realism. However, in the fifteenth century Western painting began to turn from its age-old concern with spiritual realities expressed in the form proper to it, towards an effort to combine this spiritual expression with as complete an imitation as possible of the outside world.

The decisive moment undoubtedly came with the discovery of the first scientific and already, in a sense, mechanical system of reproduction, namely, perspective: the camera obscura of Da Vinci foreshadowed the camera of Niepce. The artist was now in a position to create the illusion of three-dimensional space within which things appeared to exist as our eyes in reality see them.

Thenceforth painting was torn between two ambitions: one, primarily aesthetic, namely the expression of spiritual reality wherein the symbol transcended its model; the other, purely psychological, namely the duplication of the world outside. The satisfaction of this appetite for illusion merely served to increase it till, bit by bit, it consumed the plastic arts. However, since perspective had only solved the problem of form and not of movement, realism was forced to continue the search for some way of giving dramatic expression to the moment, a kind of psychic fourth dimension that could suggest life in the tortured immobility of baroque art. [1]

The great artists, of course, have always been able to combine the two tendencies. They have alloted to each its proper place in the hierarchy of things, holding reality at their command and molding it at will into the fabric of their art. Nevertheless, the fact remains that we are faced with two essentially different phenomena and these any objective critic must view separately if he is to understand the evolution of the pictorial. The need for illusion has not ceased to trouble the heart of painting since the sixteenth century. It is a purely mental need, of itself nonaesthetic, the origins of which must be sought in the proclivity of the mind towards magic. However, it is a need the pull of which has been strong enough to have seriously upset the equilibrium of the plastic arts.

The quarrel over realism in art stems from a misunderstanding,

---

[1] It would be interesting from this point of view to study, in the illustrated magazines of 1890–1910, the rivalry between photographic reporting and the use of drawings. The latter, in particular, satisfied the baroque need for the dramatic. A feeling for the photographic document developed only gradually.

from a confusion between the aesthetic and the psychological; between true realism, the need that is to give significant expression to the world both concretely and its essence, and the pseudorealism of a deception aimed at fooling the eye (or for that matter the mind); a pseudorealism content in other words with illusory appearances. That is why medieval art never passed through this crisis; simultaneously vividly realistic and highly spiritual, it knew nothing of the drama that came to light as a consequence of technical developments. Perspective was the original sin of Western painting.

It was redemed from sin by Niepce and Lumière. In achieving the aims of baroque art, photography has freed the plastic arts from their obsession with likeness. Painting was forced, as it turned out, to offer us illusion and this illusion was reckoned sufficient unto art. Photography and the cinema on the other hand are discoveries that satisfy, once and for all and in its very essence, our obsession with realism.

No matter how skillful the painter, his work was always in fee to an inescapable subjectivity. The fact that a human hand intervened cast a shadow of doubt over the image. Again, the essential factor in the transition from the baroque to photography is not the perfecting of a physical process (photography will long remain the inferior of painting in the reproduction of color); rather does it lie in a psychological fact, to wit, in completely satisfying our appetite for illusion by a mechanical reproduction in the making of which man plays no part. The solution is not to be found in the result achieved but in the way of achieving it. [2]

This is why the conflict between style and likeness is a relatively modern phenomenon of which there is no trace before the invention of the sensitized plate. Clearly the fascinating objectivity of Chardin is in no sense that of the photographer. The nineteenth century saw the real beginnings of the crisis of realism of which Picasso is now the mythical central figure and which put to the test at one and the same time the conditions determining the formal existence of the plastic arts and their sociological roots. Freed from the "resemblance complex," the modern painter abandons it to the masses who, henceforth, identify resemblance

---

[2] There is room, nevertheless, for a study of the psychology of the lesser plastic arts, the molding of death masks for example, which likewise involves a certain automatic process. One might consider photography in this sense as a molding, the taking of an impression, by the manipulation of light.

on the one hand with photography and on the other with the kind of painting which is related to photography.

Originality in photography as distinct from originality in painting lies in the essentially objective character of photography. [Bazin here makes a point of the fact that the lens, the basis of photography, is in French called the "objectif," a nuance that is lost in English—Tr.] For the first time, between the originating object and its reproduction there intervenes only the instrumentality of a nonliving agent. For the first time an image of the world is formed automatically, without the creative intervention of man. The personality of the photographer enters into the proceedings only in his selection of the object to be photographed and by way of the purpose he has in mind. Although the final result may reflect something of his personality, this does not play the same role as is played by that of the painter. All the arts are based on the presence of man, only photography derives an advantage from his absence. Photography affects us like a phenomenon in nature, like a flower or a snowflake whose vegetable or earthly origins are an inseparable part of their beauty.

This production by automatic means has radically affected our psychology of the image. The objective nature of photography confers on it a quality of credibility absent from all other picture-making. In spite of any objections our critical spirit may offer, we are forced to accept as real the existence of the object reproduced, actually *re*-presented, set before us, that is to say, in time and space. Photography enjoys a certain advantage in virtue [3] of this transference of reality from the thing to its reproduction.

A very faithful drawing may actually tell us more about the model but despite the promptings of our critical intelligence it will never have the irrational power of the photograph to bear away our faith.

Besides, painting is, after all, an inferior way of making likenesses, an *ersatz* of the processes of reproduction. Only a photographic lens can give us the kind of image of the object that is capable of satisfying the deep need man has to substitute for it something more than a mere approximation, a kind of decal or transfer. The photographic image is the object itself, the object

[3] Here one should really examine the psychology of relics and souvenirs which likewise enjoy the advantages of a transfer of reality stemming from the "mummy-complex." Let us merely note in passing that the Holy Shroud of Turin combines the features alike of relic and photograph.

freed from the conditions of time and space that govern it. No matter how fuzzy, distorted, or discolored, no matter how lacking in documentary value the image may be, it shares, by virtue of the very process of its becoming, the being of the model of which it is the reproduction; it *is* the model.

Hence the charm of family albums. Those grey or sepia shadows, phantomlike and almost undecipherable, are no longer traditional family portraits but rather the disturbing presence of lives halted at a set moment in their duration, freed from their destiny; not, however, by the prestige of art but by the power of an impassive mechanical process: for photography does not create eternity, as art does, it embalms time, rescuing it simply from its proper corruption.

Viewed in this perspective, the cinema is objectivity in time. The film is no longer content to preserve the object, enshrouded as it were in an instant, as the bodies of insects are preserved intact, out of the distant past, in amber. The film delivers baroque art from its convulsive catalepsy. Now, for the first time, the image of things is likewise the image of their duration, change mummified as it were. Those categories of *resemblance* which determine the species *photographic* image likewise, then, determine the character of its aesthetic as distinct from that of painting. [4]

The aesthetic qualities of photography are to be sought in its power to lay bare the realities. It is not for me to separate off, in the complex fabric of the objective world, here a reflection on a damp sidewalk, there the gesture of a child. Only the impassive lens, stripping its object of all those ways of seeing it, those piled-up preconceptions, that spiritual dust and grime with which my eyes have covered it, is able to present it in all its virginal purity to my attention and consequently to my love. By the power of photography, the natural image of a world that we neither know nor can know, nature at last does more than imitate art: she imitates the artist.

Photography can even surpass art in creative power. The aesthetic world of the painter is of a different kind from that of the world about him. Its boundaries enclose a substantially and essen-

---

[4] I use the term *category* here in the sense attached to it by M. Gouhier in his book on the theater in which he distinguishes between the dramatic and the aesthetic categories. Just as dramatic tension has no artistic value, the perfection of a reproduction is not to be identified with beauty. It constitutes rather the prime matter, so to speak, on which the artistic fact is recorded.

tially different microcosm. The photograph as such and the object in itself share a common being, after the fashion of a fingerprint. Wherefore, photography actually contributes something to the order of natural creation instead of providing a substitute for it. The surrealists had an inkling of this when they looked to the photographic plate to provide them with their monstrosities and for this reason: the surrealist does not consider his aesthetic purpose and the mechanical effect of the image on our imaginations as things apart. For him, the logical distinction between what is imaginary and what is real tends to disappear. Every image is to be seen as an object and every object as an image. Hence photography ranks high in the order of surrealist creativity because it produces an image that is a reality of nature, namely, an hallucination that is also a fact. The fact that surrealist painting combines tricks of visual deception with meticulous attention to detail substantiates this.

So, photography is clearly the most important event in the history of plastic arts. Simultaneously a liberation and an accomplishment, it has freed Western painting, once and for all, from its obsession with realism and allowed it to recover its aesthetic autonomy. Impressionist realism, offering science as an alibi, is at the opposite extreme from eye-deceiving trickery. Only when form ceases to have any imitative value can it be swallowed up in color. So, when form, in the person of Cézanne, once more regains possession of the canvas there is no longer any question of the illusions of the geometry of perspective. The painting, being confronted in the mechanically produced image with a competitor able to reach out beyond baroque resemblance to the very identity of the model, was compelled into the category of object. Henceforth Pascal's condemnation of painting is itself rendered vain since the photograph allows us on the one hand to admire in reproduction something that our eyes alone could not have taught us to love, and on the other, to admire the painting as a thing in itself whose relation to something in nature has ceased to be the justification for its existence. . . .

Eugène Atget (1856–1927) could be called the Master of Paris, so thoroughly did he capture the qualities of the city in his photographs, as the following statement by Berenice Abbott makes clear.

EUGENE ATGET

Berenice Abbott

Eugene Atget may be called one of the first great photographers. This is true in the sense that he used the camera selectively and discriminatingly for its expressive functions. Atget came late to the medium, beginning to photograph Paris and its environs when he was over forty. Thus the years of his maturity lay behind his uncanny eye. For thirty years, almost to the day of his death, he photographed his theme with perseverance and imagination, and with an unerring feeling for what the camera image can express. Perhaps the dominant attribute of Atget's work is its purely photographic nature. At no time did he confuse photography with painting. Rather, his awareness of life led him to focus on it sharply and clearly. Atget's approach to his subject was qualitative rather than quantitative, and the volume of negatives he made is to be credited to unfailing energy and industry rather than to a machine-gun system of making exposures. What was massive in Atget's oeuvre was his outlook on his material: he saw Paris as a city vast in human history and experience, and vastness was echoed in profound and poetic images. His friend, M. André Calmettes, spoke of Atget's record of the "trésors et misères" of Paris; probably the phrase does not precisely reflect Atget's view of life. He saw the old and the new, as an archeologist excavates strata of past civilizations. He admired the elegancies of Versailles and the adornments of ragpickers' huts, the life of the moment and the architectural monuments of the past. This was no program imposed on his camera by a cerebral decision but the freely chosen act of his eye. Atget followed no literary synopsis to create his series

Cour—Rue de Valence

of trees, flowers, shop fronts, grills, small tradesmen and workers, carriages, street scenes, brothels, markets, environs of Paris, interiors, street fairs, parks, and a dozen others. Not economy exacted a discipline of selectivity, but his natural sense of appropriateness: because he had lived with his Paris so long and so faithfully, he knew precisely what his subject meant in visual terms. In his love of life, Atget paralleled the indestructible vitality of Balzac. Thus he represents in photography the urbane and humane virtues of French culture. In a broader sense he stands for the best of civilization.

St. Cloud 1926

Auvers—Vieille Maison

Avenue de Gobelins

La Rue Mouffetard

St. Cloud c. 1924

László Moholy-Nagy (1895–1946) was a painter, sculptor, and designer as well as a writer and photographer. He was a major figure at the Bauhaus and later in Paris, London, and Chicago, both as artist and art theorist, the two roles in which he appears in these pages.

SPACE-TIME AND THE PHOTOGRAPHER

László Moholy-Nagy

One of the great surprises for the student of photography must be the discovery that photography follows exactly the same trends as other creative forms of expression. It is dependent on present technical, scientific, sociological trends and their relationships. As these relationships are not obvious to everyone it will be necessary to make an analysis of this statement and show by examples what its meaning is. It may become clear then, that events and actions which form the pattern of our life are more interrelated than is usually taken for granted, and that it is misleading to see photography in its mechanical aspect and for its technological miracle alone. Such an analysis may also eliminate the rather passionate discussion whether photography is art or not. Namely, if photography shows the genuine formulation of the time-bound elements with its own means, then it is doing something-plus besides its mechanical aspect. Secondly, if the thesis of interrelation is valid, then photography is not only capable of being influenced by other elements, but also has the potentiality to influence them. Thirdly, it may be proved that one can produce with photography the same content as with the other means of expression. Fourth, the range of rendering is dependent upon the human grasp, will, and skill.

The mechanical aspects of photography have already changed our technique of encompassing an object, its structure, texture and surface, and have brought us into a new relationship with light and space. But what can we do with these new experiences, how order and fit them into our life? This could be accomplished only through human initiative, thinking, and feeling built upon the new principle, integration. Integration is the attempt today to escape from the irresponsibilities of a strictly specialized existence. An early specialization leads to a mechanical perfection without the vitalizing experience of other fundamentals. Our specialist age is built upon a multiplicity of information pounded relentlessly into the individual by the daily press, magazine, radio and cinema. But tragically, the more he knows in this superficial way, the less he is able to understand, because he has not been taught to relate and integrate his casual and scattered information. Photography too, without coordination with other fields, is nothing but one of these isolated information services.

Photography, as we usually speak of it, is taking photographs with the camera. One of the obvious results is the projection of space on a plane expressed with values of black and white and gray. But what is space? The answer to this question may show the potential value of photography toward integration with many other activities. One of the methods to explain space is to show how to articulate it. Every period in human culture has developed a spatial conception. Such space conceptions were utilized not only for shelter but also for play, dancing, fighting, in fact, for the domination of life in every detail. A new space conception originated mainly through new materials and constructions introduced by the industrial revolution. However, as the technology was derived from new scientific findings, physics, chemistry, biology, physiology, sociology, etc.—all these elements have to be considered in our new space conception too. We can say that this new space conception is the legitimate successor of a space tradition giving such poor results at present. In this way architecture (mentioned here as the most easily recognizable spatial expression) became more a juxtaposition of rooms than an articulation of space.

The history of articulated space is dependent on the grasp of the dimensions: one, two, three, and more.

The magnificence of the Egyptian temple could be comprehended by walking through a one-dimensional straight line, the Sphinx alley, toward its façade. Later, the Greek architect of the

Parthenon designed the approach to the temple so that the visitors had to move around the colonnades toward the main entrance. In this way a two-dimensional approach was created. The Gothic cathedral articulated the inside most intriguingly. The spectator was set in the midst of related space cells of the naves, the choir, etc., and so was capable of a quick comprehension of their values. The Renaissance and the Baroque brought man in closer contact with the inside and the outside of the building. Architecture became a part of the landscape and the landscape was handled in relationship to the architecture. Photography can record these changes with reasonable accuracy and can help to reconstruct the spatial spirit of the past. In the last one hundred years one can find any number of photographs with congenial renderings and in the last two decades the spatial records gained much in consciousness of approach. Besides straight records, one can observe the attempt to show delicate space articulations which are often built up with elements in a vanishing-point perspective; or with linear elements, as building structures, leafless trees; or with unsharp foreground and distinctly organized subdivisions toward the background.

In the age of balloons and airplanes, architecture can be viewed not only in front and from the sides, but also from above. So the bird's-eye view, and its opposites, the worm's- and fish's-eye views become a daily experience. This fact introduces something extraordinary, almost indescribable, into our life. Architecture appears no longer as a static structure, but, if we think of it in terms of airplanes and motor cars, architecture must be linked with movement. This changes its entire aspect so that a new formal and structural congruence with the new element, *time*, becomes manifest. This brings a clearly recognizable difference between the experience of a pedestrian and a driver in viewing objects. For the motorcar driver, for example, distant objects are brought into relationship for which the pedestrian has yet no eye.

We all know that the appearance of any object changes when we move past it with speed. High speed makes it impossible to grasp insignificant details. So a new language of spatial orientation and communication is arising in which photography also takes an active part. Something similar can be observed in the advertising field, too, especially in poster making. In 1937 Jean Carlu, one of the best French poster designers, made an experiment. He mounted two posters on two conveyor belts which moved with different speeds. The one poster, by Toulouse-Lautrec, from around 1900, moved at eight miles per hour, approximately the speed of a horse and buggy. The other, a contemporary poster, moved at fifty miles per hour, the speed of an automobile. Both posters could be read easily. After this, Carlu accelerated the speed of the Toulouse-Lautrec poster up to fifty miles per hour, and at this speed the poster could be seen only as a blur. It is easy to realize the implications. A new viewpoint in the graphic arts is a natural consequence of this age of speed.

Speed itself can become the subject of a visual analysis. And here again the camera enters the field. We know of innumerable shots of quick motion, sport scenes, jumps, etc.; on the other hand we can observe unfolding buds, moving clouds taken at intervals; similarly the effect of long exposures of moving objects, streets and merry-go-rounds. Professor Harold Edgerton, of the Massachusetts Institute of Technology, made a new form of speed photograph with the help of a stroboscope. The relationship between the velocity of part-movements gave him the clue to improvements on the actions of golfers, turbines, spinning wheels and various kinds of machinery. These pictures are the unusual records of juxtaposition of frozen part-movements analyzable in each space-time unit. These speed photographs are of more recent date, but they are astonishingly similar to the Futuristic paintings, in fact, they are their exact repetition; e.g., the *Speed* of Balla, 1913. Marcel Duchamp's well-known picture of 1912, *Nude Descending the Stairway*, shows also the same juxtaposition of frozen movement parts.

In 1900 the Futurists had already begun to emphasize movement, saying, "The world's splendor has been enriched by a new beauty—the beauty of speed. We shall sing," they continued, "of the man at the steering wheel." The Futurists' aim was to represent movement, and some of their old statements from 1912 still sound fresh and enlightening. For example, "Who can still believe in the opacity of bodies, since our sharpened and multiplied sensitiveness has already penetrated the obscure manifestations of the medium? Why should we forget in our creations the doubled power of our sight, capable of giving results analogous to those of the X-rays?" Boccioni in *Power of the Street* projected such a double power of sight, such a fusion of the manifold elements of a street into one expressive representation.

The X-ray pictures, about which the Futurists spoke, are among the most outstanding space-time examples on the static plane. They give a transparent view of an opaque solid, the outside and inside of the structure. The passion for transparencies is one of the most spectacular features of our time. We might say, with pardonable enthusiasm, that structure becomes transparency and transparency manifests structure.

Cameraless pictures are also direct light diagrams recording the actions of light over a period of time, that is, the motion of light in space. Cameraless pictures, photograms, however, bring a completely new form of space articulation. It no longer has anything to do with the record of an existing space (or space-time) structure. This is usually created in the form of architecture from elements clearly circumscribed by their masses, lengths, widths, heights. Certainly these elements' masses and weights could be greatly simplified, the span of the openings enormously enlarged. Nevertheless they must be there to serve as the point of departure for the photographic record. The photogram for the first time produces space without existing space structure only by articulation on the plane with the advancing and receding values of half-tones in black and gray and with the radiating power of their contrasts and their sublime gradations. One suddenly becomes aware that here starts an invigorating investigation about the incoherent use of our rich resources. Technological ingenuity provides us with gigantic structures, factories and skyscrapers, but how we use them is shockingly anti-biological—resulting in wild city growth, elimination of vegetation, fresh air, and sunlight. To make bad worse, in the shadow of these modern buildings we thoughtlessly tolerate the slums and every bad condition that goes with them. So it seems that the most abstract experiment of space-time articulation carries a sensible reality, if the right interpretation can be made. Such experiments may signalize a spatial order in which not single structural parts, or large spans of openings, will play the important part, but the relationships of neighbor units, buildings and free areas, shelter and leisure, production and recreation; leading toward a biologically right living, most probably through a right regional planning, toward a city-land unity. Such an architecture as a new type of space articulation will bring an even more advanced solution than the present pioneers' work. These pioneers have already humanized the technological advances even if for a privileged layer. They use the new materials—glass, steel, reinforced concrete, plastics, and plywood— for dwelling purposes in the interest of a more functional and biological living. That this type of contemporary architecture is not yet accepted to a great extent, shows more the missing orientation of a tradition-bound public about their own requirements and benefits than a negative criticism of the new direction. The public accepts technical processes and new inventions more easily when they concern only details of the living standard. The acceptance becomes difficult if it seems to bring radical changes in traditional life habits. Of course many things, appearing first as gadgets or appliances, gain an enormous influence during one generation. Then it is usually too late to call for their elimination.

Our automobiles, trains, and airplanes, for example, can be viewed as mobile buildings and the fact is that this country has today 400,000 families living on wheels in trailers. These vehicles, mobile "houses," will influence the coming architecture. We know already projects of moving houses, sanitariums for example, turning with the sun. The architecture of Frank Lloyd Wright, especially the strongly cantilevered house of Kaufmann's at Bear Run, shows more similarity to an airplane than to traditional buildings. Another American architect, Paul Nelson, designed a "suspended house" where the baths, bedrooms, and library were hanging down from the ceiling. With this kind of arrangement, Nelson gained an enormous, free, columnless space inside the fenestration, which he designated as the living room. To live in such a house would create the sensation of being in an airplane with an intensified relationship to one's surroundings.

These suggestions may be disturbing to a few people, who probably would be even more aghast at the Utopian plan of Professor Bernal of Cambridge, England, to construct houses the walls of which are produced by compressed air, by rotating air streams. The walls would insulate perfectly. The question arises why one should live between stone walls when one could live under the blue sky between green trees with all the advantages of perfect insulation. There is already a house with glass walls by Marcel Breuer in Zurich where the garden grows right into the house through the wall. The trend in new architecture goes more and more in this direction. The buildings of contemporary architects with their undivided gigantic windows allow nature really to enter the house. Every Gropius, Van der Rohe, Neutra or Keck house clearly demonstrates this principle. Of course even the most modern, yet still static architecture is only a transitory step toward a future architecture of a kinetic character. Space-time is now the new basis on which the edifice of future thoughts and work should be built. Contemporary arts, rapid changes in our surroundings through inventions, motorization, radio and television, electronic action, records of light phenomena, and speed, are helping us to sense its existence and significance.

Binding different space and time levels together, we shall find that reflections and transparent mirrorings of the passing traffic in the windows of motor cars or shops belong in the same category. In photographic rendering they usually appear as superimpositions. Mirroring means in this sense the changing aspects of vision, the sharpened identification of the inside and outside penetrations.

With this instrument of thought many other phenomena (dreams, for example) can be explained as space-time articulations. In dreams there is a characteristic blending of independent events into a coherent whole.

Super-imposition of photographs, as frequently seen in motion pictures, can be used as the visual representational form of dreams, and in this way, as a space-time synonym.

The photomontage, a device often used in advertising, has a very similar technique. The cutting and assemblage of the parts is applied here on a static plane. The effect is that of a real scene, a synopsis of actions, produced by originally unrelated space and time elements juxtaposed and fused into a unity.

The acquaintance with these few attempts of a space-time visualization of which there are many more, may help to clarify the art of the motion picture. Motion pictures, more than anything else, fulfill the requirements of a space-time visual art. We can say that motion pictures can be used today even for very subtle articulation of space-time concepts.

A motion picture is the assemblage of numerous shots. In other words a film scene is "cut"—glued together from different shots. Any film sequence may serve as an example. For instance:

1. A person enters Rockefeller Center, New York.
2. He speaks to an audience.
3. A hand throws a bottle (close up).
4. Bottle flies through the air and misses speaker.
5. Hand slaps face (close up).
6. Hand pounds head (close up).

This scene suggests that one person speaking in Rockefeller Center was attacked by a man throwing a bottle. This man was then slapped and counter-attacked. Well, the peculiarity of this film scene is that all the six shots belonging to it have been photographed at six different places—some even in Europe—at six separate times.

The power of assemblage, the quick fluidity of the action structure, which seems logically to perform this incident, creates the scene as a coherent space-time reality. This, however, never existed.

It takes considerable time to grasp this miracle of illusion when so exactly analyzed. But the fact is that everyone experiences it daily in the cinema and appreciates it as normal stimulus for the senses.

Something similar may happen when one travels. Movements can be perceived on different layers: e.g., Train A is moving from the station and meets Train B slowly moving from the opposite direction. Through the windows of Train A one is watching Train B moving away and when occasionally the windows of the two crossing trains are in direct line one can glimpse beyond a street with cars and pedestrians moving in different directions. With types of relationships we are constantly heading toward dynamic, kinetic representations of time-spatial existences. The time problem today is connected with the space problem, and it is presented to us with all the elements of knowledge of our period. It involves all our faculties in a re-orientation of kinetics, motion, light, speed. Constant changes of light, materials, energies, tensions, and positions, are here related in an understandable form. It stands for many things: simultaneous penetration of inside and outside; conquest of the structure instead of the façade.

It is in our power to use this conception, and the photographer can be one of the main participants in this task. But he has to focus his attention on the facts which give an adequate record of the actions and ideas of his time. As he cannot do this without participating fully in life, consciously or intuitively his specialized field must be integrated with social reality. So naturally his visual selections will be colored by his attitude toward life. This relationship to society may have the power of rising to objective heights, expressing the constructive framework of our civilization instead of drowning in the chaos of a million details. Then the photographer will bring to the masses a new and creative vision. This will be his social significance. For culture is not the work of a few outstanding people. To benefit society their theories have to penetrate into everybody's daily routine.

Photogram

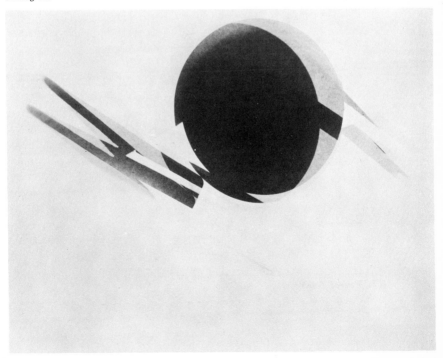

The Eternal Feminine

The Law of Series

Landscape

Light Modulator

EDWARD STEICHEN

As a practitioner of photography and organizer of spaces in which the art may best be seen, Edward Steichen (1879–   ) has no equal. He was co-founder with Alfred Stieglitz of the Photo-Secession Gallery in New York in 1902; he organized and directed the Family of Man exhibition at the Museum of Modern Art, the greatest of post-World War II photographic displays. The comments below describe the circumstances in which the following six photographs were made.

"One day . . . I borrowed from a friend a German hand camera called the Goerzanschutz Klapp Camera. Armed with this camera, I made my first attempt at serious documentary reportage. I went to the Longchamps Races and found an extravagantly dressed society audience, obviously more interested in displaying and viewing the latest fashions than in following the horse races." "The 'Wheelbarrow with Flower Pots' was certainly as realistic a photograph as I had ever made. Yet, friends remarked that it made them think of one thing or another that had nothing to do with the wheelbarrow and the flower pots. They thought of 'heavy artillery' and 'log jams,' for example. I began to reason that, if it was possible to photograph objects in a way that makes them suggest something entirely different, perhaps it would be possible to give abstract meanings to very literal photographs. I made many pictures exploring the idea." "I did a whole series with eggs and another with a harmonica and a glass bell used by gardeners for protecting plants from frost in early spring. But in trying these things out on the same friends who had responded with so much imagination to the 'Wheelbarrow with Flower Pots,' I found they were completely bewildered. Not understanding the symbolic use to which I was putting the objects, they had no clue to the meaning of the pictures. I began to realize that abstraction based on symbols was feasible only if the symbols were universal. Symbols that I invented as I went along would not be understood by anyone but myself."

Steeplechase Day, Paris (1905)

Bernard Shaw (1907)

*"There was a thrill in posing Shaw. 'He was easy
as a big dog to photograph,' says Steichen. Years
have passed since that print came forth, and Steichen
holds that it is one of the few portraits out of those
early years from his camera which stand the test
of time and are up to his later and more rigorous
standards."* CARL SANDBURG

Wheelbarrow with Flower Pots (1920)

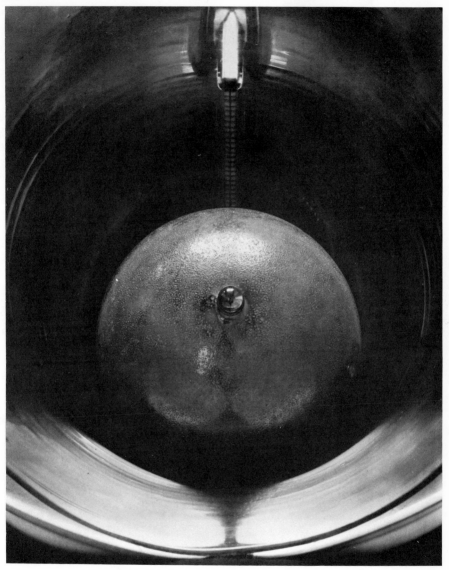

Harmonica Riddle (1921)

Foxgloves (1926)

"*Between whiles in such a week [working for Condé Nast Publications] Steichen might be working on prints of large leaves of mullein proliferant and brooding, of succulent and maternal apples, of foxglove pouring downward in a white waterfall of leaves. . . .*" CARL SANDBURG

The Shad-blow Tree

[*Since 1955*] *Edward Steichen "has been photographing* [*and filming*] . . . *a shad-blow tree at his
home in Connecticut, in every season of the year
and at all hours of the day and night. One is reminded of Monet and his water lilies. His subject
may not be a very large tree, but all of us who
know Steichen suspect that it may be the Tree of
Life. . . ."* RENÉ D'HARNONCOURT.

In the developing years of a new art form, the men
and women responsible for its development very
often work together, encourage each other, help to
find outlets and audiences or viewers for one
another's work. So it was in the formative years of
jazz and the motion picture. So it was in the development of the art of photography. A fine case in
point is that of Berenice Abbott (1898–   ). After
studying at Ohio State University, she went to Paris
to pursue a career in sculpture and drawing. There
she discovered the work of Eugène Atget, whose
photographs she introduces in another of the port-
folios in this book. She became

BERENICE

Atget's great champion, preserving his extraordinary photographic record of Paris,

ABBOTT

finding several generations
of appreciative viewers for
his work, and editing a splendid volume of his
photographs. In Paris, too, she worked as an assistant
to Man Ray, most famous of expatriate American
photographers and master of many photographic
styles, who collaborated with Moholy-Nagy in his
experiments with light upon photographic paper.
She returned to New York in 1929 to become to
that American city what Atget had been to Paris.
In her own photography, in her teaching, and in her
work as supervisor of photographic documents for
the City of New York as part of the Federal Arts
Project, she became the city's photographic historian. Her one-man shows at the Museum of the
City of New York have been important events in
the cultural history of the city. However, Berenice
Abbott is much more than master photographer of
New York City. Following the direction of Moholy-
Nagy, she has carried her art beyond its assumed
limits into the realm of science, where she worked
for a number of years at a collection of photos
demonstrating the laws of science.

Edward Hopper

James Joyce

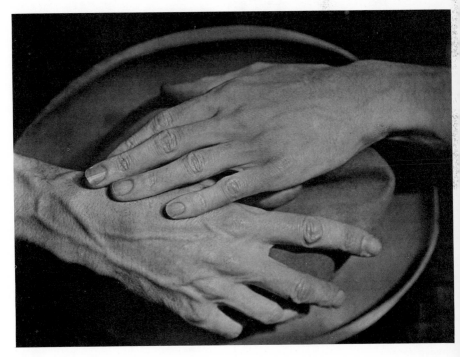

Hands of Jean Cocteau

West Street, New York

The Depression years had a lasting and curiously positive effect upon American photographers. Many of the best of them worked with the Farm Security Administration, bringing alive a rural enrivonment and people close to death. Walker Evans (1903–   ) is a major example of this kind of photographer, a camera essayist, a true stylist.

WALKER EVANS

The emergence, in some force, of serious, non-commercial still photography as an art is comparatively recent. It may plausibly be dated from the 1930's (not counting the work of a few previous, isolated individuals).

Modern photographers who are artists are an unusual breed. They work with the conviction, glee, pain, and daring of all artists in all time. Their belief in the power of images is limitless. The younger ones, at least, dream of making photographs like poems—reaching for tone, and the spell of evocation; for resonance and panache, rhythm and glissando, no less. They intend to print serenity or shock, intensity, or the very shape of love.

More soberly, the seasoned serious photographer knows that his work can and must contain four basic qualities—basic to the special medium of camera, lens, chemical, and paper: (1) absolute fidelity to the medium itself; that is, full and frank and pure utilization of the camera as the great, the incredible instrument of symbolic actuality that it is; (2) complete realization of natural, uncontrived lighting; (3) rightness of in-camera view-finding, or framing (the operator's correct, and crucial definition of his picture borders); (4) general but unobstrusive technical mastery.

So much for material matters. Immaterial qualities, from the realms of the subjective, include: perception and penetration; authority and its cousin, assurance; originality of vision, or image innovation; exploration; invention. In addition, photography seems to be the most literary of the graphic arts. It will have—on occasion, and in ef-

fect—qualities of eloquence, wit, grace, and economy; style, of
course; structure and coherence; paradox and play and oxymoron.
If photography tends to the literary, conversely certain writers
are noticeably photographic from time to time—for instance James,
and Joyce, and particularly Nabokov. Here is Nabokov: ". . .
Vasili Ivanovich would look at the configurations of some entirely insignificant objects—a smear on the platform, a cherry
stone, a cigarette butt—and would say to himself that never,
never would he remember these three little things here in that
particular interrelation, this pattern, which he could now see with
such deathless precision. . . ." Nabokov might be describing a
photograph in a current exhibition at the Museum of Modern
Art. Master writers often teach how to see; master painters sometimes teach *what* to see.

Mysterious are the ways of art history. There *is* a ground-
swell, if not a wave, of arresting still photography at this time,
and it may perhaps be traced to the life work of one man: Alfred
Stieglitz. Stieglitz was important enough and strong enough to
engender a whole field of reaction against himself, as well as a
school inspired by and following him. As example of the former,
Stieglitz's veritably screaming aestheticism, his personal artiness,
veered many younger camera artists to the straight documentary
style; to the documentary approach for itself alone, not for journalism. Stieglitz's significance may have lain in his resounding,
crafty fight for recognition, as much as it lay in his *oeuvre*.
Recognition for fine photography as art. We may now overlook
the seeming naïveté of the Stieglitz ego; it wasn't naïve at the
time, it was a brand of humorless post-Victorian bohemianism.
We may enjoy the very tangible fruits of his victories: camera
work placed in major art museums, in the hands of discriminating
private collectors, and on sale at respectable prices in established
galleries. In short, Stieglitz's art was not entirely paradigmatic,
but his position was.

As we are all rather tired of hearing, the photographer who
knows he is an artist is a very special individual. He really is.
After a certain point in his formative years, he learns to do his
looking outside of art museums: his place is in the street, the
village, and the ordinary countryside. For *his* eye, the raw feast:
much-used shops, bedrooms, and yards, far from the halls of full-
dress architecture, landscaped splendor, or the more obviously
scenic nature. The deepest and purest photographers now tend to
be self-taught; at least they have not as a rule been near any for-

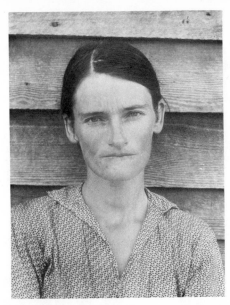

mal photography courses. Any kind of informal access to an established master is the best early training of all.

Whether he is an artist or not, the photographer is a joyous sensualist, for the simple reason that the eye traffics in feelings, not in thoughts. This man is in effect voyeur by nature; he is also reporter, tinkerer, and spy. What keeps him going is pure absorption, incurable childishness, and healthy defiance of Puritanism-Calvinism. The life of his guild is combined scramble and love's labor lost.

The meaning of quality in photography's best pictures lies written in the language of vision. That language is learned by chance, not system; and, in the Western world, it seems to have to be an outside chance. Our overwhelming formal education deals in words, mathematical figures, and methods of rational thought, not in images. This may be a form of conspiracy that promises artificial blindness. It certainly is that to a learning child. It is this very blindness that photography attacks, blindness that is ignorance of real seeing and is perversion of seeing. It is reality that photography reaches toward. The blind are not totally blind. Reality is not totally real.

In the arts, feeling is always meaning.—Henry James. Leaving aside the mysteries and the inequities of human talent, brains, taste, and reputations, the matter of art in photography may come down to this: it is the capture and projection of the delights of seeing; it is the defining of observation full and felt.

Photo-reportage is the special medium—and almost the invention—of Henri Cartier-Bresson (1908–   ). He has given long and loving thought to the photographic document, in which the presence of the photographer is all but effaced.

In my view photography has not changed since its origins, except in technical aspects, and these are not my major preoccupation. Photography is an instantaneous operation, both sensory and intellectual—an expression of the world in visual terms, and also a perpetual quest and interrogation. It is at one and the same time the recognition of a fact in a fraction of a second and the rigorous arrangement of the forms visually perceived which give to that fact expression and significance.

The chief requirement is to be fully involved in this reality which we delineate in the viewfinder. The camera is to some extent a sort of notebook for recording sketches made in time and space, but it is also an admirable instrument for seizing upon life as it presents itself. Without the participation of intuition, sensibility, and understanding, photography is nothing. All these faculties must be closely harnessed, and it is then that the capture of a rare picture becomes a real physical delight.

HENRI CARTIER-BRESSON

Photography appears to be a simple matter, but it demands powers, mental enthusiam and discipline. It is by strict economy of means that simplicity of expression is achieved. A photographer must always work with the greatest respect for his subject and in terms of his own point of view. That is my own personal attitude; consequently I have a marked prejudice against "arranged" photographs and contrived settings.

The intensive use of photographs by mass media lays ever fresh responsibilities upon the photographer. We have to acknowledge the existence of a chasm between the economic needs of our consumer society and the requirements of those who bear witness to this epoch. This affects us all, particularly the younger generations of photographers. We must take greater care than ever not to allow ourselves to be separated from the real world and from humanity.

Cardinal Pacelli (later Pope Pius XII), Montmarte, Paris, 1938

Srinagar, Kashmir, 1948

Albert Camus

Bill Brandt (1905–   ) is a generously gifted photographer whose depth of perception and wide range of interests are evidenced in his art. He was born in London of Russian parents, studied in Paris, and, like Berenice Abbott, was fascinated with the work of Atget and served his apprenticeship in Man Ray's studio, where he learned much about the surrealist view and its techniques. The influence of these years is seen in his work even today, for almost every photograph contains some element of fantasy or the irrational. In the 1930s he began to document life in England, photographing the world of the depressed and the submarginal population in the North of England, contrasting it with the life of the artistocracy in London. He captured people in all their moods, and in all their environments. During the war, he made a celebrated series of photographs of people in bomb shelters; in the years that followed he issued an equally famous set

BILL
BRANDT

of photos of literary figures in their homes. He has been a photographer of architecture and landscape for England's official archives and an innovative photographer of nudes, portraying his many interests, experiences, and styles in his studies of the female body. The poet and novelist Lawrence Durrell says of Brandt's work, "His pictures read into things, try to get at the hidden presence which dwells in the inanimate object. Whether his subject is live or not—whether woman or child or human hand or stone—he detaches it from its context by some small twist or perception and lodges it securely in the world of Platonic forms." A close examination of these photographs will show that Durrell's description is not excessive.

Francis Bacon walking on Primrose Hill (London, 1963)

Robert Graves

East Sussex

Friar's Bay

Jerry Uelsmann (1934–) speaks eloquently for the surrealist view of art in his photography, giving the worlds of dream and the nonrational every persuasive force that the camera and darkroom can provide.

Basically I am dealing with the predicament and condition of man as it directly involves me as an individual. . . . I have gradually confused photography and life and as the result of this I believe I

JERRY

am able to work out of myself at an almost precognitive level. . . . Life relates to attitudes. I have my own attitudes to

UELSMANN

work with, my own ritual, my game of involvement. Images

create other images. I cannot be asked to be something other than what I am, but I enjoy mind-prodding and mind-stretching. . . . Learn to use yourself as an instrument. . . . Although I believe my work is basically optimistic, I would like people to view my photographs with an open mind. I am not looking for a specific reaction, but if my images move people or excite them I am satisfied. . . . I have always felt I photographed the things I loved. . . . My images say far more than I could say in words. I believe in photography as a way of exploring the possibilities of man. I am committed to photography and life . . . and the gods have been good to me. What can I say. Treat my images kindly, they are my children.

Journey into Self

Quest of Continual Becoming

Apocalypse II

Fading Away

EDWARD WESTON

The great attachment of Edward Weston (1886–1958) was to natural form. Whether in the shape of a mollusk, a pepper, a sand dune, a rock, or a woman's breast, he saw intrinsic beauty and, with the large cameras on which he doted, made that beauty an enduring one. As these excerpts from his notebooks show, he was a meditative artist; nothing he did in his photography was even nearly accidental.

. . . I must dominate in a very subtle way, I must depend upon "chance"—if there is such a thing—to present to me at the moment when my camera is ready, the person revealed, and capture that moment in a fraction of a second or a few seconds, with no opportunity to alter my result. A painter or sculptor may see as quickly as I do, but they can carry their conception on mentally, change it, or if the model changes in mood or position, keep on with their original idea in mind.

Photography is not for the escaptist, the 'mooning poet,' the revivalist crying for dead cultures, nor the cynic,—a sophisticated weakling: it is for the man of action, who as a cognizant part of contemporary life, uses the means most suitable for a clear statement of his recognition. This recognition is not limited to the physical means or manifestations of our day,—such as machinery, skyscrapers, street scenes, but anything—flower, cloud or engine—is subject matter, if seen with an understanding of the rationale of a new medium, which has its own technique and approach, and has no concern with outworn forms of expression,—means nor ends.

Fortunately it is difficult to be dishonest, to become too personal with the very impersonal lens-eye. So the photographer is forced to approach nature in a spirit of inquiry, of communion, with desire to learn. Any expression is weakened in degree, by the injection of personality:—the warping of knowledge by petty inhibitions, life's exigencies.

I do not wish to impose my personality upon nature, (any of life's manifestations) but without prejudice or falsification to become *identified* with nature, to know things in their very essence, so that what I record is not an interpretation—*my* idea of what nature *should* be—but a *revelation*,—a piercing of the smoke screen artifically cast over life by irrelevant, humanly limited exigencies, into an absolute, impersonal recognition.

"Self expression," so called, is usually biased opinion, willful distortion, understatement. Discounting statistical recording, any divergence from nature must be toward a clearer understanding, an intentional emphasis of the essential qualities in things.

Through photography I would present the *significance of facts*, so they are transformed from things *seen* to things *known*. Wisdom controlling the means—the camera—makes manifest this knowledge, this revelation, in form communicable to the spectator.

. . . The pepper is well worth all time, money, effort. If peppers would not wither, I certainly would not have attempted this one when so preoccupied. I must get this one today: it is beginning to show the strain and tonight should grace a salad. It has been suggested that I am a cannibal to eat my models after a masterpiece. But I rather like the idea that they become a part of me, enrich my blood as well as my vision. Last night we finished my now famous squash, and had several of my bananas in a salad.

. . . I could wait no longer to print them,—my new peppers, so I put aside several orders, and yesterday afternoon had an exciting time with seven new negatives.

First I printed my favorite, the one made last Saturday, Aug. 2, just as the light was failing,—quickly made, but with a week's previous effort back of my immediate, unhesitating decision. A week?—Yes, on this certain pepper,—but twenty-eight years of effort, starting with a youth on a farm in Michigan, armed with a No. 2 Bull's Eye, $3\frac{1}{2} \times 3\frac{1}{2}$, have gone into the making of this pepper, which I consider a peak of achievement.

It is a classic, completely satisfying,—a pepper—but more than a pepper: abstract, in that it is completely outside subject matter. It has no psychological attributes, no human emotions are aroused: this new pepper takes one beyond the world we know in the conscious mind.

To be sure, much of my work has this quality,—many of my last year's peppers, but this one, and in fact all the new ones, take one into an inner reality,—the absolute,—with a clear understanding, a mystic revealment. This is the "significant presentation" that I mean, the presentation through one's intuitive self, seeing "through one's eyes, not with them": the visionary.

My recent work more than ever indicates my future.

. . . In selecting prints for my N. Y. exhibit, I chose, for the sake of variety from the many subjects I have used—peppers, kelp, bananas, shells, rocks, and what not, to show what can be done with anything, how each is related to all. This relativity is indicated in the course of selection: for I often place a kelp along with a pepper, or a shell with a melon, choosing on the basis of finest print quality or clearest expression in feeling, regardless of subject, for they are the same, varying only in degree.

I have on occasion used the expression, "to make a pepper more than a pepper." I now realize it is a misleading phrase. I did not mean "different" from a pepper, but a pepper *plus*,—an intensification of its own important form and texture,—a revelation.

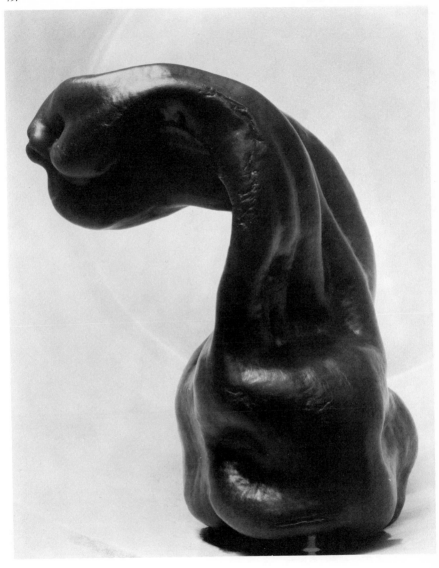

ARCHITECTURE AND DESIGN

No teaching institution has been more influential in the development of modern ways of seeing, sitting, moving, and living in the midst of designed objects than the Bauhaus, that remarkable collaboration of architects, painters, graphic artists, and philosophers, sociologists, and psychologists of design that began its life in 1919 in Weimar, Germany, and was shut down in 1933 by the Nazis. Walter Gropius (1883–1969) was its first director and as seminal in the construction of teaching ideas

SCOPE
OF
TOTAL
ARCHITECTURE

Walter Gropius

and the relationship of those ideas to students and faculty as he was in the development of modern architecture. The Bauhaus, for all its revolutionary ardor, was never out of touch with day-to-day reality. Its concepts, like its design products, were meant to fit into a machine-centered civilization and to be made available to everyone without sacrificing the freshness or individuality of the concept or the conceiver. Gropius—master designer of factories, houses, office buildings, and a teacher at the Bauhaus and at Harvard University—emerged from his years of collaboration with such artists as Klee and Kandinsky and his fellow-architect Marcel Breuer as a maker, a doer, and a thinker of central importance in the modern world of the arts.

CENTURY OF SCIENCE

I have tried to summarize for myself what the changes are that have taken place during my own lifetime in the physical as well as in the spiritual world. When I was a boy, my family lived in a city apartment with open gas jets, individual coal-heated stoves in each room, including the bathroom, where warm water was heated for the bath each Saturday: that took two hours. There was no electric streetcar, no automobile, no plane. Radio, film, gramophone, X-ray, telephone were nonexistent.

The mental climate which prevailed in the eighties and nineties was still more or less of a static character. It rotated around a seemingly unshakable conception of eternal truths. How rapidly has this conception been fading away, changing into that of a world of incessant transmutation, of mutually dependent phenomena. Time and space have become coefficients of one and the same cosmic force.

The sum of all these tremendous changes that took place during the last half-century of industrial development has achieved a more sweeping transformation of human life than those of all the centuries since Jesus Christ combined. Small wonder, then, that we feel the strain of this superhuman speed of development which seems to be out of step with the natural inertia of the human heart and with our limited power of adaptation.

Every thinking contemporary searches his mind now trying to figure out what may be the ultimate value of our stupendous scientific progress. We roar with new techniques and new inventions for speedier means of transportation. But what do we do with all the time saved? Do we use it for contemplation of our existence? No, we plunge instead into an even more hectic current of activity, surrendering to that fallacious slogan: time is money. We obviously need a clarification as to what exactly our spiritual and intellectual aims are.

Some time ago I read an article by Leo Tolstoy in which he reproaches science for studying purposely "everything." He held that mankind cannot possibly pay attention to "everything" and that we are going to tear ourselves to pieces, trying to go in a hundred different directions at the same time, unless we find out what we want most and make that the goal of our supreme effort. Of course, he thought of religion giving that final direction which establishes beyond a shadow of a doubt what should come first, after which everything else falls into place almost automatically. Well, if it isn't religion, what is it? Science has come a long way since Tolstoy's time and there are people who seriously believe that it can be the final arbiter and pass judgment on good and evil. Even if we should come to believe this, we would still have to make up our mind as to which scientific concept we want to give free rein, because, applied simultaneously, they may easily force each other out of existence and we would be the losers.

STRATEGIC AIM

I should like, therefore, to attempt to outline the potential strategic aim of planning for my own profession, architecture, within the cultural and political context of our industrial civilization. I shall try first to give a definition: *Good planning I conceive to be both a science and an art. As a science, it analyzes human relationships; as an art, it co-ordinates human activities into a cultural synthesis.* I want to put the emphasis particularly on the art of planning. Here, I believe, lie waiting creative potentialities that would give meaning and direction to our countless, isolated efforts.

We talk so much about the fact that the rapid development of science has cut so sharply into the familiar pattern of our existence that we are left with nothing but loose ends. In his eternal curiosity man learned to dissect his world with the scalpel of the scientist, and in the process has lost his balance and his sense of unity. Our scientific age, by going to extremes of specialization, has obviously prevented us from seeing our complicated life as an entity. The average professional man, driven to distraction by the multiplicity of problems spread out before him, seeks relief from the pressure of general responsibilities by picking out one single, rigidly circumscribed responsibility in a specialized field and refuses to be answerable for anything that may happen outside this field. A general dissolution of context has set in and naturally resulted in shrinking and fragmentating life. As Albert Einstein once put it: "Perfection of means and confusion of aims seem to be characteristic of our age."

TASK OF REUNIFICATION

But there are indications that we are slowly moving away from overspecialization and its perilous atomizing effect on the social coherence of the community. If we skim the mental horizon of our present civilization, we observe that many ideas and discoveries are wholly concerned with finding again the relationship between the phenomena of the universe, which scientists had so far viewed only in isolation from neighboring fields. Medicine is building up the psychosomatic approach to treatment of diseases, acknowledging the mutual interdependence of psyche and soma, the body. The physicist has contributed new knowledge of the identity of matter and energy. The artist has learned to express visibly with inert materials a new dimension—time and motion. Are we on the way to regain a comprehensive vision of the oneness of the world which we had taken apart? In the gigantic task of its reunification, the planner and architect will have to play a big role. He must be well trained not ever to lose a total vision, in spite of the infinite wealth of specialized knowledge which he has to absorb and integrate. He must comprehend land, nature, man and his art, as one great entity. In our mechanized society we should passionately emphasize that we are still a world of men, that man in his natural environment must be the focus of all planning. We have indulged our latest pets, the machines, to such an extent that we have lost a genuine scale of values. Therefore, we need to investigate what makes up the really worth-while relationships among men, and between men and nature, instead of giving way to the pressure of special interests or of shortsighted enthusiasts who want to make mechanization an end in itself.

Whom are we going to house? The people, of course, and that includes everybody. It injures the functions of our whole society if we neglect any part of it. The sickness of our present communities is the pitiful result of our failure to put basic human needs above economical and industrial requirements.

THE "COMPOSITE" MIND

If we envisage the strategic goal of planning in its vast complexity, it indeed embraces the civilized life of man in all its major aspects: the destiny of the land, the forests, the water, the cities and the countryside; the knowledge of man through biology, sociology and psychology; law, government and economics, art, architecture and engineering. As all are interdependent, we cannot consider them separately in compartments. *Their connectedness directed toward a cultural entity is undoubtedly of greater importance for success in planning and housing than finding ever so perfect practical solutions for limited objectives.* If we agree on this rank order, then the emphasis must be on the "composite mind," as we may call it, developed through a process of continuous cross-checking and balancing, rather than on the special-ized expert who shuns responsibility for the whole and divides his brain in tight compartments. During all the tedious, painstaking steps that make up his daily work, his crucial responsibility is undeviatingly to keep the broad strategic aim in mind, namely, to make segmental planning part of the total.

INDIVIDUAL FREEDOM AND COLLECTIVE ACTION

For people of totalitarian states the idea to pursue simultaneously individual freedom and collective action may appear quite incom-patible. They don't believe that it is feasible to combine a variety of form and thought with mass production of goods and with an orderly frame of law. Democracy, recognizing the autonomy of the human spirit, makes the respect for individual variety fore-most in any attempt to establish a common goal, a common denominator, laws or regulations. Intervention of government in the affairs of the people should not mean the destruction of individualism, but rather the means of preserving it. In contrast to this attitude we witness today what is happening when organi-zation and planning under dictatorial regimes are becoming ends in themselves. Man is plowed under and individual genius is paralyzed in the labyrinth of subordinated offices, forced to com-ply with the will of the self-appointed dictatorial authority. This spectacle can only strengthen our belief that democratic govern-ment in its true form must be the servant of the people. Planning, then, should grow from the ground up, not from the top down by force; ideas are put into action by individual initiative, not by bureaucratic edict. Democracy represents a widening-out, centrifugal force. A feudal or authoritarian system is, on the con-trary, a centripetal force, a straitjacket which stunts natural growth. The danger, emanating from the antidemocratic forces, has doubtlessly increased in our shrinking world with its widening net of communications and propaganda; it has made all men neighbors in spite of any imaginary curtains.

LACK OF MORAL INITIATIVE

But we should not look for danger only in subversive quarters. I believe that we must assume a much more positive attitude in try-

ing to keep creative impulses active and effective against the
deadening effect of mechanization and overorganization right
within the democratic societies. Our high-pressure, push-button
civilization is exerting a terror all of its own. It seems to fall short
of the high democratic goal of living in pursuit of happiness. We
obviously have not found the bond yet that would hold us together for a concerted effort at establishing a cultural denominator which would be strong enough to grow into a commonly
recognized form of expression, both physically and spiritually.
The great avalanche of science and progress has left the individual
bewildered and restless, unable to adjust himself and often piti-
fully lacking in moral initiative. We have developed a Gallup Poll
mentality, a mechanistic conception; we rely on quantity instead
of on quality, on memory instead of on ideas; we yield to expedi-
ency instead of forming a new conviction.

ARTIST: PROTOTYPE OF "WHOLE MAN"

Is there an antidote to this trend? Our society has certainly
recognized the essential value of the scientist for its survival. We
are very little aware, however, of the vital importance of the
creative artist when it comes to controlling and shaping our
environment. In contrast to the process of mechanization, the
work of the true artist consists of an unprejudiced search for
expression that symbolizes the common phenomena of life. This
requires that he take an independent, uninhibited view of the
whole life process. His work is most essential for the development
of a true democracy, for he is the prototype of "whole" man; his
freedom and independence are relatively intact. His intuitive
qualities should be the antidote against overmechanization, apt to
rebalance our life and to humanize the impact of the machine.
Unfortunately the artist has become the forgotten man, almost
ridiculed and thought of as a superfluous luxury member of
society. *My belief is that, on the contrary, our disoriented society
badly needs participation in the arts as an essential counterpart of
science in order to stop its atomistic effect on us.*
Examining our own experiences, we know that it is only in
isolated cases that sober scientific facts can, all by themselves, stir
the imagination to a point where people become willing to sub-

ordinate cherished personal ambitions to a common cause. Much deeper chords must be struck than those reached by analytical information if we want to call forth an enthusiastic, contagious response, capable of sweeping away barriers that stand now in the way of better planning and housing. Though scientific progress has reached us in the form of materialistic abundance and physical well-being, it has rarely matured into producing form. Consequently we find that our emotional demands remain unsatisfied by the mere material production of the eight-hour working day. This failure to gladden the soul must be the reason why we have not always been able to make our brilliant scientific and technical achievements count, and why a cultural pattern that should have emerged has, so far, eluded us.

I am convinced, therefore, that the contribution of the creative designer whose art can realize more fully the visual aspects and the human appeal of planning is essential. No society of the past has produced cultural expression without the participation of the artist; social problems cannot be solved through intellectual processes or political action only. I speak of the great necessity to recover through every man's education the lost quality of understanding and creating form.

Think of those essential imponderables, apparent in cities and towns of bygone cultures, which still have the power to move us emotionally today, though they are obsolete from the point of view of practical use. These imponderables characterize what is missing in the concept of our present communities, namely, that unity of order and spirit which is forever significant, visibly expressed in space and volume.

LACK OF RESPONSIVE AUDIENCE

Can a child, growing up in "Main Street," be expected to be in the habit of looking for beauty? He hasn't met with it yet and wouldn't even know what to ask for because his perceptive faculties have been blunted from the beginning by the ruthless assault of the chaotic colors, shapes and noises of modern salesmanship. He is left in a constant state of sensorial apathy, finally hardening into that intractable citizen who has ceased to be even aware of his impoverished surroundings. As often as not it is from this background, though, that the potential architectural client emerges, and it becomes immediately evident why he so rarely rises above creating anything but a blur or a sham when trying to give form to his environment.

None of our magnificent, practical new tools can turn "Main Street" into a beautiful pattern for living unless they are put into creative hands, unless a changing attitude of mind will bring about a fusion between science and art. But at which end shall we start to bring this about? Because what we need is not only the creative artist, but a responsive audience and how are we going to get it? Only by a slow educational process, providing comprehensive experience from early childhood on. It means, in short, that we must start at the kindergarten to make children playfully reshape their immediate environment. For participation is the key word in planning. Participation sharpens individual responsibility, the prime factor in making a community coherent, in developing group vision and pride in the self-created environment. *Such educational conception would put book knowledge in its right place, as an auxiliary only to experience in action, which alone can lead to constructive attitudes and habits of thought.* Any information given to a citizen after he has been exposed as a youth to educational practices that made planning seem everybody's concern will fall on fertile ground.

Planners experience in their daily work that the public is still very ignorant of the great benefits awaiting it from good planning. The average citizen is inclined to see an interference with his personal freedom when given direction by government agencies. The necessity continuously to inform him why communal planning is to his own best advantage calls for the highest psychological ability in a planner. A systematic psychological training in "basic politics" should give the planning student the understanding of cause and effect of human behavior. It should teach him how to put into his own practice persuasion, tact, patience and appreciation of the thought and position of others as the most effective tools of planning. It should tend to give him greater flexibility of mind, the resiliency of an alert wrestler, always ready to adjust to unpredictable situations. It should fulfill the need to develop a definite attitude of the student beyond his acquisition of the necessary knowledge and techniques.

Today we still meet too often with a deep-rooted inclination to dodge a large-scale conception for planning and housing and to add up, instead, unrelated piecemeal improvements. This will change only with a growing community spirit, carefully nurtured on all educational levels until it becomes a subconscious attitude of everybody and may finally cause a chain reaction conducive to solving our collective task.

NEEDED: EXPERIMENTS IN LIVING

Such an educational framework, as here indicated, also seems to have qualities favorable for the advancement of genuine teamwork which will naturally develop more and more in the future with the ever widening horizon of our physical knowledge of which each of us commands only a small segment. The task is too big for individuals alone. After almost twenty-five years of most valuable research and formulation of our ideas, we seem now to be in urgent need of action in groups. For in spite of the wealth of theoretical thought on community living which has been accumulated in recent years, hardly any new comprehensive "experiments in living" have been made. There is no other way toward progress but to start courageously and without prejudice new practical tests by building model communities in one stroke and then systematically examining their living value. What a wealth of new information for the sociologist, the economist, the scientist and the artist would be forthcoming, if groups, formed of the most able planners and architects available, should be commissioned to design and build completely new model communities! Such information would also offer most valuable preparatory data to solve the complicated problem of rehabilitating our existing communities. The blocks which have to be removed before we can create such laboratories for living are obviously political and legal in character. Without duly accepted legal instruments, one community master plan after the other will become a symbol of wishful thinking, of agonizing frustration.

I would propose also to bring to its test in these model units the much debated problem of how to keep more power of administrative decision down at the local level of the small self-contained unit. For any device to create more favorable conditions for direct participation of the citizen in the running of his community is essential for the attainment of an organic solution.

NOMADIC TREND

I remember that during a convention of the International Congress for Modern Architecture (CIAM) the question was raised by European architects whether Americans would ever be capable of creating a pattern for sound community life on a modern basis comparable to the closely knit townships that dominated the European picture before the advent of the machine. It was argued that the nomadic trend of the American population was so disruptive that nothing but makeshift arrangements could be expected and all local flavor would be destroyed by this mass of vacillating people in pursuit of the dollar. An American planner who was present [Martin Meyerson, Assistant Professor of City Planning, University of Pennsylvania] answered this challenge by telling of an experience he had had when he moved with his family to a place in Vermont that had always attracted him. He thought he had picked a town with the most pungent Vermont flavor, only to find, after some investigation, that the majority of the people were, like himself, born and raised elsewhere, but had selected Vermont as the place where they most wanted to live. They had come out of preference and had absorbed the local color to an astonishing degree. He felt that young Americans were not prepared to sit it out in the same towns where their parents and grandparents lived, as the Europeans have done for so many centuries; that, on the contrary, they usually became quite resentful when forced to do so. But, if given the chance to get around and look at as many regions as possible, they finally picked out one to settle down in permanently which for various reasons appealed most to them and then often became more co-operative and enterprising citizens than those who had never stirred from home. Now, if we can conceive of the future citizen as a person willing to contribute wherever he happens to settle down instead of merely looking for the easiest opening and the quickest gain, then we have, maybe, found an answer to this baffling spectacle of a nation whose citizens are, voluntarily or involuntarily, so much on the move.

To help this development we must conceive contemporary community features which would exert so stimulating an influence on the citizen who comes to live there that he will soon change from an onlooker into a participator. Such a desirable trend could well be brought about by a campaign to recapture the right-of-way for the pedestrian. As we all know, every citizen is both, now a driver, now a pedestrian; but while everything is being done for the car and its driver, the pedestrian has been pushed against the wall in the process of building up the great net of automotive traffic which has exploded our communities. I am convinced that it is just as necessary, or even more so, now to create, in addition, independent pedestrian traffic nets, separate and protected from the automobile. Such a superimposed pedestrian path pattern should start and end, not at a strung-out main street, but in a beautiful plaza, prohibited for cars, the very heart or core of the unit, to serve as the local center for the exchange of public opinion and participation in community affairs. Here, from daily social intercourse in trade and recreation, from gossip on local and world news, grow the grass roots of politics. Such a pedestrian square of human scale with its centralized social purpose would give the inhabitant a feeling of belonging and pride. It would prepare him for the sharing of responsibility, for conscientious voting and for his taking an interest in community planning which the planner needs so badly for future action. This is an ardent plea for the modern community core, the most vital organ to promote democratic process.

HUMAN SCALE FOR THE CITY

I so strongly emphasize the small self-contained unit with its community center because new experience here, on the smallest scale, will throw new light also on the more complicated problem of the larger cities and the metropolis. It will help in the gigantic task of humanizing them. For the problem of the big cities is certainly not one of building only new civic centers or piecemeal housing. It is evident that nothing less than a complete overhaul of their sclerotic bodies can turn them into healthy organisms again. We all know that their congested areas are hungry for open spaces, for nature, light and air, that their citizens long for a recognition of their identity, while the city itself needs to be protected at the same time against individual encroachment. I do not intend to elaborate on the social, political and economic procedures and implementations to reach this goal. But I wish to stress the great need of more systematic research also on the metropolitan level. How can we recapture in the city, socially and physically, the completely destroyed human scale? Research has to precede the necessary action. The growth of a living urban organism can be channeled into a superior civic form by the planner and architect only if its social functions have been recognized by new legislation, built up on the result of that preceding research. Existing law is mostly obsolete and insufficient for twentieth-century urban life, and most countries have as yet failed to put the emphasis on the whole of the communal organism, on its context rather than on its separate parts.

"HOUSING" IS NOT ENOUGH

If we try to appraise the physical achievements in housing and in organic community setup during the last twenty years, we can safely state that in several countries plan and construction of the individual family dwelling or apartment has been greatly improved with respect to livability and level of standard, but there is hardly any so-called "development" which would appeal to us as a true community, balanced in itself. Developments usually show just a quantity of streets and houses, accumulated in an additive manner without such communal features as would transform a mere housing scheme into a purposely limited, well-sized organism. They may be made up of pleasant, individual houses and often present an admirable economical achievement, but the layout of the town is usually but a dull, unimaginative conglomeration of endless strings of houses. It utterly lacks the stimulation that might have been attained from those intangibles of creative beautiful design and total conception which give life its deeper value and for which the past has given us magnificent examples of unity.

As to the conception of the contemporary dwelling itself we must first start by checking up on our own attitude toward the human and psychological components of the problem and its ever changing aspects. Only a mature mind with deep understanding of the physical and psychological requirements of family life is able to conceive a shell for living to be efficient, inexpensive, beautiful and so flexible that it will be adequate for the ever changing life cycle of the family in all its stages of growth.

OUR HABITAT

However, the greatest responsibility of the planner and architect, I believe, is the protection and development of our habitat. Man has evolved a mutual relationship with nature on earth, but his power to change its surface has grown so tremendously that this may become a curse instead of a blessing. How can we afford to have one beautiful tract of open country after the other bulldozed out of existence, flattened and emptied for the sake of smooth building operations and then filled up by a developer with hundreds of insipid little house units, that will never grow into a community, and scores of telephone poles added in place of the thoughtlessly cut trees? Native vegetation and the natural irregularities of the topography are destroyed by negligence, greed or lack of ideas, because the average type of developer regards the land first of all as a commercial commodity from which he feels entitled to reap a maximum profit. *Until we love and respect the land almost religiously, its fatal deterioration will go on.*

The human landscape which surrounds us is a broad composition in space, organized from voids and volumes. The volumes may be buildings or bridges or trees or hills. Every visible feature in existence, natural or man-made, counts in the visual effect of that great composition. Even the most utilitarian building problems, like the location of a highway or the type of a bridge, are important for the integrated balance of that visible entity which surrounds us. Who else but the creative planner and architect should be the legitimate, responsible guardian for our most precious possession, our natural habitat, for the beauty and adequateness of our living space as a source of emotional satisfaction for a new way of life? What all of us seem to need most in this hectic rush we have let life slide into is an ubiquitous source of regeneration which can be only nature herself. Under trees the urban dweller might restore his troubled soul and find the blessing of a creative pause.

I have come to the conclusion that an architect or planner worth the name must have a very broad and comprehensive vision indeed to achieve a true synthesis of a future community. This we might call "total architecture." To do such a total job he needs the ardent passion of a lover and the humble willingness to collaborate with others, for great as he may be he cannot do it alone. The kinship of regional architectural expression which we so much desire will greatly depend, I believe, on the creative development of teamwork. Abandoning the morbid hunt for "styles" we have already started to develop together certain attitudes and principles which reflect the new way of life of twentieth-century man. *We have begun to understand that designing our physical environment does not mean to apply a fixed set of esthetics, but embodies rather a continuous inner growth, a conviction which recreates truth continually in the service of mankind.*

"*I prefer the architect to 'provoke' art by means of something else besides rules . . . The architect must hear voices among the walls—women's voices, children's voices, men's voices.*" *By means of epigrams*, obiter dicta, *fleeting* pensées, *Gió Ponti (1891–) makes his vision of the architect's role come alive. In a similar spirit, with quick thrusts, elegant meditations, bold exterior lines, delicate interior detailings, Ponti has made his own contributions to architecture, to industry, to architectural journalism, and to the design of churches, houseware, hotels, hospitals, ships, and almost everything else one can create from plans on a drawing board. His magazine* Domus *is one of the most handsome and influential in the field of architecture. His work*

THE ARCHITECT, THE ARTIST

Gió Ponti

and his personality are equally striking in the development of modern Milan and much of the rest of post-war Italy. He has the necessary authority to write a book In Praise of Architecture *(from which these pages come), a "book for the lovers of architecture, for those who are enchanted by the civilization of architecture, for those who dream about an architecture that is itself a civilization . . . not a book* on *architecture but a book* for *architecture.*"

(I am evoking "the artist." Presumptuous word, obnoxious word when used professionally, as if one were always an artist, as if one could succeed in always being an artist! No, the artist is a man who has a disposition towards art, who has a vocation and sometimes succeeds.)

(We must always start by considering a work of architecture as a work of art and the architect as the artist. Buildings and builders are something else, something very respectable, but something else.)

(The real artists are not dreamers, as so many

believe; they are terrible realists. They do not transpose reality into a dream but a dream into reality—written, drawn, musical, architectural reality. Do you realize that?)

When building in the country, the architect (the artist) must imagine his walls, his spaces, and the sky (and the changing light, the fog and the multitudinous nights); he must imagine his walls, his spaces, and the waters; his walls, his spaces, and the trees; his walls, his spaces, and the people. The architect, when building in the green world, must proportion walls to trees (trees are proportioned to man).

(This is the "naturalistic genesis" of architecture. But I add that the architect reveals himself only through his imagination, an imagination independent of everything else.)

The architect (the artist) must imagine for each window, a person at the sill; for each door, a person passing through; for each stair, a person going up or down; for each portico, a person loitering; for each foyer, two people meeting; for each terrace, somebody resting; for each room, somebody living within. (The Italian word for room is *stanza*, a beautiful word; it means "to stay"; somebody staying there; a life.)

(This is the "animated genesis" of architecture. Yet architecture must reveal itself—and we must judge it—by itself, uninhabited, isolated in its own laws.)

When imagining his interiors, the architect (the artist) must hear voices among the walls—women's voices, children's voices, men's voices. He must hear a song lilting from the windows. He must hear shouted names. He must hear whistles. He must hear the noises of human work.

(This is the "sonorous genesis" of architecture. Yet architecture reveals itself by its silences; its eloquence lies in its silence.)

Blessed the ancient architect, who was originally a *muratore* or mason (a beautiful word derived from the Latin *mura*, wall). We architects of today have difficulties in understanding many things and have no feeling for them because we started out as students (what a mistake!). Things live in our intelligence before they do in our senses. For us, *nihil in sensu quod non fuerit in intellectu*, and not as for the ancients, *nihil in intellectu quod non fuerit in sensu.* Our upside-down Latin is our misfortune, a diminution of our resources, an impoverishment we have in common with engineers. Only the artists among us are saved, because poetry comes to their aid and makes them understand everything.

(What originated from the *muratore* was the "physical genesis" of architecture. Yet architecture goes beyond the senses; it is captured by means of the eyes but for the sake of the spirit.)

The architect of today, the college architect, must learn from all the artisans—from the marble cutter (his polished and smooth surfaces, hammered surfaces, sealed surfaces), from the carpenter, the plasterer, the blacksmith, from all workers and craftsmen. He must learn things made by hand. Nothing, if not first in our hands.

(This is "the manual genesis" of architecture, its living creation. Yet architecture becomes a pure, abstract form.)

The architect must also learn from the artisan how to love his trade; how beautiful it is to do something for the sake of doing. Art for art's sake is just that. It does not consist in a form of art without content but in the happiness of doing, doing without minding whether one succeeds or not. One is happy to sing just to be able to sing, and never mind how one sings; what matters is to sing; once in a while one of us will sing well.

(This is the "incantatory genesis" of architecture.)

In order to understand everything about his wonderful trade, the architect (the artist) must have his buildings in his senses, that is, foresee them (see them first); he must have a tactile presentiment of them through their materials (smooth, rough, cold, and warm). He must test them beforehand with his own prescient eyes under every possible light of the sky (calm, stormy, summer, winter, bright, dull) and under every incidence of the sun (morning, afternoon, and twilight suns).

(This is the "sensuous genesis" of architecture.)

The architect (the artist) must paint. For after all, he must compose landscapes even with his walls. Be it natural or urban, the architect is always constructing a landscape. He should paint for the sake of the appearance (the prospect) and the dimensions of his walls or surfaces; for the sake of their color; and for the sake of their relief (which he must be able to measure and have at his fingertips because of the play of the sun and light, a tactile thing).

(This is the "landscape genesis" of architecture.)

The good work of an architect may inspire a landscape to a painter. Such architecture is not scenography (no painter would make a painting of a set, for as the set is itself painted, his picture would be but a painting painted twice) but a scene of its own and a landscape grounded in life and in nature. A painting is a "test" of the architect's work.

(This is the "scenic genesis" of architecture.)

The architect (the artist) building a house should not look for praise of esthetic, formal, or stylistic values, or of values grounded in taste. These values are soon dated. The highest praise he must aspire to is to be told by the owners of the house, "Sir, in the house you built for us we live (or lived) happily. It is dear to us. It is a happy episode of our life." But for such a compliment the architect must pay more attention to the owners than to esthetics (and only thus will he reach permanent esthetic values, expressed by means of right forms, of forms esthetically beyond discussion, true forms, human forms).

(This is the "human genesis" of architecture.)

The architect (the artist) must interpret the character of the man who lives in the house, of each man in each house; he must build houses to be lived in by men who are alive. "*L'architecture est l'homme*," they say. They say. But not measured man. The man of Neufert's handbook is the measured man, and Neufert's handbook is not a technical book on architecture. Man is not to be measured; man is a character to be understood.

(This is the "psychological genesis" of architecture.)

(The architect who fails to interpret the life of the inhabitants, transforming it into an expression of civilization and culture, the architect who imposes on them his esthetic feelings only—apart from his presumptuousness—does not build a house but a show-case, an exhibition, and reduces its inhabitants from living human beings to mannequins. They, of course, rebel, and thus come about all those supposed infractions of the presumptuous order of the esthete-architect and his feelings of lèse-majesté.)

The architect (the artist) must be curious about men and women so that he may divine their characters; the true architect should fall in love with the owners, men and women, of the house he is going to build or decorate.

(This is the "loving genesis" of architecture. Yet architecture reveals itself without sin.)

The architect (the artist) is not afraid of limited means. The more limited he is, the less free to operate, the better his architecture. Then he works in desperation and performs miracles. He makes up for material difficulties with spiritual values. *Il faut décourager les arts.*

(This is the *nascita povera*, the impoverished birth of the arts. But later on everything is mysteriously rich.)

The architect must despise what is "passing" (stylistic and formal esthetics) and must look for what "remains" in life. Then he will find form (which will be what remains as life passes; a lovely contradiction).

The architect must realize that the permanent values are those of his soul, of his greatness, of his singularity as a man. Art does not consist in "formality" (any form is good, so much so, in fact, that form is continuously changing). Art is a document, a witness of man, of one man, through *one* form, *one* expression of him. That is why art cannot be repeated, why a copy is not art, why a restoration is not art. That is why a drawing by Andrea del Sarto even if beautiful and perfectly finished has *less value* than an im-perfect or unfinished design by Raphael. Because it is the document of a man who is *less great*. That is why works and monuments outside the realm of formally pure values, works like the pyramids and Milan's cathedral, belong to art. Because they are documents of grandeur, unrepeatable heroisms of history, of faith, of men. They speak.

Art, I repeat, does not lie in the form; it lies in the document of the man. Form is a thing perfect and complete. (Can we imagine an incomplete form? It would not be a form.) Nevertheless form is not indispensable to art, because a mutilated statue (the Victory of Samothrace), an altered painting (the Cimabue in Assisi), a ruin (the "test of ruin" is the great test of architecture because architecture must be able to resist all injuries and express itself even through its remains) inspire us, notwithstanding their mutilation, alteration or ruin, with an artistic emotion, because they are nevertheless *art*.

These works are documents of an artist because they emanate the spirit of the artist who created them, his magnanimity, his thought. A Man speaks.

This is the measure of art—the measure of Man. (Here the statement "Man is the measure of everything" assumes a different meaning. It becomes the measure of his heroism, of his life, of his own drama, that is, of his genuineness, of his autobiographical authenticity. Academicians are not authentic; technicians are not autobiographical; artists always are and only so. The value of Van Gogh's paintings does not consist only of their formal value, which has been copied by every imitator of Van Gogh with desolate and desolating reverence; their value lies also in his drama and in his autobiography; his paintings are its document. I say to the VanGoghists: "Go and cut your ears!" But we know that even this gesture cannot be repeated.)

Every man, I have said, shouts a cry before he dies (I do not mean the moment he dies, but before, during his life). History gathers it, if it is genuine.

The architect (the artist) should doubt esthetic and formal values. He should commit himself to the values of obligation and work. By these means he establishes his own true and valid document, the human document. The architect Muzio once said something very moving, "We have worked for a long time on this project; therefore it is beautiful." (A suggestive way of affirming those values of human obligation that adhere to a work and afterwards radiate beauty.)

This is why medieval cathedrals are beautiful, with their innumerable statues, their infinite sense of obligation and work, their infinite faith, their infinite prayer, and their infinite love (an excess of love; art is something loved excessively; but there are still rejected lovers). In the Gothic cathedrals this is true even of *the work that cannot be seen*, ornamentation and sculpture (some undercuts, some decorations in the back that nobody can see but that still exist, bestowing supreme artistic worth; an issue of love).

I realize that if an ass of an architect worked even a hundred years we could never say of his work, "Therefore it is beautiful." But I still believe in this conviction about Beauty; it is the one I like best. What is beautiful must be somehow deserved. It is something God asks of us. The architects who become infatuated with schemes, who believe in predetermined theses and rules, in proportional tracings, graphs, and other miserable tomfooleries move me to laughter and to pity (among them are some real artists, but even these seem unaware of the fact that they are artists only when they disregard their schemes). They subscribe to such theories to get out of hard work, to avoid having to aspire to inspiration, to invoke it, provoke it, and to deliver themselves painfully of it (it is not easy). If their assumptions were correct, everybody would always accomplish perfection, even they. It never happens.

On the contrary, it so happens that all of us (and they too, notwithstanding their procedures) sometimes create something fine but more often something not so fine. Art cannot be made certain or constant. This would be too wonderful! Nobody is more naive about or further removed from art than a calculating man. (It is true—I have found it to be so myself—that works of art can be schematized afterwards, *a posteriori;* we can then have fun rediscovering proportions, curves, inscriptions in circles, spirals, and the like. What cannot be done is to "produce" art by means of *a priori* rules. This would be too easy! Schemes as well as "tradition" and repetition do not exist in art; only history exists, and it does not repeat. And art is history.) Referring to schemes, Corbu says that his modulor is only for those who know nothing about proportion (*"Le modulor sert seulement à ceux qui ne comprennent rien à la proportion"*).

I prefer the architect to "provoke" art by means of something else besides rules. I mean to express this by two paintings I have never painted but that would resemble a votive diptych. One would represent the architect kneeling near his bed, praying like a child, asking for architectural grace, for inspiration. The other would represent the architect asleep, with "ideas" coming to him, through a window open to the sky, along a wire or ray. Along that wire would travel house plans, solutions of volumes, shapes of furniture. This vision is valid, after all. We have our voices, but ideas visit us at night. They are received graces.

The architect (the artist) must take time into consideration, for architecture must age well. New architecture is not yet perfect. Le Corbusier revealed to us the magic of "When the cathedrals were white." This whiteness was the beauty of those prestigious times. But the same cathedrals are now beautiful even if black. Their beauty is that they are *still* beautiful (and maybe even more beautiful.)

Every beautiful piece of architecture has survived its original appearance, purpose, and function, and many have served many functions successively. The right of an architectural work to last—and finally, its right to be—lies only in its beauty and not in its function. For it assumes a new function—beauty. Beauty is the most resistant structure and the most resistant material. It opposes the destruction of man, himself the most ferocious ally of time.

The architect (the artist) must not participate in the cult of beautiful materials; nothing is less spiritual and more material than a beautiful material. The fact that the Seagram Building of Mies was made of bronze gave me some doubts about it. Palladio worked with modest materials. A beautiful material is the same for all. Only a few are able to create beauty out of a modest material. Beautiful materials do not exist, anyway. Only the right material exists.

So-called refined people are amateurs. They are not really refined because they always want beautiful, refined materials everywhere. Rough plaster in the right place is the beautiful material for that place. This is real refinement. To replace it with a "noble" material would be vulgar.

The architect (the artist) must consider the functionality of architecture as an implicit fact, never as a goal. Functionality is the goal (and the limitation) of the engineer. A machine functions and is beautiful. Architecture that does nothing but function is not yet beautiful and is not even thoroughly functional. It functions entirely only if it is beautiful. Then it functions forever ("perpetuity," says Palladio). It must function at the artistic level, at the level of enchantment ("*Qu'elle chante*," says Corbu). It functions even when it no longer functions practically. It functions ultimately as a ruin. It functions poetically. It functions in history, in culture, in magic. This is the ultimate function of architecture—to surpass the function that originated it, to function at the level of art.

(The functionality of a machine consists of *its* motion; the functionality of a house, of a room, of a building consists of directing *our* motion.)

*Like William Morris, George Nelson (1908–   )
has not only designed furniture, but has also been
involved in its manufacture. Like Morris, too, he has
thought hard and well about the role of the designer
in the modern world, as he makes particularly clear
in the first of the two statements that follow. The
organizational principles that underlie the look of
our streets and houses rest, in a sense, on the ease
with which information relevant to their
construction can be gathered. There may also be
principles behind the way we like to push ourselves
into the corners of our houses, the "dead-end
rooms" where we can literally get our backs to the
corners. Such principles are not so easy to
arrive at, but Nelson, an indefatigable
theorist, is always willing to test a few
possibilities. The result is less than absolute
certainty but, at the same time, it is fine
entertainment and a significant contribution
to a psychology of the space which, by preference,
we like to inhabit.*

THE
DESIGNER
IN
THE
MODERN
WORLD

*George
Nelson*

The designer lives in the modern world. For him and his work it acts like a target, establishing the direction of his efforts and setting up a boundary outside which these efforts become ineffective.

The modern world—any world in its own time—is always a complex. It contains not only material that is truly of the immediate moment, but also innumerable memories of past worlds. There is also a constantly developing sense of worlds still in the making.

Any individual engaged in the effort to cope with his world is enmeshed in a tangle of phenomena relating to a near-infinity of times and places. Education is a process designed to impose something resembling a common order on this mass of events, an attempt to provide the individual with methods for coping with quantities of seemingly unrelated information.

To serve its own purposes, education must be based on social agreement. Otherwise communication between groups in the society cannot take place. During periods of great change this agreement breaks down. Certain groups react to the changes more rapidly than others, and communication becomes difficult.

The designer sometimes appears to have problems different from those of his contemporaries, such as scientists or businessmen. This is because he gives visible form to objects, an activity traditionally attributed to the artist.

Western society, during the past century and a half, has had very little use for the artist, and the feeling that he was a man apart had its basis in actual fact. But with the social isolation of the artist the myth grew up that he was *in essence* a man apart.

In the eyes of a public that had no use for him, the artist was a man who worked from "inspiration" and hence did not process the common fund of information in the same manner as other men. He was "impractical," a "dreamer." For the hard work to which other men were subjected he substituted "talent" (a very mysterious thing) or sometimes "genius" (equally mysterious but more respectable because of the long-term publicity attached to it). Because of his isolation, and the consequent loss of communication channels to the rest of society, work with the painter's brush and the sculptor's tools ceased to look like work, and it became suspect.

When Santayana said that the artist was not a special kind of man, but that every man was a special kind of artist, he was not announcing a discovery, but a re-discovery.

The industrial designer, as an identifiable category of professional, dates back barely thirty years. The importance of this phenomenon is not that the designer is anything remarkable, but that he is a conspicuous part of the new process of reintegrating the artist with society.

Two things make it hard to see the industrial designer as an artist. His activity has to do with common articles of use rather than the traditional media of painting and sculpture. And even more confusing to anyone who persists in visualizing the artist as a solitary character in a garret, is the fact that the designer is far more commonly an *organization* than an individual.

One of the most significant facts of our time is the predominance of the organization. Quite possibly it is the most significant. It will take time to realize its full effects on the thinking and behavior of individuals. In this conditioning process, few escape its influence. Even driving a car becomes part of a shifting but organized activity in which speed with safety are the result of voluntary cooperation by thousands of highly disciplined individuals.

The existence of the industrial designer marks one phase of the reassimilation of the artist into society. But because he is accepted (the criterion is very simple: people pay him money because they need what he does) he in turn must accept the beliefs of the society, and among these is the conviction that the organization is the proper form for important activities.

The existence of the organization as a dominant social form is a social response to a social problem. The problem is how to cope effectively with increasing quantities of information. A ten-year-old boy today has more information than Erasmus had at his prime. A small business or industry is already too complex to be handled by a single individual. So the specialist appears. The specialist, however, cannot exist without the organization because his particular package of information is useless unless coordinated with many others. And since this cannot be done without effective two-way communication, there arises a problem in education.

I have already described education as a method of imposing a common order on a mass of events. Specialists can communicate only if they agree on something. If I believe that fire is the expression of a particular god's wrath and you are equally convinced that it is a process of rapid oxidation, we cannot communicate, at least where fire is concerned.

The quantity of information now available has become so large that it can no longer be processed by traditional methods. This is the reason for the crisis in education and the many controversies about possible solutions. Finding workable answers is crucial, because science, business, industry and political institutions cannot continue to develop unless many people acquire a greater capacity to process information and learn better methods of communicating with each other. The industrial designer is subject to these pressures as much as everyone else.

The cultivated individual of the 18th century had a common ground with others in his class, all had studied Greek and Latin and had made the grand tour of the Continent. We enjoy no such unanimity today.

It is possible that agreement on a basic curriculum will never again be reached, that the new common ground will be found in *methods* of organizing and transmitting information.

One common element with interesting possibilities is the widespread use of abstractions. A man trained for management learns to deal with abstractions consisting of some two dozen alphabetical symbols, a handful of Arabic numerals and special kinds of pictures called charts or graphs. He does not as a rule think of these as abstractions, just as Moliere's bourgeois gentil-homme did not realize that he had been speaking prose all his life. Yet it is true that the powerful images used by management have no visible resemblance to the physical world and might correctly be described as abstractions.

The artist deals with other sets of symbols in two or three dimensions, most of which relate in some visible way to the world around him. *His* abstractions, however, are generally considered meaningless by the men who deal with letters, numbers and graphs.

Both groups, then, deal with constellations of abstract symbols that appear to have nothing in common. Yet the processing methods employed by each are not too dissimilar. And an understanding of the nature of the abstracting process might make communication possible.

When I was a student of architecture in Europe in the mid-30s, I was struck by the observation that the weights of government buildings in various countries differed greatly. Those built in Italy during the early years of the Mussolini regime were relatively light and open, but as the Italian position deteriorated in relation to Germany, the new buildings acquired thicker walls, heavier details and a generally more massive appearance. In Germany, under Hitler, the official structures from the beginning were extreme in mass and weight, and modern architecture, which is very light in structure and appearance, was forbidden by edict. In Scandinavia on the other hand, where it was not unheard of for the King and other ruling personages to be seen on street cars, government architecture had reached an unprecedented stage of apparent fragility.

So much for the observation. Now for the conclusion. After much perplexed pondering I finally decided that *the greater the internal stability of a modern regime, the lighter its buildings.* This conclusion, as it happened, was borne out by events of the next ten years, but what is important about this example is the fact that a set of esthetic symbols had been processed in precisely the same way an accountant might examine a company's balance sheet.

I believe that it is crucial for education today to explore such similarities in the greatest possible variety of activities. From these similarities we can build the bridges needed for communication.

Using such bridges, one becomes capable of exploring almost any combination of specialized activities. As an example one might say that what Joyce's "Ulysses" does to a space framework (Dublin) and to a time span (24 hours) is not unlike what the nuclear physicists did to the 19th century atom. Or what a movie director, using such devices as montage, might do with something called "boy-meets-girl." Or what the super high-speed camera does with a flame at the instant it is snuffed out. Or what Picasso does when he compresses into a single two-dimensional frame a variety of events in time and space.

Obviously these are the most loose of analogies and the comparisons could not be pushed very far. Nevertheless the space-time manipulations in each have a common—and thoroughly contemporary—character. Equally obviously, all of this activity of relating or "bridge-building" has a great deal to do with the industrial designer, who is the least specialized of all possible specialists and who must, therefore, think in terms of increasingly complex networks of problems.

In such observations as these, it seems possible that there may lie a very significant and productive concept:

The unity being sought throughout the modern world (seen from this point of view the conflicts spread over the morning paper are gropings in this direction) is not to be achieved through the reduction of complexity to simplicity, for this avenue does not exist even as a remote possibility.

It can be achieved only through the *acceptance of increasing complexity* and the establishment of a common framework within which phenomena can be related and evaluated.

The educated individual in this time does not set out to acquire more information—he enlarges his capacity to process (i.e., relate) the vast quantities he already possesses.

The industrial designer does not differ from other categories of individuals in this respect.

Because of the extreme diversity of the problems to which he is exposed, the modern designer has been compared to the artist of the Renaissance, a man who might take a commission for a portrait one day, carve a tomb the next, design a palace or work out a problem in military engineering. The similarity exists, but it is superficial. A superior individual in the Renaissance could assemble in his own head all the significant information of his time. A superior individual in the 20th Century could not possibly begin to do this. His role in this respect has had to be taken over by the organization.

For over ten thousand years the artist has been a visible landmark in the human landscape. Today is the first time in his history he has found it necessary to take out incorporation papers.

Ieoh Ming Pei (1917–   ) is an optimist among architects, but not a reckless one. He has been made cautious by his problems in designing and carrying through to fruition such large projects as the Roosevelt Field Shopping Center on Long Island in New York, the Court House Square project in Denver, the Southwest Washington, D.C., Redevelopment Plan, and the Kips Bay Plaza apartments in New York City. He is also extremely well instructed, as he argues we must all be, by the designers and planners of the past. Baroque use of space is not only theatrical in itself; it can provide the drama we need in our creation of new urban spaces. There is no brash scuttling of landmarks in I. M. Pei's speculative schemas. The past tutors the present, but in doing so does not make the present any less daring or any less our own.

THE NATURE OF URBAN SPACES

I. M. Pei

The ancient philosopher Lao-tse once remarked that the essence of a vessel is its emptiness. A city, in a sense, is a vessel, too—a container for people and for life. A city's essence, like a vessel's, also lies in its voids—its public spaces.

Most of us think of a city as a group of buildings. Yet we know from personal experience that the real flavor of a city comes from its spaces— its streets, squares, rivers, and parks. We notice that the quality of life pursued in any place has much to do with its design. Poorly designed spaces inhibit life and movement. Well-designed ones raise the ordinary rituals of life to a high level of intensity and purpose. The conclusion seems to be that a city, so far from being a cluster of buildings, is actually a sequence of spaces enclosed and defined by buildings. The thought may seem strange; yet it is, in fact, the very essence of urban design. And every architect who enters this interesting field will soon find himself designing buildings and spaces as a single entity. More often than not, he is likely to be more concerned with voids rather than volumes, surfaces rather than solids, for the character of a space is determined by its bounding surfaces—the façades of the enclosing buildings.

In attempting to speculate on the nature of urban spaces, I shall limit myself to the aesthetic factors. It must be taken for granted that no urban space can ever be successful, however well designed, unless there is a social, economic, and political reason for its existence.

The first factor, and perhaps the most important of them all, is scale. To develop a space to its highest intensity, the scale of the façades that enclose it must match the scale of the space itself. A large square needs important, monumental structures around it. A narrow street should have small-scale buildings along it. The idea seems self-evident, except that scale is often confused with sheer size; they are by no means the same thing. The Piazza San Pietro in Rome is an enormous oval of 650 feet by 500 feet, whereas the surrounding colonnade is only 65 feet high. Yet it is one of the world's most majestic urban spaces. The reason is that Bernini's colonnade, despite its modest overall height, is conceived on a huge scale. Scale here alone sustains an enormous space.

A second and a far more complex factor is the shape and extent of the space's bounding surface. To be felt as a space, an open area, as a general rule, needs to have enough of an enclosure to define it. If there are too many openings or too many interruptions in the surrounding façade, the space will drain away. In Venice the designers of the Piazza San Marco felt the need for enclosure so strongly that they finished off the surrounding buildings on three sides with an unbroken façade and even forced approaching streets and alleys to enter through arcades so as not to interrupt the continuous fabric of the architectural envelope. This piazza is one of the most extreme examples of complete enclosure that comes readily to mind. The continuous buildings around it are as solid as anyone could wish. Yet they are experienced as surfaces and are meant to be. It may be surprising that a space as large as the piazza could be so intimate; but the almost total enclosure makes it so. The more completely a space is enclosed, the smaller, tighter, and more intense the space appears to be.

Applying this principle to present-day planning experiences, we may observe that long-slab buildings enclose a space more completely than point buildings or towers. In the Kips Bay apartment project in Manhattan, a pair of twenty-story, 400-foot-long buildings stand parallel to each other. A distance of about 300 feet separates them. It might have been more economical of available space to build them closer together. But this space, though open at its two distant ends, is nevertheless substantially enclosed by the length and the bulk of the two buildings and therefore seems smaller and more confined than its actual dimensions would suggest. In the Society Hill section of Philadelphia, on the other hand, three tall apartment towers stand grouped around an open space that is a mere 180 feet across. There is no sense of confinement here even though the buildings rise over it to a height of thirty-one stories. The reason is that the space is far less enclosed than at Kips Bay. There are wide gaps between the towers through which the space can leak out into the beyond. This leakage reduces the intensity of the space. The Society Hill towers could have been considerably higher and a pedestrian on the ground would not feel any additional sense of confinement as he walks between them. To express it differently, the space between the Society Hill towers is actually a fluid space: the stream of movement flows into it, around it, and out again with ease. The space at Kips Bay lacks this implied movement. It is more intense. It is static and therefore needs more room to breathe.

Closely related to the scale and extent of the architectural development is a third factor—the formality of its design. A space gains immensely in intensity, in grandeur, and in importance when the buildings around it are conceived within the framework of a single formal design. The Piazza San Pietro again furnishes a striking example. Others are the Place Vendôme in Paris, the Piazza San Carlo in Turin, and the Place Stanislaus in Nancy, where the formal symmetry of the buildings, the strict axial arrangement, and the rhythmical repetition of motifs raise the quality of the space to a level of ceremonial impressiveness.

Here, it should be mentioned that the three-dimensional accents within a space often play an important part. Paris' Place de la Concorde is almost unique in that, with the exception of the Madeleine block, it has virtually no surrounding façade at all.

Yet it is clear, intense, and articulate, and the chief reason for this, I believe, lies in its interior accents—its two great fountains and obelisk, lanterns, and paving patterns—which actually create a form of their own. In the Piazza del Popolo in Rome, the one central obelisk, together with Renaldi's twin churches opposite the Porta, performs a similarly effective function.

A fourth factor in the design of open spaces is one that is imposed by nature rather than by man. It is the element of light. Everyone knows that light and climate affect architecture; for instance, large windows in the North let in the weak sun and little windows in the South keep out the glare. But light also affects our experience of spaces. The bright sun of Mediterranean lands tends to make spaces look bigger than they really are. The grey light of the North makes them look smaller. The alleys of Mykonos, for example, seem far more spacious than the streets of Chartres. Differences in the scale of buildings undoubtedly play a part, but the quality of light remains the determining factor. The Grande Place in Brussels, with its dark buildings under the Northern sun, looks relatively small; Constitution Square in Athens, though similar in scale, looks immense in the blinding Aegean light.

Up to this point, I have discussed urban spaces as if they were isolated entities, separate and self-contained. But the effectiveness of a space also depends upon its neighbors. When we walk through a city, we actually experience a series of spaces in sequence; and the impact of any particular space, whether a street, a passageway, or a square, is multiplied many times over by what we have already seen before and by what follows afterward. The classic example is in Nancy, where three spaces are lined up along a single axis. The two terminal spaces are broad, monumental, and ceremonial squares; the connecting space is long, narrow, residential, and divided by rows of trees. The effectiveness of the two ceremonial squares is tremendously heightened by the change of pace provided by the central residential space, the Place Carrière, which is designed on a far smaller scale. Conversely, the residential space seems all the more intimate and human because of the contrast it affords to the large scale of the two terminal squares. Each reinforces the character of the other when experienced in sequence. Architects, then, must think of urban spaces as a sequential experience and strive to orchestrate them into an effective ensemble. They should alternate wide spaces with narrow ones, constriction with expansion, concealment with revelation, so that each space intensifies and dramatizes its neighbors until, as a result, the whole becomes something greater than the sum of its parts. In this, I think, we become close at last to part of the secret of a city's visual quality.

These are a few of the factors that seem to me relevant to the aesthetics of urban spaces. They are hard to rationalize and harder yet to measure, for urban space is a medium that still remains elusive, immeasurable, and often more successfully approached by intuition than by logic and mathematics. Sometimes, as if to mock our efforts to understand, a successful space will result from a wilful breaking of all the rules. I am always astonished by Rockefeller Plaza, a space that by all rights ought to be oppressive because of its comparatively small area, the almost total enclosure, the immense scale and size of the surrounding buildings and the deep shadows in which most of it lies throughout the year. And yet Rockefeller Plaza is one of the most exciting urban spaces I know of. One can only speculate. Most beautiful things, they say, contain within them some exaggeration. Can it be that in New York, whose special beauty rests in the spectacular, in the exaggerated, a space as far-fetched and beyond all bounds as Rockefeller Plaza is the only kind that can capture the spirit of the city and intensify it?

Baffling questions like this remind us how little we really know about urban design. The elementary principles I have touched on here were once common architectural currency during the Baroque period. It is no accident that I have drawn most of my illustrations from that extraordinary era. From Bernini to Gabriel, the great Baroque space-makers translated order and discipline, the powerful instincts of their age, into the fabric of their cities. They mirrored the strict hierarchy of life in architectural subordination and emphasis. They expressed the ceremonial spirit of the age—its endless processions, parades, and spectacles, secular and religious—in elaborate and formally planned public spaces that heightened its solemnity. The Baroque sense of the theatrical became, in the hands of these architects, a dramatic sequence of spaces. And the delight in movement was satisfied by great boulevards carefully framed to lead body and eye onward with irresistible momentum.

Order, drama, movement—these were the impulses that produced the majestic plans and spaces of the great Baroque cities of the Continent. To these England added an important ingredient—the human touch. In England the ceremonial and public aspect of cities was balanced by the domestic and private. England's first contribution to urbanism was Inigo Jones's Covent Garden which was designed in the classical manner. Subsequent to this, trees and greenery began to invade English public spaces. The architectural setting followed suit with small-scale residential façades in place of the exclusively monumental ones. The Royal Crescent at Bath forms an immense elliptical arc of almost 600 feet in length, yet the scale of the continuous façade and the corresponding intimacy of the tree-filled park make the ensemble seem warmly personal. The Baroque sense of order is not once compromised. Nevertheless, the human scale asserts itself.

Today in America we stand on the threshold of an exciting era of urban planning and development. The public mind, now familiar with the splendors of Europe's cities, looks for similar beauty, spirit, and vitality in its own. Ever since the introduction of the National Housing Act of 1949, and particularly since its amendment in 1954, large segments of cities are being replanned and rebuilt. Architects are once again confronted by the challenge and the opportunity to create the kind of urban spaces that mirror our lives and aspirations.

In searching for guidance, it is only natural that we should turn to the Baroque planners. Admittedly, they gave scant attention to satisfying the social needs we consider important in our time. The social relationships for which they sought to provide a framework are not, despite the passage of centuries, so very different from our own. We, too, need order and discipline in our cities. We, too, need to provide for movement, though of a different sort. We also need a sense of drama to provide for a ceremonial side of life that seems to be re-emerging. And yet we have forgotten the very fundamentals on which the Baroque planners built their cities. To plan wisely and well, we must first relearn what they knew. This does not bind us to a slavish imitation. Much has changed since then. The high population density of most of our cities rules out the leisurely residential solution reached by the English planners, at least in strictly urban areas.

And the development of new building techniques and materials has opened up new opportunities for exciting urban designs far beyond the reach or imagination of the Baroque masters. But the fundamental discoveries they made about the nature and aesthetics of urban spaces are as valid today as then. In this respect, the careful study of Baroque cities is still deeply rewarding and is likely to remain so for years to come.

CBS building.
Photograph, CBS Photo.

"*As a nation we have often been hesitant and apologetic about whatever has been made in America in the vernacular tradition,*" John Kouwenhoven (1909–   ) *says at the end of his book* Made in America. "*Perhaps the time has come when more of us are ready to accept the challenge offered to the creative imagination by the techniques and forms which first arose among our own people in our own land.*" *Certainly John Kouwenhoven has himself accepted that challenge in the essays and books he has written on the American vernacular, on architecture, machinery, typography, on bridges, on interior decoration, on jazz. For nearly two hundred years, the technology of industrial democracy has shaped and reshaped environments and the people in them, but we go on thinking and teaching and talking as if our world had only barely changed since the eighteenth century. It is against the unwillingness to accept the real world for what it is and what it might be, that Kouwenhoven has set himself in essays like this one. One of their delights is the amount of incidental cultural history that they offer. Even if one cannot accept the present world, he can still enjoy the antiquarian games with which Americans have for so long and so happily evaded reality.*

WHAT IS "AMERICAN" IN ARCHITECTURE AND DESIGN?

Notes Toward An Aesthetic of Process

John A. Kouwenhoven

All of us at times need to confirm the continuity of our culture with that of the past, in order to reassure ourselves in the midst of bewildering flux and change.

We may ask what is "American" in architecture and design because we want to establish their continuity with buildings and objects of the past. And if this is our motive in asking the question we will, of course, be most interested in those buildings and objects whose structure and aesthetic effect are clearly related to, and thus comparable with, those of their predecessors in the Western tradition. We will concern ourselves, that is, with architecture in its textbook sense, as a fine art which has developed continuously, with local and national variants, throughout the Western world.

If we approach the question in this way, taking "architecture" to mean churches, government buildings, and palaces (for princes or merchants), and taking "design" to include what the nineteenth century lumped as "Industrial Art" (manufactured objects to which one could apply "arts and crafts" decoration, such as pottery, textiles, bijouterie, and the printed page), we will probably conclude that the "American" quality is catholicity. We can find in the United States an imitation of almost any architectural style or decorative mannerism which ever existed in any other nation. And when we have done so, all we shall have demonstrated is what we already knew: that Americans came from everywhere, and brought with them the traditions—architectural and decorative as well as social and religious—of which they were the heirs. We shall have learned what is English or Spanish or German about our architecture, and our design, and therefore how they relate to the Western tradition; but we shall know as little as ever about their "American" quality, if such there be.

There is, for example, nothing "American" about New York City's Cathedral of St. John the Divine, except perhaps the fact that it is unfinished. It is an important and lovely fact of our cultural history and of the history of architecture in this country, but it tells us more about what is not "American" than about what is, just as a Coca-Cola bottle made in France tells us more about what is "American" than about what is French.

The question can be asked, however, not in hopes of establishing ties to the past but in hopes of discovering those elements of creative energy and vitality which can evolve forms and structures appropriate to a world of flux and change—the "American" world—even at the risk of devaluing or destroying much that we have cherished and loved in the past. If this is our motive, we must look at those structures and objects which were not thought of as "Architecture" or "Industrial Art" by those who designed or paid for them. We must look, in other words, at those structures and objects which have been unselfconsciously evolved from the new materials, and for the unprecedented psychological and social uses present in the "American" environment.

THE VITALITY OF THE VERNACULAR

If we go at the question in this way, we will discover, I think, that the "American" quality is the product of a vernacular which has flourished in the United States but is by no means confined to it, which has deep roots in Western Europe, and which is rapidly establishing itself wherever modern technology and democracy are working together to recast our consciousness of our relations to one another, to external nature, and to our Gods.

I am again using the term *vernacular* as a descriptive label for the patterns and forms which people have devised, usually anonymously, in attempting to give satisfying order to the unprecedented elements which democracy and technology have jointly introduced into the human environment during the past hundred and fifty years or so.

Actually there are two ways in which people can order the elements of a new environment. One is to cramp them into patterns or forms which were originally devised to order other and quite different elements of another and quite different environment. Hence the mid-nineteenth-century blank verse "epics" about backwoodsmen in Kentucky; hence the flying buttresses of Raymond Hood's Chicago Tribune Tower: hence "symphonic" jazz and amphora-shaped cigarette lighters. The forms or patterns in such instances will often have a symmetry and finish which give genuine (if nostalgic) pleasure, but only at the cost of considerable distortion of the elements which have been worried into them. It would be interesting to consider, for example, how we warped the development of a system of higher education appropriate to an "American" world by corseting it in pseudo-medieval cloisters and pseudo-Renaissance palaces.

The other way is to shuffle and rearrange the unfamiliar elements until some appropriate design is empirically discovered. The vernacular patterns or forms so devised will often be ungainly, crude, or awkward in contrast with those evolved and refined over the centuries to order the elements of the pre-democratic, pre-industrial world, but they will at least bear a vital relation to the new environment of whose elements they

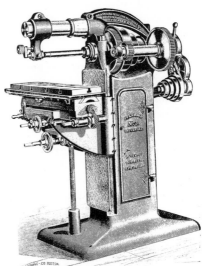

Top, Robertson's milling machine, patented 1852 (from a wood engraving in an advertisement in David Bigelow, History of Prominent Mercantile and Manufacturing Firms in the United States, *Boston, 1857); center, a Brainerd Universal milling machine of 1894 (from a wood engraving in* Illustrated Price List *of the Fairbanks Co., 1894); bottom, the Cincinnati Milling Machine Company's Universal milling machine of 1943 (from the* American Machinist, *May 27, 1943).*

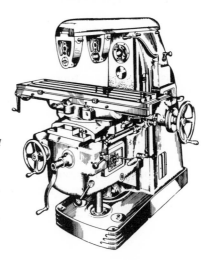

are composed. More importantly, they will contain within themselves the potentiality of refinement and—God willing—of transfiguration by the hand of genius.

As an example of the characteristic evolution of vernacular form, we may take the development of a machine tool such as the milling machine. Three stages in its design are illustrated. The earliest machine shown in the series was made forty years after Eli Whitney created his first practical machine tool of this type, but it is still a gawky four-legged object which has not yet discovered the so-called "knee and column" form appropriate to its functions, in which both of the later machines are made. Bearing in mind that each stage in the development of this machine represents an advance in the magnitude and complexity of the operations it is designed to perform, even a non-mechanic will be able to observe the increasing simplicity and refinement of the over-all design.

If we turn from mechanics to building we may perhaps more easily see the way in which vernacular forms and patterns can become expressive elements in creative design. In the past thirty years many structural elements which were developed in vernacular building have become characteristic features of contemporary architecture. One has only to look at the accompanying pictures of a century-old iron loft building, the glass-enclosed verandahs of a seaside hotel of the eighteen eighties, and an abandoned tobacco factory, to be aware of the vernacular roots of important elements in the architectural design of such buildings as Albert Kahn's tank arsenal, the Farm Security Administration's utility building for a California migrant camp, and Raymond Hood's magnificent McGraw-Hill building—done after he had learned to dispense with the Gothic trappings of the Tribune Tower.

Thus far we have touched upon examples of the vernacular which were evolved primarily to cope with or exploit those elements of the new environment which were introduced by technology—by developments in the machining of metal, in frame construction, and in the manufacture of glass. But the vernacular as I have tried to define it is by no means the product of technology alone. It is a response to the simultaneous impact of technology and democracy. Watt's first practical steam engine and the Declaration of Independence became operative in the same year, we should remember. Technology by itself can become

Above, Cast Iron Building designed and built by James Bogardus, 1848, on the northwest corner of Washington and Murray streets, New York (photograph courtesy of Gottscho-Schleisner); below, the Hotel del Coronado, on San Diego Bay, California, 1889 (wood engraving from promotional pamphlet, Coronado Beach, *Oakland, 1890); bottom, abandoned tobacco factory in Louisville, Kentucky (photograph 1943, courtesy of Reynolds Metal Co., which bought the building that year for conversion to aircraft-parts manufacture).*

the servant of a tyrant, as has been amply proved in Hitler's Germany and Stalin's Russia and, on a smaller scale, in some communities closer to home. But it is the peculiar blend of technology with democracy which produces vernacular as opposed to merely technological forms. New technics and new materials have not been the only constituents of the new environment for which men have had to discover appropriate forms. There have also been new amalgams of thought, of emotion, and of attitude.

If, for a moment, I may use the term "American" in its conventional and limited sense, as referring to whatever has to do with the United States, it is a very American fact that we are chiefly indebted to a European for calling our attention to the anonymous and "undignified" sources of many of the creative elements in contemporary architecture and design. It was the Swiss scholar Siegfried Giedion, who, in the Norton lectures at Harvard in 1939, first showed many of us that such utilitarian structures as the balloon-frame houses of early Chicago, and such utilitarian objects as nineteenth-century water pails and railway seats, were often more prophetic of the essential spirit and creative force of our contemporary arts than the buildings and objects which have been acclaimed for their "artistic" quality.

By now it is clear that many of the constituents of contemporary design which at first struck us as alien and strange evolved from our vernacular. The molded plywood which seemed so startling when it appeared in chairs exhibited at the Museum of Modern Art in the late thirties and early forties was the conventional material for seats in American ferryboats in the 1870's. The spring-steel cantilever principle, which attracted world-wide attention when Mies van der Rohe used it in a chair he designed at the Bauhaus, had been standard in the seats of American reapers and mowers and other farm machines since the 1850's. Built-in furniture, the "storage wall," and movable partitions to create flexible interior space, all three were employed in an ingenious amateur house plan worked out in the 1860's by Harriet Beecher Stowe's sister, Catherine Beecher, a pioneer in the field now known as home economics. The provision of storage facilities in interchangeable units, which can be rearranged or added to, as changing needs and circumstances require, had a long history in office equipment, kitchen cabinets, and sectional furniture before it was recognized as an appropriate element in creative design.

Right top, Chrysler tank arsenal, designed by Albert Kahn, 1940 (Hedrich-Blessing Studio, courtesy of Architectural Forum*); right below, utilities building, FSA Camp, Woodville, California (photograph courtesy of the Library of Congress); below, the McGraw-Hill building, West Forty-second Street, New York, designed by Raymond Hood, 1931 (photograph courtesy McGraw-Hill Studio).*

What is important about such instances, from the point of view of this article, is that so many of them reflect a concern with process, especially as it is manifest in motion and change; for it is this concern, as I have said, which seems to me to be central to that "American" quality which we are trying to define.

THE AESTHETICS OF PROCESS

The quality ·shared by all those things which are recognized, here and abroad, as distinctively "American"—from skyscrapers to jazz to chewing gum—is an awareness of, if not a delight in, process: that universal "process of development" which, as Lancelot Law Whyte has said, man shares with all organic nature, and which forever debars him from achieving the perfection and eternal harmony of which the great arts of Western Europe have for centuries created the illusion. In the hierarchical civilizations of the past, where systems of status kept people as well as values pretty much in their places, men were insulated against an awareness of process to an extent which is no longer possible. In an environment dominated by technology and democracy, a world of social and physical mobility and rapid change, we cannot escape it. And our awareness of process is inevitably reflected in the vernacular, just as our occasional dread of it is witnessed by our continuing commitment to the cultivated forms inherited from a world in which permanence and perfection seemed, at least, to be realities.

It is the ideas, emotions, and attitudes generated by this conscious or unconscious awareness of process which account, I think, for a basic difference between the aesthetic effects of vernacular forms and those of the cultivated Western tradition. Inevitably, the forms appropriate to our contemporary world lack the balanced symmetry, the stability, and the elaborate formality to which we are accustomed in the architecture and design of the past. They tend, instead, to be resilient, adaptable, simple, and unceremonious. Serenity gives way to tension. Instead of an aesthetic of the arrangement of mass, we have an aesthetic of the transformation of energy. Only in some such terms as these, it seems to me, can we describe the so-called "American" quality which we detect in our architecture and design.

It is not possible in a brief essay to do more than suggest the implications of such an approach to the question asked in our title. Obviously it restricts our attention to a limited field of structures and objects, and diverts it from some of the most charming and interesting things which have been produced in this country. But it has the merit, I think, of converting a question which can easily become a mere excuse for a naïvely nationalist antiquarianism, or an equally naïve internationalism, into one which may help us discover the aesthetic resources of an "open-ended" civilization, of an "American" environment which reaches far beyond the borders of the United States. It also has the modest merit of requiring us to look with fresh eyes at things around us—not just the things in the decorators' shops and museums, but the humbler things which, because the people who made them took them, as we do, for granted, are often spontaneously expressive of those elements in our environment which do not fall naturally into traditional forms and patterns.

One way to emphasize the point I am trying to make is to contrast a product of the vernacular with a masterpiece of the cultivated tradition. Books on the architecture of bridges do not, so far as I know, refer to structures such as the bridge built in 1882 across the Canyon Diablo in Arizona, on what is now the Santa Fe Railroad. Seen in contrast with the majestic Pont du Gard, one of the most perfect examples of Roman masonry construction, which rises 155 feet above the river Gard near the French city of Nîmes, this spider-web truss of iron, carrying heavy locomotives and cars 222 feet above the bottom of the canyon, dramatically illustrates the utterly different aesthetic effects produced in response not only to new technics and materials but also to new attitudes and values. The two structures, embodying fundamentally different conceptions of time, of space, of motion, and of man's relation to external nature, make essentially different demands upon our attention.

If we can put aside, for the time being, all question of which structure is the more beautiful, there will be no difficulty in recognizing which of the two is embodied in a scheme of forms that is capable of becoming a vehicle for an architecture expressive of the American environment.

In the triumphant composure of its daring triple arcades the aqueduct calmly declares that by its completion, almost two thousand years ago now, its builders had accomplished, once and for all, a tremendous task. Hewn stone lies on hewn stone or thrusts diagonally downward against hewn stone, each held immovably in place by its own dead weight. The railroad bridge, by contrast, is entirely preoccupied with what it is doing. Its trusses and girders are a web of members in tension and members in compression, arranged in supple, asymmetrical equilibrium. The stones of the aqueduct rest there, block on block, sustaining the trough through which water once flowed. But the bridge's trusses gather up and direct the forces set in motion by the trains which the structure quite literally "carries" across the canyon.

Anyone who looks at the Canyon Diablo bridge with eyes accustomed to the forms and proportions of traditional Western European construction will feel a disparity between the apparent fragility of its members and its demonstrable capacity to bear weight. An architecture based on the scheme of forms the bridge embodies would disappoint all the expectations which Western architecture has ratified for centuries. For the disposition of mass, in architecture, had traditionally conformed to what Geoffrey Scott[1] called our sense of "powerfully adjusted weight." Architecture, indeed, has selected for emphasis those suggestions of pressure and resistance which, as Scott says, clearly answer to our "habitual body experience" of weight, pressure, and resistance.

Since a scheme of forms based upon the tensile strength of steel does not answer to this internal sense of physical security and strength, we cannot enjoy it, Scott insists, even if we can understand intellectually why the structure does not collapse as our eyes convince us it should. "We have no knowledge in ourselves," he says, "of any such paradoxical relations. Our aesthetic reactions are limited by our power to recreate in ourselves, imaginatively, the physical conditions suggested by the form we see."

This so-called "humanistic" conception, of architecture as an art which projects into concrete, three-dimensional form the image of our bodily sensations, movements, and moods, would necessarily exclude all structures based upon the system of tension embodied in the Canyon Diablo bridge. But many structures embodying a scheme of forms in tension do, in fact, give genuine aesthetic delight—including, most notably perhaps, the great suspension bridges of our time. One suspects that Scott's elaborate

---

[1] My quotations from Scott are to be found in his eloquent study of *The Architecture of Humanism*.

Top, the Pont du Gard, near Nîmes, France (photograph reproduced from Charles S. Whitney, Bridges, A Study in Their Art, Science and Evolution, *New York, William Edwin Rudge, 1929); bottom, the Canyon Diablo Bridge in Arizona, on what was then the Atlantic and Pacific Railroad. The ironwork was fabricated by the Central Bridge Works in Buffalo, New York, and shipped to the site for assembly (photograph reproduced from an original in historical files of the Santa Fe Railway).*

thesis is in essence only a subtly conceived justification of a long-established "custom in the eye."

The science of the modern engineer, which evolved the unprecedented structural webs of tension and compression, is like nature in that it requires from objects only such security and strength as are in fact necessary. One has only to think of the spider's web or the sunflower's stalk to realize the truth of Scott's observation that the world of nature is full of objects which are strong in ways other than those which we are habitually conscious of in our own bodies. But although there is an order in nature which the scientist can comprehend, it is not, according to Scott, an order which can be grasped by the naked eye. It is not "humanized."

There is an implication here that the eye of science—what we can "see" with the aid of photomicrographs, X rays, stroboscopic cameras, microscopes, and so on—is not "human" vision, and that human life, and the arts which express its significance, are alike alien not only to science but to nature itself. It may be so, but there is much in the vernacular which argues the contrary, and much to suggest that the technological forms which are a part of that vernacular can beget a new "custom of the eye." We would do well, therefore, to set against this concept one which was expressed by a Tennessee architect named Harrison Gill.[2]

What distinguishes all truly modern architecture from all architecture of the past is, Gill argues, the very fact that it does not rely on compression alone, but employs tension as well. By its use of tension it "comes closer to the forces and mechanics of nature than ever before . . . The ability of a stalk of corn to stand erect lies in the tensile strength of its outer layers. Man and beast can move and work because of the elastic tension of tendon and sinew. All living things exist in a state of constant tension. . . . All truly modern building is alive."

Here, then, from vernacular roots a scheme of forms has evolved which is capable of expressing a humanism which takes man's mind as well as his body, his knowledge as well as his feelings, as its standard of reference, a humanism which sees man not as a stranger trying to assert his permanence in the midst of nature's inhuman and incomprehensible flux, but as a sentient part of nature's universal process.

[2] In his article, "What Makes Architecture Modern?" *Harper's Magazine,* July, 1953.

At once utopian and visionary in the matter of how men should live, Paolo Soleri (1919–   ) was a student of Frank Lloyd Wright but over the years rebelled against the master's precepts. A central concept of Soleri's thought is the "arcologies," megalopolitan structures designed to encompass every purpose for which mankind may require shelter. For example, one model of an arcology, dubbed "3-D Jersey," would house 1 million people under one roof, stand 300 stories high, and cover about 14 square miles of land; by contrast one West Coast city in America requires about 46 square miles to house 700,000 people. Soleri's goals are urban efficiency, economic use of land, freedom from pollution, and the implied banishment of the automobile; these goals also contemplate human enrichment. Soleri's basic assumptions may be questioned on the grounds of implied inflexibility (the basic supportive structure cannot be varied or substituted for without endangering the entire structure), and there remain questions of financing and the problems of maintaining a balance between the arcology and the surrounding environment. A critic of Soleri observes that "Utopian dreams . . . can be hallucinatory and thus . . . add to our frustrations." Presently Soleri lives in the Arizona desert.

ARCOLOGY: THE CITY IN THE IMAGE OF MAN

Paolo Soleri

The concept is that of a structure called an arcology, or ecological architecture. Such a structure would take the place of the natural landscape inasmuch as it would constitute the new topography to be dealt with. This manmade topography would differ from natural topography in the following ways:

1. It would not be a one-surface configuration but a multilevel one.

2. It would be conceived in such a way as to be the carrier of all the elements that make the physical life of the city possible—places and inlets for people, freight, water, power, climate, mail, telephone; places and outlets for people, freight, waste, mail, products, and so forth.

3. It would be a large-dimensional sheltering device, fractioning three-dimensional space in large and small subspaces, making its own weather and its own cityscape.

4. It would be the major vessel for massive flow of people and things within and toward the outside of the city.

5. It would be the organizing pattern and anchorage for private and public institutions of the city.

6. It would be the focal structure for the complex and ever-changing life of the city.

7. It would be the unmistakable expression of man the maker and man the creator. It would be diverse and singular in all of its realizations. Arcology would be surrounded by uncluttered and open landscape.

The concept of a one-structure system is not incidental to the organization of the city but central to it. It is the wholeness of a biological organism that is sought in the making of the city, as many and stringent are the analogies between the functioning of an organism and the vitality of a metropolitan structure. Fundamental to both is the element of flow. Life is there where the flow of matter and energy is abundant and uninterrupted. With a great flow gradient the city acquires a cybernetic character. The interacting of its components erases the space and time gaps that outphase the action-reaction cycles and ultimately break down the vitality of the system.

These are mechanical but fundamental premises for functioning metropolitan life. In reality the idea is that of a very comprehensive "plumbing system" for the social animal, which the city is. The plumbing system consists of the previously mentioned man-made topography. Social, ethical, political, and aesthetic implications are left out, as they are valid and final only if and when physical conditions are realistically organized.

To dispel the aura of cerebralism or utopianism from the concept presented, there is another way to see the central problem of the city: The degree of fullness in each individual life depends on the reaching power unequivocably available to each person. In turn this reaching power is in direct proportion to the richness and variety of information coming to and going from the person.

Information means not only sounds, sight, and so forth, but all the sensorial data, all the physical intermediaries that make any sensitivity possible; all kinds of inorganic, organic, organized, or man-made matter or material or instruments, from foodstuff to wireless, from toilets to television, from mothers' reprimands to theater. This wholeness of information must include packaged and remote information such as television, radio, telephone, and the communications media, as well as environmental information. Environmental information calls in the technology of transportation, distribution, and transfer, and calls for the no less fundamental quality of the environment itself.

This combination of remote and synthetic information and environmental information is indispensable to the nature of metropolitan life. In physical terms it means that the distances, the time, and the obstacles separating the person from all civilized institutions have to be scaled down to the supply of energy available to the person himself.

If we inject into the picture the sheer bulk of products and devices wanted by and forced upon each man, we can see the dimension and the absolute priority of the logistic problem. The burden of matter, part of the environmental information weighing on every man, is impressive and also irrational. This matter has to be transformed, manipulated, moved, serviced, stored, exchanged, rejected, and substituted—the warehouses of arcology will have to be enormous. One thing nomadism has not been able to teach us is frugality. What is the mechanism by which the rich and complex life of society can flow back into the structure of the city?

In a society where production is a successful and physically gigantic fact, the coordination and congruence of information, communication, transportation, distribution, and transference are the mechanics by which that society operates. It is not accidental that these are also dynamic aspects of another phenomenon, the most dynamic of all: life.

In every dynamic event of physical nature the elements of time and space, and thus acceleration, speed, and deceleration, are crucial. The speed of light, a space and time shrinker, well serves the communication of information of the packaged kind—television, radio, telephone—the synthetic information. Thus a good supply of synthetic information can reach even the scattered suburbanite (for him environmental information is and remains monotone, bone stripped).

The picture is totally altered when we come to transportation and distribution. Unless the feeding in and feeding out of these two is highly centered and axialized, the laws of matter and energy will see that sluggishness and possibly stillness prevail. *Swiftness and efficiency are inversely proportional to dispersion. Scattered life is by definition deprived or parasitic.* This can be verified by approaching the problem from the opposite end: The environment is vital and living information; it is the bulk of information available to man.

Blighted environment is blighted information. The cause of blighted environment is the breakdown of environmental information occurring when there is not follow-through from synthetic information to transportation, distribution, and reach. When this occurs, the energies of the individual are exhausted in the struggle to keep the avenues of environmental information open, to keep the flow of things going. Man's mechanically low-grade energies are absorbed, not euphemistically, by cement, asphalt, steel, pollution, and all sorts of mechnical, static, and dynamic barriers in an ever-enlarging frame of space and time. The flow becomes sluggish, if it does not come to a standstill. This blighted environment is a direct consequence of sluggish or dying flow.

Impaired flow is ultimately the disproportion between the validity of the individual reach and the amount of energy that is expended to make the reach possible.

One may thus say that because of the biophysical make-up of our world, rich flow—that is, rich potentiality—is the direct consequence of minimal separation between components. *Minimal separation between components cannot be achieved by using only two or three coordinates of space. Minimal separation between components is structured three-dimensionality, or it is not feasible.* The solid and not the surface is the environment where adequate flow is possible, thus where environmental information is rich and where life can flourish.

The surface of the earth, for all practical purposes, is by definition a two-dimensional configuration. *The natural landscape is thus not the apt frame for the complex life of society.* Man must make the metropolitan landscape in his own image: a physically compact, dense, three-dimensional, energetic bundle, not a tenuous film of organic matter. The man-made landscape has to be a

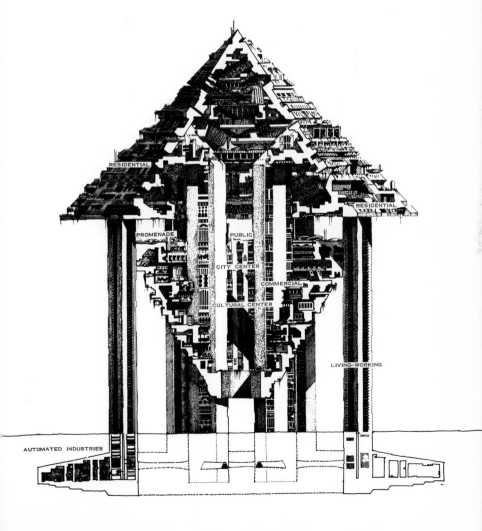

multilevel landscape, a solid of three congruous dimensions. The only realistic direction toward a physically free community of man is toward the construction of truly three-dimensional cities. *Physical freedom, that is to say, true reaching power, is wrapped around vertical vectors.*

There is a further and reinforcing reason for verticality. As individuals we act horizontally and need horizontal dimensions up to six to ten times the vertical dimensions. Thus, the compactness and richness of social collective life can be found only vertically. *Around vertical vectors, megalopoly and suburbia can contract, moving from flat gigantism toward human and solid scale.*

If this concept is valid, as it seems to be in view of the nature of the physical and energetic world, then a dense urban structure is mandatory, regardless of the what, how, where, or when. A few generations of men reared and grown in an environment badly stripped of cultural and aesthetic scope may be sufficient for the brutalization of society. Signs that such brutalization is already at work are abundant and impressive. If man is quality against quantity, then the priority is clear. It is much too late for our present generation, bound to the spell of arrogance and license. It may even be quite late for the just born, but there is hope for the children of our children. The when is now, for lack of any reachable yesterday.

*What dimension is to Henry Moore, illusion is to
Richard Lippold (1915–   ). A master of the
delicate art of wire-sculpture, Lippold jumps, skips,
and pirouettes through space like a high-wire artist.
He does as much again in his teaching and writing,
forcing his reader to confront illusion not only in
words but in the non-verbal elements that are so
much a part of our experience of the modern book
or magazine page. We must "read" Lippold's black
and white pages and the two with what he
calls "a cryptic diagram" as carefully as the
text that contains them. For what they
promise is a deeper grasp of illusion and thus, in
Lippold's terms, of life itself.*

ILLUSION AS STRUCTURE

*Richard
Lippold*

Structure is illusion. The greatest wonder of the
many wonders of this century is this fact. For
the first time in his history, man is able to prove
—or at least is on the verge of proving—that all
of the means he has ever used to define the
nature of nature, and thus his own nature, is the
illusion afforded him by his meager senses and
sensitivities. His ever-changing definitions, calculations, analyses, measurements, descriptions,
propositions, proofs, answers, certainties—even
uncertainties and questions: all are illusion. Even
the disillusion so produced becomes illusion. A
few decades ago such utterances might have
come only from an Eastern mystic, surely not
from a Western artist, let alone a Western scientist; yet I, as a Western artist, base these
remarks not on the currently fashionable mystique of Zen Buddhism, but on the almost identical findings, if different phrasings, of Western
science.

It can almost be said that this age of disillusion
is in reality an age of dissolution. The rapid
succession of theories destroyed by science has
left even the scientist with grave doubts as to the
meaning of *anything* beyond its own momentary

mention. A young Nobel Prize scientist, still in his twenties, speaking recently at a Massachusetts Institute of Technology symposium, said that things were happening so fast in physics these days that he could not understand at all what the "younger" men were talking about.

On what is this dissolution based? Insofar as I, as a layman, can understand it (although as an artist I have long "known" it), what seems to have happened to an understanding of the structure of matter (the same process applies to psychic, social, and philosophical structures as well) is that with every effort to describe it from one point of view, a new point of view manifests itself. Just when the most minute particle, for example, has been described for us, it seems to disappear, or at least to transfer its "true" existence to some other area of "reality"—from physical matter to electrical energy, for instance. Recently even the smallest electrical particle has been assumed to be a tiny bit of whirling space, inexplicably thrown into a dervish-like vortex, emanating energies as by-products whose illusory forms (waves, electrical impulses) we interpret as "matter" through our limited perceptions. We have come, since my childhood, from the "knowledge" that we are chemically ninety-five percent water to the "certainty" that we are physically one hundred percent "empty" space!

However, it may only seem to our impoverished intelligences that the tiny vortexes of our atomic "structure" are whirling, or are even what we call Space. Even if they can be said to be whirling, we know now that movement is relative, and their speed may be such that they are also standing still, as we are told *we* would be if we "traveled" at the speed of light. Or their movement in space, which we now "know" is infinite and endless, would imply that they really are going nowhere, because there is no "where." We can no longer ask "where" or "when." (As I write this, an astronaut has just flown out of February twenty-first into February twentieth and back again, not only once, but several times! If we cannot say "where" he is or "when" he is, can we even ask "what" he is?) On the one hand then, we seem to have come empirically to the same point of view as the religious one which has warned us for a long time that "all is vanity."

On the other hand, no sooner has all matter, all identity of place and time thus vanished into the greater "void" of space,

than science suspects, by observing nature's penchant for symmetry, that space cannot be empty. Apparently it seems "empty"
only because of our meager access to its "total" properties. Space
is now supposedly *stuffed* with conjectured, therefore as yet
immeasurable, Matter and Anti-matter. We are, according to
recent reports, merely the lucky (or unlucky) debris of a constant warfare between this Matter and Anti-matter, which fills
up the interstices of space whose most minimal, detectable
particles are merely a kind of dead residue of the battle. We are
like the slower lemmings who escape suicide through native
lethargy—or at least our atomic particles are, if we still wish, as
"whole" men, to remain blameless in this newer situation. Yet it
must seem small comfort that we "exist" because our most minute
particles are either ashes or pacifists.

Again we are confronted by a new version of a familiar duality: all or nothing. Like previous alternatives, innocence or
experience, grace or disgrace, they provide for the return of guilt
through doubt.

But are they alternatives? Is perhaps "all" also "nothing" and
"nothing" also "all"? To swing for a moment a few degrees on
the inflexibly mounted axis of human perception, the seeming
alternative can be viewed in another way. The alternative exists
because what we call Nature is always posing paradoxes. As has
been pointed out, Nature has a penchant for symmetry, but she
has as much a penchant against it, by means of the chance effects
of the inter-relation of all things. So the "laws" of Nature which
seem to cause each member of her family to establish its unique
identity (we plant an acorn; we do not get a monkey), are modified by the accidents which befall existence (rains may sweep
away the nut, enemies consume, or friends nourish it). The "law"
is the ideal form (the potential "void" of static, timeless space),
"chance" is the modifier of the ideal (the unseen warfare of
Matter and Anti-matter, charging and shaping "space").

Together, the peace *and* the war, the empty *and* the full, are
responsible for the existence of form.

Thus has science, at long last, later than art and philosophy,
brought us face to face with the necessity to see that we cannot
choose between the empty and the full and pretend to be alive,
because they are the same thing. I have attempted to express this
situation visually by four of the six pages in the center of this
article.

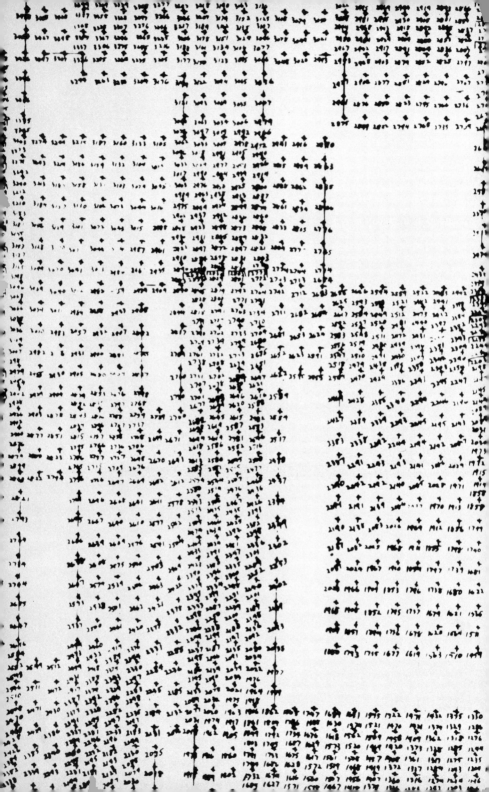

The first two pages are white ("empty") and the last two pages are black ("full"). In graphic terms, these are as opposite qualities as I am able to produce to make my point. But in actuality what are they? Of course the white pages are "inexperienced," and the black pages are "experienced," full to the point of literal saturation. No room is left for another event. In relation to the consideration of matter in science as I referred to it above, the white pages are like the seemingly pure state of absolute space, of the "nothing" whose self-movements may generate energy; and the black pages are the material sediment of all the apparent energy which fills the void of non-being: a dense, solid, tangible mass of total "stuff." But are they? Or, more properly, is it?

The answer is self-evident: the white pages are stuffed to the full with "emptiness," while the black pages are deliciously void of "nothing." Thus each is equally empty and equally full. There is no choice as to condition. Even if we attempt to choose on the basis of white and black alone, who can say, except from prejudice, that white is empty, is nothing, and black is full, is everything? Or vice versa? All we can attempt to say is that white is the absence of black, and black is the absence of white; by this very implication the existence of the other is assured.

If, then, both are possible, yet neither is sufficient, it would seem, as I began by stating, that if only paradox is "real," all other "reality," or form, is illusion.

We in the West particularly have been prone to accept the deceits of "calculable" or "definable" structures and to defend them to the death. As seen in the arts, we have insisted on every conceivable "truth" about form, from the security of the "mass" of the pyramids to the security of "pure space" in the empty walls of an Yves Klein exhibition, with, of course, every imaginable variant and combination to suit our changing concepts. (Yet a close look at "mass" reveals that even the densest metal is so full of "space" that all kinds of energies pass through it unimpeded. Cosmic rays and television shows pass through any mountain—as well as the "mass" of our own bodies—quite freely. As for "pure space": a cubic centimeter of the space in Mr. Klein's "emptiness" has enough cosmic energy in it to populate a universe.)

We have embraced symmetry as an ideal and we have rejected it as an empty conceit. We have reduced vision to a calculated formula of constructed elements, and rejected it for an "auto-matic" compilation of the debris of order. Who of us has been "right"? "Neither, said the moon" (said Emily Dickinson), "That is best which is not. . . ." Not mass, not void; not anything in between. Not symmetry, not law, not disorder, not chaos; not anything in between. Only NOTHING. . . .

But NATURE! we cry. NATURE is not *Nothing!* NATURE has evidence for whatever we wish to believe! NATURE *loves* sym-metry; look at the human body, or a snowflake; read this news item: "Sundsvall, Sweden, July 27 (AP)—Two cars of the same make and the same color collided head-on outside Sundsvall. Both drivers were thrown against their cars' windshields and were treated at the local hospital for cuts. One driver was Finn Gagner, aged twenty-five. The other was Dag Gagner, twenty-five. They are identical twins. . . ." What a magnificent, symmetrical, or-derly event!—except that it was, of course, an accident.

For those who seek to prove it, Nature can be said to *hate* symmetry. Look *closely* at the right side and left side of a face; no two snowflakes are ever identical; chance events are the only real determiners of character, from the shape and size of a tree to the "choice" of one's love.

But these are the very clues to our contemporary feelings about structure. Symmetry is an accident of disorder, yet acci-dent is the order of non-symmetry—what Hans Arp calls the "Laws of Chance," or the scientist approximates with his "Second Law of Thermodynamics." The wildest of neo-Dada "happen-ings" can be as carefully calculated and reconstructed as a master plan for the sewers of New York City. In fact, since there is no "time" and "space," *all* events and objects are merely immediate sensations. Order is but an event of the briefest duration, for nothing is identical from moment to moment. The warfare of Matter and Anti-matter is in us all, growth and decay rotate in their orbits as steadily and simultaneously as Venus and Mars about the Sun, pursuing and pursued. What can be left but staticity and the total "mass" of nothingness? Obviously what can be left can just as well be called everythingness. It is true that Nature is not only Nothing; Nature is also Everything.

In the face of this totality, revealed for us now by Science as well as by Philosophy and Religion (in this sense, Science *be-comes* our contemporary Philosophy and Religion), how can this be made visible, sensible to our human equipment?

Between the white pages and the black pages in this article are two pages carrying a cryptic diagram. Into the space of the white pages have filtered energetic particles of black, or one can say that the space of the black pages has fissured, and whiteness has isolated the particles of black, like a gigantic magnification, revealing the inner "structure" of black. Because of this "space," as in the mountain or the metal, the "solid" black has only been an illusion all along. Referring back to the white pages, we can say the same. This is a magnification of them also, revealing the invisible energies inherent in what seems to be pure space, like Matter and Anti-matter made visible.

It will be noted on close inspection, that there is an "order" to the little particles, yet it is as deceptive an order, in its relation to "reality," as is the order of the chaotic struggle of Matter and Anti-matter in relation to the form of shapes in space. Its deception lies in the fact that this diagram is part of a study for a piece of sculpture which in its finished state is never seen to have the symmetry and systematic arrangement of this, its inner "structure." I have chosen to leave the drawing unidentified, because the sculpture exists and is experienced on its own terms beyond this part of its creation, much as we exist and relate to what we call "life" beyond and in addition to the interstices of our atomic structures, the vacancies in our psyches, the silences in our senses, and the various energies which occupy all of these in part.

This drawing then, is both something *and* nothing; it is black *and* white, it is empty *and* full. It is as "abstract" as the principles behind the operation of all things, and it is as "real" as the operation of those principles. It is a visual set of laws which in the finished sculpture are broken by the "accidents" of four-dimensional existence, of light, of point of view, and of perspective. It is also, conversely, the accident of a particular artist's vision in a particular moment in "history," thus becoming a specific, identifiable entity, a "law"—a formula for these particular chance occurrences.

In all these respects, this drawing and the kind of sculpture which it represents, is relevant to the point of view to which Science is bringing us, and which frees us for the first time from decision as well as from indecision. Without "time," we have all of Time; with all of Space, we have no need to choose a particular "space." Like this sculpture, we know the "mass" of space, and the "movement" of staticity; for, although the sculpture's own movement, or activity between its parts, or human movement in relation to it may or may not exist, its very being in a state of relationship is no more nor less than the great staticity of all universal events at a given instant, and, as I have already pointed out, at the very next instant everything will be (apparently) different again. Another static moment will have appeared, and, together with the first, will be assumed to be movement by our feeble perceptions and the deceptions of memory. Like all assumptions, this is illusion.

It is quite true that our arrival at a point of no decision in the arts and sciences, more or less simultaneously at this "moment," is in itself another illusion. True to human form, the general awareness of this illusion at this juncture has effected another choice: acceptance of the illusion, or rejection of it (which is to say acceptance of disillusion). But it is quite natural that in being free *from* decision, we are at once free *for* it as well. Our "moment" still triumphs!

The proof of this paradox is visible in the world of sculpture, as I have already pointed out. The decision to abandon law and order, as in the selection of debris and automatism, leads at once to the proscribed law of anarchy—a law none-the-less, and inviolable in the direction of any "outer" law. The decision to employ pristine materials and "orderly" procedures, "free" from predetermined forms and processes, exposes it to the hazards of the evolution of its own growth, and the distortions of external efforts, like the "growth" of all living things in Nature. Which is free, and which slave?

Seen in this light, works evolved from interests described above operate either as protest (through disillusion) or as illustration (through dedicatory illusion) of the same current attitudes. The black is contained in the white; the white is possessed by the black. All structure in contemporary sculpture, to be a part of this "static" moment, must be a part of this new illusion, just as sculptural structures of the "past" were a part of the illusions of those moments. "Ultimate Reality" is so far removed still from our awareness that we have only contemporary illusions on which to erect our forms. It is irrelevant whether they come from science or from somewhere else. The delight of science at this point is its surprise with its discovery that it too is only a small illusion in the mind of man.

In this way, the scientist, the artist, and the prophet are one, for it is the general acceptance of a particular illusion which motivates and unifies mankind at any given time. To abandon this illusion to chaos or to embrace previous illusions is to die. Creativity, like life and like love, depends on a man's ability to accept an illusion, to be aware of it, and to sustain it. Only in this way can he find a structure for his life and for his work. Illusion *is* structure.

Author Index

Title Index